DANCE FLOOR DEMOCRACY

★ ★ ★ ★ ★ ★ ★ THE SOCIAL GEOGRAPHY OF MEMORY AT THE HOLLYWOOD CANTEEN ★ ★ ★ ★ ★

SHERRIE TUCKER

DUKE UNIVERSITY PRESS   DURHAM AND LONDON   2014

Printed in the United States of America on acid-free paper ∞
Designed by Heather Hensley
Typeset in Minion Pro by Westchester Book Group

Library of Congress Cataloging-in-Publication Data
Tucker, Sherrie, 1957–
Dance floor democracy : the social geography of memory at the
Hollywood Canteen / Sherrie Tucker.
pages   cm
Includes bibliographical references and index.
ISBN 978-0-8223-5742-1 (cloth : alk. paper)
ISBN 978-0-8223-5757-5 (pbk. : alk. paper)
1. Hollywood Canteen. 2. World War, 1939–1945—Social aspects—
United States. 3. Memory—Social aspects—United States. 4. Los
Angeles (Calif.)—Social conditions—20th century. 5. Dance—Social
aspects—California—Los Angeles—History—20th century. I. Title.
D744.7.U6T83 2014
940.53'1—dc23   2014000772

Cover art: Actress-hostess Faye McKenzie jitterbugging with military
guest; unknown aerial hostess and soldier to the left; and onlookers. By
permission, Bruce Torrence, hollywoodphotographs.com.

Duke University Press gratefully acknowledges the Society of American
Music, H. Earle Johnson Publication Subvention, which provided funds
toward the publication of this book.

Contents

Acknowledgments

Many people danced with me as I researched, thought through, wrestled with, and wrote this book. I know things looked differently from all of your many sides. I appreciate your time, enthusiasm, patience, push-backs, good humor, support, hospitality, readings, and reality checks. I don't claim to speak for you, but I couldn't have spoken without you.

My first debt of gratitude goes to the people who shared their memories of the Hollywood Canteen and of Los Angeles during World War II. I wish I could have included all of your stories, but please know that my moves in this book are shaped by conversations with all of you and I am deeply grateful. I hope I have left room for your footsteps. Sadly, I note that nearly everyone interviewed for this book is now deceased. I also thank your families and friends for sharing your time with me.

Families and friends of former Canteen-goers connected me with loved ones and helped to facilitate interviews. I would not have found the range of people I was able to speak with if you hadn't come forward, offered to help, vouched for me, and negotiated the parameters of the dance in such caring ways (*don't call her before noon; if he can't hear you over the phone, send him a cassette, etc.*). Many people came forward, but I especially thank Clora Bryant, Josh Curtis, Mary Letterii, Margaret Nevarez, Catherine Ramirez, Rick Ruvolo, Julie Dawn Smith, Ian Walters, Kim Warren, Valerie Yaros, and Elisa Foster.

I benefited from generous material support for research, travel, and writing time for this project, including a National Endowment for the Humanities "We the People" Fellowship in 2010, a Haynes Foundation Grant from the Historical Society of Southern California, a Beveridge Research Grant from the American Historical Association, and several rounds of generous support from the Faculty General Research Fund from the University of Kansas.

I could not have gathered the support to finish this project without Kathy Porsch and Victor Bailey and everyone at the Hall Center for the Humanities. Kathy deserves full credit for securing external funding for this book—she molded my proposal like a hunk of clay and a lot of her brilliant handiwork remains in the finished book. In addition, I was supported by a Hall Center for a Humanities Travel Grant and a glorious Hall Center Faculty Fellowship in 2006. The Louis Armstrong Visiting Professorship at Columbia University in 2004–5 provided a year of incredible access to archives, jazz scholars, and feminist musicologists. Time away from teaching is impossible without the support of colleagues, chairs, and departments, and I am grateful to my colleagues in American studies at the University of Kansas for covering for me, sometimes at times when our faculty and staff were already greatly over-stretched. I am proud to work among colleagues so interested in and supportive of each other's work. Terri Rockhold and Kay Isbell, I am humbled by and grateful for everything you do, for your top-notch skills and dazzling patience while keeping so many people whose heads are mostly in the clouds all moving in the right directions. You both are amazing. I began this project as an adjunct in women's studies at Hobart and William Smith Colleges and I am grateful for their gift of the first travel grant that launched this work. I am also grateful to the Society of American Music for the H. Earle Johnson Publication Subvention Award that assisted with production costs.

I am indebted to the generously critical anonymous reviewers who read numerous iterations of this book for Duke University Press and helped me make it better. Many others who read drafts of chapters include: Tami Albin (more than anyone), Michael Baskett (thank you, also, for all of the instant film history expertise), Brian Donovan, Lindsey Feitz, Michelle Heffner Hayes, Tammy Kernodle, Monique Laney, Cathy Preston, Nicolas G. Rosenthal, and everyone at the Los Angeles History Research Group and the Autry Western History Workshop (2009), Ayu Saraswati, Kim Warren, Chris Wells, Robyn Wiegman and fellow workshop participants at Dartmouth "Outside American Studies" Summer Institute (2003), and my wonderful writing partners, Nichole T. Rustin and Akiko Takeyama. Thank you to Robin D. G. Kelley, George Lipsitz, and Ingrid Monson for writing the same grant letters year after year. Thank you, Gerald Early, for including sections from this book in the special "American Music" issue of *Daedalus*, Fall 2013, and for your and Mina Yang's wonderful suggestions and edits.

Dozens upon dozens of people in addition to those named above helped me work out concepts, listened to my ideas, and offered feedback and consultation on particular aspects of the research and analysis: Giselle Anatol, Crystal Anderson, Lisa Barg, Chuck Berg, Maylei Blackwell, Donald Bogle,

Zanice Bond, Jayna Brown, Joselin Buckner, Philip Cairns, Darshan Campos, Anne Choi, Susan Cook, Suzanne Cusick, Angela Y. Davis (always my advisor), Ryan Dohoney, Raul Fernandez, Krin Gabbard, Tanya Golash-Boza, Brenda Dixon Gottschild, Farah Jasmine Griffin, Michelle Habell-Pallan, Tomie Hahn, Ellie Hisama, Kyle Julien, Florice Kovan, Josh Kun, George Lipsitz, Tiffany Ana Lopez, Renita Lorden, Anthony Macias, Jacqui Malone, Ken Marcus, Carol Mason (thank you for the fabulous research road trip to Minnesota), Juliet McMains, Tracy McMullen, Mark Miller, Keta Miranda, Martha Mockus, Terry Monaghan (tragically no longer with us, but to whom I and many others who write about swing dance are indebted), Fred Moten, Naomi Pabst, Eduardo Pagan, Nicole Hodges Persley, Ben Piekut, Eric Porter, Ailicia Ruscin, Ursel Schlicht, RJ Smith, Eric Usner, Deborah Vargas, Lindsay Vogt, Penny Von Eschen, Gayle Wald, Megan Williams, Pete Williams, Mike Willard, Kevin Whitehead, and Deborah Wong. Swing dancers, many of whom are also scholars and historians, helped me to interpret photographs and films, and helped me to better understand torque: Lance Benishek, Ada Emmett, Bayliss Harsh, George Hildebrand, Peter Loggins, Eric Usner, Chris Wells, and members of the Kansas University Swing Club. I am grateful to the many co-presenters and audience members who shared comments, leads, and feedback at numerous conferences and talks. Among the many generous people who issued invitations that provided pivotal conversations for me at departments, universities, and centers in the United States, Canada, and Germany were Birgit Bauridl, Charles Carson, Maryemma Graham, Udo Heble, Jann Pasler, Josh Kun, Ken Marcus, Carol Mason, Tracy McMullen, Louise Meintjes, Jenni Veitch Olson, Ron Radano, Willy Raussert, Nicolas G. Rosenthal, Cotten Seiler, Louise K. Stein, Yoko Suzuki, Judy Tsou, Allison Varzally, Ellen Waterman, Lloyd Whitesell, Mike Willard, and Deborah Wong.

One of the great pleasures of my life is working with the terrific graduate students at the University of Kansas. Some of you who helped me figure out my way in this book are named above, but I also want to send a special thanks to those of you who showed up to read, and didn't drop the seminar when you found out that I wanted you to dance: Trevor Grizzell, Rich Housh, Liam Lair, Megan Lease, Ashley Mog, Michelle McCudden, Marion Probst, Chris Robinson, Claudia Trotzke, Kay Walker, and Pete Williams. My deep gratitude and respect goes to Michelle Heffner Hayes for the improvisatory team-teaching adventures that facilitated such meaningful embodied pedagogy and to my colleague Ray Mizumura-Pence for adding so much to the experience.

I am endlessly grateful to Tami Albin, Garnette Cadogan, Nicole Ishikawa, and Florice Kovan for research assistance, to Nicole Ishikawa again for transcriptions, and to Tami Albin for driving on those freeways that freak me out and for operating the video equipment. For helping me prepare the manuscript for submission, I thank Tami Albin and Bobbi Rahder. Down-to-the-wire photograph and permissions assistance was expertly performed by Nicole Ishikawa and Kelly Ishikawa and by cartographer Andrew Gottsfield.

As far as I am concerned, nothing is possible without archivists, curators, librarians, and library staff. Among those to whom I am indebted are: Tami Albin, Sara Morris, Scott McEathron, Rhonda Houser, and Billie Conway of KU Libraries; Valerie Yaros at the Screen Actors Guild; Susan D. Anderson, Claudia Horning, and Tom Hyry at UCLA Library Special Collections; Jonathon Auxier at the Warner Bros. Archive at University of Santa Cruz; Ryan Bean at the Kautz Family YMCA Archives, University of Minnesota Libraries; the late great Mayme Clayton, whose collection now lives in the Library and Museum in Culver City that carries on her work and bears her name; JC Johnson at the Howard Gotlieb Archival Research Center at Boston University; Sarah Cooper at the Southern California Library of Social Science Research; Kevyne Barr at the Tamiment Library at New York University; Marva Felchin at the Autry Library; and numerous librarians and staff of the New York Public Libraries (especially at the Schomburg and Library of Performing Arts), the Los Angeles Public Library, the Margaret Herrick Library Special Collections at the American Academy of Motion Picture Arts and Sciences; the American Film Institute; the American Jewish Historical Society; Sterling Memorial Library, Yale University; and the Wisconsin Center for Film and Theater Research. Numerous private collectors were generous with knowledge and resources, including Josh Curtis, Bruce Torrence, and Marc Wanamaker.

In the early 1990s, Ken Wissoker called me at my secretarial job to ask about my research on all-girl bands. I have been loyal and grateful ever since. Thank you for making my dreams of being a writer come true. And thank you for continuing to ask me about the Canteen book and for assuring me that I wasn't alone in struggling with the "second book thing." Everyone at Duke University Press has been professional, warm, and meticulous every step of the way. Special thanks to Jade Brooks, Katie Courtland, Jessica Ryan, Bonnie Perkel, and to the brilliant copyeditor, Martha Ramsey.

My approach to embodied navigations of space, theorizing communities-of-difference, and weight-sharing is shaped by several very exciting and transformative collaborative opportunities. I am thankful to Robert O'Meally for creating the Jazz Study Group at Columbia and for bringing me into it. Everyone who was there contributed to the impact of those unforgettable sessions, but I was especially inspired by interactions with Krin Gabbard, John Gennari, Maxine Gordon, Farah Jasmine Griffin, William J. Harris, Diedra Harris-Kelley, Robin D. G. Kelley, George Lewis, Jacqui Malone, Ingrid Monson, Fred Moten, and Salim Washington. Over the past seven years, I have been indelibly shaped by Ajay Heble's work and vision, and the brilliant teams he initiated and facilitated through the Improvisation, Community, and Social Practice (ICASP) Research Initiative. Out of these joyously unpredictable settings I gratefully became involved in Pauline Oliveros's Adaptive Use Musical Instrument (AUMI) project and the new ways it made improvising across abilities possible. Thank you to Pauline for her collaborative community-formation philosophies and practices, and to Leaf Miller, Jackie Heyen, Gillian Siddall, Ellen Waterman, and Eric Lewis and the rest of the AUMI Research Group. I am grateful to my brilliant and multiply talented colleagues in the KU AUMI-InterArts from the core research team of Kip Haaheim, Michelle Heffner Hayes, Nicole Hodges Persley, and into the wider "(Un)Rolling the Boulder" community that we have become. I am grateful to the KU Interdisciplinary Jazz Studies Group for our fabulous interdisciplinary conferences (2003–8). Over the last couple of years, I have had the pleasure and honor of exploring collaborative research with the Melba Liston Research Collective, whose members include Lisa Barg, Monica Hairston-O'Connell, Tammy Kernodle, and Dee Spencer. Thank you to Michelle Habell-Pallan and Sonnet Retman for the wonderfully creative, brilliant, and collaborative Women Who Rock UnConference, another place where I've been learning critical methods for how to do together what we can't do alone, a core theme of this book. To CV Hawkins, wherever you are, this book has been brewing in me ever since the social geography of Los Angeles impinged on our plans to be roommates in Hollywood. That two acting students and retail workers of exactly the same age could not find a convenient place to share the rent in the late 1970s did not seem to surprise you, but came as a shock and lasting source of regret and shame for me, and introduced me to the questions that ultimately led me to and through this book.

Many friends have supported me emotionally and in so many other ways throughout the years of writing this book, and I want to thank, especially, Julia Beyer and Mary Letterii. Thank you, Emily Kofron. In addition to human friends, a plethora of excellent cats kept me company during long periods of sitting in one place. It is with no offense to Maggie, Casey, Idgie, Birdie, or Bowie, that I single out little Angel, who spent most of her Nora Desmond years helping me to not lose my ding dong. With apologies to all of the cats with whom I actually lived, I send a special shout-out and blade of grass to another late great writing cat and unparalleled task-master, Tux, with whom I had the incredible good fortune to spend a productive six weeks. For that opportunity, I am grateful to Ellie Hisama, Anton Vishio, Hana, and Liam.

Tami Albin has already been listed in nearly every category of gratitude, but I owe her much more. She joined me after this book was under way and has stuck with me while I carried it (literally) on my back for fourteen years. As grateful as I am for all her help with the Canteen research and writing, I am even more grateful to her for dragging me off the dance floor from time to time and to live in our own times. I would have been lost without you. I hope I am as much of a rock for you now, as you write your book, as you have been for me.

Marilyn and Roy Tucker, to whom I dedicate this book, were the first people I ever met who remember World War II, and no doubt, their many interests, commitment to living in the present, and eclectic musical tastes gave me my first hunches that their generation was far more than a monument to war. I wrote this book, as I have written everything else, in close play-by-play dialogue with them and their friends. I wish all writers could be so lucky. To my parents I say thank you for creating an environment rich in inquiry, stories, humor, friends, and music, and for your relentlessly convincing interest, from the very get-go, in what I have to say. I am embarrassed by how much time you have spent listening to me hash out ideas, but so grateful. We have covered topics A-to-Z. So now hear this: I love you. Thank you for everything.

Prologue

Dance Floor Democracy?

There Is No Color Line at This Coast Canteen
—*CHICAGO DEFENDER* (JANUARY 30, 1943)

What does it mean to have a body that provides an institution with diversity?
—SARA AHMED, *ON BEING INCLUDED* (2012)

Democracy! That's what it means, Slim! Everybody equal. Like tonight! All them big shots, listening to little shots like me, and being friendly!
—A SERGEANT BROOKLYN NOLAN, *HOLLYWOOD CANTEEN* (1944)

This is a long book about a small place, a military recreation spot operated for three years by motion picture industry workers in Hollywood (October 3, 1942–November 22, 1945).[1] There are larger rooms with longer (earthly) life spans. But this one's fame extends beyond walls and years. Even so, this long book does not deliver a comprehensive history of the Hollywood Canteen— there are far more detailed accounts of the nuts and bolts of its operation. A reader seeking such a resource would do well to consult Lisa Mitchell and Bruce Torrence's book *The Hollywood Canteen: Where the Greatest Generation Danced with the Most Beautiful Girls in the World* (2012).

At the same time, this is a small book about a large topic. I began by interviewing people about their memories of dancing in this particular patriotic swing station, and I wound up rethinking my position on enduring linkages between democracy, war, and swing. I push off from the Hollywood Canteen to ask broader questions about relationships between big band music, jitterbug, and U.S. nostalgia for World War II. You might say I write less *about* the dance floor than *on it*, approaching it from many routes. I wrestle with it, cruise it, and squeeze through the crowd. I dance in the archives and sit on people's sofas. I meet some former Canteen-goers through the papers they left for posterity and interact with others in a shared moment when we ask one another questions, compare interpretations, and push back. I hope this book bears traces of embodied transmissions with different implications and outcomes. This is a dance floor that means something to people: those who remember it and those who recognize its nostalgic style. I approach with respect and suspicion. I spy on it, screen it, and experiment with its pressures.

Before we take off, I offer a few questions to set the ground. First, what was the Hollywood Canteen and why go there now? What does it tell us about 1940s swing culture and the continuation of romantic attachments to World War II in the United States? Finally, why study a dance floor in the past if the object of study is the lingering power of swing culture to move U.S. Americans to think fondly of World War II in the present?

What Is This Place?

The Hollywood Canteen was a uso-like nightclub that was operated by volunteers drawn mostly from the guilds and unions of the motion picture industry. Patterned after New York's Stage Door Canteen, the Hollywood Canteen opened on October 3, 1942. During the three years of its existence, volunteers entertained drafted and enlisted members and soldiers of the army, navy, Marines, Coast Guard, and Allied nations. Bette Davis was the president. John Garfield was vice president. The Hollywood Canteen became a powerful backdrop for publicity photos of movie stars performing patriotism through dancing with soldiers, feeding them, signing autographs, and generally being friendly and generous with their time, beauty, and fame during a relatively "popular" war. Volunteers were drawn from across the ranks of motion picture industry workers and supplemented with others. Publicity images leave the impression that all of the volunteers were movie stars and everyone socializing on the dance floor was white.

Yet, the Hollywood Canteen was also the site of brouhahas that broke out when Canteen board members fought over whether or not people could dance across race lines. When challenged by members and volunteers less keen on integration, Bette Davis and John Garfield, along with the segregated locals of the Los Angeles musicians unions, threatened to pull their support, and the color line purportedly was broken. Stories about these civil rights battles appeared in the national black press, popular front press, and the music magazine *DownBeat*, if not the mainstream press. It is the story that dominates the FBI files and morphs into happy multiculturalism (among the extras) in the 1944 feature film about the Canteen. Later on, this angle resurfaced as something to be proud of in biographies and autobiographies of celebrities and other film industry personnel and as evidence of racial tension (with varying degrees of resolution) in excellent histories of jazz and swing, World War II, and Los Angeles.[2]

Nonetheless, the lasting image that circulates in national memory is the jitterbugging white starlet and soldier. Sometimes a photograph is juxtaposed that shows a black entertainer on the stage and bears a caption that celebrates the club for its racial integration.[3] By *national memory*, I do not mean to imply that everyone in the nation shares the same memory, nor that this form of memory bears traces of every national subject. National memory is not social memory in the sense of being co-created by members of a community remembering together.[4] What I mean by national memory is a multisensory look and feel, a story and a soundtrack, a pallet of colors, a style of commemoration of imagined coherence that is stirring enough to bring the nation to the nation-state. So dominant is such a national memory that all who claim positions as national subjects must grapple with it from time to time, one way or another, whether they see themselves reflected in it or not.

Photographs and newsreel footage of the white starlet-and-soldier couple recur in documentaries about the wartime home front and Hollywood's patriotic service in World War II. In recurring nostalgic production, the recycled and reenacted white jitterbugging man in uniform and actress volunteer instantly evoke the friendly nation at war. In this book, I ask: what is the connection between the integrated dance floor as a symbol of democracy and the white dancing couples that provide so much of the readymade stock footage of swing culture—in its incarnation as the national memory of the "Greatest Generation" in the "Good War"? What is this gap between the iconic photos of white starlets and soldiers in Hollywood and the disappearing/reappearing "battles" over mixed-race dancing?

There is something about this contradiction that looms larger than the Hollywood Canteen and, in fact, resembles the conundrums surrounding the way democracy is typically conceived in the United States and in swing and jazz history. Indeed, the more deeply drawn I was into the research, the more I was convinced that this small place could be a window onto bigger questions of swing, democracy, race, gender, war, and national memory.

The typical Hollywood Canteen story goes something like this: selfless movie stars roll up their sleeves and boost morale. The servicemen are bashful boys in uniform who want nothing more than a glass of milk, an autograph to send home, and a spin around the dance floor with a modest (yet pretty) starlet-hostess to the energetic sounds of swing music, heard as optimistic, youthful, and utterly "American." Lists of donations figure prominently in the telling, the thousands of pounds of butter donated, the numbers served, and the sweet things GIS uttered when Hollywood personalities treated them as though they were important. Often the soldiers are depicted as adorably shy and homespun, country bumpkins in the court of the rich and famous. A typical story in *Screenland* tells of a "husky Marine [who] keeps dancing with [glamorous movie star] Alexis Smith until she suggests he meet some of the other girls. 'Oh no,' he says, 'I'd be scared stiff to dance with a glamorous movie star. I like a regular girl, like you.' "[5] In telling after telling, the Hollywood Canteen unfolds as a utopian tale of national unity and innocence, its characters exemplars of "towering achievement and modest demeanor," to borrow from Tom Brokaw's consecration of an entire generation.[6]

The narrative was already in place on the club's opening night, when Colonel Harold E. Shannon, commander of the Midway forces of the Marines, claimed to speak for "every leatherneck, gob, and buck private" when he told the overflow crowd and radio audience: "these boys here tonight will be going out to our battle fronts and in the tough moments that may come they will have a memory of the warm friendliness that is being shown by you folks."[7] This tone carried over in the self-congratulatory status-reversals that would become characteristic of Hollywood Canteen–style democracy. Celebrities performed humility from the grandstands by cheering the "real stars"—the GIS—as they filed in to dance with movie stars, including Ann Sheridan, Rita Hayworth, Hedy Lamarr, and Deanna Durbin, to the big bands of Duke Ellington, Jimmy Dorsey, and Kay Kyser.

The basic narrative is typical of patriotic World War II musical films. In fact, Warner Brothers made one of those features about the Hollywood Canteen during the run of the club, featuring many of its actual volunteers. In *Hollywood Canteen* (1944), Sergeant Brooklyn Nolan (Dane Clark) delivers a soliloquy on the topic of democracy. He is speaking to his buddy, Corporal Slim Green (Robert Hutton), after an exhilarating night of dancing with Ida Lupino and Janice Paige.

"You know, I don't want to get sloppy about this, but it kind of got me, all them famous people being friendly and democratic." Sgt. Nolan surprises himself with the word. He says it again. "Democracy." (And again!) "Democracy! That's what it means, Slim! Everybody equal. Like tonight! All them big shots, listening to little shots like me, and being friendly." Suddenly, his thoughts turn to his body, injured in battle. It turns out that democracy-as-friendliness not only feels great, it has tremendous healing properties for the individual, the military, and the nation. Sergeant Nolan leaps from his bunk with a bodily epiphany: "I DANCED TONIGHT! LOOK! I don't need my cane no more!"

As contemporary political theorists, philosophers, and activists continue to point out, the very definition of U.S. democracy uttered by the fictitious Sergeant Brooklyn Nolan was a common one in the World War II era and remains so in the present. When presidents, pundits, and politicians bother to define "democracy" at all, they characterize it vaguely. It is still *not that unusual* to find liberal institutions in the United States that profess democracy without defining it or define it as "big shots" being friendly to "little shots."[8] How often is an undefined, but emotionally charged evocation of democracy hailed as *proof* of America's friendly intentions toward "little shot" nations? How often is America's performance of friendliness taken as *proof* of its democratic spirit? How often does one hear the call to war as protecting "democracy" from her "enemies" without a definition of "democracy" (and sometimes without a clear definition of "enemies" except as "enemies of democracy")?[9]

Like a large budget studio feature film, the Hollywood Canteen was produced, performed, advertised, represented, filmed, written about, and documented in ways intended to stimulate larger-than-life and certainly larger-than-local experiences, memories, and identifications. Indeed, the usual story seems to know no temporal bounds. The image of the (white) jitterbugging starlet and (white) GI at the Hollywood Canteen assumed a place in contemporary World War II national identity and never seemed to go away, and never seems to lose its ability to evoke a sense of familiarity to new viewers, whether as retro-style in Christina Aguilera's video "Candyman" of 2007 or as misty amateur evocations of the United States home front of World War II in countless reunions, reenactments, and commemorations or as historical and educational materials. As narrator of a 1988 documentary on Hollywood and World War II, actor Van Johnson, historicized the Hollywood Canteen as "a real fairy tale of democracy."[10]

Why Go There Now? Swing Culture as War Memory

When I began this project in the summer of 2000, the history of the Hollywood Canteen felt historical. The pairing of civilian women with military men on a swing dance floor, as an expression of national consensus for going to war, seemed a quaint artifact of another era, pitched to a naïve population that I thought had been replaced by the far more sophisticated audience celebrated by cultural studies. Sure, I had noticed the connection between 1940s pop culture and war when the swing revival accompanied the seemingly endless fifty-year anniversary commemorations of World War II and coincided with the supposedly one-year-long Gulf War in the early 1990s.[11] Somehow this memory didn't prevent me from being stunned anew post–September

11, 2001, when World War II popular culture once again demonstrated its efficacy to mobilize Americans for national love and war.

Eerily, the style and content of the network news quickly resembled the propaganda of the 1940s that I was studying as part of my research on World War II popular culture. Barely two months after September 11, while researching the government censorship of popular culture enacted by the Office of War Information in the 1940s, newspapers reported on meetings between the federal government and Hollywood producers about how to combine forces to create the kinds of images and narratives Americans need during difficult times. A page 1 editorial in the *New York Times* used the subheading "Firing Up the Hollywood Canteen" to tell us that "Karl Rove, a senior Bush adviser, is to meet today with senior Hollywood executives to see how they might contribute to the war effort, possibly with public service spots and documentaries on terrorism." To this reminder of Hollywood's cooperation with the Office of War Information and the cascade of patriotic films of the 1940s, the editorialist, Clyde Hyberman, connected other developments that harkened back to World War II, including George Bush's sudden shift from "lone cowboy" to "born-again nation-builder and multilateralist" and the Pentagon's blockage of "access to independent information about the war."[12]

To conduct any kind of research about World War II history and culture during these years was to dance with the past and the present. My interactions with former Canteen-goers were shaped by the high level of "wartime consciousness" afoot—that is, the World War II memory that Torgovnick tells us lies dormant but is ready to spring into action at times of national crisis, often through 1940s-style national rhetoric and popular culture.[13] The years in which I conducted these interviews are certainly not the first time that popular artifacts of the World War II era resurfaced as national culture, but the effects were difficult to miss. Who could fail to notice, for example, the relentless references to the bombing of Pearl Harbor following the attacks of September 11, 2001,[14] or the recirculation of iconic World War II images in the months that followed, such as the reworkings of the Norman Rockwell Four Freedoms series of illustrations in the *New York Times*?[15] Searching the web for "The Hollywood Canteen" in November 2001, I learned that Los Angeles had caught "forties fever," according to a review about a popular night spot called the Hollywood Canteen at a location mere blocks away from the original (demolished in 1962). Only this one charged for food and operated in reverse: instead of military personnel being served by celebrity volunteers, celebrity customers were served by waitstaff dressed as World War II military personnel and pinups. By 2004, the Bob Hope USO Club at Los Angeles

International Airport had tripled in size. Its connections to World War II also expanded, with the addition of a library named after General Doolittle, a snack bar called the "Hollywood Canteen," and a TV lounge named after Johnny Grant, honorary mayor of Hollywood and one of my interviewees.[16]

In short, my research of the Hollywood Canteen ceased to feel like a social and cultural history of race and gender relations during the 1940s and morphed irrevocably into a history of the present, specifically focused on contemporary production of memories about World War II. My study retained its emphasis on contradictory connections between race, gender, democracy, and swing on that 1940s dance floor that was configured, more than any other, as the dance floor of the nation—but that emphasis became a way to study the relationship between the various ways World War II is remembered and memorialized in the United States and the ways official memories are recruited to justify national actions globally.

It may sound naïve to say that I did not realize that this exploration of skirmishes over democracy on the dance floor at the Hollywood Canteen would also be about national memory and embodiment in the present. Nonetheless, I found myself a subject who, like Canteen hostess Jane Lockwood, "danced as never before." For me, this entailed revisiting swing historiography and stepping into scholarly spaces I had not yet explored—fields of memory studies and dance studies—in search of new ways to approach, in the present, multiple perspectives on swing culture of the past. It has been crucial to this project not only to study cultural struggles historically on one dance floor in the 1940s but also to explore what happens to diverse social memories, and ways of telling those memories, when a dominant strain manages to masquerade as everybody's memory of the "dance floor of the nation."

The management of whiteness and multiculturalism in the representations of the Hollywood Canteen in revivals displays a striking continuity of 1940s images and current revivals. Although the photographs, the newsreels, and the feature film of the 1940s occasionally include people of color, they are presented almost as scenery, with the focus clinging to the white jitterbugging couples. The absence of people of color presented as subjects of the narrative of "inclusion" has changed little in the revival images I have tracked throughout the years of writing this book. In 2007, Christina Aguilera's video "Candyman" includes nonwhite soldiers and hostesses in the Hollywood Canteen–inspired background, but Aguilera's uncanny trio performance with herself as an Andrews Sisters knockoff (spectacularly in three hair colors), and the jitterbug scene are presented as white.[17] World War II nostalgia production—from immediately after the war to this day—has issued many re-enactors of the Andrews Sisters, as well as bandleader Glenn Miller, including the "In the Mood Singers and Dancers" and "String of Pearls Orchestra," who played the string of World War II anniversaries that accompanied the Good War Memory Boom and continue to tour. Their advertising promises that they are as "authentic as it gets."[18] Not all "white" nostalgic reenactments are performed by white people. They don't need to be. Tracy McMullen argues that the Glenn Miller reenactment band at Yale managed to enshrine a memory of World War II swing culture as an all-white, all-male orchestra in spite of its inclusion of people of color and white women.[19]

As I worked on this research, my own workplace, the University of Kansas, repeatedly hosted events that enacted connections between World War II commemoration and wars of the present. The Dole Institute of Politics broke ground the month after September 11, 2001, and finally opened four months after the launching of "Operation Iraqi Freedom" with the invasion of Iraq on March 20, 2003. The opening started the Institute off with a bang: a four-day celebration that included the Glenn Miller Orchestra (the "ghost orchestra," that is, to use the chilling term for bands that played on, replacing original members as mortality rotated them out), a "USO show," a World War II–era air show, and World War II military reenactments. The grand opening of the institute building itself, with its "World's Largest Stained Glass American Flag," concretizes the associations between World War II with the very different wars of the present. At the end of a display of artifacts from Senator Bob Dole's military career in World War II stands a pair of glass-encased steel fragments from the fallen towers of the World Trade Center. A plaque explains they are there to "remind us that each generation faces its own call to service."[20]

As an especially beloved artifact of World War II swing culture nostalgia, the Hollywood Canteen fits squarely into the cultural repository that Marianna Torgovnick calls "the War Complex," or the particular ways that national memory of the World War II continues to express, for many Americans, "how we like to think of ourselves and to present ourselves to the world, even at those times when, the United States has been a belligerent and not-much-loved nation."[21] Stories of uncomplicated American goodness during the World War II have played, and continue to play, a powerful role in constructing national memory and recruiting national identity, even for those too young to remember that war. A Hollywood Canteen memory of volunteer movieland hostesses jitterbugging with wholesome boys in uniform is a powerful backdrop for narrations of a controversial nation that inscribe the national "we" as innocent, benevolent, and united. This book is about that vision, but it is also about the visions that are forgotten when that one is the only one that is remembered.

Why Dance in the Past?

There are many routes one could take to explore the complex cultural work of the Hollywood Canteen. A history of the club might have told us more about the place behind the memory—but this presumes that the "place" and the "memory" might be disentangled, that one is literally the referent for the other. This didn't seem to get at the questions I wanted to ask, although I did indeed conduct extensive archival research on the club and other sites of soldier entertainment in Los Angeles during the 1940s. At the other end of the spectrum would be a cultural study of reenactments of the Hollywood Canteen, along with other swing culture performances of World War. Indeed, I collected evidence of nostalgic afterlife and read with great interest other scholarship on World War II nostalgia performance, reenactment, and stimulation of particular forms of national memory. But I wanted to do something slightly different. I wanted to better understand my own fascination with, and fear of, World War II nostalgia, particularly as it travels in swing culture, and I wanted to do it in conversation with people who had attended the Hollywood Canteen.

Some white former Canteen-goers talked about racial tensions but most narrated the dance floor as completely integrated, friendly, and uncontroversial. One after another insisted that it was a "wonderful" place where "everyone was together" and "there was no prejudice." However, when asked if they had ever danced with a person of a race other than their own or saw people of other races dancing, many replied "I don't remember," followed by "but I'm absolutely sure it was integrated. I would have noticed if it wasn't." One white man told me, "Those problems hadn't started yet."

Canteen-goers of color more often narrated a segregated or at least partially segregated environment. When I asked Mel Bryant, an African-American veteran, about the extent to which the dance floor was integrated, he replied, "Don't you believe it." He added that it was "a different thing, a wonderful thing to have a place where soldiers could go, but it wasn't integrated in an equal way."[22]

Most of those who had been civilian volunteers at the club remembered both military men and women as being welcome there. However, women veterans most often narrated the club as a place where they were shunned or sent upstairs. Navy veteran Lorraine (Mitchell) Bear recalled being turned away from the door when she and her fellow WAVES (Women Accepted for Volunteer Emergency Service) traveled from Port Hueneme for a night on the town.[23] Other servicewomen remembered being allowed in the building but barred from the dance floor.

Whether the interviews happened before or after September 11, 2001, profoundly affected them. While I agree utterly with Marianna Torgovnick that the words "After 9/11" have "become a cliché that can set the teeth on edge, identifying powerful memories, potent emotions, and a political code," it also seems necessary to comment on the presence in my interview sample of emotional and rhetorical distinctions between those that that occurred in the months following 9/11.[24] In October 2001, a white starlet, Andrea King, told me this about the Canteen:

> It's one of the earliest instances I can remember when a night club was racially mixed. And I'm proud to say I never personally heard anyone complain about it. There were much greater concerns of the day. Just like what's happening now, with the tragedy of the Trade Towers attack, everyone comes together for a single cause. For a while at least, other prejudices are put aside.[25]

King's perception that World War II promoted racial integration in the United States and that this was an uncomplicated policy eagerly supported by all is paralleled by her perception that prejudices were now set aside and responses unified in the United States post–9/11. There is ample evidence to the contrary in both cases, yet my aim is not to produce a historical study that would prove her incorrect but to listen in relation to many versions. Narrated memories of people who attended the Hollywood Canteen cannot be taken as an accurate map of social relations sixty years ago. Nonetheless, they can offer insights into a "struggle over memory," in the very serious sense in that Alessandro Portelli develops in his groundbreaking work.[26] For Portelli, oral historians must work "on both the factual and narrative planes." It doesn't matter, then, whether memory is true or false. "When an incorrect reconstruction of history becomes popular belief, we are not called on only to rectify the facts but also to interrogate ourselves on how and why this common sense took shape and on its meanings and uses."[27]

Listening for struggles over memory, I conducted oral histories, interviews, conversations, and corresponded with over sixty people who had visited the Hollywood Canteen. For simplicity's sake, I will use the terms "interviewee" and "narrator" interchangeably. However, I do mean by "oral history" something different from "interview." I define "oral history" as a narrator-led interpretation of the past in the present in which the oral historian listens and tries to follow (and follow up) wherever the teller leads. Both participants still may ask and answer questions, and both impact the interaction, but there is a looser sense of time, place, and story, and the details and events selected as important may not be at all what the researcher anticipated. The "interview" is also a dynamic interaction but one that is structured around a specific object of inquiry and unfolds in a more contained question-and-answer-driven pattern, even when those questions are open-ended. Though the parameters are tighter, surprising answers do occur, stories do get told, and the lead and follow may switch off. My preference is the former, but I was also happy to lead the Q&A when my partner preferred to dance within more structured guidelines. In my experience of both forms of exchange, there is nearly always slippage between them. What is important is that the parameters are discussed and mutually agreed on before the session begins.

In listening to many struggles over memory, I trained my ear to notice instances of critical commotion, by which I mean moments in which the speaker seems to narrate ways of being that are both in and out of sync with the dominant "official" version. The significance of the Hollywood Canteen interviews is not in what they can reveal about "what really happened" but in the ways people remember and narrate themselves in relation to such a narrow and persistent available framework. Often, narrators and interviewees identified with the familiar version yet in some way or another also identified limitations in the democratic fairy tale. In this way, in remembering and describing their own bodies as moving both with and against the official national narrative, tellers situated themselves as particular kinds of national subjects.

When narrators told how their bodies were embraced or rejected by the social geography of race, gender, class, sexuality, and American-ness, they shared ways of remembering and telling that were shaped not only by that night sixty years ago when they attended the Hollywood Canteen, but by national historical events and official stories told about those events both at the time and in the present. Because I see these memories as socially constituted, as embodied, I am interested in how people *place* themselves in an imagined landscape that represents a kind of dance-floor-of-the-nation. To what extent do narrators identify with the Canteen of national memory? To what other community memories (neighborhood, familial, ethnic, racialized, occupational, political, etc.), do they connect their re-membered visits to the Canteen? Narrative theory helps me to listen to how people make order from the disorder that is opened up when I ask, and they begin to respond, to the question "What do you remember about the Hollywood Canteen?" We covered lots of territory. But it was the focus on the small place—the club grounded in time and place—that allowed us to do this, even when it catapulted us to other times and places.

The research for this book has felt like walking slowly and respectfully through a roomful of people at the end of their lives who are all talking at once. I hear them talking about the same thing and different things simultaneously. From this perspective, it is difficult to make out more than one person's words at a time. I hear each person's story when we are briefly face-to-face but always remain aware of the dissonant surround-sound of other voices, living and dead. Reveries of nostalgia suddenly spring bolt upright as conversation shifts from distant memory to diverse responses to the evening news: "... *just like what's happening now* ..."[28] "*We're at war, but I don't think the people realize we're at war.*"[29] Because my own feelings of rage, terror, and fear of U.S. militarism are so great during this research period, I cannot bracket my feelings about current wars as we talk about the past—and neither do my interviewees. I step on their feet, and they step on mine. I am one of the embodied participants, partnering in brief but intense conversations about a distant past that urgently matters. They tell me what they hope I will write. I feel the weight, knowing that my own perspective more closely mirrors those of some interviewees than others; I feel the weight of wanting to democratically represent not just one point of view but the tangle.

Therefore, I have attempted to write this book as though it is a dance floor of memory. I am one of the dancers. As a reader, you are another. Sometimes I take the liberty of referring to us as we, though I know we are not the same. Previous jitterbug experience is neither a plus nor a minus—this is a dance floor famous for its stated commitment to democracy and tolerance for dancers of all levels, novice to pro. As I shall elaborate in the introduction, I worked to write in such a way as to represent my interactions with people connected with the Hollywood Canteen as accurately as I could, while leaving space for questions I didn't ask, people I didn't meet, and various possible interpretations, including yours. I want to get at the crowdedness of this dance floor as it moves with and against the trademark simplicity of representations of World War II swing memory, and the jitterbugging starlet hostesses and GIs at the Hollywood Canteen, that have been invested with national nostalgia.

In the introduction, I walk through my writing strategies for dancing in a small place in order to explore large questions. I stretch out on the peculiarities of writing connections among swing culture, democracy, and war memory. I conclude with a map of the approaches that make up the remainder of this long book, a foray occasioned by a small—and very crowded—space.

Introduction

Writing on a Crowded Dance Floor

I have come to believe that improvised dance involves literally giving shape to oneself by deciding how to move in relation to an unsteady landscape.
—**DANIELLE GOLDMAN**

What we manage to do each time we win a victory is not so much to secure change once and for all, but rather to create new terrains for struggle.
—**ANGELA Y. DAVIS**

What would history look like if it were to acknowledge the fact of improvisation?
—**SUSAN LEIGH FOSTER**

Writing from the Tangle

How does one write on a crowded dance floor—*any* crowded dance floor— never mind a *famous* crowded dance floor that existed over sixty years ago?[1] The writer can interview people who were there, read what others have written, and sift the archives for photos, ephemera, and newspaper clippings, but she cannot actually perch in the rafters and record the interactions below. Nor can her interviewees actually recreate their points of view from the dance floor. Even if total recall was an option, eyewitnesses could never identify all of the bodies that affected their experiences and memories. They wouldn't have been able to see beyond the heads and shoulders of those with whom they danced any more than I can see beyond those with whom I spoke. Nor would our interactions be the same on a different day. Oral history, like dance, is dynamic, interactive, and shaped by embodied knowledge of participants.

FIG I.1: Dancers at the Hollywood Canteen, around 1943. PHOTOGRAPH TAKEN BY GILBERT SPRECKLES, PART OF A ROLL INTENDED FOR THE NAVY NEWSPAPER THE *GOLDEN GATOR*, NAVAL AIR STATION, ALAMEDA, CALIFORNIA. COURTESY OF R. JANIE TILBURY.

So is writing, though it doesn't usually feel that way. To write on a crowded dance floor is to practice intentional awareness of contingencies among ourselves and those we face, as well as those of unknown bodies and perspectives that jostle the social geography on which we move.

To add another layer of crowdedness—how does one write meaningfully about a *famous* dance floor that has been relentlessly depicted in particular ways in newspapers and newsreels, movie magazines, radio broadcasts, and elsewhere throughout, beyond, and even *before* its earthly existence? Truly, this dance floor was saturated with all of the ingredients of national nostalgia before the opening night crowds were so thick that Bette Davis had to crawl through the bathroom window to deliver the welcome speech,[2] and Betty Grable danced with forty soldiers, sailors, and Marines in ten minutes,[3] and the paparazzi discovered the simple poignancy of Marlene Dietrich sweeping the floor between stampedes. A sturdy patriotic narrative about this dance floor had been erected before the first three thousand hostess-soldier couples shook the foundations of the old barn, even before the paint dried on its immediately legendary murals. People who shared their stories noted the difficulty of distinguishing between their own memories of the dance floor and what they remember from the feature film *Hollywood Canteen* (1944), other people's memories, or any number of newsreels, Hollywood biographies, histories, and documentaries, most of which repeat the nostalgic presentation of wartime publicity. How does one write through this thick sea of narrative in which public relations storytelling cannot be separated from personal memories? How does one balance, in writing, memories shared by people who danced at the Hollywood Canteen once or twice a week for three years, with those who danced (or tried to) once or twice *period*? How should the writing balance the striking similarity of some people's memories to official Canteen narratives—with the equally striking differences of others?

To write about swing dancing at the Hollywood Canteen demanded, unavoidably, that I tangle with one of the many potent sites of America's nostalgia for itself as innocent, heroic, and virtuous during World War II. My use of "tangle" as a methodological verb is deliberate. I do not hope to "untangle" the various layers of significance wrapped up in the Hollywood Canteen, in other words, but to "tangle with" cultural memory as "a field of contested meanings," drawing from Marita Sturken's conception of the relationship between personal and cultural memory and history as "entangled."[4] Diverse memories and narratives jostle and bounce one another around the room when they *take* to this crowded iconic space, yet in doing so are somehow never completely free from a simple "coherent" national version. Writing—even historical writing—is embodied. Dancing—even social dancing—inscribes subjects, democratically or otherwise. And remembering one's body in motion is different from remembering "what happened." In the sections of the interviews when people narrated their bodies moving across the crowded dance floor of the Hollywood Canteen, the vantage point tended to shift from a "big picture" of "it was like this" to the type of bumpy, idiosyncratic view one might expect from the revealing limits of a handheld movie camera that cannot see above the heads of others. In discussing the challenges of filming the Lindy Hop, and its mainstreamed doppelgänger the jitterbug, Robert Crease noted that neither the proscenium view nor the cutting from one close-up to the next is able to render the sense that "the performer of vernacular dance is always alongside others in an organic and multiperspectival event."[5] In this way, oral history may be better suited than film to represent these fleeting perspectives.

But people are not cameras, and even a cinema verité–style personal narrative of flying, bouncing, looking at others looking at me and you is not a record of what happened but what is fashioned in the act of re-calling one time, space, and performance into another and performing it via the narrative possibilities of an interview, which is also a dynamic social interaction that occurs in time and space. Nonetheless, it was in these complex moments when narrators spoke from a sense of being embodied, of relating fleeting focal points limited and facilitated by flesh and matter, that I learned what this book would be about—struggles over democracy at the dance floor memory level—and knew it would be tricky to write. Like the dance theorists who contributed to Susan Leigh Foster's *Corporealities*, I became convinced that I must somehow turn myself "(in)to writing to dance with this figure," which for me is the nostalgic hold of World War II swing culture on U.S. nationalism at a moment when those who could help us to factor in social and political difference, improvisation, tension, injury, and torque were becoming scarce.[6]

Democratic writing on a crowded dance floor must acknowledge bodies of interviewees, as well as the interviewer, as more than the vehicles for heads full of memories, analyses, and meaning. How can one write in such a way that the historian is also embodied, thinking of the past in the present, and trying to "think together" with one narrator at a time, sometimes briefly once, and sometimes in repeat performances? Dance scholars are far ahead of the game in developing methods for embodied writing. Dance theorist Marta Savigliano has coined the term "choreocritic" in her search for an embodied writing position suitable for analyzing dance and "the sociohistorical conditions it expresses and produces." [7] Picture me a dizzier, untrained (though enthusiastic) social-dance version of the "choreocritic"; not so spectacularly qualified as dance scholars in this business of writing about bodies but perhaps well matched to partner with many of the amateur dancers who visited the Canteen and sharing Savigliano's interest in trying to "imagine stories about people who move for and against each other, articulating webs of power."[8] I want to write as an embodied narrator grappling with constraints, making palpable the "weight" of my "presence" and "present" as storyteller—an aspect Savigliano accurately notes is often the part we forget to tell, so fascinated are we "by the past we are enticed to imagine."[9]

My writing goal, then, has been to find a textual practice crowded with different bodies and voices, positions, and experiences, suitable for narrating the "break-aways" as well as the basic steps. While asking people to share memories of the Hollywood Canteen was not exactly the same as channel-surfing the reruns of national memory, it sometimes had that feel. The Hollywood Canteen—though crowded, divergently remembered and narrated in interviews, and slippery in meaning, especially in the "break-aways" of embodied memory—retains an uncanny ability to adhere to its own special nostalgic gloss. Dancing with these narratives and their relationships, I have tried to write in a way that accommodates narratives that critique and narratives that prove the ready-made story about a "democratic night club." I've tried to write the power of the tangle without throwing out the power of the gloss: the story of friendly volunteers from the motion picture industry dancing new social relations with soldiers, sailors, and Marines; rendering chaos of war, of mass migration, of racism, of overcrowding, of uncertainty, of separation of loved ones into a national memory as harmonious as the Andrews Sisters.

Benedict Anderson used the term "unisonance" to refer to the effects of singing together with strangers a national anthem on a national holiday as "the echoed physicalization of the imagined community."[10] This "remembering-together" of the Hollywood Canteen as the benevolent, uncomplicated "dance floor of the nation" also seems to have this effect when narrated as personal memory. Over the telephone or in person, in isolation or within earshot of spouses, family, friends, or nurses, or others, participation in what Anderson might call the "simultaneity" of Canteen narrative seems a ready-made inducement for interviewees to place themselves in a larger context of national belonging. As Anderson put it, "How selfless this unisonance feels!"[11]

At the same time, many interviewees who were familiar with the dominant mode of Canteen memory voiced narrative dissonance even as they reprised the consonant strain. To a greater and lesser extent, narrators troubled particular aspects of the national memory, relating anecdotes and interpretations that criticized the exclusions intrinsic to that selfless "We" of national sing-along. It is tempting to view the "dissonance" as individual memory versus "unisonance" as national memory, but I will argue that dissonance is also achieved through "remembering together." In other words, dissonance is not just an accidental result of "not fitting" but the powerful "out of tuneness" that Ajay Heble compares so fruitfully to other kinds of critical practice.[12] Francesca Cappelletto argues that "community itself is built on narrative acts."[13] Dissonant narrativity builds critical communities, in which members sustain important differences, building on practices of sounding and listening that resist resolution.

The Writing That Drew Me to This Dance

There is nothing like an archive to reveal the unsteady ground of a story you think you know. It was, in fact, the dissonant range of perspectives on "dance floor democracy" evident in the writing of contemporary observers that drew me to this project. The Hollywood Canteen first tugged at my attention as a particularly intriguing site of national memory while I was conducting newspaper research for my first book, *Swing Shift: All-Girl Bands of the 1940s*. While perusing microfilm evidence of the hundreds of all-woman bands that had been omitted from jazz and swing historiography (but included in women-in-jazz historiography), I kept noticing, from the corner of my eye, claims about the Hollywood Canteen for its inclusive democracy. This surprised me, as I would have considered the Canteen part of the nostalgic bundle of overrepresented swing narratives that eclipsed critical counternarratives. Nonetheless, the black press, the Communist and Popular Front press, and the mainstream newspapers all praised the Hollywood Canteen. In story after story, it was depicted as both typifying a nation that was jumping with soldier-hostess dance spots and at the same time, for many different and contradictory reasons, hailed as utterly unique—the very pinnacle of democracy.

Refractions of this theme stemmed from a variety of values and positions, each of which identified a special form of democracy at the Hollywood Canteen. "Democracy" adhered to a variety of visions of inclusiveness, even in ways that were atypical of the nation. Such claims were usually supported by gestures toward a boundary-breaking dance floor. This basic narrative was repeated, with different stakes by very different sources addressing different constituencies, including the black press, Hearst papers, entertainment guild and union publications (including the *Overture*, the official paper of white Local 47 of the segregated musicians union in Los Angeles), and the Popular Front press (including the Communist paper the *Daily Worker*). Stories in these papers claimed the dance floor of the Hollywood Canteen as a space where lines of social division could be crossed in the name of American democracy. Somehow, by enabling the crossing of lines that typically served as barriers to U.S. democracy, the Hollywood Canteen accrued status as simultaneously unusual within the nation and representative of the nation.

For the mainstream press, the list of social barriers broken at the Canteen usually highlighted the crossing of the great gulf that lay between movie stars and regular folk, as when the *Los Angeles Times* praised the Hollywood Canteen as a place "where Joe Dogface can dance with Hedy Lamarr."[14] This is Sergeant Nolan's definition of democracy as "big shots being friendly to little shots."[15] Repeatedly, in the mainstream newspapers, movie magazines, and newsreels the Hollywood Canteen was constructed as a great leveler of class hierarchy through narratives that equated screen careers with elite status. Stars were not capable of run-of-the-mill volunteerism (which was seen as civilian obligation); their friendliness was magnanimous. But these stories of Hollywood royalty who conferred national belonging to the "common people" were not the only awkward proofs of democracy.

Other divisions bridged through Canteen stories in the mainstream press included national boundaries between the Allied nations. The *Los Angeles Examiner* once referred to the Canteen as "the bright crossroads of the world" where "uniforms from Great Britain, France, Greece, the Netherlands, China, Belgium, Russia, Brazil and other lands blend happily with olive drab from Nome and Key West."[16] Such happy blendings, for the black press, were located across race lines, with the Canteen as a place where, according to the *Chicago Defender*, "the sepia boy in uniform is as welcome as the fairest Caucasian, and where sepia hostesses dance with both nationalities."[17] Though the civil rights story later made its way into Canteen historiography, in the 1940s the possibility of racial mixing went mostly unmentioned in the mainstream press, but was an achievement the black press emphasized throughout the war.

Other papers that sometimes emphasized racial mixing were the socialist, liberal, and labor papers. The *Daily Worker*, which also advocated integration of baseball, described the integrated Canteen as "an example of community solidarity behind the war effort," going on to explain that inclusiveness would strengthen "the bond between the fighting forces of democracy and the people."[18] Numerous stories in the black press, the socialist press, and labor publications repeated the same quotation from what must have been an early press release about the Canteen: "military men and women regardless of race or creed, wearing the uniform of any one of the United Nations will be admitted to the canteen."[19]

These claims would pique the curiosity of anyone who knows a thing or two about U.S. social history during World War II. How did a *racially integrated* dance floor in the United States in the 1940s express democracy for such differently situated groups? This was, after all, a country that was busy fighting fascism with a segregated army, segregated Red Cross blood supply, and legal mandatory segregation in many states; a country with a Congress unable to pass an antilynching bill, a defense industry that had to be forced by presidential executive order to hire nonwhite workers during a labor shortage, and an administration that rounded up and interned people of Japanese descent by another executive order? And how was the Hollywood Canteen able to symbolize a space of comfort and belonging and support not only for military men but for *military women* in the newly formed women's branches of the armed forces, against stereotypes of servicewomen as deviant women—either heterosexually "loose" or lesbian?[20] How could diversity represent patriotism in a nation plagued by race riots, especially in 1943? Los Angeles loomed large in the violence, while its mainstream press, police department, and city government fanned the flames. How could integration symbolize the democratic spirit as white sailors in uniform enacted their patriotism by beating up racialized young people in zoot suits, primarily Mexican Americans but other nonwhite youth as well—African Americans and Filipinos?

Guided by these questions, I began seeking people to interview who had attended the Hollywood Canteen between 1942 and 1945. What was the Hollywood Canteen, why did they go, how did they get there, what happened inside, who was there, who danced with whom, and what did it all mean? Sometimes in person, sometimes over the phone, sometimes in letters, sometimes via email or even cassette tape exchanges, sixty members of what Tom Brokaw has called the "Greatest Generation" responded to my request for memories about a crowded dance floor on which they had moved or gazed, weekly or once, well over half a century ago. One by one or in pairs, and sometimes in consultation with memorabilia, media, family, and friends, my small sample of respondents in their late seventies, eighties, and nineties narrated their youthful bodies in motion, crowding with other bodies through the Canteen's wooden entrances—the back for volunteers, the front for service personnel—in wartime Los Angeles.

On some general narrative points, these embodied memories moved together: the dance floor was small and crowded, the Canteen was run by the guilds and unions of the Motion Picture Industry, the soldiers, sailors, and Marines were young and preparing to risk their lives, sandwiches were served, there was always a stage show of some kind.

On other points, memories swing out in wildly different directions: it was racially integrated, it was racially segregated; military women were welcome equally with military men, military women were not allowed to dance; it was a hotbed of political difference, it was a place where politics were set aside for a greater good.

Many interviewees warned me that my request for Canteen memories was impossible to fulfill; sixty or sixty-five years seemed too long to reach back for a clear picture (if that is ever possible, even of yesterday). From limited vantage points that swayed in and out of focus, narratives emerged nonetheless. Disclaimers of blurriness often gave way to sudden convictions of certainty about one thing or another. Such moments of surety most often staked claims not only about what remains to be said about the Hollywood Canteen but also about what the Hollywood Canteen might tell future generations about democracy, war, race and gender, the United States and its own people, and the United States in the world.

The fact that these conversations took place during the war years of 2000–2010 accelerated the usual past/present double-time of oral history interaction. Across vast differences in times, wars, and cultural sensibilities, narrators frequently compared their Hollywood Canteen memories to the national "present"—which encompassed, in the course of our conversations, such events as the attacks on the World Trade Center and Pentagon on September

11, 2001, the vaguely defined U.S. "war on terror," wars in Iraq and Afghanistan, Libya. In speaking of the World War II period, my interviewees and I often spoke about at least two wars at once (what some scholars refer to as "war memory"), even when we thought we were talking about dancing in the past.[21] Our equilibrium was affected by our inevitable guessing at each other's political leanings in the present. My interviewees held political stances all over the map. Nonetheless, they all seemed to agree that the Hollywood Canteen could tell people in the present something about democracy in America (and sometimes, its limits).

Swinging War Memory

"Without music for dancing we would have had no canteen," proclaimed Bette Davis, thanking the musicians union for contributing the bands.[22] To that I would add: without swing music and dance, the Hollywood Canteen could not have become a site of war memory that continues to inspire visions of democracy.

Swing was not the only music performed at the Hollywood Canteen, nor was jitterbug the only dance. Other forms abounded—fox-trot, waltz, even square dance—inviting other subject positions and social relations. Nonetheless, it was the jitterbug that narrators tended to describe, and it is swing, coded as "American," that lives on in Canteen and other nostalgia about World War II. Maurice Halbwachs has written of music as a particularly evocative form of memory.[23] As the dominant soundtrack of national memory of the United States during World War II, swing memory demands a careful listening station for writers tackling the "democratic dance floor," past and present.

As Perry Hall and others have argued, the ability of swing to represent American identity tends to be theorized at one end or the other of two poles: (1) swing was an unusually integrated cultural formation, expressing populism and multiethnic, multicultural, and interracial mixing as particularly American, or (2) swing represented a blatant example of white American appropriation of black American culture. Rather than arguing one side or the other, I am interested in swing's capacity to slip between these poles. If, as Inderpal Grewal argues, "America" continues to be imagined as simultaneously multicultural and white, both within the United States and about the United States in other nations,[24] then the easy slide between swing as multicultural populism or white domination defines its symbolic potency. How neatly the popular national narratives about swing musicians as pioneers who integrated a segregated industry, and patriotic jitterbug dancers as integrating the dance floor, fit what Nikhil Pal Singh has called "civic myths about the triumph over racial injustice" that have become "central to the resuscitation of a vigorous and strident form of American exceptionalism."[25]

When swing is presented as America's "triumph over racial injustice," this narrative drowns out critical opportunities for examining continuing inequalities. In his remarkable study of a predominantly white neo-swing subculture in late 1990s Southern California, Eric Usner has pondered identity formation through a dancing nostalgia that emerged in tandem with white youth anxieties about multiculturalism. Through articulations of historical reenactments of dance, dress, and style with values presumed "authentic" to the 1930s and 1940, the neo-swingsters claimed identities "akin to ethnicity," which they also conceived as "mono-cultural," or at least as a joyful and distinctly "American" blend in which cultural difference was irrelevant.[26] Similar strains are audible in the narratives collected for this book, both in sing-along form and in counter-points of contention. Perhaps it is precisely swing's history as *musical melting pot* and *crime scene of appropriation* that positions it to acquire such a seductive national memory as "universally" American and democratic. In other words, perhaps swing excels as a "national" music not in spite of but because of its ability to mean different things to many people while instantly signaling a unified wartime "America." Listening to former Canteen-goers remembering their young swing-dancing bodies helps draw connections between the smooth surface of a nostalgic "dance floor democracy" and the noisy commotion of a "dance floor democracy" of different dancers with varied perspectives, experiences, and memories, thus offering a way to explore in swing memory the tensions of "America" as the many and the one.

While I admit that I am most drawn to the diverse, complex, and often critical swing dancing narratives of the members of a generation that is often celebrated as unified, I agree with Portelli that the point of oral history is not to replace "previous truths with alternative ones" or to choose between historical "fidelity" and "subjectivity" (as a historically contingent, ongoing process of becoming)—but to listen to them together, for the way "each provides the standard against which the other is recognized and defined."[27] Listening to the oral narratives, in relation to one another, to the official story, and to archival documents, I am not sifting evidence for a preferable version of the past to write. Instead, I listen for, and try to write, relationships—coming together while leaning away, gathering momentum, releasing without letting go—as I try to better understand the persistence and performativity of swing culture in animating Americans' thoughts and feelings about democracy, the nation, and past and present wars.

Swing: From Time to Torque

When swing scholarship shifts from music to dance, the analytic center tends to pivot from time to torque. The verb "to swing," defined by jazz and swing scholars who focus primarily on music, tends to apply to conjugation of rhythm, tempo, pulse, and the forward motion that is often, but not always, achieved in the activated second and fourth beats of the 4/4 rhythm. Kevin Whitehead describes swing as a "headlong, but relaxed sense of propulsion, as if the music was skipping down the sidewalk. It often relies on small surges and hesitations, on placing a note or accent just in front of or behind where a metronome or tapping foot would put it." However, he adds, "Count Basie's bassist Walter Page could place his notes squarely on the beat and swing like crazy."[28]

When dance scholars talk about swing, however, we enter a world of physics, the "centrifugal force, torque, and momentum" that "keep the partners spinning smoothly," writes Joel Dinerstein.[29] Lewis Erenberg emphasizes the role of the "intimate communication" of the "dance's hand clasp," necessary in order to ensure "that the couple could survive the centrifugal force and the obstacles of the dance" while "the rooted quality of the beat balanced flight."[30]

Howard Spring argues that the new musical approaches to swing, in rhythm and timbre, responded to new ways of dancing that were more physical and involved more parts of the body and more movements per measure (four instead of two). Dancers increasingly required music with more rhythmic drive, noisier textures, and momentum than earlier styles.[31] Changes in music and dance occurred within a close, mutually inspirational relationship between the fast, flowing, forward-moving big band swing surge and the energetic yet smooth horizontal swing of the lindy dancers.

Many scholars highlight the "break-away" as the defining property of the lindy and jitterbug, representing the integration of individual and community, improvised solo and ensemble—the dance version of what has been celebrated as the democratic principle of jazz. "In most couple dances (the waltz and the fox-trot, for instance)," writes Robert Crease, "the partners hold each other closely enough so that they generally need to do identical footwork with reverse parity lest they tread on each other's feet." What was radically new in the lindy, then, was the "development of the break-away," which "made possible a flexible couple dance with room for improvisation. Partners could do markedly different steps—even ones unknown to and unanticipated by one's partner—as long as the basic rhythm was preserved."[32] Dinerstein breaks down the requirements: the "fast, fluid steps demanded improvisation *and* precise motion."[33] Prior to the break-away,

FIG I.2: Actress Faye McKenzie negotiating torque with a Hollywood Canteen guest. BY PERMISSION, BRUCE TORRENCE, HOLLYWOODPHOTOGRAPHS.COM.

the couple connects by first walking toward each other, grasping each others' waists, and then spinning quickly in place, creating a torque-like motion across the hips. The "swing-out" move that follows involves the leader letting the partner out and away by extending the hand. At that point, either or both dancers can improvise. During this "break-away" step, partners literally break away to improvise steps of their own or remain attached to their partner by a light touch.[34]

To onlookers, swing dancing may look like a back-and-forth, in-and-out motion. But to dancers, to "swing" is less like the sway of a pendulum and more like what would happen if you could "swing" that pendulum at the end of a string around and around over your head.[35] The heavy end becomes airborne and seems almost weightless only when you achieve the optimum combination of force, rotation, and distance. Swing it too placidly, and it doesn't get off the ground. Swing it too hard, and the string slips out of your hand and the pendulum flies through the neighbor's window. But swing it just right, just fast enough, with just enough bend to the arm to adjust the speed for the weight—*torque it accurately*—and you and the pendulum—or better yet, you and your dance partner—achieve a heightened level of turning power that neither could achieve alone.

In their book, *Physics and the Art of Dance: Understanding Movement*, physicist Kenneth Laws and dance pedagogue Arleen Sugano, define *torque* as "a kind of force that causes a rotation, like the hand turning a screwdriver or two hands turning a T-shaped wrench to tighten bolts on a car wheel."[36] For solo dancers, torque is applied to the floor through the feet, one pushing one way and one the other. In partner dance, the floor and feet still do this work but in relation to the torque dancers apply to one another. Like a physicist, the experienced swing dancer *appears* to defy gravity, not by fighting it but by knowing its rules; and using this knowledge to accurately apply the laws of turning power, weight, velocity, distance, and shape. The swing, then, for the lindy or jitterbug, is not all in the rhythm, the tempo, or even the steps. Swing is in the crouch, bend, lean, weight, speed, balance—torque. Music that swings, for experienced swing dancers, is music conducive to the achievement of torque—music that supports embodied knowledge that may achieve instant, kinetic adjustments of power, weight, and speed.

Dinerstein locates the torque of the lindy in a cultural history of survival technologies developed in African American culture. While white dancers in the 1930s were drawn to the lindy, he writes, they tended to embrace it as a "hopping vertical motion," whereas "black dancers tended to dance in the crouch, low to the ground, and smooth," working "with, not against, the laws of gravity." For white dancers, socialized in a culture that constructed blackness as "primitive," undisciplined, and prone to sexual abandon, the swing-out was about letting go of all control, missing altogether what was new in the lindy for black dancers.[37] By the 1940s, the lindy's cross-over to the more mainstream jitterbug obscured its origins in black culture for some white Americans, for whom the dance craze connoted "youth" culture. Nonetheless, the jitterbug retained "primitivist" attractions for many white dancers who saw it as pulling out all the stops rather than as a communicative partnership between a lead and follow that sought flight through balance. At a democratically conceived patriotic dance spot like the Hollywood Canteen, all kinds of approaches, skill levels, expectations, cultural associations, and experiences with the jitterbug were brought to the floor. If a space opened on the floor, and the crowd sensed excitement and edged out of the way, an inexperienced lead might fling his partner around like a rag doll, or a pair of complementary dancers might achieve torque.

It was *possible* in the jitterbug, as with the lindy, to connect with another through touch and feel, find the point of connection in which bodies move one another, improvising across shared or different orientations (including degrees of resistance, centers of gravity, mass) and strike a balanced pattern of tension and release that maintained "I" and "we," the individual and the collective—what one might call the physics of swing democracy. The break-away didn't facilitate this on its own. Neither did the couple steps. The swing is in the torque, without which the break-away and coupling have no connection. Torque, then, is the turn that facilitates the democracy that so many attribute to swing cultural formations. As such, dance floor democracy, even at a famous soldier-hostess World War II canteen, is collaborative and physical and not guaranteed.

What difference would it make for students, consumers, and participants of World War II nostalgia to rearticulate democracy and swing culture in the "torque" and not in the reassuring (for whom?) rocking motion of the pendulum swing or in the patterned opportunities for relative freedom (individualism?) in the break-away? Is there a way to store past torque for the future, in self-narrative, for example, in stories of improvised moves on the dance floor? Nostalgia, as a longing for a past that never was, is emptied of torque. However, some ways of remembering and telling find footholds that aid in turning nostalgia into something else, through tone and gesture, humor, and critique. How do people apply turning power to narrative performances of memory? Sometimes the torque is in the telling.

Torquing Back

I have mentioned that I hear the "official" memory of the Hollywood Canteen in virtually every interview; sometimes in unison with it, and sometimes in dissonant relationship to it, and sometimes a little of each. In some, I hear swing culture as mutual, easy, and "friendly." In others, I hear the connection with nostalgia through rebuttal. In most interviews, there is some point when I hear the familiar tune "torqued" in the telling; a moment when the teller moves with the official memory, while leaning away from it, and applies a bit of pressure that changes its direction or meaning.

One dancer narrates her body dancing in an unexpected way: perhaps she breaks the rules, dances across race. Somehow this breach creates an even more democratic dance floor than the one in the movies. Another would-be dancer describes the impact of rejection on the "inclusive" dance floor, maps what it should have been like as a vision of democracy. Another compares the Hollywood Canteen with another even more democratic dance floor. Another ascribes the democratic achievement of the Hollywood Canteen to the radicals on the staff rather than the naïvete of a simpler generation.

National nostalgia about the Hollywood Canteen is an unsteady landscape, navigated differently by different narrators. Sometimes its most forceful currents take narrators to a happy place in the national body. Sometimes the nostalgia is invoked as a constraint and danced against. The official story often opens the interview as an anchor of alignment, which the personal account may affirm or deny—usually a little of each. In this way, the narratives of Canteen memory resemble the various ways people danced the jitterbug in crowded social space. A connection between moving in sync and releasing apart is built into the structure of the dance, but what happens in each instance is open to variables affecting the kinetic relationships of the "we" of the couple and the "me" of the individual in the break-away, feet pounding the floors among the "we" of the other couples.

My accumulation of personal accounts people shared with me form another "we," not a complete one (for it is never complete) and not a unified one (for it is never unified) but one that enables me to explore one remembered negotiation of the possibilities and constraints of the dance floor, and then another, and then another. From my own dance as an interviewer, researcher, scholar, and writer, with a variety of "I"s narrating the possibilities and constraints of a variety of interpretations of the national "we"s of the jitterbugging soldier-hostess dyads of the Hollywood Canteen, I try to learn different kinds of critical engagements with swing culture as war memory. I consider Canteen-goers' narratives as they tell me about the club's interior, as well as the social, geographical, and historical ground navigated on their way to the building, their travels after exiting the premises, all the way up to the present moment of the interview. I listen carefully to which memories are connected to each of the narrator's Canteen stories. I ask for the dance, then try to follow—though I am, of course, active throughout the process, initiating the event, operating recording equipment, asking questions, reflecting intended and unintended responses as a listening body that my interviewees interpret as they decide to what to tell me, knowing that I will try to write about it—and, of course, I do. Through all of this, I try to follow interviewees, wherever they go, in their navigations of a past in the present, what I think of as a "social geography of memory." These narratives, taken one at a time and in relation to one another, help me think about a different kind of critical engagement with swing memory as war memory, one that I call "dance floor democracy."

In the prologue, I noted that politicians and pundits have appealed to "democracy" as worth defending but not defining. As I close this introduction, I admit that jazz and swing scholars, including myself, have often invested hopes of democracy, resistance, and freedom into jazz and swing history and practice in ways that tend to fall short of defining what we mean by democracy, resistance, and freedom. Danielle Goldman makes this point powerfully in the opening pages of her book on "improvised dance as a practice of freedom."[38] Nonetheless, she also argues that no single definition of any of these terms is capable of fitting the desires and needs of all subjects and to presume so actually diminishes one's understanding of the social potential of improvisation. Assumptions of "sameness" in dance experience blocks one's ability to appreciate the political power of dancers' interactions within constraints and therefore of "the possibility for meaningful exchange."[39]

Addressing social dancing at New York's Palladium in the 1950s, Goldman writes that although this dance hall was unique for its racial integration, it was still "not a 'free' space where everyone was equal and anything was possible." Rather than interpreting contradictions as evidence of failure (a move that often accompanies the "appropriation" pole of swing scholarship), she emphasizes the importance of attending to multidirectional desires—and interpretations. In her analysis of improvised dance as a "practice of freedom," she acknowledges that a "variety of constraints imposed by racism, sexism, and physical training shaped how people moved" and that individual dancers' experiences of a powerful moment, however meaningful, "were neither shared by, nor identical for the dance hall's many patrons."[40]

The Hollywood Canteen in 1940s Los Angeles was a different kind of social dance space from the 1950s New York Palladium, with different constraints, but I approach the Hollywood Canteen with an ear for difference, negotiation, and "moments of resistance" and do not presume that these will match or add up to a "one-interpretation-fits-all" conclusion. I listen for "torque" and "torque potential" as requisite components of a democratic dance floor. It is those moments of telling in which dancers reorder the "official story" from the perspectives of their re-membered orientations to the nation, where history might "acknowledge the fact of improvisation."[41] To reconfigure World War II home front memory as an "unsteady landscape"[42] is not to dispense with the potency of swing memory but to break up the old patterns and improvise on "a new terrain of struggle."[43] If one can think of the democratic dance floor of the nation as a site of constraints and possibility, rather than a magical past where "big shots are friendly to little shots," one might even discover useful inclusive democratic dance floor strategies for the present, by listening more closely to the volunteers and military guests who attended the Hollywood Canteen in World War II.

Stepping onto the Dance Floor . . .

The place of the Hollywood Canteen, then, in this book, is not so much a site of history as it is a hub of memory, where competing identities, histories, and definitions of democracy converged and clashed from interview to interview. In this introduction, I have discussed some of the research and writing challenges posed by this dance. I have outlined some of the "moves" I brought from my previous work in oral history, swing historiography, and jazz studies, as well as some of the new "ways-of-working-a-room" I tried to pick up along the way from dance studies, theories of embodiment, and memory studies, all while scrambling to meet the demands of writing on such a crowded dance floor. Some of my techniques were transmitted by one-on-one encounters with interviewees, some from careful listening to the archival records, some from transformative interactions with archivists, librarians, fellow researchers, and dancers.

Working with the concept of "torque" has helped me to rethink linkages of swing, democracy, social change, and writing. I feel that the radical potential of swing culture resides in torque. Nostalgia masks the balanced pulling away that creates the productive tension that gets people to move and change. In writing this book, I've tried to cultivate a practice of feeling for pulls from various corners of the room—in archives, in interviews, in narrative—to develop a sensitivity to other bodies in motion that may be headed in directions I hadn't imagined, and to my own responses, impulses, and habits. Like the narrated memories of the Canteen visitors and volunteers with whom I spoke, this book draws toward and leans away from its own mixed impulses to deny narrative authority and to inscribe "what really happened" (or "what *else* really happened") in the barn-like structure that once stood at Cahuenga and Sunset Boulevards (now the site of the CNN parking structure). "It's a long time ago" and "I only went there once or twice" give way to "I'm absolutely sure it was like this . . ." Between my own disclaimers of "I am interested in what is remembered today, not in what happened back then" spill traces that betray my own inevitable guesses at what may have been. In this way, I remind myself (and readers) of my presence in the cultural tangle of interviewing people in time and space and writing a book. I also keep visible the spurious sense of time I often share with my informants: never quite isolating the World War II years from the kinetic present yet never quite getting them in sync—and never giving up the idea that sharing memories of a crowded dance floor that closed over sixty-five years ago might yield insights into a usable past.

Organization of the Book

Although this book is more about the various ways people narrated their memories between 2000 and 2010 than about "what really happened" in the 1940s, I also take as significant the specificity of the social geography of 1940s Los Angeles when listening to people narrate their memories of traveling to, and moving across, that "crowded dance floor." The Hollywood of the 1940s was not only a dreamscape but a highly demarcated place in which race, nationality, ethnicity, politics, economics, gender, and sexuality differentiated experience. Different bodies traveled in different ways to and through the geographical vastness of Los Angeles long before they arrived at the "crowded dance floor," and these travels are remembered in different ways by people whose bodies traveled differently since. Therefore, the chapters in part I wrestle this star-studded nightclub to the map, grounding it in the social and cultural geography of its particular neighborhood in wartime Los Angles. I argue that Hollywood's localism, as well as its unparalleled ability to defy geography and history, together contributed to the Hollywood Canteen's ability to become such a potent symbol of American exceptionalism. Through a comparison with other self-consciously constructed "democratic dance floors" in Los Angeles during the World War II years, this chapter observes that what happened at the Hollywood Canteen was not identical to, or isolated from, the ways such experiments could and did happen elsewhere in Los Angeles. The place of the Hollywood film industry in Los Angeles ensured that the reach of the vision of democratic dancing that was possible at this particular "local" spot would exceed its "city limits" in special ways that would soon be exported to national and global audiences. In addition, the transhistorical travels of the Hollywood Canteen, through the feature film about it, as well as reenactments, and its reliable presence in documentaries about the U.S. home front, has ensured that its Westside–centric "city limits" (to play on the title of Josh Sides's excellent Los Angeles history)[44] have maintained dominance in World War II nostalgia. Place, in other words, affected how the swing dancing nation could be imagined and enacted locally, nationally, and internationally and continues to affect the vision transmitted as effective war memory, not just about Hollywood but about the U.S. home front spirit during World War II.

The next two parts focus on dance floor narratives gathered from archival sources and interviews that I conducted between 2000 and 2010, in which I employ a self-consciously imposed embodied approach to explore a variety of personal orientations to the democratic dance floor. Part II engages the memories and narratives of enlisted men and young civilian women who volunteered as junior hostesses. In this part, I listen carefully to the narratives constructed by individuals who once occupied a position in (or near) the jitterbugging couple that has since become an icon in the national imaginary of the United States in World War II. Though I keep in play the figure of the ideal soldier-hostess dyad, I overlay, often in tension with the ubiquitous ideal, narrators' self-animations of Canteen dancing, stories that often included other events. I include whatever else they seem to connect in significant ways to their memories of traveling to, from, in, and through this famous Hollywood night spot. To what other improvisations and constraints are their memories mapped in individual Canteen memories? What social memories are activated in these narratives? How did these travels inform the expectations and experiences of Canteen-goers, and how did these and subsequent travels shape and reshape interviewees' memories and narrative strategies in relaying them? The existence (or not) of a dance floor color line, and the possibility of dancing across it (or not) produces much, though not all, of the narrative tensions—the pull between unisonance and dissonance—(sometimes achieving torque) for differently positioned military men and civilian hostesses.

Part III focuses again on military guests and civilian volunteers who were, like those in part II, members of what became known as the "Greatest Generation." However, the two groups visited in part III were not incorporated into the national body in the same ways. The chapters in part III explore narratives of military women and draft-age civilian men who were present at the Hollywood Canteen, though usually not as dancers. Some military women remembered not being allowed through the door at all, a smaller number remembered dancing, and most with whom I spoke remembered being admitted to the Canteen but restricted from the dance floor. Draft-aged civilian men told different kinds of stories that similarly took them to marginal places and that usually did not include dancing. The color line is one of many barriers to full inclusion, it turns out. Military women and draft-aged civilian men of all races were met with an unpredictable, questioning public, one that was heightened at sites of military recreation.

The color line is the focal point once again in part IV, in which I follow the special agent(s) who spied on the Canteen and filed regular FBI reports on it (which were then forwarded to the Departments of the Army and the Navy). The FBI asserted that its concern with the Canteen, as well as with other people, places, and organizations in Hollywood and elsewhere, was the possible presence of Communists. Indeed, though there were not as many

Communists as the FBI seemed to think there were, some of the volunteers (and possibly visitors) were members of the Communist Party—not an illegal activity. The possibility of racially integrated dancing, even as an unsettled debate, and the strong showing of Jewish executives and workers (particularly writers) in the film industry were reason enough for the FBI to view the Hollywood Canteen as a hotbed of Communism and therefore as dangerous enough to warrant expenditure of taxpayer dollars for FBI surveillance throughout the war. In addition to studying the FBI files on the Canteen, I draw from narratives—archival and oral history—of Hollywood leftists who were followed by the FBI and were involved in the Canteen's struggle over the integrated dance floor. In both chapters 10 and 11, I consider the relationship of state memory and national memory in the swing dancing nation-state. By state memory, I draw from David Theo Goldberg's analysis of the way the modern state is constitutively "racial" and often racist yet represents itself as instrumental or uninterested in social categories such as race. By national memory, I mean a dominant articulation of remembrance and amnesia that invites national identity without claiming the baggage (like racism, conquest, and colonialism).[45]

Chapter 11 revisits the most widely circulating vehicle for the "official story" of the Hollywood Canteen as national memory: the 1944 Warner Brothers feature film directed by Delmar Daves. I return, in other words, to the film with which I opened this introduction, in which Sergeant Brooklyn Nolan defines "democracy" as "big shots" being friendly to "little shots." Rather than limiting my reading to what lives on within the frame, I sneak backstage and rummage through early scripts and treatments, company memos, and other archival holdings in search of evidence of struggles that will tell us more about what it was that writers, directors, and other individuals representing interests ranging from the studios to the unions and to the state wanted from this film. How did these various players navigate the shifting landscape of film production about a site where many of them volunteered? What were the tensions at work in the collaborative and embattled process of the creation of this film— not just the tensions at work in the creation of any film but specifically the tensions that produced this lasting edifice of swing memory as war memory? I see this chapter as dancing closely with chapter 10. While the FBI files show the way the state collected and classified information about attempts at intentional integration at the Hollywood Canteen, the studio files on the making of the war musical show how the people who were under surveillance balanced notions of democracy and difference as patriotic moviemaking. As a result, much of what the FBI classified as "suspect" in state memory was respun in the national memory that lives on in the film as color-blind multiculturalism in the casting of extras. Studio documents make it possible to track the multiple levels of memory management of the kinds of inequities, exclusions, and diverse navigations of socially loaded space that were blatantly promoted by the state in the FBI files and Shore Patrol documents that I consulted. The torque often winds up on the cutting room floor, in rejected scripts, memos, lawsuits, labor struggles, or, sometimes, small on-screen traces left from larger tugs and pulls. This chapter also continues to incorporate the dissonant social memories that are made audible through oral history in order to understand how conflicting memories comprise crucial ingredients in the "makings" of compelling national unity, even when directed to the background or cut from the frame. Difference is not only different from but is justification for the unified vision.

Cecelia O'Leary illuminates the fact that even such ubiquitous symbols of U.S. patriotism as the Pledge of Allegiance, Memorial Day, and "The Star-Spangled Banner" are relatively recent inventions and "emerged, not from a harmonious, national consensus, but rather out of fiercely contested debates."[46] Not a national symbol in quite the same way as, say, the Pledge of Allegiance or even the Statue of Liberty or the Lincoln Memorial, the Hollywood Canteen nonetheless has accrued national memory with which I and my interviewees have contended. It is remembered as a popular site of a particular time—famous, but not timeless. Its hold on national imagination is ephemeral; not on the tip of everyone's tongue but somehow familiar and unsurprising when it shows up in nostalgic evocations of World War II. The Hollywood Canteen is recalled as singular (the only place like it ever in history) and generic (typical of the American spirit in World War II). It is lauded as wholly unlike other sites of soldier comfort at the time—distinguished by celebrity volunteerism yet also the most representative of patriotic dance floors, its movie industry hosts and hostesses interpreted simultaneously as royalty and regular folk and peculiarly "American" in this achievement. Imagined as unique and typically national at the same time, the Hollywood Canteen assumes its place in national memory through its exceptional performance of American exceptionalism, in much the same way that swing assumes its ability to represent the nation.

While this book is critical of some representations of the World War II generation, it is not meant as a criticism of the generation itself. In fact, my critique of the most reductive evocations of the "Greatest Generation"—so frequently celebrated during the time in which I wrote this book—is driven by my own admiration for members of this generation with whom I have spent a great deal of time. This book is, perhaps, even a bit of a love letter to the complexity and diversity within a generation too often celebrated as simple, unified, and uncritical.

"Greatest" or not, the World War II generation is dying. And in spite of all the increasingly critical scholarship on the diversity within this generation, it is in danger of being remembered as a heroically unified one. To speak of its complexity and contradiction and to engage the intellectual and political variety within it is itself in danger of counting as national disrespect in times when World War II is invoked as national consensus. But national memory is dangerous when it becomes a national monument that obstructs the memories of multiple publics—the Third Reich is a tragic example, however no nation is immune. In the eloquent words of Phil Melling, "to challenge the role of memory is not to destroy or defile, but to invigorate. When memory is beyond reproach it is deadened and emptied of all responsibility, deprived of the sustenance of legitimate enquiry."[47]

This book moves from the conviction that the struggles and thoughts of the generation that remembers World War must not be reduced to the unified feel-good version that still so effectively mobilizes support for military actions. As the last members of the World War II generation exit the dance floor of the living, this book is an attempt to amplify their diverse perspectives on war, culture, and democracy—their dissent and struggles—in order that they may invigorate perspectives of those who remain. Too often, the critical insights of the World War II generation have been conscripted into service of national unification. By listening to this generation's multivocal complexity squarely on a site of memory that more often stands in as a symbol of its simplicity, this book is an attempt to listen to, dance amid, and remember the critical commotion of democratic struggle. I hope that readers enjoy, as I did, picking up the various tips passed along by dancers about the democratic potential of swing culture beyond nostalgia for national friendliness. Friendliness can be pleasant on the dance floor but proves a poor substitute for torque.

PART I ON LOCATION

★ ★ ★ ★ ★ ★ ★ ★ ★ ★ ★ ★ ★

SITUATING THE HOLLYWOOD CANTEEN

(AND SWING CULTURE AS NATIONAL MEMORY)

IN WARTIME LOS ANGELES

CHAPTER 1

★ ★ ★

Wrestling Hollywood to the Map

Race is not simply a category of analysis that can be applied or removed from a map of the "real" urban landscape like a thematic overlay. Rather, it is a concept that has been integral to the way American cities have developed and the way urbanites of all backgrounds have made decisions.
—JOSH SIDES, *LOS ANGELES CITY LIMITS* (2003)

It took me weeks to get it through my head that Hollywood's bravery was to be as glittering and glamorous as always, to provide escape and memory of times when all was well, to inspire others by their example.
—ADELA ROGERS ST. JOHN, "DEAR READER: HOLLYWOOD HAS CHANGED!" (MARCH 1943)

Nostalgic love can only survive a long-distance relationship.
—SVETLANA BOYM, *THE FUTURE OF NOSTALGIA* (2001)

If swing culture became national memory—a sonic-kinetic *nostalgia express* from the ever-complicated present to a simpler, more unified dance floor imaginary characterized by a mood of friendliness, innocence, and spunky energy as emblematic of democratic spirit (with a special ability to slide between multicultural and white), it did so, one might say, *via* Hollywood.[1] This is a simple and not particularly original argument. Swing scholars have documented well the effects of the industrial, economic, and westward geographic shifts of the culture industry that would render swing available as a national symbol in World War II.[2] What is less understood is the dance between the local and the national through West Coast production of swing culture as war memory. How did the social geography of Los Angeles shape the look and feel of patriotic dance floors throughout the region, and how did the understandings of motion picture industry volunteers at the Hollywood Canteen and other local USOs and USO-like clubs impact the lasting feel of swing culture as war memory?

To answer these questions is to apply some torque to the national swing imaginary about World War II, and to the local ground from which those dreams push off. In this chapter, I attempt to connect swing culture as war memory to Hollywood's ground as a particular neighborhood among neighborhoods. I know it won't stick, but I hope to close the distance long enough to recognize the local in the national. In this, and chapters 2 and 3, I approach Hollywood as (among other things) a place in Los Angeles. I imagine many "ways in" and consider the effects of different routes taken by different Canteen-goers before they ever set foot on the democratic dance floor.

(West Coast) Swing Culture as War Memory

By the late 1930s, mainstream swing success required entrée to the West Coast mechanisms of the culture industry, which had already gone west with the movies. Branding and bundling of swing through the multiple packaging of motion pictures, broadcasting, and radio took on new importance when the United States entered the war.[3] All that was popular with the youth who would later be called the "Greatest Generation" was rallied to recruit popular support for the war effort—and most propaganda was produced in Los Angeles, buoyed by government contracts. Out of this convergence emerged the legacy of the look and feel of wartime swing culture as patriotic, the long-lived nostalgic effects of the jitterbugging soldiers and hostesses in feature films such as *Stage Door Canteen*, *Thank Your Lucky Stars*, and *Two Girls and a Sailor*, not to mention *Hollywood Canteen*.[4]

In considering this new articulation of Hollywood swing culture as national memory, one might specifically think of the film representations of the "typical" GI (played by a draft-exempt actor) dancing with the glamorous actress to a live famous big band as a particular production of yearning—then and now—for supposedly "simpler" times. Another approach would be to think of the celebrity status of name bands and bandleaders, detectable through film references and cameos, in full-length features, as well as shorts, including the short-lived "soundies," the music films that played on jukebox-like machines called Panorams.[5] Consider the famous "Hollywood" romances between white swing bandleaders and white movie stars and starlets in the 1940s that so appealed on the pages of movie magazines—Harry James and Betty Grable (who met at the Hollywood Canteen), Artie Shaw and Lana Turner. And then there is the Hollywood Canteen as it is evoked in black-and-white footage of soldiers streaming in to get a sandwich and cut a rug with Rita Hayworth, Marlene Dietrich, and Hedy Lamarr, accompanied by descriptions of the Canteen's glamorous premiere-like grand opening on October 3, 1942.

"Huge klieg lights sent beacons swirling into the low-hanging clouds in the sky over Hollywood," wrote Bette Davis biographer James Spada. "Swing music blared from loudspeakers and filled the night as thousands of servicemen jamming the street cheered every time they caught sight of one of their favorite movie stars pushing through the throng."[6] Klieg lights, *despite wartime blackouts*—some accounts take pride in noting this detail, as though the act of catapulting great cylinders of light into the coastal wartime night sky was itself a vivid example of "Hollywood's bravery."[7] Like the music, the beams travel beyond the site itself; in fact they overtake and outdistance the brightest star and hottest tune (except on radio). The winning combination of stars, swing, and soldiers represents national civilian hospitality for the troops even as it trumps all other local canteens. It attracts national love, while signaling the on-site swarm of bodies that gathers to fill every inch of the sidewalk, the landscaping, the nearby gas station parking lot, and the other free space for blocks and blocks and blocks.

The backstory includes such details as the massive influx of newly arrived defense workers and military migrants getting ready to ship out to war, and the somber roll call of wartime precautions—dimmed lights, limited travel, the coastal vigilance of plane spotters. But this is mere setup, really—a stage for the *real* story, in which Hollywood goes to war by doing what it does best: demonstrating the power of its major industry to brighten spirits. Glamour trumps gloom as Hollywood throws a party smack dab in the middle of a designated military highway (police had their hands full keeping the throughway clear of frenzied onlookers). Two big bands played outside, and others accompanied the dancers inside. Big stars paid $50 each to sit in bleacher seats and cheer the GIs as the "real" celebrities. And glowing from the pages of many a star-struck, star-authored, or ghost-written account published later, a "blaze of klieg lights" pierced the cloud cover with the usual Hollywood hoopla, an assurance that all would be well again.[8]

The centrality of the Hollywood Canteen in this loop of swing, war, and nostalgia is part of what I mean by "situating the Hollywood Canteen (and national memory) in wartime Los Angeles." Swing goes national *via* Hollywood. And the nation goes Hollywood *via* swing. But what is "Hollywood" in this cultural alchemy? Is it an ideology, an industry, a brand name, a style? Does place have anything to do with it? If so, what is the *place* of Hollywood as a particular part of Los Angeles? And how does that neighborhood travel in the configuration of swing culture that travels as war memory? Where does Hollywood (the neighborhood) go when Hollywood (the industry) represents the nation in a Hollywood manner? Some definitions are in order. It turns out that "Hollywood," like "democracy," requires parsing before it is possible to use the term in a meaningful way.

Hollywood (the adjective): "Hollywood" quickly describes the style of the best known products of Hollywood (the industry)—the big *Hollywood movies*—not only as the cinematic texts but as widely shared, intimately familiar dreamscapes, structures of feeling, and ways of telling a story. In swing contexts, Hollywood (the adjective) references a media shift in the national-popular, and attendant gatekeeping that determined which bandleaders became pop icons and which bands mushroomed in visibility through the movies. For dancers, Hollywood represents a style shift associated with white swing dancer Dean Collins, who saw himself as an East Coast Lindy-Hopper of the Savoy Ballroom in Harlem but whose individual stamp on the dance became associated with the West Coast, whiteness, and the movies. All of these style markers—look, sound, and movement—travel in nostalgia shows, reenactments, commemorations, and the "retro" grab bag of popular culture. Dreamscape is the most tangible definition of "Hollywood"—instantly evoking name brand recognition, unapologetic artifice, and a national *common-ground-that-never-was* that binds imaginaries, like it or not, across time and space.

Hollywood (noun: the industry; or proper noun: the Industry, if we are in Southern California): In this definition, Hollywood is not the style of the brand but the corporations that brand the style through the manufacture of the many kinds of media products (not only feature films). As an industry, Hollywood historically employs workers, attracts (too many) aspiring professionals, populates a sprawling city, promises to return investments, and is repeatedly organized and disorganized in class struggles.[9] "Hollywood" in this definition does not include all the companies that make movies, nor is it limited only to companies with offices and studios in Hollywood (the place), for it identifies a group of companies that coalesced around the district called Hollywood by the early teens and twenties but even in the 1940s spilled beyond the neighborhood, over the mountains, scattered itself in studios in the San Fernando Valley (Republic, Warner Brothers, Disney) to the north and in Culver City (MGM) to the south and west. Nevertheless, this Hollywood without boundaries is more readily grasped than the neighborhood among neighborhoods.

Hollywood (proper noun: the place): Hollywood is the name of a district of Los Angeles that was only briefly a town in its own right. Founded as a real estate investment by Horace H. Wilcox in 1887, the town joined the city of Los Angeles in 1911 in exchange for water. In the early teens, it became associated with the film industry, as studios migrated west. Hollywood (the place) borders other districts and has a local history. Nonetheless, this definition, the most concrete definition—the part-of-town—is the most difficult to ground. If I don't take an extra beat to say "Hollywood as-a-part-of-town," my meaning will be construed as style, theme park, and industry.

In pinning Hollywood down as a part of town, I am not advocating a mind-body split between fantasy and reality, national and local, dominant dreamscape and differently situated experiences but am instead trying to consider the interplay between embodied knowledge of people moving in and out of Hollywood on-the-ground, in relation to Hollywood as an industry (also grounded and embodied, people going to work and then going to volunteer at the Canteen), and the place of Hollywood as a dreamscape in producing swing culture as war memory, which, as I have already argued, bears ramifications for identities and bodies across time and space.

In this respect, the klieg lights provide an attractive image. These contraptions are tools of the trade, used in the making of movies; but they are also rolled out and swiveled skyward for glamorous events like premieres and nightclub openings. If you followed the lights, you arrived at the ground where the action was, or at least at the outer perimeter of its thousands of spectators. At the same time, the klieg lights, as a cliché of Hollywood glamour, are helpful because they *dislocate* Hollywood from its place-ness, in the sense described by the California historian, lawyer, and activist Carey McWilliams when he wrote that Hollywood "exists only as a state of mind, not as a geographical entity."[10] If Hollywood is a "state of mind," it is one produced by an industry named "Hollywood," situated, in part, in proximity to a "geographical entity."

In Norman Klein's provocatively entitled chapter "The Most Photographed and Least Remembered City in the World," the film historian argues that the "erasure of memory" of particularly often-filmed Los Angeles places and their histories is a specialty of the industry. In fact, he writes,

> the mood of erasure is fundamental to the spectator's pleasure. However, beneath the charming effect lie the actual sites where a film is shot. These cannot surface, even when they are in plain view; and they are very rarely sensed offscreen either. Once a city or an event is enshrouded by this pleasure, there is almost no way to make it visible again.[11]

What is left out of cinematic renderings of Los Angeles, he argues, is evidence of the "twin beasts of racism and ruthless city planning." Extending Mike Davis's observation that Los Angeles is imagined as either sunny or noir, Klein notes that the Westside, home of Hollywood and Beverly Hills, is filmed on the sunny side, contributing to visions of Los Angeles as carefree, opulent, and white. The whiteness of Los Angeles lives in a cinematic world in which "ethnic stories are New York stories."[12]

This "erasure of memory" of place in film is in cahoots with other histories of forgetting in and about Los Angeles. A different kind of place than other U.S. cities in the 1940s, Los Angeles possessed a very particular and complex social geography and a history of civic promotion and identity that was adept at translating historical, social, and political contradictions into a myth of leisure, friendliness, and multicultural compatibility. Los Angeles was a place that embraced the romance of "old Mexico," in its architecture, iconography, and narratives, while erasing the violent colonial history of conquest, war, statehood, and Americanization of California, continuing to displace Mexican American and Mexican residents of the formerly Mexican, formerly Spanish colonial city.[13] It takes many steps to re-member Hollywood's gravity as a material, historical, and social place, but only through this connection can its mighty weightlessness as national memory be understood.

Location isn't *everything* in this chapter and chapters 2 and 3, but it is *something*, which is seldom the case when one speaks of Hollywood. Following the lead of the meticulous Los Angeles historians Carey McWilliams, George Lipsitz, Scott Kurishige, George Sanchez, Josh Sides, Anthony Macias, and others, I work to *locate* the Hollywood Canteen in the complex social geography of wartime Los Angeles.[14] The translocality of Hollywood shaped Canteen-goers' travels to and through the city, the neighborhood, and the nightclub in disparate ways, and this requires a close examination of race, national and colonial history, labor and housing. The nationalizing of swing culture as war memory, then, is not only about Hollywood movie memory of Canteen-dancing, or about the swing bands, dancers, and styles popularized through the circuits of the industry on the West Coast, but the effects of the local terrain on bodies in motion.

Follow the Lights

Klieg lights aimed skyward signal the glamorous event at their root. They designate the place to see and be seen, while signaling the distance and direction between where you are and the center of that action. A vision in which this luminous premiere-like Hollywood welcome is extended not just to the usual suspects—screen royalty and those who worshiped at their feet—but to draftees and enlisted military personnel lifts Hollywood from the local, while addressing population shifts on the ground. The movie town welcomes the troops with beams usually reserved for glorifying its own stars.

It doesn't seem to matter that the literal presence of klieg lights is doubtful. Dimout regulations had forbidden their use so near the coast, and they were banned from premieres commencing August 20, 1942.[15] In fact, Hollywood's first "dimout premiere" was a benefit for the Hollywood Canteen on August 29, just a month and a half before the grand opening. Columbia Pictures donated ticket sales from the Four Star Theatre launch of *Talk of the Town* (Columbia Pictures)—the first "dimout premiere." "Dim Outs Fail to Dim Preview," wrote Maxine Bartlett in her column for the *Los Angeles Times*, explaining that "searchlights and batteries of arc lights were missing Saturday night when 'Talk of the Town' was shown at the Four Star Theater with proceeds going to the Hollywood Canteen fund," but "the jewels of the guests glittered just as brightly."[16] Another *Times* writer, Philip K. Scheuer, searched for words to describe the phenomenon, settling on "'premiere party,' something new under the dimout."[17]

The black press emphasized an angle the mainstream largely ignored—the news that not only the benefit premiere but the after-party at Ciro's were racially integrated. Free tickets were distributed to fifty to seventy-five soldiers in black segregated troops (numbers vary according to the report). Also emphasized was the bright showing of black Hollywood stars (who did not live in Hollywood). With or without klieg lights, the Hollywood Canteen story splits in two: one version evades race and marvels at the glitter; the other emphasizes (black-white) integration and marvels at the glitter.

Photographs taken of the Hollywood Canteen's actual grand opening a month and a half later indicate floodlights, by no means "dim," aimed earthward toward the thousands of celebrity, military, and civic celebrants. Lighted space stakes out a circle of ground crowded with bodies but still doesn't catch Hollywood where it never likes to be: on the Earth, as a small dot in the western and northern end of the 496 square miles that make up the city limits of Los Angeles, itself a fraction of the boundary-defying four-thousand-mile expanse of Greater Los Angeles.

If I were a filmmaker, I might *keep* the "blaze of klieg lights" but make a point of dimming it from time to time, catching their beams in shifting frames from center to so far back you can hardly see them, maybe splice night shots abruptly next to pale scenes shot in available light. Or maybe start with a typical luminous opening, then fade through a shot that is similar but lit in a contrasting design: dozens of loopy neon lines on a giant map, extending backward behind the estimated twelve thousand attendees who danced and cheered and lined up in the streets that night, thousands more for the volunteers. I'd angle the cameras down to the *shoes* (note to wardrobe—find footwear indicating different *walks of life*) and then get the cartoonists to paint footprints behind them, marking their routes.

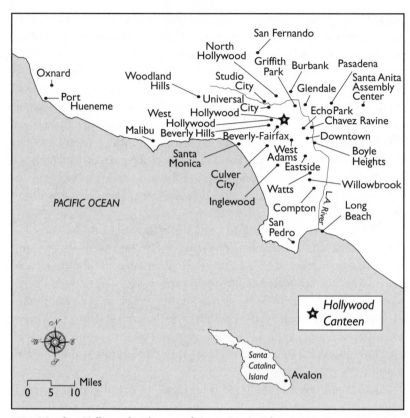

MAP 1: Wrestling Hollywood to the map of greater Los Angeles. MAP BY ANDREW GOTTSFIELD.

The sound department could mix a recording of Rudy Vallee's Coast Guard Band so the volume goes up and down according to spatial travels suggested by the jarring cuts between street scenes of many neighborhoods: Beverly Hills to Bunker Hill, Studio City to Central Avenue and to San Pedro and Beverly-Fairfax. An unruly web of converging and splitting lit-up routes expands across the screen. Some lines cross Santa Monica, follow along Broadway, east to Boyle Heights, or south through Central Avenue, Watts, Compton, and all the way down to the Port of Los Angeles. I'm no filmmaker, but if pressed to speak in the language of the "swing culture as national memory," I might zoom out even farther to accommodate the accelerating proliferation of pathways over broader swathes of the map (note to sound: pick up tempo). Get in as many routes as possible, the many orientations to Hollywood, and within Hollywood, the other places occupied and visited the same work-, school-, or leisure-day, the same liberty weekend.

The travels are long and the city is large. To get them all in, I'd need to pan to the north, then west, then south, then east, across this extended map. Many stretch from the two entrances (military guests on Cahuenga and volunteers around back on Cole) and head north, meandering a bit at nearby Hollywood and Vine. The routes behind them lead on up through the mountains to origin points in studios, bases, and defense plants in Burbank, Studio City, and throughout the Valley wherever troops encamped, movie people worked and lived, and war workers commuted to and from on shifts that spanned all hours of the day and night. Some paths lead west, to Oxnard, Camarillo, and the deepwater navy base at Port Hueneme. Other routes from the Canteen head due west from the door to Santa Monica to the coast, winding down to San Pedro and the Port of Los Angeles, Long Beach, and all the way to San Diego.

A more direct and traveled pathway to the southern navy bases cuts directly through the middle of downtown, through the largely racially unrestricted Eastside, home of the Central Avenue district (a mixed area with many black-owned businesses and homes), and through the uneasy borderlands of Watts and Willowbrook, which stood between the concentrated sphere where most of the African Americans in Los Angeles resided and the white residential strongholds of the industrial hub of Compton and Inglewood. Thousands and thousands of paths do not originate that far south but stem from Union Station and the Greyhound bus station downtown. Many routes converge on Broadway, some originating from troop trains and buses and others from the Mexican American and multiethnic neighborhoods (due to fewer racially restrictive housing covenants) east of downtown in Boyle Heights. Some routes begin from the northeast, from Glendale (with its whites-only after sundown policy), Pasadena, and beyond—skipping over the Santa Anita Racetrack, now Assembly Center: volunteers and guests will not be drawn from that spot (though it is possible that army soldiers who rounded up the Hollywood residents of Japanese descent and moved them to the horse stalls may attend the Canteen). Points east in the desert extend from the many bases in Riverside, such as the Desert Training Center, where soldiers trained under General Patton,[18] and San Bernardino. Zoom out again to take in the ever-shrinking map as more and more itineraries radiate from the tiny dot on Cahuenga and Sunset—three years' worth of routes through the Greater Los Angeles region—encompassing over two million visitors alone and who knows how many volunteers. A sped-up montage could cut in bright zigzag lines to indicate hitchhiking, horizontally hatched parallel lines for the troop train tracks, something different for bus routes (Greyhounds,

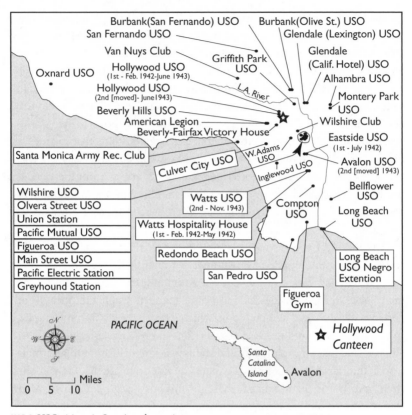

MAP 2: USO sitings in Los Angeles region, 1942–1945. MAP BY ANDREW GOTTSFIELD.

city buses, street cars, and "Liberty buses," provided to deliver troops from bases to sites of leisure and recreation), carefully planned gas-rationed automobile itineraries, and footpaths of military sojourners looking for the bright lights of Hollywood from wherever they've been dropped off. The lines will also indicate the pathways in and out of the dozens of other canteens where soldiers danced with hostesses. The Hollywood Canteen was unique, but it was not the only game in town. In fact, some of the other canteens in Greater Los Angeles provided name bands, floor shows, and movie stars.

USO Sitings in Greater Los Angeles

Founded in 1941, the United Services Organization (USO) coordinated efforts of six organizations that had provided home front services for military personnel during World War I: the Young Men's Christian Association (YMCA), the Young Women's Christian Association (YWCA), the Salvation Army, the Jewish Welfare Board, Catholic Community Services, and Traveler's Aid. The

USO clubs were often housed in the recreation facilities of these member organizations, as well as in American Legion halls, other community centers, and hotels. The first USO club in Los Angeles opened in a tent downtown in Pershing Square. It later moved to the Biltmore Hotel, before settling in the Pacific Mutual Building. According to the *Los Angeles Times*, one of the first USO volunteers in Los Angeles was the wife of the actor-director Jean Hersholt.[19]

By February 1943, twenty-four USO clubs had cropped up throughout Los Angeles, in which "twenty-eight thousand women representing 375 groups and organizations volunteer thousands of hours."[20] Among these thousands, a staple role was the USO junior hostess, a prominent "home front service" was dancing, and a widely popular choice was jitterbugging to big band swing bands or records.[21] The USO clubs and other canteens were located in neighborhoods with differing but interconnected histories of race and varying relationships to the motion picture industry. Many were located near popular nightclubs where swing dance prevailed, albeit with a divergent set of demographic parameters, management policies, police interest, and military approval ratings.

Local USO clubs in Los Angeles had a different look and feel from those in other towns and cities throughout the country, and the USO clubs that blanketed the Greater Los Angeles region also varied greatly according to their places in the spatially dispersed social geography of race in that city and region. Whiteness dominated the USO landscape in Los Angeles in alternately overt and unspoken ways, mirroring and often drawing into relief the uneven and unevenly experienced social geography of race in the city itself. Assessing the city's racial climate in 1944, an official navy report concluded that Los Angeles was "not a particularly satisfactory liberty city for Negro naval personnel, except for those that live there and know it well." The report noted that the city was too confusing, its rules too varied and unstated, for African American military migrants to navigate. Without experiential local knowledge of the racial map of this huge city, one was more likely than not to wander into unpleasant conditions.[22]

The navy was also worried about the wanderings of white sailors. Of particular concern was their presence in the same neighborhoods the navy thought most appropriate for black military, the Central Avenue district.[23] The Shore Patrol had the power to police only navy personnel, but with a long reach that included maneuvers that were very invasive to all businesses and patrons onshore. The Patrol could enter private businesses the navy had determined "off limits" and remove navy personnel. On the street, they could harass mixed couples involving navy personnel (the Los Angeles Police

Department—LAPD—handled the others), often justifying this action with the presumption that racial mixing meant prostitution. The Shore Patrol and the LAPD routinely harassed black women on the streets—sometimes USO hostesses—whom they presumed to be prostitutes (and therefore disease-spreading predators of navy personnel), discouraged white sailors from entering the district, and even removed them from it. Shore Patrol officers were instructed to "stop white naval personnel in the area and warn them that they are in a tough district and advise them to keep out of it. If they do not take the advice," they were "to pick them up for a uniform violation or on some other pretext."[24]

Whereas in some racially restricted white parts of the Westside, such as Hollywood, it was easy for white residents to live largely unaware of racially restrictive housing policies and attendance policies in nightclubs and restaurants, this "power evasive" white experience of race did not did not characterize all the predominantly white neighborhood of the city.[25] Inglewood and Compton, for example, were in the 1940s intentionally white communities that shared borders with districts with significant areas of unrestricted housing. As migration of defense workers and military personnel and families intensified and housing became increasingly scarce, battles also intensified over racially restrictive covenants. Such battles spilled onto the ground of patriotic soldier recreation in heated debates over where to open USO clubs and who could attend. Because of the USO's adherence to a "community standards" model to determine the look and feel of civilian soldier-hospitality, the social geographies of USO and USO-inspired canteens, rather than setting an organization-wide imperative for racial integration, for example, or inclusion of military women on canteen dance floors, tended to mirror the most conservative versions of local social geography wherever they appeared. An organizer at the Inglewood YMCA-USO reported that the community surrounding the club was "very prejudiced against racial groups. Some people are proud of the fact that there is an unwritten law that Negroes must not be seen on the streets of Inglewood after sunset, and the original charter prevents Negroes from owning property. So it was with real concern that the USO staff learned that Negro troops were being sent in to this vicinity."[26]

The solution in this case was to consult the African American director of the Central Avenue's Woodlawn Branch YWCA to help the Inglewood USO to "interpret . . . inter-racial policies of USO" and organize training for volunteers. As a result, wrote the Inglewood USO representative, "the United Daughters of Confederacy who had charge of snack bar refreshments on Sunday evening came along beautifully and served Negro soldiers without question." This change in attitude did not extend to the dance floor. Instead,

"Negro hostesses were imported from Los Angeles and Negro dances were organized at the army base. A high grade variety show was organized with several Hollywood Negro stars participating."[27]

Other USOs on the southern border of racially unrestricted residential areas of the Eastside were not so accommodating. A 1943 YMCA report from the Compton USO drew on the language of war to describe the expanding presence of people of color in the communities surrounding the center of industrial Los Angeles. "The community of Watts, which adjoins Compton Township, and Willowbrook, which is in the township due north of the City of Compton, are infiltration centers for both Mexicans and Negroes. Negroes are restricted from Compton city limit residential area." The proposed solution to this "infiltration" was: "Let the Watts USO handle the Negro units."[28]

Just north of Compton, 1940s Watts was more diverse than neighboring communities. (In 1940 the population was 50 percent white or Mexican American, 35 percent black, 13 percent Mexican immigrants, 1.5 percent Asian.)[29] But that does not mean it was a haven of multicultural harmony. When Henry and Anna Laws, an African American couple, built a house in Watts in 1942, a white homeowners' association pushed back. Scott Kurashige writes, "for three years, civil rights advocates battled proponents of restrictive covenants until the municipal court ordered the Laws to vacate in November 1945. Defying the order, the Laws were sent to jail for living in their own home."[30] Two predominantly black USO clubs were created in Watts, beginning with the short-lived Watts Hospitality House on 112th Street east of Central Avenue. In August 1943, the Watts USO club held its grand opening, ten blocks from where the Laws housing battle yet raged.[31] An easy walk from the Watts USO (primarily set up to entertain black solders) was the Plantation Club with its famous chorus line and top bands. Patrons of all races were admitted to this nightspot. Not so at another big nightclub two miles to the west and north in South Gate. The Trianon Ballroom featured many famous, popular African American big bands but did not admit black customers.[32] Soldiers who found themselves in Watts, looking for something to do with their precious little spare time, navigated a tense and uncertain racial landscape. During the decade of the 1940s, the black population of Watts increased from 8,814 to 92,117, making Watts the "largest black residential area in the city."[33]

The mostly black, but integrated, Eastside USO at the Twenty-Eighth Street YMCA, located within an easy walk to the center of black businesses, churches, recreation, and community life, opened in July 1942 (three months prior to the Hollywood Canteen) and then in 1943 moved to a new location on Avalon and Forty-Third Street. It was to this club that Chester Himes's protagonist sarcastically referred in *Lonely Crusade*: "not a segregated center . . . just a center in a Negro community, staffed by Negroes, served by Negroes, and serving Negroes. But not segregated, no."[34] Himes's critique of the covertly segregated city stands in contrast to the war work of his wife, Jean Himes, who held a post with the USO in Los Angeles during World War II and devoted the war years to helping provide black soldiers with recreation.[35] Volunteers from the Eastside USO also served heavy duty in supplying black hostesses to far-flung bases and other clubs where black soldiers arrived but black people did not reside. Other canteens in the Central Avenue district included those operated by the American Volunteer Women's Services and the Congress of Industrial Organizations (CIO). All of these canteens were within easy reach of black nightclubs and theatres: the first location of the Eastside USO was an easy walk to the Lincoln Theatre to the north or the Elks Hall to the south. The Avalon USO was right around the corner from the Alabam, the Downbeat, and the Last Word. The CIO canteen was a few blocks further south. Like other CIO canteens, this one maintained an integrated policy.

Though the clubs on Central Avenue were integrated, they were also, as Himes pointed out, located in segregated Los Angeles, in that so much of the rest of the city was restricted—not by schools, not by zoning, but by real estate practices enabled by legality of covenants, custom, and neighborhood associations. White people could, and did, attend Central Avenue nightclubs, which were, indeed, frequently attended by white Hollywood movie stars on a night out, but white military men were discouraged from venturing in that direction by both the LAPD and the Shore Patrol.

In some predominantly white but mixed areas with growing populations of people of color, "extension" clubs were established. An "extension" was what the USO added when an existing club required an additional building to support (white) industrial workers or Negro soldiers. Such was the case in San Bernardino (sixty miles east of Los Angeles) and Long Beach. A USO administrator reported that the separate Long Beach clubs were serving an important role as "a step toward interracial parity" in a community where "tolerance" was turning to "alarm" among the white population worried about the "consequences resulting from influx of new families and interracial emphasis."[36] At the same time, while volunteers at the Long Beach Negro Extension were drawn mostly from the local African American community, they included several white volunteers interested in interracial advancement. In addition to recruiting and organizing hostesses for the Long Beach Negro Extension, the burden was on explicitly "colored" clubs to provide black hostesses to USO clubs and military camps where black soldiers appeared but black civilians did not reside. Mae Mack at the Long Beach Negro Extension pleaded for a more reasonable schedule in the demand to supply black hostesses beyond the active schedule of dances at the Extension and ship parties "which came to us without much warning." Of the sixty-five women available for local activities, fifteen were available for caravans but were also committed to the local club. Mack proposed a less grueling, but still rigorous, caravan schedule for her volunteers and suggested that some of the Los Angeles clubs leaning on the Long Beach Negro Extension might find black women volunteers in closer vicinity.

Although the main Long Beach USO club, the Municipal Service Men's Club at 2601 East Main, did not prohibit black soldiers from entering, hostesses were given special instructions for what to do "when negro personnel do come into the Service Men's Club"; the official word was that they should "face each situation separately." An official memo posed several possible scenarios. The USO worker should try to ascertain whether the black soldiers have come to the white club intentionally, "perhaps even with the intention of making an issue of their presence in the place where white people are entirely predominant," or whether this has happened "quite accidentally," in which case a soldier "may consider that he has been favored when given the information that he might feel more at home at the [Negro extension] USO center on Anaheim." A third possibility was the "negro service man who feels that he has been pushed from pillar to post, has grown weary, and would just like a place to sit down and relax and observe what is going on."[37]

Most USO clubs were housed in the existing buildings of the various member organization branches in Los Angeles or buildings secured and operated by them, thus inheriting histories of community service from a wide range of local YMCAs, YWCAs, and Jewish community centers. The downtown Figueroa USO club was in a YMCA branch located near downtown nightspots popular among Mexican Americans who liked to jitterbug, including the All Nations Club at First and Main and the New Mexico-Arizona Club at Second and Spring Streets, only two blocks from the Zenda Ballroom. For Mexican Americans, writes Anthony Macias, "swing was not only fun to dance to, but it was 'American,' and as such it helped them to further differentiate themselves from the traditional Mexican music of their parents' generation."[38]

Of all the organizations of the USO, the YWCA was most committed to and experienced in racial integration, but even with pressure from the national organization, regularly scheduled visitation reports from traveling YW executives, and integrated national meetings, some YWs in Los Angeles, such as Glendale, were steadfast in their resistance to integration. The general YW commitment to integration also often set them in tension with more conservative, racist, and anti-Communist members and organizations in their communities.

Housing covenants had restricted Jewish residents of Los Angeles, albeit with more mobility than African Americans and Mexican Americans. Jewish residents were migrating out of downtown and Boyle Heights in the teens and twenties and into the Fairfax and Pico districts. The Beverly-Fairfax Jewish Community Center opened the Beverly-Fairfax Victory House at 8008 Beverly Boulevard on July 11, 1943.[39] The junior hostess program resulted in tripling the female membership in this community center. On the other hand, the Soto-Michigan Jewish Community Center, which didn't attract many military personnel due to location, had difficulty maintaining its female membership.[40]

There was a USO in Beverly Hills, and home-cooked meals were available for soldiers every Sunday at the Beverly Hills American Legion Hall.[41] In 1942 the Hollywood USO Hospitality Center was already in full swing in Hollywood just a few doors up Cahuenga from the future site of the Hollywood Canteen. In fact, when this center opened on February 2, 1942, it also did so under pre-dimout conditions. Edward G. Robinson presided as starlet hostesses welcomed one thousand military guests in a "kleig-light [sic] ceremony and fanfare."[42] Until the planning of the Hollywood Canteen, the Hollywood USO club was often referred to as the "Hollywood Canteen."[43]

"If New York Can Do It, Why Not Hollywood?"

Many of the USO clubs throughout Los Angeles were established before the Hollywood Canteen, and many came afterward. But none of them appears in origin stories about the Hollywood Canteen, which invariably look to New York. It made professional sense for the organizers of the Hollywood Canteen to link their efforts to the Stage Door Canteen in Manhattan, which opened in the spring of 1942. The Theatre Wing found a way to operate a USO-like club outside USO control, retaining agency among entertainment workers, who sought to organize their own patriotic volunteerism in ways that served the troops while sustaining their jobs, industries, and reputations throughout the war. Two other Stage Door Canteens had opened in quick succession in Philadelphia and Washington, D.C.[44] It made sense for film industry workers to do the same.

Workers in the entertainment industries were particularly vulnerable to overvolunteerism: the expectation that they could interrupt their work schedules to entertain the troops for free, their professions were frivolous, and the only reason an actor or actress would turn down an appearance at a military camp or hospital was that they were selfish, spoiled, and unpatriotic. Industry workers could organize their own volunteers, control service obligations, present their own versions of their industry, and wield their own star power. Nonetheless, the operation of the Hollywood Canteen could never be wholly worker controlled, because of the financial and labor contingencies of the motion picture industry as a big business, including fierce competition for contracts, powerful agents and studios, and rampant un- and underemployment and exploitation of casual labor—even for many unionized workers. Nor could it be free from blurry lines between service for the troops, publicity, and professional networking.

Those who organized the Hollywood Canteen also worked to brand their club differently from the Stage Door canteens, drawing on the stylistic vocabularies of West Coast versus East Coast that marked rivalries between the centers of the motion picture and the theater businesses: the wagon wheel chandeliers, for example. But when these organizers rallied interest within the motion picture workforce, they did so by way of comparison with New York. John Garfield credited his trip to the Stage Door Canteen as the inspiration for approaching Bette Davis about founding a similar operation in Hollywood; never mentioned in this story line is the nearby Hollywood USO already in operation. Stories in the black press often referred to the Hollywood Canteen as a West Coast version of New York's Stage Door Canteen, even though the Eastside USO in the African American district south of Main and East of Broadway had already opened and had been celebrated for its interracial "democracy" and movie star presence.[45]

Writing about the plans for the Hollywood Canteen in one of the three local black newspapers, the *Los Angeles Tribune*, Wilma Cockrell informed readers that "the Canteen will be based on the one in New York that has been successful in giving service men, regardless of race, creed, or color, the finest entertainment that money can buy, provided free by the world's greatest actors, entertainers and musicians." The story emphasized interracial planning in the cooperation between the Los Angeles musicians of the segregated union locals 767 (black) and 47 (white), while adding that a similar idea had been percolating in Hollywood between Bette Davis and John Garfield, and these efforts would be combined. "If this can be put over, it will prove a Godsend to our boys."[46]

While it was certainly newsworthy that the segregated musicians union locals were cooperating to open an integrated club for soldiers and Hollywood stars were joining in, what this New York inspiration angle overlooks are other local efforts outside Hollywood and the vast differences between the social geographies of New York and Los Angeles, and how these differences might result in different dance floor democracies. In New York, for example, people who lived in different neighborhoods citywide were more likely to encounter each other in public space than those navigating spatially dispersed Los Angeles.

As Hollywood columnist Hedda Hopper put it, in New York "everything is concentrated within a few blocks. [In Los Angeles] we're spread out like the tentacles of a giant squid."[47] The contributors to David Halle's edited volume *New York and Los Angeles: Politics, Society, and Culture, a Comparative View*, provide a complex multidisciplinary comparison. At 303 square miles, New York is geographically tighter, more densely populated, and more concentrated around a single urban center than the rambling, geographically blurry, multiply centered Los Angeles. Whereas Los Angeles is only 200 square miles larger than New York City, it is a multicentric urban arrangement that has historically ignored its own cartography, spreading far beyond its spatial, environmental, and governmental limits, throughout the wide-ranging four-thousand-square-mile expanse of Los Angeles County. In addition, the white populations of New York and Los Angeles have vastly different immigration histories. White migrants to Los Angeles were more likely to come from the Midwest, more likely to have established white U.S. identities prior to the move. Whiteness itself was differently constructed in the two cities. In New York, self-identified white Americans were often no more than one migration away from another national/ethnic identity, more connected to a homeland outside the United States, and more tolerant in general of other immigrants. In Los Angeles, the whiteness that had been advertised and constructed in the real estate boom and later in the film representations not only reflected but targeted Midwest migrants, depicting a form of whiteness that was disconnected from memories of international immigration. This whiteness was less identified with "ethnic whiteness" and hyphenated identities and those who identified with it tended to be less tolerant of immigrants overall, including African Americans (thought to have migrated west much later, even though black migrants were among the first settlers in Los Angeles), Mexicans (even though, of course, California had been part of Mexico), and indigenous people if they strayed too far from white romantic fantasies of the past.[48]

Racially, while both New York and Los Angeles were residentially segregated, New York contained multiple areas where African Americans lived, though Harlem was the largest and the African American cultural center. In Los Angeles, however, from 1915 through World War II, there was one African American district in Los Angeles, stretching south from downtown along Central Avenue. In 1940, 70 percent of the 63,774 African Americans in Los Angeles lived in the section east of Main Street, then known as the Eastside and now known as South Central Los Angeles.[49] Because of the more concentrated urban center, there was more public mixing in Manhattan—on the streets, on transportation, in shops—and more pervasive visibility of racial stratification.

On the other hand, 80 percent of the residential acreage of spread-out Los Angeles was covered by racially restrictive housing covenants.[50]

Some white people did, indeed, live in or near unrestricted areas of the city. Most, however, lived in restricted areas where it was easy to miss the ethnic and racial variety of people in the city and live unaware of the segregation in housing, labor, hotels, restaurants, nightclubs, and healthy-lifestyle leisure activities for which Los Angeles was known. A swimming pool in a racially restricted residential area need not post rules about race in order to enact segregation. It just needed to restrict users to those who lived in the neighborhood. Schools, however, were not limited to those who lived in the vicinity.[51] One effect of residential segregation and school integration was that it enabled many white people in restricted neighborhoods to carry memories of the few people of color in their schools as evidence of a racially integrated upbringing.

Los Angeles maintained its national reputation for relaxed attitudes toward race, even for the national black press. At the same time, it maintained a social geography organized largely around racially restrictive housing covenants on an immense spatial scale that made it possible for most white people to not realize how many nonwhite people lived in the city or question why they did not encounter them. This was certainly true in Hollywood. Cushioned by layers of other neighborhoods whose demographics were also defined by racially restrictive housing covenants, Westside communities such as Hollywood were far from the border skirmishes of white neighborhoods adjacent to multiracial neighborhoods. Hollywood was one of many neighborhoods in Los Angeles that could be experienced by white residents as socially inclusive and by people of color as both covertly and overtly segregated.

Community Standards at the Dance Floor of the Nation

Just as operating a canteen in Inglewood, Glendale, or the Eastside shaped what happened on the respective democratic dance floors differently, so did the placement of the Hollywood Canteen in its particular neighborhood in wartime Los Angeles. In fact, it was because of the particularities of its local primary industry that it could also *exceed* (though not transcend) its locale, as traces of Los Angeles social geography were tracked back into on-screen versions of the democratically dancing nation. Many of the people who worked on "canteen-theme" films (wherever they were set)—as actors, dancers, writers, painters, editors, janitors, producers, office workers—also produced this particular club in time and place, a place defined by a particular social geography of race, whether most of the people who arrived at its doors knew it or not.

Although making a canteen is not the same as making a movie, they are closely entwined when it comes to the Hollywood Canteen. Stars and extras who played the jitterbugging soldiers and hostesses in films that framed canteen dancing as epitomizing U.S. democracy also volunteered and made appearances at the Hollywood Canteen and other canteens and USO clubs throughout greater Los Angeles. So did the writers, producers, secretaries, painters, camera operators, and others. Like residential Hollywood, the industry and its guilds and unions, were shaped by race in mostly exclusionary ways, and populated by people to whom racial exclusions were mostly invisible. The industry was also traversed by people for whom the lines of race materialized at every turn, in thwarted attempts to rent or buy property, find acceptable employment, or gain entrance as customers in nightclubs, restaurants, and hotels. It was also populated by people whose consciousness was expanded through activism, friendships, and work. For some, segregated, color-blind Hollywood constituted a battleground with powerful ramifications for producing new visions of democracy. Others defended race-based exclusions and hierarchies in housing, city space, employment, labor, representation, and leisure—all of this affected dance floor democracy at the Hollywood Canteen.

People with all of these different orientations to Hollywood—as an idea, industry, and part of town—planned, built, decorated, donated to, and volunteered at the Hollywood Canteen. They made sandwiches and phone calls, programmed the acts, worked the door, raised money, paid the bills, managed crowds, bused tables, argued over the rules, obeyed them, differently interpreted them, and sometimes broke them—and they danced. They made slow decisions in board meetings and quick decisions on the fly, improvising on the theme "What would Hollywood do?" when fights broke out, hostesses were manhandled, and people danced across race. Like all canteens and USOs, the Hollywood Canteen applied local spins to national style. What makes the relationship between the local and national at the Hollywood Canteen unique, however, is the unparalleled national reach and utterly elusive local that meet on this ground.

Volunteers fed, comforted, and danced with soldiers, sailors, and Marines at hundreds of sites across the nation, including many in Los Angeles. In that respect, the Hollywood Canteen was no different. But it did stand out in special ways: volunteers were movie industry workers, including stars; the president was Bette Davis, and the vice president was John Garfield. Though other canteens boasted celebrity volunteers and special appearances, this club was the one that the guilds and unions opened, that the producers and agents invested in, and that was produced as the most glamorous canteen of all by people in the industry whose job it was to produce Hollywood movies. The club stood in the middle of the place that was movie industry capital, tourist destination, and stuff of dreams for people far and beyond the reach of the klieg lights—literal or figurative—of Hollywood. And unlike most clubs of its type, the Hollywood Canteen was (and is) sometimes remembered for racial inclusiveness, which is sometimes held up as its proof of American democracy. Unique within the nation yet somehow symbolic of the nation, the Hollywood Canteen remains the most remembered, represented, and reenacted of wartime patriotic nightclubs of the 1940s—it was one club among others, but its memory stands in for the rest. It is national memory, locally produced.

Among the people whose accounts of the Hollywood Canteen I explore in this book, orientations to Hollywood on the ground and Hollywood as an industry swiveled in many directions. They lived in the many neighborhoods across the great expanse of Greater Los Angeles, including Hollywood. Some of the military migrants I spoke with were from Los Angeles or settled there later. But all of the volunteers I talked to lived, at least during the war, somewhere in the greater Los Angeles region. Some came from families who had lived in Southern California for generations. Others had been drawn in the twenties, thirties, and forties by the Hollywood motion picture industry itself. Others had come in search of defense work in the booming war industries at the start of the war.

Hollywood was many things to many people. Here, I "break-away" to assorted itineraries of people who worked in Hollywood for short or long times. These are not meant to be representative but to evoke a proliferation of routes, destinations, and outcomes.

Routes 1–5: Assorted Pathways to Star(let)dom

Various distances, directions, and degrees of arrival.

For Margie Stewart, a white model from Wabash, Indiana, the road to Hollywood lay ahead when it turned out that demonstrating how to open and close a car door in a bathing suit could lead to a movie contract at RKO.[52] Nancy Marlow's Hollywood was both place and time: "Living in Hollywood is part of the Canteen story and I was part of the old Hollywood," she explained. Her move south from the San Francisco area happened soon after high school graduation, when her mother "decided I was going to be a big star and we moved to Hollywood."[53] Like Stewart, her status as a wartime RKO starlet led to being recruited to dance with the soldiers. From her home in the Hollywood Roosevelt Hotel, she could walk to the Canteen.

For dancer Jeni LeGon, Hollywood was never home, but a big part of her career. She moved to Los Angeles by virtue of being stranded with seventeen other Chicago-based African American musicians and dancers who had traveled west by bus for to work in a show that didn't materialize.[54] Upon finding work in another show, she caught the eye of an RKO director who cast her in her first film. She spent her years in Los Angeles, living, working, and teaching dance in the Eastside, sharing space with her brother, who opened the first African American bookstore in Los Angeles. For a short time, she held a multiyear contract from MGM—a first for an African American woman. Hollywood, for LeGon, was not her whole career, but part of it, and an archive of all-too-brief glimpses of her dance performances of that period. She believed that the truncated footage is shaped, in many ways, by the jealousy of white women stars, especially dancers, who influenced edits. Nonetheless, her dazzling performances survive in two dozen films.

Not so fortunate in her screen career, but fortunate in other ways, was Los Angeles-born Helene Angus (stage name: Helene London), whose father worked in the banking side of the industry, affording a cushion and connections that allowed her to maintain a steady audition effort that nonetheless did not result in a fabulous screen career. From the family home in the Beverly-Fairfax district, she was geographically and socially well-positioned to audition for everything. Like most hopefuls, she answered "yes" to all queries— "Can you ride a horse? Yes. Can you ice skate? Yes"—confident she could learn on the job.[55] Her biggest role in the 1940s was "uncredited cowgirl" in *Take It Big* (Paramount 1944). And, of course, she danced at the Hollywood Canteen.

Virginia McDowall moved to Beverly Hills in 1940, when her father joined the British Merchant Marine, and her mother thought it safest to take the rest of the family away from London. It was also an opportunity to see if the children's success in British film might translate to Hollywood. It was her little brother Roddy's career that took off, but both worked in the movies, and all three volunteered at the Canteen. In addition to entertaining soldiers, McDowall remembers socializing with the colony of British character actors in Santa Monica, mourning the deaths of the "English fellows in our life who were killed," and waiting for her father to visit from the war.[56]

Routes 6–8

Arizona to Hollywood via East LA; West Virginia to Hollywood (boxcar accommodations) via Manhattan; Detroit to Hollywood via Little Rock.

Maria Luisa Ramirez moved from Nogales, Arizona, to Los Angeles as a child with her Mexican immigrant parents and three brothers in the early 1930s. The family lived in East Los Angeles, though starting in the fall of 1941, her brothers one by one began to enlist, the two older brothers in the army and the youngest in the navy as soon as he was old enough to get in. "Mary Lou," as she was called, belonged to the downtown YWCA, and began serving as a hostess at "Y"-sponsored dances both downtown and on the Desert Battalion, where she sometimes danced with Italian prisoners of war, who were housed at the camps where hostesses traveled in caravans to entertain the troops. Sometimes she and a friend traveled west and north by bus to the Hollywood Canteen.[57]

Jean Lewin, born in Morgantown, West Virginia, in 1909, came to Hollywood after the Great Depression forced her to leave New York. She had left home for New York City right before the Crash. ("She wanted 'big time,'" her sister, Marjorie Lewin, explained).[58] The New York adventure had burned brightly for a time. (Her widower, Bernie Gordon, told me she worked for June Mansfield, who was seeing Henry Miller at the time. Part of Jean's job was to safeguard Mansfield's other love affairs from the famous writer.) When the economy dropped, Jean rode the rails in a boxcar and hitchhiked to California, where she found secretarial work in the motion picture industry. Once she was established in the studios, her mother and sister joined her. When the opportunity for a more interesting post as the paid secretary for the Hollywood Canteen arose, Jean was glad to leave the studio and take it. She and Marjorie were volunteer numbers 1 and 2 at the Hollywood Canteen.

When Aniela McAuliffe and her mother left Detroit in 1942, they were heading for Florida, seeking some control over the changes in their lives since McAuliffe's brothers had enlisted. "But you never know what circumstances will bring."[59] When they stopped to visit one of her brothers at an airbase in Little Rock, Arkansas, her mother had a conversation with a stranger in the hotel lobby. "When I came to join them at the counter, my mother turned to me and said, 'Why don't you have this gentleman talk to you? Because he thinks California would be a better selection.'" They changed their course and drove west. McAuliffe sought employment and a way to complete her education. She shared a bedroom with her mother, who rented the other room to soldiers on leave. She scrambled for work, learned new skills, took classes, and volunteered on weekends at the Hollywood Canteen.

Routes 9–10

New York to Hollywood: 2,795 miles east.

For aspiring screenwriter Bernie Gordon, Hollywood was the only place where people wrote movies for a living and therefore a destination worth selling his Graflex camera and microscope to scrape up enough cash for a $16 ride-share from New York with three total strangers. "The few gold coins from my bar mitzvah were long gone," he wrote in his autobiography. "I had about sixty dollars to get me to California. The very word was thrilling. I must have felt something like my forbears who left for America, the promised land."[60] On the West Coast he would reunite with his friend from school Julian Zimet, who had already been busy cashing in family connections, getting his foot in the door at Republic, trying his hand at writing Gene Autry westerns, and befriending interesting secretaries (including the Lewin sisters from West Virginia). Hollywood would be Gordon's home during the years of the Canteen and during the years when I paid him visits while working on this book. In between, Hollywood would be a place to leave. Blacklisted for his political commitments, he spent those interim years occupying other places and other pen names so as to continue writing for the movies.

On a rainy November day in 1943, another aspiring writer, Donald Vining, rolled into Los Angeles on a bus from San Francisco and set out to find the downtown YMCA. In his diary, he recorded his first movements through the city as "grueling," traversing pavement and trolleys lugging "two heavy bags and a typewriter slung by a strap over [his] shoulder." He located the YMCA, only to be told that there was no room for him, despite his reservation, because of the flow of military and defense industry migrants and travelers. "They sent me to a nearby hotel but there was nothing there either. The clerk told me to park my stuff there before searching further. I went around the block to a number of hotels but there was nothing." Fatigued, he retrieved his bags and headed back to the bus terminal for the night, where he "had plenty of company sleeping there" but was targeted for a vigorous questioning by the police. This was no case of racial profiling—Vining was white. "I told [the station cop] my story. He suggested I try a couple of the hotels I'd already been to, and when he saw my plight he let me stay there. Servicemen and sleeping women he didn't bother but all civilian men got questioned."[61] The next day, he tried the Hollywood Y. Again, no room. While standing in the lobby, contemplating his next move, someone mentioned a nearby apartment vacancy. The location couldn't have been better suited for planning to get janitorial work in the studios and volunteer at the Hollywood Canteen.

Route 11

Jim Crow Texas to "Black Hollywood": 1,425 miles west.

Mel Bryant had Hollywood in mind when he piled into a car with friends from his high school graduating class of 1942 and drove 1,425 miles west to Los Angeles. Of his hometown of Denison, Texas, he told me, "being black, it was rather difficult for you to get anything of merit in that small town." His father had encouraged him and his siblings to expect more from life than their lot in

Jim Crow Texas. Hollywood seemed a logical destination for this young man whose talents had been recognized by his community in his high school production of *Dust of the Earth*. Once in Los Angeles, he scrambled for odd jobs, living "like a domino piece that just moves from place to place."[62] He lived for a time at the New Morris Hotel on Fifth Street downtown, followed by a string of rooming houses in the West Adams neighborhood. But his life took a fortuitous turn one night when he was discovered at his busboy job by the biggest movers and shakers in black Hollywood, the actor-agent Ben Carter and actor Mantan Moreland. It is his own Lana Turner Cinderella story—one day he is in a cafeteria, and suddenly he is playing the lead in a short patriotic feature for MGM. The studio had other plans for him, but so did the draft. He enlisted in the Marines and was sent to North Carolina for training. One year later, he spent his furlough making his second journey to Los Angeles. He stayed as a guest in Carter's house and devoted his time to renewing the professional relationships he had established before enlisting. Naturally, this entailed more than one trip in the Pacific Electric Red Car up to the Hollywood Canteen.

The improbable "blaze of Klieg lights" appears again and again in nostalgic recollections, a confounding flicker in my research notes and reminder of the dreamscape on which we tread. Literally, these lights connect the ground to the ether. They proclaim the "place to be and be seen," yet literally reach only so far. They connect an event in time and place to a dream that lasts forever as local and national nostalgia.

Accordingly, the lights will come and go as I continue to situate the Hollywood Canteen in wartime Los Angeles. I allow them to fill the page from time to time, lest author and readers forget to factor in the material and ideological effects of happy Hollywood hoopla, and then I swivel them outward to the far corners of the frame. Each time the beams pass overhead, I travel to a different set of coordinates in the vast and shifting ground of Los Angeles, to locations that are differently oriented in relation to Hollywood and its famous Canteen. One might not see the lights at first, or perhaps only dimly, as one rides the Red Car up from the (southeast) Eastside, or drives west over the mountains from Pasadena, or takes the Liberty Bus from Port Hueneme, east through the valley and then down through the mountains, or rides into town in a stranger's car, having hitchhiked up from San Diego.

These angles are meant to evoke Hollywood's pull, keeping the visibility of the material and ideological effects of that locally produced, widely exported state of mind. But these angles also highlight the provincialism of Hollywood's claim to be the center of culture in so vast a city (let alone the nation and world). Bright as they were, klieg lights—originally designed for shooting daylight scenes in the nighttime—could not illuminate so boundless and boundary-defying a place as Los Angeles. The pivoting columns of light would not have stretched to most parts of the city. For those on the ground nearby enough to see them, the lights would appear bright or dim, welcoming or alienating or a little of both, apprehended from a variety of routes and approaches.

Had klieg lights been on the scene that cloudy October evening, they would surely have been seen throughout the Westside neighborhood of Hollywood on-the-ground and perhaps as far to the east as Griffith Park and as far west as Santa Monica. They would not have registered as far south as downtown. They most certainly would not have been able to scale the San Gabriel and Santa Monica Mountains to the north, even if they fell from time to time on the southernmost entrance to the Cahuenga Pass.

CHAPTER 2

★ ★ ★

Cruising the Cahuenga Pass(t)

It is a far cry from the "Cantina" of almost one hundred years ago when California was in the making—and the ribald laughter of merry-making soldiers rang through the Hollywood hills—but its ruins have risen to glory once again, and the colorful gaiety which typified the place in the days of the Dons and the pioneer Ybarras, is once more happily on the loose in the "HOLLYWOOD CANTEEN"—FOR SERVICE MEN!
—LEO "K" KUTER, *WARNER CLUB NEWS* (FEBRUARY 1943)

I was in the doctor's office and somebody said, "How come there are so many Mexicans here?" I said, "Well obviously, you haven't read your history."
—THERESA NEVAREZ, INTERVIEW WITH AUTHOR (APRIL 11, 2009)

Route 1.a

Burbank, gazing toward Hollywood, which is seven miles south, February 1943.

One cannot see Hollywood—the part of town—from the northern side of the mountains. Nevertheless, this valley lives in the thick of Hollywood-as-an-industry.[1] This has been true since 1915, when Carl Laemmle gambled everything on 250 acres of rough terrain off the beaten track from the existing Los Angeles studios, gathered his scattered East Coast companies, and sent them west to try their luck in California as Universal Studios.[2] He christened the land of his West Coast experiment with a brand name: Universal City. Studios already on the West Coast followed Laemmle's suit, claiming their own rangy acreage for northern expansion. Having just won another gamble (the race to sound), Warner Bros. invested its unexpected windfall into absorbing

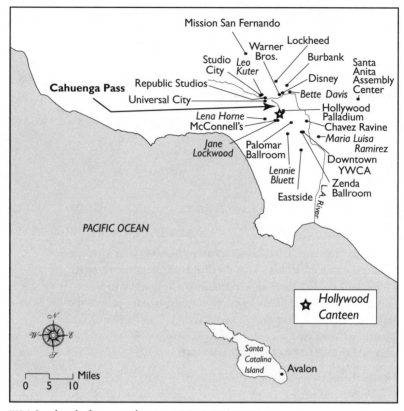

MAP 3: Landmarks for assorted routes. MAP BY ANDREW GOTTSFIELD.

First National's lot in 1928. The following year, the Warners headquarters shifted from Hollywood (Sunset and Bronson) to Burbank. In this very spot, the Midwest migrant Leo "K" Kuter, art director at Warners, sits down in February 1943 to write the "colorful gaiety" of the Hollywood Canteen in historical perspective.

He hammers out his essay for Warners in-house company magazine from his Burbank office, or maybe from his home, six miles to the west, in the aptly named Studio City (also a convenient commute to Republic, Universal, and Disney). Either way, he writes from the San Fernando Valley. Kuter doesn't need to wrestle Hollywood to the ground. His readers are Warner Bros. employees who are well aware of the difference between Hollywood as a part of town and an industry and the connections between them. His challenge is to find a distinctive spin to please his insider audience, acknowledge their service, and recruit new volunteers.

Despite historically different working conditions, Kuter and I face similar snags in our attempts at fresh Canteen-writing. Only four months into its operation, the Hollywood Canteen has inspired buckets of ink but only a handful of narratives. Some of these have already gelled into forms that reproduce themselves again and again in the 1940s and will continue to fuel Hollywood home front nostalgia in documentaries, biographies, and popular and scholarly histories sixty-five years later. There's the "Andy Hardy" spin (so named by California historian Kevin Starr), in which Bette Davis and John Garfield plan the whole operation over a casual chat in the Warners Green Room. Certainly, the readers of *Warner Club News*, many of whom were active volunteers at the Canteen, were already familiar with this well-publicized anecdote.[3] But Kuter doesn't go there. Indeed, given his readership, it would have been a mistake to explain away all that hard work of hundreds of workers as spontaneous party planning by two top Warners stars. (Davis and Garfield also consistently included the vast numbers of volunteers from the guilds, unions, and studios in their accounts.)[4] Other options already growing redundant included recounting lists of the massive amounts of donated food (in the first month alone, four thousand loaves of bread, two hundred pounds of butter, and one million pieces of cake).[5] But Kuter is an artist, not an accountant, and a grocery list is not a story. He will include the food inventory—it is impressive—but in his telling the recitation of donations is the icing, not the cake itself.

The spectacular grand opening of October 3, 1942, had proven an attractive and lasting story. This is the angle I wrestled with in chapter 1: the conspicuous display of humility of movie stars cheering the enlisted men as the *real* stars. But that story is ancient history by this newsletter's standards, and many of Kuter's readers were *there*. Also already established was the infantilizing "soldiers-say-the-darnest-things" approach, in which the beauty, glamour and kindness of the stars brings the troops to their knees. Sometimes the man in uniform is so floored by his proximity to the stars that he misspeaks (or faints, as does Brooklyn in the movie *Hollywood Canteen* when it dawns on him that he is dancing with the real Joan Crawford, not just a "dead ringer" for her). And sometimes the GI fails to recognize the famous person and utters something adorably homespun. But Kuter does not opt for this routine favored by movie magazines and gossip columns.

From the dawn of Canteen planning, stories promising and defending the racially integrated dance floor had appeared in the black press, the Popular Front press, and the union paper of Local 47 of the American Federation of Musicians (AFM). Just one month prior to Kuter's article, the first news item to champion Bette Davis as a protector of the mixed dancing policy had already appeared in the black press as a syndicated story of the Associated Negro Press. A senior hostess, alarmed at what she saw as the impropriety of a black hostess dancing with white soldiers, telephoned the Warners star. Davis purportedly responded, "Let them dance if they want to."[6] But the issue of upholding mixed dancing (a controversial matter for the studio heads, who were worried about the PR of their stables of stars and starlets) did *not* circulate in the *Los Angeles Times* or newsreels or movie magazines, nor does it appear in Kuter's story.

Instead, Kuter—a creative professional, after all (the following year he will serve as art director on the feature film *Hollywood Canteen*)—finds an innovative approach. He will tell the history of the *building*—a structure that predates the Hollywood Canteen, World War II, the motion picture industry, and the founding of Hollywood itself. Weaving the Canteen's future home into a thin but lengthy swathe of Los Angeles history, his origin story does not begin in the late summer and fall of 1942 with the planning, refurbishing, and premiere-like opening. Instead, he locates his Canteen story of place and war with the Spanish "discovery" of the natural pass in the mountains between Hollywood to the south and the San Fernando Valley to the north. He invites his readers to imagine colonial history as a familiar commute.

Route 1.b

Pueblo de Los Angeles to Burbank: twelve miles north on horseback, 1769.

From his desk nearly two centuries in the future, a white man faces south, imagining the arrival scene of "the first white man" (among many) to cross into Burbank.

> "As you go whizzing over Cahuenga Pass, it is very difficult indeed to realise [sic] that only one hundred and seventy-three years have passed since Don Gaspar de Portola—the first white man to gaze upon and use this now celebrated and essential arterial highway to the Motion Picture Studios, in search of a way to the North, made the acquaintance of the Cahuenga Indians who then occupied this Valley. [7]

The Warners headquarters sits on that route, just north of the Pass "discovered" by de Portola. The Canteen is not yet visible in the narrative. It is historically in the future but geographically to the south, newly accessible (for the Spanish explorers) via this passageway. Kuter guides us there across time and space, through an uncritical but enduring narrative of conquest, colonialism, and whiteness. "San Fernando Valley exceptionalism," writes Laura R. Barracough, is distinguished by narrative emphasis on "friendship, the romantic but impracticable virtues of Mexican honor, and presumptions of indigenous extinction," all of which serve "to justify and legitimate the American conquest."[8] Kuter situates the motion picture industry as heir to colonial progress, in partnership with "gentleman farming," suburbs, and modern industrial growth (and in the 1940s, air bases and defense plants).

Though distinct from other origin stories of the Hollywood Canteen, this picture of a quaint, peaceful colonial past was, and is, in fact a popular way of imagining Los Angeles history. The "Spanish Fantasy" narrative, as the term was coined by Carey McWilliams in 1949, functions to obscure the historical and contemporary realities of Mexican Americans in Los Angeles.[9] Filtered through this narrative's romantic lens, stories of colonial encounter are stories of strangers becoming friends, war is an occasion for adventure, and land and power grabs become tales of natural progress, slow and consensual. Kuter's treatment integrates the busy commute between Warner Bros. and Hollywood into the rhythms of this take on the Spanish (and later U.S.) colonial project. In tracking de Portola's expedition northward, during which he became the "first white man" to pass through the natural gateway through the mountains, the story both cites and obscures violent histories of the way Burbank became white. Kuter's unapologetic nod to the white conquest of Burbank elides Mexican and indigenous removal, residential housing covenants, and the very recent relocation of farmers of Japanese descent from the San Fernando Valley to internment camps.[10]

The story also misses racial discrimination in nearby defense plants such as Lockheed and Vega. Along with Glendale, Burbank was one of the Southern California locales that had a "sundown" policy for African Americans that aimed to restrict residence to white people.[11] The intentional whiteness of Burbank was no secret to the national or local black press but was only summoned into white consciousness when black soldiers and defense workers begin to cross into the city limits. Kuter does not mention the 369th Coast Artillery, a celebrated black unit that carried the legacy of the Harlem Hellfighters of World War I, or the subsequent residence of black troops near Burbank who had trouble finding a place to eat in town. There is more to this story, but Kuter doesn't go there. I will catch up with the 369th in chapter 3.

Kuter's historical travelogue continues its picaresque march through the land grant period and statehood. In typical "Spanish Fantasy" narratives of the road to California statehood, he telescopes successive battles into a quaint account of the second (1845) battle of Cahuenga Pass, rendering a whole violent period as a sleepy two-day episode of Los Angeles history. "The Mexicans had three cannon, and the Californians two. No lives were lost, but one mule is said to have laid down its life in the two day 'battle.'"[12] Warners employees would have been well aware of this bit of local color, having heard about, seen, and maybe even dug up some of the cannonballs that were frequently discovered by farmers, construction workers, and homeowners. (You can still see cannon balls in Burbank; one resides at the local historical society.)

Omitted are the casualties of other wars, the tragic fate of most of the indigenous people with whom de Portola had become "acquainted," and the twenty-four-year period of Mexican independence. Sites worth noting, however, include the place where the Treaty of Cahuenga, which "secured California for the United States of America," was signed on July 13, 1847 ("just across the street from Universal Studios").[13] Whitening is not hidden, nor is it narrated, but rather spreads as an effect of progress. Unmentioned is the fact that Americanization, like most colonial regimes, came with its own system of racial reclassification and attendant rules, in this case the massive relocation of most Mexicans to the "disenfranchised non-white category," except for a small number of powerful landowning families of the previous ruling class. The 1880s usher in what one historian describes as the "dramatic shift toward Anglo domination of Los Angeles," with "a new class of rulers" with names like "Otis, Chandler, Doheny, Huntington, and Getty."[14]

Kuter did not invent this mode of highlighting explorers, missions, and haciendas while downplaying native people, Mexican independence, and Mexicans. His romantic passage through what McWilliams has called "the Unending Mexican War" follows a well-traveled path, entrenched in boosterism, urban planning, and historical tourism. It serves him well as he bypasses mention of the common motivators of "available" land and cheap labor that were shared by Spanish colonizers, American colonizers, and the westward movement of the motion picture industry in 1910. The Motion Picture Producers Association had been founded to protect the open shop.[15] For union members reading the *Warner Club News*, a reminder of the producers' attraction to Los Angeles as a nonunion paradise would have rendered the "cheap labor" aspect unsavory. But the reminder might also have elicited a chuckle from those who participated in the subsequent labor movement that established the guilds and unions whose members founded and operated the Canteen. For those in management, a reminder of "cheap labor" as an incentive for westward expansion might have touched a nerve, an unpleasant reminder of the labor movement's successes in organizing motion picture workers, as well as other sectors in Los Angeles. All in all, one can talk about the weather and scenery, but "cheap labor" is a divisive topic in a story about the Hollywood Canteen, which is, among other things, a rare instance of union-management harmony. Unionized actors, carpenters, and secretaries, and historically anti-union producers washed dishes together and rubbed elbows on the Board of

Directors. Like so many other contested frontiers, this one is made palatable through Manifest Destiny. As such, Kuter's narrative bridges the past and the present by situating the Hollywood Canteen not as a *new* development but as a traditional site of military leisure on the march to nationhood. Canteen history does not begin in 1942, but spans uncertain periods of national, imperial, and village battle (once again rendered as colorful and gay) in which soldiers roved the land and vaguely specified armies vied for its control.

Now, from the Mission at San Fernando to the Pueblo de Los Angeles, it is roughly a matter of twenty-five miles on horseback. And horses, like men—get thirsty. They like to "stop awhile" and slake their thirst, stake a rest—and go on their merry way. So—what more natural than some canny soul should establish a "cantina" midway between the two objectives? A man must "look after" his horse! And legend has it, that in the years that followed, many a weary caballero put up for the night at the cantina which spread its adobe walls along the south side of the dusty road that is now Sunset Boulevard, at the intersection of Cole Avenue, just east of Wilcox Avenue—so named in honor of Horace H. Wilcox, who started the subdivision of his 160-acre ranch in 1887 and called it "Hollywood." [16]

With the naming of the intersections, even the most obtuse reader will recognize the contemporary relevance of this lesson in architectural, industrial, and military history. Almost primordially (as though modern history begins at statehood), the Hollywood Canteen emerges as a traditional watering hole for soldiers. At the time of publication, the building is a destination for soldiers, sailors, and Marines who pour out of the newly constructed, old-Spanish-styled Union Station by the hundreds and walk, take buses, or hitchhike up Sunset. However, it has already been the destination of thirsty soldiers, who have rested their bodies and their horses at the halfway stop between the old city of Los Angeles and the Mission, only twelve miles from the future site of Warner Bros. Studios.

The San Fernando Mission, named for King Ferdinand III of Spain, was founded in 1797 as a result of de Portola's expedition. This mission, like others in this colonial process, played a central role in diminishing the native population. Historians have documented well the slavery, danger, and outright brutality committed against native people in the California missions, a system that one historian has called the "first great crime against humanity in the region." [17] But this is territory far outside the "Spanish Fantasy" and certainly does not appear in *Warner Club News*. Kuter's (tongue-in-cheek?) "encounter" scene has de Portola greeting the local Indians as a sort of California-casual act of interracial friendliness. He does not mention that the Gabrieleno, or Tongva people, had used the Cahuenga Pass as a footpath through the mountains long before de Portola's "discovery." (In fact, "Cahuenga," according to some historians, is a Gabrieleno/Tongva word for "place of the mountains.")[18] From the present in which I write, it is important to observe that the descendants of those "Indian enough" to meet the Franciscans' qualifications for childlike converts and slave labor are *still* not considered Indian enough for federal recognition by the United States Bureau of Indian Affairs and are therefore not eligible for Indian Health Service care and other benefits.[19] But this is not the objective of this story. We return to the soldiers' journey.

South of the watering hole that will become the Hollywood Canteen, at the other end of the route traveled by the timeless march of soldiers leading up to World War II, sits the Spanish-founded city that would soon become the "Spanish Colonial"–style city of Los Angeles, California, USA. Kuter's narrative, like other "Spanish Fantasy" renderings of Los Angeles history, takes a detour around Mexican rule, although some of the soldiers in the sweep of his cantina story are surely soldiers involved in the Mexican War. This mode of remembering and forgetting, as McWilliams and others have pointed out, drives architecture and city planning as well as storytelling. While the Mexican past and Mexican and Mexican American people were increasingly pushed out of the Los Angeles landscape, the Spanish-style "look" of the city proliferated. As William Deverell writes, the "Spanish Fantasy" narrative was "integral to the city's cultural and economic rise during the period between the Mexican American War and World War II."[20] It not only continues, but accelerates in the 1940s. The new architecture of the City Hall, the Hall of Justice, and Union Station, all of which further displaced Mexican and Mexican American residents to smaller and smaller areas of the city, was fashioned in twentieth-century "Spanish Fantasy" style.[21] Even the new all-white Naval Training School (or Armory) was erected with an old "Mediterranean" look when it was planted in the midst of a largely Mexican and Mexican American working-class neighborhood in Chavez Ravine in 1940.[22]

Eduardo Pagan argues that it is the decision of city planners to build a "million dollar training school for the all-white Navy" in "low-income Mexican American neighborhoods," more than any other factor, that explains the violence between white sailors and local Mexican American youth, the worst of which would be called the Zoot Suit Riots.[23] In order for navy men stationed at the Training School to get to Hollywood or downtown Los Angeles, they had to cross through three predominantly Mexican working-class neighborhoods, a situation that was exacerbated by the tendency of white servicemen to believe that Mexican American women were more sexually available than white women. Elizabeth Escobedo's interviews with Mexican American women who lived in these neighborhoods during this period attest to the harassment stemming from these assumptions. These tensions were exacerbated by the broader public acceptance of increased visibility of young Mexican American women as "wartime defense workers and patriotic morale boosters," a gendered shift that was not extended to Mexican American men, who continued to be criminalized and policed in public space, especially outside the barrio.[24] Many scholars have noted that although the Zoot Suit Riots were sensationally interpreted (and produced) by the mainstream press as crimes of unruly and outrageously dressed Mexican American and other men of color who had set out to violate white women and white space, such propaganda masked the violence of the "unending Mexican War," a continuation of the colonial and racial project of Americanization.[25] Escobedo also notes that whereas Mexican American women were welcomed as USO hostesses in Los Angeles (unlike the Southwest), when Mexican American women's clubs organized hospitality geared toward "Spanish-speaking and Latin American origin servicemen" that emphasized Mexican culture, cuisine, and Spanish-speaking hostesses, the USO was less supportive.[26] They could entertain soldiers, but even in a Mexican American soldier-hostess dyad, the "Mexican" had to be erased. Colonial gender politics rendered Mexican American women available to white soldiers and disloyal if they focused on Latinos as Latinos.

Catherine Ramirez writes of the proactive responses of Mexican American women against defamation when newspapers characterized them as "cheap prostitutes" and the Red Cross refused their blood donations because they were Mexican. She also points out that when stereotypes were fought on the grounds of respectability politics that insisted on Mexican American women's moral and sexual purity, they erased the subjectivities of young women who formed subcultural identities through zoot suit culture, sometimes known as (and not always identifying as) pachucas, but who were no more eager to serve as "pawns among warring men" than women whose gender identities as Mexican women were shaped along more traditional paths.[27] The spatial, racial, and gendered tensions and violence that led to and made up the Zoot Suit Riots were surely felt at the Hollywood Canteen premises, in the navy curfew that followed, and in the hysteria about Mexican youth that surely affected attitudes and behaviors of volunteers and military guests. But it also contributed to the magnetic attraction that drew white sailors away from the place where the navy had put them and to Hollywood and downtown, walking through the spatially dwindling Mexican American neighborhoods in a longer history of colonial displacement. Among the many navy participants in the Zoot Suit Riots violence was J. C. P. Miller, who in March 1943 was sauntering back along Broadway on his return trip from the Hollywood Canteen and wound up fighting with young Mexican American men dressed in zoot suits who allegedly hurled obscenities at him as he passed through their compromised neighborhood.[28]

Current racial tensions, racialized sex and gender constructions, and continuing military takeovers, however, are out of place in the world of *Warner Club News*. While Kuter writes in February 1943, twelve of the six hundred young people, mostly Mexican American men, who had been rounded up by the Los Angeles Police as suspects in what would become known as the Sleepy Lagoon Murder case, are one month into their incarceration in San Quentin, where they will stay until the case is dismissed (for lack of evidence) in October 1944. Inflammatory newspaper coverage condemned them. Civil rights activists, including many in the Los Angeles film industry, fought for their release. But Kuter does not mention this or any other rumblings of the violence that will soon explode in the spring and summer of 1943. Tensions have been brewing throughout the military buildup in California since 1940 (and, according to McWilliams, had never stopped since the days of de Portola). But Kuter doesn't go there. Instead, he returns the readers of *Warner Club News* to the "ribald laughter of soldiers" in the romantic history leading up to Americanization. Safer than historical continuities of race and space is the recognition of a shared road trip on the busily traveled thoroughfare between the Mission and the Pueblo. Workers who volunteered at the repurposed cantina would, in fact, reverse de Portola's expedition in private automobiles, car pools, or Pacific Electric Red Cars. And when they arrived at their destination, the site of laughter and soldier recreation, they would be in the same building as of old, or at least parts of it.

It is a long history, and good storytelling requires leaving something out. Although he skips the twenty-four years of Mexican independence, Kuter does, however, make room for the seven years of Hollywood's independence as a city, which ended in 1910, "when, in order to get an adequate water supply, it surrendered its Charter, and by annexation, became part of the ever expanding City of Los Angeles." He stretches out his picaresque descriptions of the dilapidated old cantina, which "went the way of all things, and except for a few adobe wall ruins, and an old wooden barn." He supplies a personal note—in 1920, he himself used to frequent the structure when it was used by "a small group of artists and actors who worked in 'motion pictures'—a booming young business which had come to Hollywood some ten years previously."[29] The next paragraph brings it home: "Strange, how this particular area has always seemed to have an especial attraction for the military, thespians and artists!"[30]

Past and present merge as he tells how the "old wooden barn" was rotated to face Cahuenga Avenue, where, from its new orientation, it functioned briefly as a "quaint nightclub" before once again falling into disuse. Finally, it is discovered by Bette Davis and John Garfield, who lead the industry campaign to "remodel the old barn into a suitable and proper place in which to entertain Uncle Sam's Service men."[31] He describes a humble assembly on September 3, 1942. "Amid the ruins and wreckage of the old wooden barn, strewn with broken tables and chairs, covered in dust, a little group of interested people, headed by Bette Davis, gathered together in candlelight."[32] Kuter's story begins to resemble the usual press lists of the food provided and the great service being performed by the people of the motion picture industry when exactly one month later the candles are eclipsed, if not by klieg lights, then flood lights as the Hollywood Canteen becomes, "overnight," to quote the *Los Angeles Daily News*, the most popular "entertainment center for servicemen in the Los Angeles district."[33]

If you were a reader of *Warner Club News*, you probably recalled that evening well. No one would need to remind you that celebrities paid for bleacher seats to cheer the GIs. You would already have known—from memory, office buzz, reading or listening to news, or a blur of all of these—that the military guests and civilian hosts and hostesses who could squeeze into the club that night danced crowdedly in it. The rest among the estimated twelve thousand attendees watched from the sidewalk. As a reader of the newsletter, you might have recalled the police efforts to keep these attendees on the curb. "Move back! Get out of the street! Cahuenga is a military highway for the duration." You already knew that not everyone could fit in the building and that the Canteen board had rented the Shell Oil Company gas station on the corner for its commodious parking lot and runways, on which "the servicemen . . . dance[d] with the Hollywood girls" and installed "a cordon of military police . . . to guarantee decorum."[34] You already knew—but it may have been pleasant to hear again—that among the crowd of celebrities, soldiers, and dignitaries milled Hollywood residents. Many of them worked in the industry; others lived in the neighborhood and had ventured down the street to check out the excitement. Whether you were inside dancing to Duke Ellington's orchestra or outside dancing to Rudy Vallee's Coast Guard Band or just standing on the curbstone, you were still right at the root of the glamorous lights, at the center of action. And now, thanks to Kuter's article, you could remember this glamorous "first dance" of the stars and soldiers with a sense of Los Angeles history.

Route 2

Hollywood to Santa Anita Assembly Center, twenty miles east,
March 27–October 27, 1942.

On the other hand—if you and I were among the revelers at the Hollywood
Canteen grand opening, we probably would not know about a starkly different
(and perhaps even more startlingly similar) articulation of swing music, jitterbug, military, and notions of American belonging taking place only twenty
miles to the east at the Santa Anita Assembly Center. At this (barely) recon-
verted race track, the Starlight Serenaders, a swing orchestra formed by forcibly removed Japanese American Southern Californians, played for dislocated dancers bidding farewell on eve after eve of further dislocation to more
remote and longer term internment camps. Some among the jitterbugging
Nisei teenagers were Hollywood residents who would have been able to stroll
down to cheer the soldiers and gaze at the stars, or even see the glow and hear
the festivities of the Canteen grand opening from their homes, if they had
not been rounded up with their families by the army. This was not the first
time that Hollywood residents of Japanese descent had been threatened by
removal. In 1923, the "Keep Hollywood White" campaign of the Hollywood
Protective Association had targeted residents of the Tamarind-Bronson
neighborhood south of Sunset.[35]

In operation from March 27 to October 27, 1942, Santa Anita was the largest
"assembly center" among those that sprang up on fairgrounds and race tracks
to temporarily house the ninety thousand Isei and Nisei evacuees slated for
the camps. People slept in horse stalls. Over a four-day period in mid-April
1942, 5,204 residents of west Los Angeles, including Hollywood, Beverly Hills,
and Westwood, joined the nearly 6,715 temporary inhabitants who had arrived
over the previous two weeks at the Santa Anita Racetrack.[36] By June 1942—
while the Hollywood Canteen was still in the planning—the Santa Anita Assembly Center was the thirty-second largest city in California.[37] The average
population at Santa Anita was nearly thirteen thousand.[38] Before evacuation,
Ryohei Nomura, a student at Hollywood High School, had lived at Cahuenga
and Santa Monica, a block away from the barn that housed the Hollywood
Canteen.[39] With his family, he was removed to Santa Anita and soon removed
again to the internment camp at Heart Mountain in Cody, Wyoming. In 1945,
he was allowed to join the army, the same organization that had relocated his
family from their home.[40]

In imagining the Hollywood Canteen as part of an interconnected swing-
dancing landscape at the Santa Anita Assembly Center, we might conceive
the latter as a tiny community gathering. Nonetheless, according to George

Yoshida, the Sayonara Balls held under the stars and in front of the grand stand accommodated up to two thousand dancers at a time, many more than could be served at the Hollywood Canteen (where military guests were limited, by fire regulations, to five hundred at a time),[41] or for that matter any but the more extravagant Los Angeles ballrooms (the Hollywood Palladium housed six thousand).[42] The Hollywood Canteen moved its guests in and out, entertaining up to three thousand per night, but in shifts. Twenty miles to the east, two thousand evacuees attended a Saturday night dance "to honor the former residents of San Diego who were leaving Santa Anita for an undisclosed destination," Yoshida writes. The next weekend a dance was held for "transferees of San Jose, Santa Clara Valley, Hollywood and part of Los Angeles."[43]

Other assembly centers, including Tanforan (380 miles to the North) and Pomona (35 miles to the east), had swing bands of Nisei musicians playing for dances.[44] Charles Kikuchi, interned when he was a Berkeley graduate student, noted in his diaries that the Saturday night dances at Tanforan were "jammed to capacity" with Nisei teens. On May 17, 1942, he wrote, "many of the parents who would never let their daughters go to dances before do not object so strenuously now. They are slowly accepting the fact that their children cannot stay home night after night doing nothing without some sort of recreational release."[45] The next month, he observed, "the jitterbug craze is still strong with the young kids and for them nothing else exists. . . . Last night at the dance they were all dressed up in their draped pants and bright shirts."[46]

As evacuees were relocated, musicians among them formed new bands in new internment camps. By the time the Hollywood Canteen opened, Nisei teenagers had already jitterbugged to the music of the Jive Bombers at Manzanar, two hundred miles to the north.[47] Santa Anita would cease its operation as an assembly center three weeks after the opening of the Hollywood Canteen, but Nisei musicians and dancers, including former Hollywood residents, continued to produce and participate in swing culture—nine out of the ten permanent camps had swing bands.

Reiko Nagumo, born in Los Angeles in 1933, was too young to have danced at the Hollywood Canteen, even if her family had not been uprooted from their home six blocks south of Hollywood Boulevard. Still, she was a Hollywood child, and, as she would tell students at the Elk Grove Unified School District many years later, she spent her years at the camp at Heart Mountain, Wyoming, writing to movie stars for their autographs. Embarrassed by her Japanese heritage by that time, she used an Anglo pseudonym for these transactions. Maybe the Heart Mountain return address gave her away to some stars and publicity assistants, or maybe it didn't. In any case, by the end of the war, she had acquired sixty-eight photographs from stars including Bette Davis, Tyrone Power, and Rita Hayworth, all signed "to Virginia" instead of "to Reiko"—mementos of her connection and disconnection with that world; the movies, the nation, her hometown.[48] George Yoshida tells a similar story when he describes the way he and other interned Nisei jazz and swing musicians, dancers, and fans listened to the sound of Tommy Dorsey's trombone as it floated out from the Hollywood Palladium "through barrack radios, but that music was being played on the outside—forbidden territory to us 'enemy aliens.'"[49]

The Palladium, which opened in 1940, was forbidden territory to African Americans as well. It was a fact well known to African American residents of Los Angeles that black people were not allowed to enter most of the night spots and eateries in the vicinity of the Hollywood Canteen. Mexican American civilians were often, but not always, admitted to the Palladium and other Hollywood venues, hinging on such factors as skin color and dress and if anyone in the party could be read as a pachuco. If you were a black military traveler from out of town, you might not find out that nightclubs near the Hollywood Canteen were off limits until you were refused entrance, but this situation was well known by African American volunteers at the Canteen. The actor, dancer, musician, and former Canteen volunteer Lennie Bluett told me in our 2003 interview that he *still* won't go to the Palladium, after being excluded from the audience when "Frank Sinatra made his great debut with Tommy Dorsey." He described what he could have witnessed had he been admitted. "Jo Stafford and the group were singing behind him, like they did," Here, Lennie broke into song: "Dream, when you're feeling blue." His voice was lovely, smooth, he nailed the band crooner style of the era, singing in what must have been the higher end of his baritone voice, and there were no cracks—none, at eighty. He stopped and leaned back. "We were not allowed to go. No black people were allowed to go . . . so I won't even walk into the Palladium today, I don't care what's there."[50]

Route 3

Hollywood swing (the westward expansion narrative):
New York to Los Angeles / black to white / subculture
to national culture.

The place of Los Angeles in swing history and mythology is not so very different a site of remembering and forgetting from that of Los Angeles itself. Accounts of swing on the West Coast are polarized between an uncritical "arrival" story of swing becoming national culture—and local histories of Los Angeles that attend to geographies of race. Swing historiography, after all, has its own national fantasy to grapple with—if it functions, in part, as a story of national unity, of the time when all Americans shared a common musical culture—so it is not surprising that swing carries its own colonialist discourse of westward expansion, whitening, and mainstreaming.

So the story goes: when Benny Goodman arrives at the Palomar Ballroom in Los Angeles in 1935, the West Coast audience, who live life not only on a sunnier shore but in an earlier time zone, is already familiar with the more adventuresome swing music that Goodman saves for later in the night on his live broadcasts from New York. When Goodman pulls out the stops at the end of his otherwise disastrous coast-to-coast tour, all of (white) Los Angeles jumps to its feet, and soon the whole nation is doing the jitterbug. American popular music is born and with it, the swing era. Swing as black music is a "New York story." If swing is white on the West Coast, it is because the West Coast is white. If it is more relaxed on the West Coast, it is because the West Coast is relaxed. If it is more lucrative on the West Coast, it is because the West Coast is bountiful.

Los Angeles holds a special place in "Swing Era" history as the site where Goodman is crowned the "King of Swing." In this respect, Los Angeles attracts dubious renown in jazz and swing historiography as the locus of swing's shift from "verb" to "noun"—from African American dance music to a national (white dominated) "craze" in Los Angeles; from black culture to white commodity.[51] Granted, being the King of Swing is not the same as being the King of Spain, but it is worth noting the colonialist pattern in the Goodman myth. Like the Palladium, which would open five years later, the Palomar was a whites-only club or, more accurately, a club that might admit Mexican Americans but was closed to black audiences and bands. In this westward expansion narrative, Goodman's storming of the Palomar is still a story of white conquest written on racial, spatial, and economic shifts in who owns swing. The special place of Los Angeles in this story of how swing goes white and national has a history older than swing, older than Goodman, and older than California statehood.

In critical jazz and swing historiography, the underlying colonial narrative is exposed by revealing African American roots of the music and the fact that earlier black swing bands, including the magnificent orchestra Fletcher Henderson led, which would not have access to the kinds of markets Benny Goodman's would enjoy even though Henderson's arrangements for Goodman's orchestra were embraced by the mass crossover audiences of the Swing Era. Historians of the evolution of jazz in Los Angeles made a double intervention when they set out to document that "West Coast Jazz," like the "Swing Era," was a marketing label that left out many scenes, sounds, and players, even as it promoted the music and constructed audiences. "West Coast Jazz" would become a brand name in the 1950s for laid-back, cool sounds of artists such as Chet Baker and Shorty Rogers. Though these white jazz artists themselves worked in racially integrated groups, they benefited, like the white swing artists, from legacies of race that they didn't invent. Historians of black Los Angeles and of jazz in Los Angeles and Los Angeles musicians who wrote memories and contributed oral histories took on the task of reperiodizing and remapping popular notions of jazz and swing on the West Coast, therefore going against the grain of popular understandings of the jazz and swing period. Ample scholarship is now available on preexisting jazz and swing on the West Coast prior to Goodman's arrival (still not part of the canon but perhaps a respectable "extra credit assignment"), particularly in the African American business district on Central Avenue. The Eastside, as the neighborhood was more often called at the time, not only a lively music scene but one of the few neighborhoods in Los Angeles where African Americans were allowed to live (and even then some blocks were off limits), was home, business place, and leisure site to musicians, actors, dancers, bankers, teachers, merchants, newspaper editors, and some of the preeminent civil rights lawyers of the period. It was also home to a YWCA and YMCA that were mobilized for entertaining soldiers during World War II.

Histories covering the Eastside and histories of what Donald Bogle has called "Black Hollywood" (people hired to play the black roles in the movies but largely banned from residing near the studios) are other places where one can find testimonials of racial restriction throughout Los Angeles. Unsurprisingly, the Palomar, which was located not in Hollywood but downtown on Third Street and Vermont, was a segregated ballroom, as were most places where white people danced in Los Angeles in the 1930s and 1940s. Anthony Macias points out that even most race analysis of the whitening of swing on the West Coast elides the participation of Mexican Americans, who were sometimes and sometimes not admitted to white Hollywood night spots, including the Palladium, and who could even have been among those dancing to Goodman's band at the Palomar in 1935, an observation that disrupts even the whiteness of the swing frontier narrative, as well as the black/white color line of most, but not all, the critical jazz and swing historiography of Los Angeles.[52]

Goodman may have called the tunes, but he didn't call the shots that catapulted him to his dubious throne in the frontier myth of swing. A parallel, lesser known story from the dance side of equation is that of Dean Collins, who, like Goodman, was from the East Coast, a child of Jewish immigrant parents, and steeped in the black cultural developments of his day. Col-

FIG 2.1: Theresa and Joe Nevarez outside the Hollywood Canteen, 1944.
COURTESY THERESA NEVAREZ.

lins arrived in Los Angeles a year after Goodman, in 1936, dancing Savoy Ballroom–style lindy with his own personal touch. Swing and jazz scholars have addressed the ways black music has served as sites of aspirational whiteness and American-ness for "ethnic white" children of immigrants. Collins rejected claims that his dancing created a new category separate from that of the black dancers he admired. Nonetheless, Collins was afforded more mobility throughout Los Angeles, and especially in Hollywood, than local African American dancers, or even Whitey's Lindy Hoppers from the Savoy Ballroom, who traveled west to the movies around the same time. His dancing—in contests and on the screen—and his teaching and choreography in swing films were embraced and canonized, or "ballroomed," to use the dance vernacular, as "West Coast" style against his own objections. It was Collins's version of the lindy—not the Mexican American Pachuco Hop, a variation that actually did develop in California, or the Lindy Hop as danced by the Savoy dancers of whom Collins saw himself as a fellow stylist—that became California's state dance in 1987.

Route 4

East Los Angeles to Hollywood with Theresa Nevarez, seven miles to the northeast, 1944.

Theresa Nevarez could not recall if she and her husband had actually danced *inside* the Hollywood Canteen, but she did possess a beautiful photograph of herself and her husband standing *outside* the club, in broad daylight, smiling with the happiness that was theirs during the furlough when Joe came home and they married in 1944. Our telephone conversation was arranged by her daughter, Margaret Nevarez, whom I met when I gave a talk on the Hollywood Canteen at the Autry Center in Griffith Park. Margaret was accompanied by her cousin, a volunteer at the Bob Hope USO at Los Angeles Airport. Margaret had brought a copy of the photograph of her parents in front of the Canteen. I asked if I might interview her parents. Her father wasn't well at the time, but she checked with Theresa to see if I could interview her about her Canteen memories.

Theresa agreed. She narrated a vivid picture of Los Angeles in her memories from World War II. She remembered that people went to Tijuana to buy shoes, which were rationed in the United States. She bitterly recalled being tracked into beauty school from Lincoln High when a counselor "in a little cage" made up a program and handed it to her.

"You didn't choose to go to beauty school?" I asked.

"No," she replied, adding, "There is still racism." She shared the measures she took to protect her daughter and the way her daughter protected her daughters when counselors and teachers said, "You don't belong here, you belong over there."[53]

When I asked her if she ever danced at the Hollywood Canteen or any of the USOs during the war, she told me no, she lived at home still, near Alpine and Figueroa in East Los Angeles, with her protective, tightly knit family. "You had to be home by ten o'clock, even if you had a boyfriend." But her family was involved in a fraternal society that offered many opportunities to socialize at dances. It was in fact on the dance floor at such an event that she met her future husband. A more serious dancer than she, Joe Nevarez coaxed her onto the floor.

Everyone told her, "Don't dance with that man. He's too old for you." She told them, "I'm not marrying the man. I'm just dancing." She laughed. This is an old family story now. Joe had crossed from Juarez to El Paso with his parents as a three-month-old baby during the Mexican Revolution. Now in his early thirties, he was the first and only Mexican American staff reporter for the *Los Angeles Times*. Joe recognized Theresa as the pretty woman he had previously glimpsed through the beauty shop window where she worked downtown. He began to court her, but just as they got to know each other, he was inducted into the army. They wrote to each other, and during his furlough visit in May 1944, they married. After a few brief days of celebration in Los Angeles, they returned as a couple to Joe's base in Texas. Whether or not they danced at the Hollywood Canteen (it doesn't seem likely, since Theresa wasn't a volunteer), the photograph of the beautiful young civilian woman and the handsome man in the army uniform posing in front of the iconic Hollywood wartime landmark depict the couple, and Mexican Americans, at the center of national and local memory, which more often excluded them.[54]

Route 5

Los Angeles to Hollywood, Los Angeles to Hollywood, Los Angeles to Hollywood (via Culver City) with Lennie Bluett.

World War II brought a great increase in the overall population, but the demographic with the greatest percentage of growth was represented by the influx of African Americans, drawn, like other civilian migrants, to promises of jobs in defense plants and shipyards. Lennie Bluett did not "migrate" to Los Angeles. He was already there. "My mother was a school girl here." Born in the city in 1919, Lennie spent his life just about as close to the center of Los Angeles history as a person could while existing on its margins. His grandparents moved to Los Angeles in the 1890s, where they lived at Henry Huntington's estate, in the gardener's quarters. During the Great Depression, his mother moved to Beverly Hills, where she lived with Humphrey Bogart and later with Bogie and Bacall (every day except Thursday and every other Sunday afternoon), as their cook. From the time he was a teenager, Lennie attended the Bogarts' private parties, where he met everybody who was anybody in the motion picture industry, while entertaining at the piano. A longtime member of the Screen Actors Guild, Lennie appeared in many of the films that defined the era, including *Gone with the Wind*, playing a wounded Civil War soldier ("a *Confederate* soldier," he would tell an NPR interviewer). On the eve of World War II, he led the battle to desegregate the portable toilets on the set.

"Back lot MGM that's Culver City, California, *right here*," he tells me in 2003, gesturing with his extended arm toward the south wall of his Hollywood apartment. He tells the story of arriving at the set at 6 a.m. for makeup and costume (in this case blood and bandages). He was walking out to the makeup tent through the realistic set of the Civil War battlefield when he was confronted with a living legacy of the confederacy.

> I walked along a row of outdoor toilets like they have at venues outside, you know, and I looked up and saw, "white, colored, white, colored, white, colored." Two or three hundred of them. And I swear to god on my dear mother's grave—I loved her dearly—I said, this cannot be. This is 1938, '39. We're getting ready to go into war to fight for this country. And on the back lot and we can't go number one or number two where we want to? And we've got to go fight for this country? I can't believe this. I'm all of eighteen and a half, nineteen. So we got together with the older guys. The older guys said, "Oh, man, don't rock the boat . . . I got babies at home to feed." I said, "What about your pride? What about your dignity?" They said, "Yeah, we've got dignity, but . . . [what if] they told us to go home?" I said, "They cannot bring four hundred Mexicans out here to look like blacks. They're not going to look like blacks on film. They got dark skins, but they aren't going to look like . . ." So they said, "Okay, whatever you guys decide to do, we'll stand behind you."

In Lennie's narrative, it seems to be the possibility of being replaced by Mexicans, a legacy of divide-and-conquer racism in Los Angeles, that moves his coworkers to support his action. He then narrates his younger self as he marched up to knock on the door of Clark Gable's dressing room.

> Gable's makeup man said, "Yes?" And I said, "I have to speak to Mr. Gable for two seconds. It will not be more than two seconds." And so Gable said, "Who is it?" And I said, "Mr. Gable, I worked with you on *Mogombo* with Grace Kelly but you won't remember me, but I'm one of the black guys." And so the minute I said "black guys" he said, "Let him in." So the dresser let me in and he said, "Yeah, what is it? Hi." He was very nice, very affable. He said, "Yeah, come in." And I said, "Mr. Gable, would you give me one minute of your time to come out? I want to show you something."

The star of the film took off the towel that had been around his neck for makeup and followed the extra out into the MGM back lot, stepping over the cables until they came to the line of outdoor toilets.

"I said, 'Would you see those signs up there?' He swore like a sailor and he got on the phone. He called Victor Fleming, the director. He called over to the property master. He said, 'If you don't get those goddamn son-of-a-bitch signs down, I'm going to walk off this production.' That was Clark Gable."

Before, during, and after the making of this Civil War film in Culver City, Hollywood was a battleground for Bluett. It was the industry, workplace, and neighborhood where he carved out a career as an actor, singer, and dancer while fighting to gain entry to nightclubs, living quarters, restaurants, and studio commissaries. In 1940, he, the actor and agent Ben Carter, and three other black men took McConnell's Restaurant to court when they were refused lunch service. Years after winning the battle of the segregated toilets on the set of *Gone with the Wind*, he was still fighting for professional, private, and public accommodation. The case against McConnell's was represented by the African American attorney Walter L. Gordon as part of a longtime battle fought by black residents of Los Angeles who took the time and trouble to draw legal attention to racial exclusions throughout most of the city.

Route 6

South of Beverly to Hollywood with Jane (Josephs) Lockwood,
two and a half miles north.

Every week from 1942 to 1945, Jane Josephs left her house on Sycamore, walked one block north, turned left at Beverly, and waited at the next corner for the La Brea bus. She might ride to Hollywood Boulevard and transfer to an eastbound bus, or she might decide to get off at Sunset; the Canteen is less than a fifteen-minute walk from there. At the volunteer entrance to the back, she showed her Canteen ID with her (anglicized) professional name, Jane Lockwood (her mother's maiden name). It was as Jane Lockwood that she danced with soldiers and observed the stars. Later that night, she would take the same route back, where her mother met her at the bus stop (unless her father, a well-known physician, picked her up at the Canteen and took her out for a late-night bite in Hollywood). She would tell her parents about her evening's adventures and then write it all down in her diary. The next week, she would go back via the same bus stop, the same route, the same routine. Should her gaze drift east while waiting for her bus, she might even see, without noticing, McConnell's Restaurant. Four blocks away, the local eatery was an ordinary blip on the horizon. I don't know, but I imagine, that she would have been surprised that its management would turn anyone away.

Like most white people in Los Angeles, Lockwood lived in an area where she could easily miss the evidence of structural racism. People restricted by housing covenants, neighborhood-watch-style protective associations, and admission policies to public places knew full well that the city was segregated. So did those living in the fiercely guarded white communities, such as Compton and Inglewood, near unrestricted mixed areas.[55] But white people in areas at a remove from the covenant border wars, whose communities were buffered by other restricted communities, could easily live without this knowledge. Hollywood was such a place.

Even explicitly "white" communities, such as Glendale, could be experienced as incidentally, rather than intentionally, white if one traveled the landscape in an apparently white body. Did Bette Davis know—when she bought her home at 1705 Rancho Avenue on the Los Angeles River in Glendale, in 1940—that the city enforced an illegal sundown policy that did not permit African Americans to spend the night within the city limits? Glendale's whiteness was defended not only by realtors, homeowners' organizations, and covenants but the city police. The ordinance may have been only a rumor, according to the civil rights and fair housing lawyer Loren Miller.[56] Nonetheless, it might as well have been official, since it was enforced as such. Davis would not have had to sign anything or even know about this racial contract in order to enter it. Did she fight it? Was she aware of it? If so, it is not mentioned in her autobiographies or biographies, though her commitment to the integrated dance floor at the Hollywood Canteen is mentioned, along with her commitment to breaking down racial barriers by entertaining black troops in an otherwise all–African American caravan led by Hattie McDaniel, and in her work on the film *In This Our Life*.[57] But African American residents of Los Angeles were aware of Glendale's danger for black travelers after sundown, as was the national black press. Even the national headquarters of the YWCA was aware of it, from visitation reports filed by YW executives over the years, at least as early as 1936, alerting the head office of the refusal of the local executive board of the all-white Glendale YWCA to take a stand against racist exclusion in their community.[58]

In 1941, the national YWCA representative Winifred Wygal visited the Glendale YWCA and reported that officers and board members "reiterate[d] in the course of the day that Glendale has no race problem, meaning no Negro problem," but that she later learned that "the reason that there is no Negro problem there is because Glendale does not allow a Negro to stay overnight in the town."[59] Wygal, a white woman long active in YWCA integration drives, wrote, "I do not believe that the general secretary is lacking in sensitivity on this point except in this instance that she has never had an opportunity to think through such an implication of such a decision on the part of the town fathers." Wygal recommended guidance be provided to the Glendale YWCA from the national office. In 1945, another officer from the national headquarters visited the Glendale YWCA in order to try to convince the board and officers to assist with the formation of a club for formerly interned Japanese and Japanese American girls and women living in a nearby housing project. The Glendale YWCA refused and in fact also declined to reemploy the part-time gardener who had previously tended the YWCA grounds and had lived in Glendale for twenty years before being forcibly relocated to an internment camp.[60] As late as 1947, the visitation reports by the national YWCA noted that some of the young white women in the Glendale membership had attended summer conferences where they became aware of racially restrictive housing, studied the issues specific to Glendale, and began "discussing them in their club and interest groups at home." The experience of going to conferences "where race relations are discussed in interracial gatherings" motivated them to invite "girls of other races to meet with them in occasional club meetings."[61]

Route 7

East Los Angeles to Hollywood to downtown:
Mary Lou (Ramirez) Ochoa.

Although Mary Lou (Ramirez) Ochoa enjoyed the Hollywood Canteen, she recalled that the YMCA was easier to get to by transit from her home in East Los Angeles. The downtown "Y" was near the Zenda Ballroom, one of the nightclubs that Anthony Macias lists as places where Mexican Americans jit-terbugged in the 1940s.[62] She recalled that there were more Latinos at the USO in the "Y" than at the Hollywood Canteen and that she felt more "protected" at the "Y." (I wonder if she might have crossed paths with a young writer, his typewriter hanging by a strap on his travel-weary frame, who, when turned away from the "Y," stumbled back to Greyhound to get some sleep?) She de-scribed what downtown was like during the war. "I remember seeing a lot of Marines and sailors." She then shifted into the present to explain that down-town today isn't what it was like when it used to be a good place to go to shop. "But I haven't been downtown in years. It's so changed, everything is so different." During the war, it was different, too. "On Broadway, the streetcars and buses were full of Marines and sailors, always flirting, trying to pick up girls down there. And there were always a lot of girls who would try to meet them, and date them. But they were not part of the 'Y.'" These other girls, she said, "would be necking on the corners" with the sailors. "It was totally different from the way I was brought up."[63] (It is possible, Macias writes, that Mary Lou's brother, Randolph Leon "Ron" Ramirez, danced at the Palomar the night of Benny Goodman's splash success.)[64]

Throughout the years when the Hollywood Canteen was planned, opened, and operated, stories in the black press, jazz and swing periodicals, and Pop-ular Front press continued to gesture hopefully toward its lack of Jim Crow.

But this was not a story covered in movie fan magazines, the *Los Angeles Times*, the *Los Angeles Examiner*, other mainstream local and national newspapers, or Leo "K" Kuter's story in the *Warner Club News*.

One month before Kuter's story appeared, battles among volunteers and members of the board and executive committee of the Hollywood Canteen over mixed dancing there made their first appearance in the black press and were ignored by the mainstream (white) press.[65] In the coming months, a different story about battles over race and proximity in Los Angeles would dominate the news. This one was not ignored by the white press. Instead, the mainstream press, most particularly Joe Nevarez's employer, the *Los Angeles Times*, blamed flurries of racist violence against criminalized Mexican American youth on young people of color. The black, Latino, and Popular Front press defended the Mexican American young people who were most egregiously affected by the vigilante violence in their communities, the inflammatory journalism, and the racially imbalanced response of the police and courtrooms that listened to white people and ignored people of color. In the same papers, stories appeared that presented the struggles over mixed dancing at the Hollywood Canteen as significant civil rights battles.

The *Los Angeles Times*, while having a great deal to say about the delinquency of Mexican American, Filipino, and African American young people in zoot suits, was silent on the "knock-down, drag out fights" over mixed-race dancing that occurred at the Hollywood Canteen in 1943.[66] Instead, the club was depicted as a haven of kindness of stars to soldiers. Race wasn't mentioned. The apparently harmonious, homogeneous whiteness of the club in photographs was unremarked. The presence of Canteen volunteers who had been active in organizing for the defense of the young Mexican American men who had been scapegoated in the Sleepy Lagoon case since August 1942 was unmentioned. While racial tensions and violence permeated Los Angeles and race riots heated up and raged through the nation, the mainstream (white) press presented the Hollywood Canteen as color-blind and white at the same time. And the black press, Popular Front press, Communist press, and some trade union magazines declared the Canteen's dance floor integrationists victorious.

Was the Hollywood Canteen of 1942 a "far cry from the Cantina of almost 100 years ago?" Yes and no. Kuter's story, uncritical though it is, is unusual among newspaper and magazine stories about the club written in the 1940s in that it locates the Canteen on the ground in a particular part of Los Angeles and in a historical context that includes pre–Pearl Harbor militarism, colonialism and conquest (interpreted as friendly and relaxed), and whiteness. Nonetheless, his story does so without questioning the paradoxes this history of place raises for present democracy and without reservations about his ability to so seamlessly place World War II Los Angeles within a historical narrative of colonial continuity. Indeed, the narrative participates in an ongoing colonial and racial project in which Mexican Los Angeles and racialized people in Los Angeles continued to be under siege. The whiteness of the landscape was still being achieved, as Kuter wrote, through racial regulation that was largely invisible to those who benefited and starkly apparent to those who did not.

In the next chapter I invite you to reorient with me again, this time swiveling south, to move even farther from those resilient improbable klieg lights, and this time from a vantage point from which racial overlays on the map are well known by residents whose travels they shape. We shift our perspective to eye level, through points of view of people operating from a different curbstone—not at the corners of Cahuenga and Sunset or Hollywood and Vine but much further south and east of Main. The Central Avenue district was far from Hollywood—"more than an hour's cab ride," as Lena Horne described the distance between the black neighborhood of Los Angeles and the apartment in the whites-only Hollywood neighborhood that her agent found her at the start of her movie career.[67] It seemed even farther, writes Kyle Julian, for African Americans traveling the other direction.[68]

★ ★ ★

CHAPTER 3

Operating from the Curbstone

A quiver went through the Negro community when these men poured
in. "Our boys have arrived" were headlines in one of our papers.
—DOROTHY GUINN, " 'OPERATING FROM THE CURBSTONE' " (MAY 15, 1942)

To travel to the communities near Los Angeles where several hundred
Negro men are stationed requires the volunteer service of persons with
cars.
—MRS. BERT MACDONALD, *CALIFORNIA EAGLE* (FEBRUARY 5, 1942)

As if to show that the U.S.A. can make democracy work, there was a
sprinkling of white soldiers among our guests. Of course they were
treated the same as our own boys and enjoyed the occasion just as much
as did our colored boys.
—"WATTS USO HOSPITALITY HOUSE HAS BRILLIANT OPENING," *CALIFORNIA EAGLE*
(FEBRUARY 26, 1942)

Route(s): Multiple, Unpredicable

*The few places black people could live in Los Angeles to everywhere
black soldiers were stationed in greater LA. Miles: countless.*

Ten miles due south of Hollywood and as far west of Main as black people
could generally reside in Los Angeles, the elite West Adams neighborhood
known as Sugar Hill was home to black celebrities, including Ethel Waters,
Louise Beavers, and Ben Carter, who might have lived in Beverly Hills had
it not been for residential segregation.[1] On May 15, 1942, soon after she pur-
chased her own Sugar Hill home, the actress Hattie McDaniel greeted fellow
members of the Negro Sub-Committee of the Hollywood Victory Committee (HVC). Among her guests were black actors who, like herself, achieved

Hollywood screen success, mostly playing roles of servants, including Beavers, Leigh Whipper, Lillian Randolph, and Eddie Anderson.[2]

The larger HVC was formed in order to organize Hollywood's contributions to the entertainment of troops, such as USO "Spot" (local) camp shows. Members of the HVC sought to manage volunteerism in their industry in ways that provided ample patriotic service while protecting workers from having to make excessive unpaid appearances—always a hazard in the entertainment business.[3] They held this goal (if not all the details, such as chain-of-command) in common with the organizers of the Hollywood Canteen (and some, like Bette Davis, served with both). The primary charge of the HVC Negro Sub-Committee was to organize black entertainers for USO "Spot" performances for black troops stationed throughout Greater Los Angeles. But the Sub-Committee also provided opportunities to strategize on issues off the radar of the "parent" organization: for example, how to ensure that black entertainers would not be disproportionately "volunteered" when their services were requested both for the black segregated shows and for the integration of white shows? This meeting at McDaniel's mansion was the first of many in which the Negro Sub-Committee both executed its charge to plan black entertainment for black troops and raised matters less easily addressed in racially mixed Hollywood company.

Dorothy C. Guinn was not present at that meeting. There is no reason she would have been. This fifty-two-year-old African American YWCA director and social worker was decidedly *not* a member of the entertainment industry. However, she did hold, among her many accomplishments, a national reputation as a celebrated playwright, at least in "Y" circles. Her best known pageant, *Out of the Dark* (copyrighted by the YWCA in 1924 and later collected in Willis Richardson's *Plays and Pageants from the Life of the Negro*, 1930), depicted the horrors of slavery, followed by a series of inspiring historical vignettes about African American men and women. Aimed at ensuring that black history was taught in meaningful and memorable ways, *Out of the Dark* was designed to be performed by community groups, not professionals, and included practical suggestions for casting, staging, and tips on low-budget stage effects.[4] In the late 1930s, while McDaniel, Beavers, and Randolph made the most of their roles as servants to characters played by Bette Davis, Claudette Colbert, and other white stars, Guinn provided dramaturgical leadership across town at the Twelfth Street YWCA, where the household employees among its members produced and performed plays that "interpret[ed] the efforts of domestic workers to secure social recognition through opportunities for better hours of work."[5] In one of these educational plays, Dorothy's much younger sister, Elmira—who lived with her

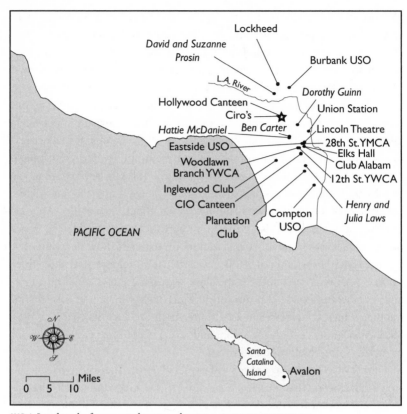

MAP 4: Landmarks for assorted routes, chapter 3. MAP BY ANDREW GOTTSFIELD.

and was sometimes employed as a domestic worker—played the role of an employer.

But on the day in question, May 15, 1942, Guinn composed a different kind of educational literature, neither skit nor pageant but another rhetorical form at which she excelled: the official organizational report. Across the top, she (or perhaps Elmira?) typed: "Operating from the Curbstone." This catchphrase had been coined within the membership of the USO-YWCA Committee of Negro Women in the early months of 1942 to describe the emplaced and improvisational character of her committees' war work. The charge of this committee came from national headquarters but was experienced at ground level by black clubwomen who resided in geographically small and racially unrestricted pockets of the city's southeast, as they scrambled to meet the needs of black soldiers throughout the sprawling expanse of mostly segregated Greater Los Angeles. More organized and professional than "flying by the seat of our pants," the phrase, "operating from the curbstone" captured just the right combination of duty, excellence, and exasperation. Guinn must have felt some satisfaction when she redeployed it toward national YWCA headquarters. She wrote in a measured tone—businesslike, meticulous, and, in the rousing conclusion, passionate and persuasive. She had to inspire YWCA executives in New York to imagine the view from a curbstone they could not imagine, and she did it through the dramatist's flair for point of view, tension, and narrative twist.

A Tale of Two Committees

I picture these parallel events on a split screen. Members of the HVC Negro Sub-Committee nominate and vote for officers in the lavish Harvard Boulevard home of the Academy Award–winning daughter of former slaves. The most prominent black actors in the industry plan how to present their concerns to the larger HVC. Who will challenge the white membership to spare a white star or two for black shows? How might white Hollywood actors be convinced that integration must run both ways? They listen to their guest, Edward Arnold, president of the Screen Actors Guild, who speaks on the importance of black entertainers in the USO. But the best part, according to the columnist Ruby Berkeley Goodwin (who was also McDaniel's friend and adviser), is when the Sub-Committee informs their esteemed guest of "the unfairness of segregated camps, which deprived colored soldiers of practically all entertainment."[6] (The 1944 feature film *Follow the Boys* will depict the black actors of the HVC happily sitting together in their own section of a town hall meeting and offering stereotypical services. Louise Beavers will speak the line "You can count on me for anything from singing to cooking."[7] The strategic and organizational work of the Negro Sub-Committee—especially its challenges to white Hollywood—will be screened from memory.) Five miles to the east, the Columbia University–educated YW director and social worker sits in a rundown branch perusing her notes on six months' worth of meetings, activities, and observations of the USO-YWCA Committee of Negro Women—work that will be even more thoroughly forgotten.

Like the initiatives raised by the HVC Negro Sub-Committee, Guinn's month-by-month report and recommendations simultaneously deliver and critique the assignments leveled at the Committee of Negro Women of Los Angeles by the paired national organizations represented by the USO-YWCA. She writes with authority, tact, and rhetorical prowess that subverts the form:

> In the opinion of the writer, what Negro citizens seem to be trying to say is that the concept concerning physical facilities like Hospitality Centers should be such that these centers demonstrate a truly American way of life

in which all men of the armed forces regardless of race or color who fight for democracy are welcome wherever the U.S.O. banner flies. The Center in the Central Avenue district will be established with the same principle in mind, although accessibility to the more thickly populated Negro community would mean that most of the men served will undoubtedly be Negroes.[8]

She presses incisive critique into deceptively passive language. The "writer" offers her "opinion" not on what "Negro citizens" say but on what they "seem" to "try" to say. Nonetheless, packed into this two-sentence bundle is (1) an argument for the establishment of a USO in the Eastside; (2) a critique of the USO hypocrisy that necessitates it; and (3) a claiming of patriotic moral high ground for the segregated black Angelenos who, unlike the USO, conceptualize entertaining the troops as extending to all "who fight for democracy" (or at least the men), "regardless of race or color." The USO and "Negro citizens" may share a vision of serving the troops, but because the USO is limited by its unwillingness to challenge segregation, it is unable to fulfill its vision. "Negro citizens," on the other hand, would prefer all clubs to be inclusive and will carry out the integrated policy in the small part of Los Angeles where most black people live. It is the USO—not black citizens of Los Angeles—that fails to lay the groundwork for "a truly American way of life." But that is just the "writer's" observation of what the "Negro citizens" are "trying to say."

I never interviewed Dorothy Guinn. She died in 1971. I encountered her words in the stillness of my own university library, the urgency of her tone reaching me through several layers of technology not exactly conducive for transmitting emotional response. It was after a full day of scrolling through hundreds of pages of typewritten and photographed YWCA documents, including visitation reports and bylaws, chugging through a jerky microfilm reader, that I found myself sitting up, feeling that I could almost hear her furious typing. Her documents bristled with purpose. I am always amazed by the intimacy of such moments, when even under such humdrum conditions it is possible to feel touched beyond context or data through the ephemeral leavings of a person. Passionate oral historian that I am, I also know that there is no guarantee that I will be more or less moved by an archival encounter or an in-person interview or that the voice in a live interview will ring more vividly than the voices of those whose traces are stored in the archive. The dance is different, but the difference is not one of life and death, flesh and paper (or in this case microfilm) but one of orientation. The oral history narrator, in conversation with an interviewer, reflects back and delivers a story that makes sense of the past in the present. The writer one meets through archival letters or reports appeals to another audience in another present. Sometimes, a voice, frozen in text, is nonetheless molten with immediacy, commitment, and purpose. Such was the voice of Dorothy Guinn, who moved me to rethink my assumptions about middle-class uplift and respectability politics as black YWCA workers' modus operandi.

Route 1

Massachusetts to Los Angeles, one "colored" YW at a time.

Born on June 11, 1890, Guinn arrived in Los Angeles at the end of a long and winding westward trail of "colored" YWCAs. After establishing herself through her YW work in Bridgeport, Connecticut, and Brooklyn, and earning a master's degree in social work from Columbia University, she accepted leadership posts at a series of "colored" branches: St. Joseph, Missouri, in the 1920s; Denver in 1930 (perhaps crossing paths with Hattie McDaniel, who, five years her junior, grew up in that town before she headed west in 1931 for a career in the movies); and finally Los Angeles. Crossing that blurry line between research and surveillance, I learn that she registered Socialist throughout her years in Los Angeles—that she selected that exact box, rather than "Decline to State" (DS), a safer option, given the historic red-baiting of left-leaning YW workers.[9] What would she have thought of the "democratizing" effects of voter registration data available to me now on ancestry.com? That she checked the "S" during the war years tells me something but, sadly, not something I can ask her about. It does tell me something, however, that changes my dance with other "Y" workers and my assumptions about who, and where, were Socialists in wartime Los Angeles.

Her new post in 1937 placed her at the center of black clubwomen's organizing in Los Angeles and in contact with a class-diversified range of predominantly, but not exclusively, black working-class girls and women in the Los Angeles Eastside, who sought the services of and sometimes lived at the branch she would direct. It also introduced her to members of Black Hollywood, who could be called on to entertain at events, and civil rights leaders. Mae Muse, daughter of actor (and HVC member) Clarence Muse, sang at her gala welcome reception.[10]

But the building that awaited her leadership was far from glamorous. Its facilities were poorly appointed, overcrowded, and in a terrible location. Its neglect seemed to be symbolized by its name, which missed the mark of its actual address by a good thirty blocks. When Guinn assumed her post, the Twelfth Street YWCA still bore the name of its original address when it had been founded as the branch for "colored girls" at 1108 East Twelfth Street in 1919. As the new director, Guinn's top priority was to acquire a better building.

To assist her was an impressive board of directors, a who's who of well-connected, university-educated, politically astute black women, including Juanita Miller, a social worker committed to nondiscriminatory public housing policy. Miller was an active member of the Delta Sigma Theta sorority, she served on the Council of the Los Angeles Civic League, and she was the first African American appointed to an executive administrative post in the State Relief Administration. Miller would lose that position in what she believed was a "race-based dismissal" in early 1940, soon after suing a restaurant that refused to serve her and her Delta sisters (represented by her husband, the civil rights attorney Loren Miller).[11] During the war years, she served as a field representative of the housing authority of the city of Los Angeles, working to ensure that "public housing in Los Angeles is working successfully along the democratic plan." Miller told her Delta audience in 1942 that "a11 of the 10 new developments are open to citizens of all races, regardless of color, creed or political affiliation. . . . There are southerners who have just arrived from Oklahoma, Arkansas and Texas, living side by side with their Negro and Mexican neighbors in the greatest harmony."[12] At the same time Juanita fought for fairness in public housing, Loren was busy fighting and winning cases against racially restrictive housing covenants. He won his first case around the time Dorothy Guinn arrived in Los Angeles. The new building for the Twelfth Street YW would be in the same neighborhood as the group of houses that served as the battleground of that legal victory.[13] Miller would try most of the restrictive covenant cases in Los Angeles, including the precedent-making Sugar Hill case, which led to the U.S. Supreme Court finally overturning restrictive covenants as unconstitutional. Guinn's YWCA board also included Vertner Gordon, the mother of another of Los Angeles's civil rights attorneys, Walter Gordon Jr., and wife of real estate agent, loan officer, and notary public Walter Gordon Sr., whose offices were in the same building as one of the three local black newspapers, the *California Eagle*.

By the time the seasoned YW executive directed her attentions to composing a narrative worthy of the hard work and need for better support of the overextended black professional women in the Negro Women's Committee, she had been "operating from the curbstone" at the misnamed Twelfth Street YWCA (on East Forty-Third) for four and half years. Established in 1919, this YWCA for "colored women," like most of black Los Angeles, was multiracial—a place that could be utilized by people of all races and ethnicities. As early as 1926 a traveling YW executive noted its inclusive membership of "white, 'colored,' and Japanese."[14] Other than the drastic interruption of Nisei and Isei participation in civic life for the period of internment, the constituency continued to be mixed, though predominantly black, throughout the war.

From 1937 to the fall of 1941, Guinn focused most of her attentions on seeking better facilities for the uniquely multicultural club in her charge, a multiplatform task that involved improving the club's relationship with the Los Angeles YWCA headquarters and building up the committees, clubs, activities, and networks necessary to improve the morale and activities of the branch. At the same time, she watched as war loomed in the news, erupted abroad, and exerted ramifications at home. In 1940, the impending U.S. entry into the war drew the national YWCA into the newly formed conglomeration of the USO—a tight and contradictory dance, as it would turn out. The change-of-address of the "colored women's branch" would improve the base of operation, but the operation itself would change drastically with the new pressures on black YWCA women to meet the demands of USO war work on behalf of black soldiers in Los Angeles. The city's expanse, the vast local military and defense buildup, mushrooming migrations of workers and troops across the racially restricted landscape (governed by covenant and custom, thus mystifying to newcomers) meant that "operating from the curbstone" from the city's only "colored branch" YWCA to wherever black soldiers might land held particular challenges for black women in Los Angeles.

Six months after filing her report of May 15, 1942, Guinn will move her branch to greatly improved facilities on Woodlawn. But today she writes from the rather shabby building that greeted her in 1937. Either that, or she writes from the home that she shares with her sister to the north on Occidental and Temple near Elysian Park. In either scenario—in relation to Sugar Hill or Hollywood—she writes from the racially mixed neighborhoods to the east, where most of the African Americans, Mexican Americans, and other people of color of Los Angeles reside.

If the title "Operating from the Curbstone" draws attention to a local, street-level view that those in the head offices of the YWCA or USO cannot see, the subtitle of the report privileges local raced and gendered standpoints of those working the territory: "The Experiences of the U.S.O.-Y.W.C.A. Committee of Negro Women, November 5, 1941–May 15, 1942." In categorizing six months' worth of work as "Experiences" rather than "Activities," "Achievements," or even "Recommendations," the report suggests that the embodied difference it would make to "operate from the curbstone" as black Los Angeles women could prove instructive to USO and YWCA headquarters. This is not a story of a chain of leadership in which local officers implement a portable national plan. Instead, Guinn weaves a tale of overextended, highly skilled black women organizing on the ground and on the fly, working under conditions that can only be apprehended at close range, and achieving their goals in spite of poor national planning and precisely because of their experiences as black clubwomen. This is a committee capable of carrying out their tasks but also critical of their charge to compensate for the ongoing historical effects of residential segregation in Los Angeles, USO executives' conservatism and inexperience with race, and the clashing goals of the new USO and the YWCA.

Of the six organizations that formed the USO in 1941, the YWCA was alone in its official commitment to racial integration and programmatic history of field reporting on race at local branches nationwide. At the end of the war, the USO surveyed the six organizations for evaluations of numerous operational points of the umbrella agency's war work, including race relations. The most critical evaluations came from the YWCA. Under "Major satisfactions in the agency's participation in service to Negroes," the YWCA identified "Freedom within the six agencies—which made it possible for the YWCA to function in line with their basic beliefs and experience in interracial matters." Regarding the question of "Basic gaps in services and practices," the national YWCA responded: "It is now evident from many quarters that USO might have been more aggressive in operating on a less segregated basis in those communities where 'community mores' did not impose the pattern. Unfortunately USO has to its credit the introduction of segregated services to many communities." In addition, the YWCA lamented that the "USO did not see the value in its incipiency of aligning with the more progressive elements in communities."[15]

Thus, another challenge of the USO-YWCA Negro Women's Committee was to serve two national organizations: one dedicated to meeting the needs of girls and women, the other mobilized to serve men headed for war; one that had fought segregation for decades through specific programmatic strategies (including interracial conferences, racially diverse leadership, and regular visitations of local branches), another that espoused democracy and racial equality but refused to rock the boat of conservatively interpreted community standards of race. Therefore, in addition to juggling these conflicting definitions and strategies for democracy within the YWCA-USO partnership, the Committee of Negro Women was charged with interpreting and translating contradictory policies to local African American community members, on whom they relied for volunteers.

This new committee, and the new focus on entertaining the black troops throughout Greater Los Angeles, came at the same time that Guinn was finally acquiring the much-needed new building and better location for her YWCA branch. The national YW was already aware of Guinn's skills: one visiting executive in 1941 reported that she was "by all odds the strongest member on the Los Angeles staff. In spite of her vigorous opinions, she seems to hold the respect of even conservative members of the board, staff and community."[16] Under her leadership, the YWCA board for all of Los Angeles mobilized to invest scarce resources into the "colored women's" branch, a consensus that struck one visiting YW executive as "one of the finest episodes in Association history."[17] But no sooner were these wheels finally set in motion than the impending entrance of the United States into the war added new priorities, including the work of this committee, formed in response to and anticipation of racial and spatial effects of the war in relation to Los Angeles. Beginning in November 1942—*before* the bombing of Pearl Harbor—the USO-YWCA Negro Women's Committee held community meetings, organized entertainment and housing for black troops throughout the region, set up task forces to investigate allegations of USO neglect of black troops, and recommended solutions. When complaints from the black community reached the committee alleging that Traveler's Aid was ignoring black military troops at Union Station, the committee dispatched members to study the traffic patterns of detraining troops. What they found was that the service was equally distributed to all comers but black soldiers rarely approached the booth. Was Traveler's Aid neglecting black troops? No—and yes! The committee recommended that the USO include black volunteers at Traveler's Aid. As summarized in the report: "The USO Traveler's Aid worker said she herself was willing to consider this suggestion, but would have to consult the Board which was meeting during the next week. This was April 9th; to date May 15th no report having been received from this meeting, we are now requesting a statement from USO Traveler's Aid in order to inform the Negro civilians who are interested in this situation."[18]

Guinn's report tells of the contradictory positions occupied by the USO-YWCA Committee of Negro Women as they simultaneously worked with the USO to meet the needs of black troops and tried to make sure that the USO did not discriminate against black soldiers throughout Los Angeles. Equally contradictory was simultaneously working to organize USO services for black troops in the black community while dealing with the fact that black members who were very concerned about the welfare of black soldiers and were eager to provide services and entertainment tended to trust the local branch YWCA but not the USO. After all, the USO had early on demonstrated its willingness to impose Jim Crow in camp shows, so the odds of the USO integrating its recreation centers did not look good. Throughout her long, detailed narrative, she voices the Committee's concerns that the USO not just fight "for the ideals of democracy" but work to put democracy "into practice." This included "anticipating pressures rather than taking action after compulsion with its unpleasant concomitants."[19]

In their efforts to improve communication and understanding among the Central Avenue community and USO leadership, the Committee of Negro Women organized a citizens' meeting with the director of the USO. The consensus message of the community attendees, as summarized in Guinn's report, was the request that the USO not place the burden entirely on black citizens to provide comfort and entertainment for black soldiers but that "all centers should be open to all men regardless of color; that Negro volunteers should be used in centers wherever possible and Negroes should be employed on the USO staff."[20] Only after USO policy proved inflexible toward proactively integrating all its recreation centers, not only those in black communities (where black troops were not usually stationed), did the Committee turn its attentions to creating an official USO center in the Eastside. "Operating from the Curbstone" without an integration policy from the national USO headquarters contributed to the frustrating experiences of many different groups and individuals working with the USO, or working independently from it, who found themselves at cross-purposes, despite similar goals, in their scattered improvisatory efforts to meet the needs of black troops all over the city and region.

Guinn's report "from the curbstone[s]" of the Eastside compiles a list of contradictions that conspired to pile the brunt of black soldier entertainment in Greater Los Angeles on black YWCA women and other black clubwomen and civilians in the Eastside. For example, black soldiers, unlike black Los Angeles civilian residents, were often stationed in otherwise white communities who resented their presence and refused to entertain them. In theory, the commanding officers (nearly always white) would contact the Central Branch USO to plan for their recreation, but this was not always something that officers were aware of or prioritized. The arrival of troops could be sudden and unexpected. Although the Central Branch USO in downtown Los Angeles was charged with the task of organizing the neighborhood efforts of USO clubs, YWCAS, YMCAS, and Jewish community centers, black community members often learned of the locations of black troops earlier than the Central Branch did. The news traveled a variety of routes, ranging from family connections to the occasional white officer wandering the streets of the Central Avenue district attempting to single-handedly recruit black women to visit the troops. Because of a widespread (and well-earned) distrust of the USO, black community members were more likely to contact the local YWCA than the Central Branch USO, and sometimes decided to organize soldier entertainment on their own. The Committee of Negro Women responded to sudden notices from community members, as well as referrals from the Central Branch about the arrival and location of black troops, and attempted to provide some organization of the largely improvised efforts of many different people and groups.

Even when the notification system worked as intended, the brunt of the labor fell on black Eastside women. For instance, the white officer of black troops stationed nearly two hundred miles north in San Luis Obispo was going through proper channels when he contacted the central USO office in Los Angeles in search of entertainment for the soldiers under his command. Likewise, the central USO officer correctly referred him to the USO-YWCA Committee of Negro Women. The ball was now in the court of the Committee, whose job it was to quickly organize the community, the army, the USO, and the standing committees of the "Colored Women's Branch" of the Los Angeles YWCA. Guinn elaborated:

> The Entertainment Committee brought together eighty-five young women representing different interests and back grounds. The Home Hospitality Committee secured donations for refreshments. Entertainers for the motion picture colony were invited. An evening of fun was held at the Jefferson High School Gymnasium. A Sightseeing Tour was held the next day. Transportation was made possible by the use of Army trucks. In the evening came a dance with the hall donated by the Elks.

The next day, the men were guests in local churches, and later that afternoon the women were invited to visit the soldiers in their camp near Exposition Park.[21]

"Soon after," Guinn wrote, "the U.S.O. Traveler's Aid began calling on our committee to provide the entertainment for soldiers who had a few hours leave. This was difficult service to render since it came unexpectedly."[22] Requests came for entertainment for men on leave, some arriving in twos and threes, groups of men who were "in transit," and entire encampments of men, some of which were some distance away. Factors such as racially restrictive housing covenants, the vast expanse of the city, and the national reputation of California for being more racially progressive than it actually was contributed to the challenges of intercepting and caring for the black troops who were dropped into this confusing landscape. The responsibility for entertaining black troops fell largely on black community members, who were restricted by the same sets of barriers that rendered these difficulties.

Another side effect of the USO's refusal to advocate for integration in areas where it was not already practiced was the preference of black community members for coordinating local efforts to entertain black soldiers outside the organization. From Guinn's perspective, this led to well-meaning individuals taking action that undermined the work of the USO-YWCA Committee of Negro Women. One of many examples was the case of the choral director Frieta Shaw, who set out to provide entertainment for a camp of black men stationed in racially hostile territory near Compton. Guinn explains that the Committee of Negro Women and Twelfth Street YWCA women were not convinced that this location represented the most sensible investment, but they agreed, at the request of the central USO office, to hear Shaw's ideas for a "center for Negro Soldiers." After they toured the building Shaw wanted to rent and visited the soldiers at the camp, Guinn wrote, the Committee remained hesitant because they lacked information about how long black soldiers would be stationed in that location, the "accessibility to the focal point of Negro population in Angeles," and the increasing numbers of black troops scattered throughout Southern California, which indicated the need for a larger and more centrally located club. These concerns proved valid when "the boys moved from the camp" several days before the new center— named the Watts Hospitality Center and located at the southern tip of Watts, just north of Compton—held its grand opening. It was too late to shift gears.

> The young woman had gone ahead with enthusiasm. She had done everything herself and indirectly the USO Committee of Negro women learned she had selected a place different from the one discussed with the chairman and secretary. Her invitations were ready and the public had been invited to the opening.[23]

Despite the Committee's concern, from the perspective of the black press there was nothing not to like about the new USO club in Watts. The *Pittsburgh Courier* noted that the Watts USO "Hospitality House" had opened "with all the fanfare of a Hollywood premiere."[24] The *California Eagle* described the ceremony as "one of the most strikingly brilliant spectacles we've seen in years. With our own soldier-boys in their natty uniforms, and the pretty junior hostesses in their pretty afternoon frocks, it was enough to thrill and warm the coldest heart." Entertainment was provided by African American actors of stage and screen, including Ernest Whitman, Clarence Muse, Ben Carter, who played boogie-woogie piano for the occasion, and Mantan Moreland, whose storytelling "caused a riot of laughter." The *Eagle* did not mention the absence of the troops for whom the center had been established but reveled in the hospitality shown to black troops who had been brought from Riverside, as well as the "sprinkling of white soldiers among our guests" who were "treated the same as our own boys and enjoyed the occasion just as much as did our colored boys."[25]

While more reserved about its promise for democracy, Dorothy Guinn admitted the success of the ceremony.

The center was opened with a splendid program planned by the young woman herself. The chairman of the Board of Directors of the Los Angeles USO Board and others were present. Soldiers from a nearby camp were present to lend atmosphere. It was indeed a creditable affair.[26]

However, Guinn was less concerned with ceremony than with the viability of the center to contribute to black soldiers' well-being for the duration. As the USO-YWCA Committee of Negro Women had speculated, the existence of a black encampment in Compton was a singular event. "As days passed into weeks and the months ended, no soldiers appeared at the camp for which the center was opened," she wrote. Subsequently, the YWCA recommended to the USO that "support be withdrawn and consideration be given to a permanent center accessible to all types of soldiers from all places." The USO approved. That "more central" location turned out to be the YMCA located in the midst of the Central Avenue district on Twenty-Eighth Street.

In lobbying for a club for "all types of soldiers" and identifying this location as the best choice, the plan combined two commitments: to have integrated USO clubs and to establish a club in the center of black Los Angeles. It would be not be limited to black soldiers but would be located in a neighborhood where black military personnel would be welcomed in nearby restaurants, theatres, stores, and churches. The USO accepted the proposal.

Guinn has thus far written fourteen detailed pages on the recent past. Her prose style becomes more dramatic in her final notes, separated into three brief stanza-like paragraphs. Her flair for community pageantry is palpable in these closing remarks.

As we write Negro troops have arrived in the town immediately adjacent to Los Angeles. A quiver went through the Negro community when these men poured in. "Our boys have arrived" were headlines in one of our papers.

"There are 2800. Sixty two officers are with them. The 369th Coast Anti Air Craft Coast Artillery base here" so goes the conversation.

Thus ends chapter one in the six months of USO experiences from the point of view of Negro women.[27]

Two weeks after she filed her report, black newspapers around the nation announced the arrival Dorothy Guinn predicted: the 369th landed in Burbank. "For years there has not been a colored person residing in Burbank," reported the *Baltimore Afro-American*, along with other black papers. Now that this community's apprehension about "colored making their homes in the vicinity" had been replaced by fear of becoming a bombing target with so many defense plants in operation, the Associated Negro Press reported, Burbank citizens were said to be feeling much more secure with the 369th keeping twenty-four-hour watch.[28]

The 369th Coast Antiaircraft Artillery Regiment was distinguished by its earlier history as the renowned "Harlem Hellfighters," a black regiment who had fought bravely in Europe in World War I and had been welcomed home by a big parade in Harlem. As in World War I, even the officers of the 369th were black, a rarity in the segregated military. The Burbank encampment generated nearly daily stories in the black press, often emphasizing the entertainment of the black officers.[29] A photograph in the *Chicago Defender* showed "Lieutenant Frasier of the crack 369th Coast Artillery" being entertained by "Mrs. Art Tatum" among the "society matrons" who are "visiting the men while they are bivoaced [*sic*] in southern California."[30]

When the 369th moved on to San Francisco, where further orders awaited, its place in Burbank was filled by the 76th Coast Artillery Regiment, an African American regiment with white officers.[31] The local black press held onto the celebrated regiment, however, and continued to refer to the members of the 76th as the 369th in much of its coverage.

On June 27, 1942, a story broke in the black press concerning a white family who had entertained members of the "369th" (probably the 76th) in their North Hollywood home six miles west of Burbank (and three miles east of Leo Kuter's home in Studio City). Because of their cross-racial hospitality, the family was now being harassed by neighbors. David Prosin, a twenty-eight-year-old carpenter and son of Jewish immigrants from Russia and Romania, had met a group of African American soldiers in North Hollywood who told him of their many failed attempts to find a restaurant that would serve them. He invited them to his house, where he and his wife, Suzanne, "fed and entertained them." Later, Suzanne visited the camp and asked officers what she could do to help. She then invited more black soldiers to their home and invited black sorority women from Alpha Kappa Alpha to entertain and dance with them. Neighbors met to protest against "Negroes socializing in North Hollywood homes." David's volunteer position as an air raid warden was revoked, and the family was threatened with removal from their home.[32] The Prosins' persistence made them heroes in the black press. But entertaining the black troops was tricky on the ground just in terms of organization. People operating on one curbstone could be at cross-purposes with people operating on another. When Suzanne contacted the Burbank USO for help with generating "favorable publicity" about a party, they turned her down, explaining that they were already providing services for black soldiers.[33] In fact, this was true, thanks to the efforts of Guinn and others on the USO-YWCA Committee of Negro Women.

From the point of view of Dorothy Guinn's "curbstone," the Prosins' efforts, like those of Frieta Shaw, were duplications of effort caused by the USO's unwillingness to integrate all of its facilities. At the same time that the Prosins threw private parties in their home without the support of the Burbank USO, the Eastside-based USO-YWCA Committee of Negro Women worked with the Burbank USO to facilitate caravans of hostesses, Eastside dignitaries, and entertainers twenty miles north to entertain the black troops stationed in white restricted space.[34]

The Prosins did not live in Hollywood but in North Hollywood, west of Burbank. Still, editors could not resist the punch of "Hollywood" in headlines such as "Hollywood Hostess Defies Neighbors and Fetes Colored Soldiers" and "Social Equality Irks Hollywood Haters of 369th." Sometimes the text included a disclaimer, as when one reporter explained that "North Hollywood is not Hollywood, the movie capital, but a self-governed village north of it. Hollywood screen folk and resident[s] like to have either soldiers or civilians of the race among their guests."[35] Hollywood may have been more welcoming than North Hollywood, but the inclusion of "race" members as "guests" is telling terminology in this sweeping, overly optimistic nod toward the warm welcome available in a part of town that was mostly off limits to black homeownership and renters.

Nonetheless, there were people in Hollywood and the Hollywood industry who worked with one another across race on committees, such as the defense of the young Mexican American men who had been incarcerated without due process in the Sleepy Lagoon case, and/or who knew each other from movie work, though usually playing master and servant. Cross-racial organizing efforts on behalf of racial social justice did take place in soldier-entertainment efforts in Hollywood movie industry settings, across differing orientations to the social geography of Los Angeles. In addition to meeting at Hattie McDaniel's house in Sugar Hill, the members of the Negro Sub-Committee of the HVC counted among the nine black members in the integrated HVC and served on its other subcommittees. In reading the minutes of the meetings, I notice that action items on issues of racial justice seem only to have come up when African American members were present. However, I also notice that action did, indeed, take place.

On July 16, 1942, Hattie McDaniel, representing the Information Subcommittee at a combined HVC Actors Subcommittee and Advisory Committee meeting, presented a report "on the availability of colored actors and volunteered their cooperation."[36] The minutes of an HVC Educational Committee meeting on July 21 record the opinion of "Miss Ethel Waters" that "the colored entertainers should not be restricted to the entertainment of the colored troops alone and that there should not be straight colored shows but that white artists should occasionally appear with a colored troop in the same manner that the colored entertainers have appeared and will appear with the white entertainers in the future."[37] Only two days after that, at the July 23 meeting of the Actors Committee (at which Ethel Waters, Hattie McDaniel, and Clarence Muse were all present), Muse reported on "Miss Bette Davis' willingness to participate on an all colored show before the colored soldiers of Lockett Field, and thanked her on behalf of colored actors."[38]

Davis and McDaniel knew each other from the movies. In fact, the (relatively) progressive Warner Brothers film *In This Our Life* had opened a week before the first meeting of the Negro Sub-Committee of the HVC. In it, Davis plays a blatantly racist white woman willing to frame her black driver, a promising law student played by Ernest Anderson, for a fatal hit-and-run accident she has caused. McDaniel, playing the young man's mother, delivers an unprecedented line about the futility of telling the police that her son was in fact at home at the time of the accident since they "won't listen to what a colored boy says." On July 28, just one week after Ethel Waters raised the issue at the HVC Actors Subcommittee meeting, Hattie McDaniel led a USO caravan into the desert to entertain the black troops at Lockett Field that carried the legacy of another historic black regiment, the Buffalo Soldiers. Joining her were Ethel Waters, Clarence Muse, and Bette Davis, who performed together on stage and signed autographs. Among the dozens of black entertainers on this caravan was the concert violinist Victoria Rice, who later served as a captain of black hostesses at the Hollywood Canteen.

The next month, Bette Davis made (black) news by inviting black soldiers to the "Talk of the Town" premiere benefit for the Hollywood Canteen and to the after-party that broke the color line at Ciro's, one of the many historically white and glamorous Hollywood nightspots. The Associated Negro Press presented the gesture as a follow-up to Davis's tour with Hattie McDaniel.[39] "Bette Davis Invites Boys to Premiere," the *California Eagle* announced two days before the event. "Seventy-five Negro army boys will be special guests of Bette Davis and the Hollywood Victory Committee."[40] Among "the celebs and movie personalities" present were Ben Carter, actress Tommie Moore, and actor-dancer-musician Lennie Bluett. Not only was the premiere significant in its intentional inclusiveness and breaking of historical color barriers, explained the *Courier*, but the "proceeds of the show and the supper party held afterwards at Ciro's went to the maintenance" of the Hollywood Canteen, which the paper described as "the canteen opened to all nationalities."[41] The Popular Front and Communist press also emphasized the explicit racial integration of the premiere. Dalton Trumbo (under his pseudonym John Gunn) wrote in *People's World*: "the guests drawn from the fighting forces included 50 Negroes who were seated on an equal basis with everyone else."[42] Racial integration is all but missing from the *Los Angeles Times* and *Los Angeles Examiner* coverage. An exception is a throwaway line in Hedda Hopper's column about a "colored girl" who charmed actress Norma Shearer by wearing a "replica" of her wedding dress at the Ciro's party.[43]

Previously, in August, Hopper had noted that the young man who played the framed lawyer in *In This Our Life* had joined the army. On the following Christmas—the first at the Hollywood Canteen—Bette Davis presented Corporal Ernest Anderson to the crowd. Highlights of the evening for Sidney Skolsky of the *Hollywood Citizen-News* included Jewish Santa Claus (Eddie Cantor) taking off his fake beard and joking with the crowd, "Who am I fooling?" and Corporal Anderson gazing out at the audience and saying, "I probably realize it more than you, but I know that this is the real democracy, and worth fighting for."[44]

But before all of this—preceding Hattie McDaniel's caravan with Bette Davis by two weeks, Davis's invitation to black soldiers to the *Talk of the Town* premiere by five—a USO opened in the Eastside.

No klieg lights nor even rumors of klieg lights radiated skyward; instead, carrier pigeons took to the sky, trailing red, white, and blue streamers, when they were released at the corner of Paloma and Twenty-Eighth Street at 3 p.m. on Sunday, July 12, 1942, at the dedication of the Eastside USO. This ceremony, which preceded that of the Hollywood Canteen's opening by nearly three months, consisted of music and speeches, performances by major bands, appearances of Hollywood stars, welcome speeches by dignitaries both national and local, and public acknowledgements of the sacrifice and labor of service personnel and volunteers. Just one short block west of Central Avenue, Paloma Street (*not* a designated military highway) was blocked off to traffic between Twenty-Eighth and Twenty-Ninth Streets to make room for the overflow crowds of military personnel, volunteers, civic leaders, military and celebrity well-wishers, and local residents. The festivities began with a concert by the 76th Coast Artillery Regiment Band, which had come down from Burbank for the event. Then came a flag salute, patriotic songs, speeches from representatives of the mayor's office, national USO dignitaries, and local representatives from the six organizations of the USO.

"Hollywood was well represented," one reporter noted, naming Hattie McDaniel "Academy award winner, member Hollywood Victory Commit-

FIG 3.1: Hattie McDaniel signs autographs at Lockett Field. BETTE DAVIS COLLECTION, HOWARD GOTLIEB ARCHIVAL RESEARCH CENTER, BOSTON UNIVERSITY. BETTE DAVIS™ IS THE TRADEMARK OF THE ESTATE OF BETTE DAVIS. WWW .BETTEDAVIS.COM.

FIG 3.2: Bette Davis with black enlisted men and white officers at Lockett Field. BETTE DAVIS COLLECTION, HOWARD GOTLIEB ARCHIVAL RESEARCH CENTER, BOSTON UNIVERSITY. BETTE DAVIS™ IS THE TRADEMARK OF THE ESTATE OF BETTE DAVIS. WWW.BETTEDAVIS .COM.

FIG 3.3: Entertainers on HVC caravan to Lockett Field, July 28, 1942. Bette Davis stands between Hattie McDaniel and Ethel Waters. Ben Carter is left of McDaniel. Seated directly below McDaniel is Clarence Muse, with Mantan Moreland to the right. The tall man in the back row, left, is Lennie Bluett. Violinist Victoria Rice (standing, third from left) will become one of the eight black hostess captains at the Hollywood Canteen. The front row of the large audience of black soldiers seems to be reserved for white people. BETTE DAVIS COLLECTION, HOWARD GOTLIEB ARCHIVAL RESEARCH CENTER, BOSTON UNIVERSITY. BETTE DAVIS™ IS THE TRADEMARK OF THE ESTATE OF BETTE DAVIS. WWW.BETTEDAVIS.COM.

tee"; members of the cast of the *Oxbow Incident*, including Henry Fonda, Leigh Whipper (uncredited in this and many other films, but always a star as far as African American audiences were concerned and founder of the Negro Actors Guild), Harry Davenport, and Jane Darwell; and many other stars, including Mantan Moreland, Ben Carter, Jesse Graves, and Ernest Whitman.[45] A "roll call of Negroes in War Organizations" recognized local members of the American Red Cross, Nurses Aids, the Women's Ambulance and Nursing Corp., the American Women's Volunteer Service, American Veterans of Foreign Wars, and enlistees in the Women's Auxiliary Army Corps.

The actual door-opening was initiated by a ceremony titled "Three Pals of the USO." Sergeant Henry Williams, soldier; Miss Marilyn Warren, junior hostess; and Elrum Tatum, of the navy, linked arms and marched up the stairs of the clubhouse and stood at attention for the official dedication. The absence of a Marine is significant, in that the Marine Corps had only recently been forced to include African Americans. No black Marine had yet completed the first basic training, because the Marine Corps had yet to finish construction of the segregated training camp in North Carolina that had been built for the purposes of accommodating a Jim Crow Corps in response to pressures to admit black men.[46]

The trio of the black soldier, hostess, and sailor stood before the door, which was barred with red, white, and blue ribbons fashioned into a Double V, the symbol of antiracist patriotism initiated by the *Pittsburgh Courier* but adopted widely by African Americans during the War. The Double V linked victory against fascism abroad with victory against racism at home, a salient theme for this opening ceremony. The ribbons were cut, the door opened, and the carrier pigeons were released into the sky. Even with their red, white, and blue streamers, the pigeons must have registered as doves of peace as they soared above Paloma Street to carry the "message of the open door of the uso club."[47]

At this point, the "procession of hostesses," drawn from Eastside social clubs and the YWCA, set the mood for the entrance of military guests into the interior of the club, beautifully renovated by Paul Williams, the famous black architect (who also lent his expertise to the renovation of the new Woodlawn branch YWCA). Continuing with the dove imagery, the *California Eagle* described the "bevy of attractive coeds and young women who have served as junior hostesses" and who "flocked into the Center to receive the men of the armed forces."[48]

Among the many, varied activities that would be offered at the Eastside uso were "jitterbug contests."[49]

Route 2

Minneapolis to the Eastside USO.

The first time I telephoned Avanelle Harris, I asked her directly about the Hollywood Canteen. I knew she had spent most of the on-screen portion of her dance career amid the choruses of black women who appeared behind Lena Horne. I knew that Horne had volunteered at the Canteen and wondered if Harris had done the same. She was sure she had not. "I may have been there for a photo shoot or something," she told me. "Dorothy [Dandridge] and Lena may have been there, but it didn't happen for *us* at the Hollywood Canteen."[50] A few years later, I found a similar statement she made in 1946 in an *Ebony* story with her byline titled "I Tried to Crash the Movies": "I've been around Hollywood 20 of my 25 years and been in 18 movies—but it's always a dancer, extra chorus girl. I've learned that as far as Negroes and star roles are concerned, it can't happen here."[51]

Later, when I came to the realization that I could not comprehend the social geography of the Hollywood Canteen without considering the other soldier-hostess canteens in Los Angeles, I called her again and asked if she had volunteered at any USOs. Our conversation lasted longer this time. It turns out that she and other members of the chorus line at the Club Alabam had volunteered every Monday night at the Eastside USO. She invited me to her apartment in the Crenshaw district, where I sat on her couch and listened to her stories about Los Angeles, Hollywood, and the Eastside, from a long career spent "trying to crash" the movies.

In her late eighties when I visited her in 2006, Avanelle Harris looked to be a good two or three decades younger. She began by telling me that she should have listened to her mother and developed her singing—"singers last longer than dancers." I knew she meant professionally, but what occurred to me was how youthful she was—how *lasting*, compared to so many. She was energetic, found her words without visible effort, and just as easily got up and down out of her chair to show me pictures that illustrated the points she wanted to make. I asked about the 1940s, the height of her dance career in the movies. She began by linking dance to family history.

"I danced all my life. My father before me was a dancer and died doing one-night stands. Please mention my father." Roscoe Harris had been set to open in a big Ziegfeld show in New York as Burt Williams's straight man but had contracted pneumonia on the road and had died just months before the rehearsals would have begun that could have spelled his big break. Avanelle was three years old, a frail child. A relative, a railroad porter based in Los Angeles, suggested to her mother, Eula, that a move to Los Angeles would be beneficial to her daughter's health. (In another version of the story that appeared in the *Ebony* article, she attributed the move to her mother's hopes that her daughter would land a career in the movies. Both scenarios came true: Avanelle's health did improve, and she did work in the movies.)

Her mother's transition to the West Coast was difficult. Eula had worked in a Bullocks Department Store in the Twin Cities. As Harris tells it, in her first attempt to find work in Los Angeles, "Mother went down to the Bullocks, the same Bullocks here owned the same store in Minnesota. And mother went down there and asked for a job and they thought she was crazy. No way! It was very prejudiced in California at one time." Eula and Avanelle lived where most African Americans lived—east of Main Street in the Central Avenue district. Her mother took in sewing, and later worked for the Works Progress Administration. Avanelle began studying dance with a teacher on Central Avenue, Loretta Butler, whose students included Dorothy and Vivian Dandridge. By the time World War II broke out, Avanelle was dancing in the

FIG 3.4: Civilian women entertaining soldiers, Los Angeles region, 1940s. PHOTO 0287, WALTER GORDON COLLECTION (COLLECTION NUMBER 1867). UCLA LIBRARY SPECIAL COLLECTIONS, CHARLES E. YOUNG RESEARCH LIBRARY, UCLA.

FIG 3.5: Avanelle Harris, 1940s. COURTESY CLORA BRYANT.

FIG 3.6: Some of the dancers from the Alabam chorus line, 1940s. PHOTO 1021, WALTER GORDON COLLECTION (COLLECTION NUMBER 1867). UCLA LIBRARY SPECIAL COLLECTIONS, CHARLES E. YOUNG RESEARCH LIBRARY, UCLA.

chorus line at the Club Alabam and working in numerous Hollywood films. She appeared in the black Hollywood musicals, including *Cabin in the Sky*, *Stormy Weather*, and *I Dood It* (1943);[52] in lines of beautiful, talented, and underutilized young black dancers (some of whom, like her, were actresses) who were mostly used for ambience. These dancers were celebrities in the Eastside, known for their glamorous performances at top Central Avenue nightspots.

"[The Club Alabam] was very famous," she said. "Everybody wanted to be there. They had the best bands." But there were many clubs, and "the big bands played up and down the avenue. The Club Alabam had a big show and the Plantation had a big show. The Alabam was known all throughout the whole country." The show that provided the Monday night entertainment at the Eastside USO, in other words, was celebrity caliber.

I asked if the Eastside USO was integrated. "It was," Harris replied, adding that it was "predominantly black, but mixed." The top-flight entertainment spanned the entire week. The Alabam took care of Monday, but other nights featured entertainment from the many floor shows, local acts, and headliners all up and down Central Avenue.

She showed me pictures from her career and told me stories about dancing on stages and in the movies, and later in Las Vegas. Suddenly, she laughed.

> I'll tell you a funny thing that happened to me. I'd taken a girlfriend of mine to the airport in Las Vegas. I was walking back up, after I'd said goodbye—she was going back to New York. And I was walking back, just dah-dee-dah. And we had been out so I was dressed kind of nice. And there was a group of men. . . . One man turned, and it was Bob Hope. And, he just turned and looked right at me as I was walking by and I said "Hi, Mr. Hope!" and he said, "You know me?" I said, "Oh, yes!"

She began to list the Hope-Crosby vehicles in which she had appeared in the background: "*Road to Morocco, Road to Zanzibar . . .*"

> "'Really?' he said. 'The Lord sure has been good to you, girl!' And I said, 'Not as good as he's been to you!'"

Harris and I laughed. It is a story well told; a story that *torques back*. She recalled that Hope and his friends also burst out laughing and wanted to talk more. "They said, 'Come back! Come back and talk to us!' I said, 'No, I'm double parked. I gotta go.'"

Rumors of Inclusion

On June 29, 1942, during the same week that the USO-YWCA Committee of Negro Women, the Burbank USO, and the Prosins of North Hollywood were at cross-purposes in their mutual efforts to entertain the troops of the 76th Coast Artillery Regiment, pianist-accompanist Carroll Hollister presented a report to the Civilian Defense Committee of Local 47, the white segregated local of the AFM. He spoke of the Stage Door Canteen in New York, describing it as "a new sort of 'people's night club'" where "no racial distinctions or national prejudices can inject their vicious poison into this democratic club, for there is no 'Jim Crow' here!"[53] His stirring speech was soon published in the union's publication, *Overture*, along with plans to start a democratic club without Jim Crow in Hollywood.[54] Other papers—the local and national black press, the Popular Front and Communist press—were also trumpeting the news that would lift the Hollywood Canteen into its historical achievement of racially equitable dance floor democracy. At the same time the plans and rumors flew, African Americans could not live in Hollywood (unless they *lived-in* in Hollywood) and could not enter most Hollywood eateries, nightclubs, and ballrooms. A Hollywood dance floor that envisioned democracy as inclusive of African American soldiers and hostesses depended on participation from local African American civilian volunteers, for whom

Hollywood was decidedly *not* inclusive—as an industry, a dreamscape, or a neighborhood. For most of these volunteers, it was not so far as Burbank but a rather inconvenient trek.

I invite you to return with me north to Hollywood, imagining the route that the Shore Patrol advised white sailors to take, vigilant to keep them away from the Central Avenue "dives and saloons"[55]—including the "Negro Owned Club Alabam," which "features dancing by Negroes and whites" (the club Harris described as having the "best bands" and lavish shows, the place where "everybody wanted to be"). This was also the route Jeni LeGon took after receiving a call to bring her dance students and chorus line up from Central Avenue to dance with black soldiers (though apparently not on the nights Mel Bryant visited as a black Marine in the spring of 1944).

This is also the route Dorothy Guinn traveled on June, 25, 1942, when she proceeded north with a caravan of members of the USO-YWCA Committee of Negro women and other clubwomen, entertainers, and other civilians, bypassed Hollywood, and wound right on up through the Cahuenga Pass to visit soldiers stationed in San Fernando Valley.[56] Also heading north from the Eastside and traveling into the mountains were a group of young women praised in Freddie Doyle's *California Eagle* column: "One dozen roses to the Club Alabam chorus girls; they are putting all their cigarettes, books, magazines, candy and what have you in their cars and taking them up to our boys in camp some where [*sic*] in Burbank, Calif."[57]

As Avanelle Harris and her coworkers whizzed north through the Cahuenga Pass to comfort and entertain the black soldiers of the 76th Coast Antiaircraft Artillery Regiment, perhaps they crossed paths with a southbound car carrying workers home from Lockheed. Carey McWilliams wrote that in 1940 none of Lockheed's forty-two thousand employees were black.[58] It took an executive order from President Franklin D. Roosevelt to integrate the war industries, a threatened march on Washington to get the executive order, and watchdog committees to see that the order was followed.

Among the Lockheed workers traveling across the expanse between the unrestricted neighborhoods of south and east Los Angeles and the aircraft industries in Burbank were Amanda Perez and Sylvester Davis, longtime Los Angeles residents, who might never have gotten to know each other had it not been for their war jobs and long commute. Perez was Mexican American, subject to racism yet legally white in 1941, when she met Davis, who was African American. Their carpool romance resulted in marriage—and the legal battle that finally ended the antimiscegenation laws in California in 1948.[59] Also in 1948, racially restrictive housing covenants were ruled unconstitutional by the U.S. Supreme Court. It took three years to strike down the legality of these covenants, and many of the people involved in entertaining the black troops were among those who participated in the landmark Sugar Hill class action suit brought by Loren Miller against the West Adams Improvement Association, including Hattie McDaniel, Ethel Waters, and Ben Carter. After October 3, 1942, as the southbound Lockheed workers continued to cross paths with the northbound caravans of Eastside volunteers en route to visit black soldiers, they were joined in the flow of traffic by carloads of secretaries, starlets, stand-ins, inkers, writers, and other studio staff and day workers all heading south to volunteer at the Hollywood Canteen. Many served as "junior hostesses" and jitterbugged with soldiers, sailors, and Marines. Some experienced the democratic dance floor as racially integrated; all understood it as "Hollywood" and a symbol of the industry's patriotism. Some defense industry workers also headed south to dance as Hollywood Canteen hostesses, including a group from Lockheed who called themselves the Blue Stars.[60]

We will catch a ride with them.

The wartime changes in Los Angeles shuffled the rules of race enough to pave the way for significant postwar shifts in civil rights. But these were not changes wrought by the consensus democracy of a unified Greatest Generation, nor were they brought about solely by Hollywood people doing the right thing. The battles to lift racial restrictions were not simply addressed by new policies, laws, or cartographies drawn by a nation coming to its senses. These changes emerged from battles waged on and through bodies-out-of-place; bodies in motion, racially marked in white space, or white in racially marked space; bodies pushed and pulled, and that sometimes torqued back in ways that affected the dance for selves and others. Dancing the confusing parameters of an unruly city in uncertain times, out-of-towners, new migrants, and longtime Angelenos moved with and against the contradictions of a city that advertised itself as white and racially relaxed at the same time; a city in which most white residents remained unaware of why their neighborhoods were white. National memory about Los Angeles lodges in Hollywood fantasy. But this is a fantasy produced in a particular spatial/racial orientation to colonial place. Swing memory also lodges in Hollywood fantasy, shaped by Los Angeles, and received as the sound and feel of American democracy in World War II.

What happened at the Hollywood Canteen happened within a network of other swing-dancing sites in wartime Los Angeles, including the Eastside USO, the Santa Anita Assembly Center, the Hollywood Palladium, and Watts Hospitality House. A grounded understanding of Hollywood's orientation to Greater Los Angeles tells us how and why that network is so easily forgotten.

An isolated, demapped memory of the integrated dance floor in Hollywood as a symbol of carefree jitterbugging multicultural harmony is intimately compatible with American exceptionalism; it stimulates national memory in the same ways and for the same reasons.

As Peggy Pascoe explains, "American racial systems have always worked most effectively when they are taken so completely for granted that their structures are more or less invisible to Whites."[61] The impressionistic association of swing dancing, friendly boundary crossing, and patriotism in "glittering and glamorous" Hollywood adds up to an extremely effective vision of national "memory of times when all was well." In doing so, however, such an association bypasses the knowledge of those who remembered what was *not well* and who struggled and sometimes jitterbugged toward futures they hoped would be better. Subjects of reshuffled crowds in uncertain times— bodies wedged in motion—strangers in front and strangers behind—drafted, enlisted, policed, invited, volunteered—comprised a social body of many different embodied knowledges, orientations, and dreams. How did they, and how do we, move in a place?

I see we've made it to the door. Shall we try to squeeze inside?

PART II PATRIOTIC JITTERBUGS

★ ★

TRACING THE FOOTSTEPS OF

THE SOLDIER-HOSTESS DYAD

CHAPTER 4

★ ★ ★

Dyad Democracy

I'm a patriotic jitterbug—yeah, yeah, that's what I am.
—PATTY ANDREWS, SINGING IN *HOLLYWOOD CANTEEN* (1944)

Have you ever seen a soldier fresh from three months in the California desert, jitterbug? Ladies and gentlemen, you ain't lived!
—KATE HOLLIDAY, "TROOPS GALLOP TO THE DANCE" (DECEMBER 6, 1942)

I was asked to dance by a "jitterbug" and I danced as I have never danced before. Egad.
—JANE LOCKWOOD, DIARY (FEBRUARY 13, 1943)

On the night of February 13, 1943, twenty-year-old Jane Lockwood hopped off the bus and walked with her mother the short block and a half to their house.[1] Once alone with her diary, she scribbled a breathless "Egad!"[2] Since Halloween, she had been boosting morale on the dance floor of the Hollywood Canteen. A dozen times she had worn her red, white, and blue armband, dancing four to five hours each double shift, working alongside Rita Hayworth, Olivia De Havilland, Marlene Dietrich, and other big stars. By the second month, she was so frequently "cut in on" that she could write, "I really lost my envy for the 'glamour girls' and there are plenty around too."[3] Already, she had acquired the ability to stand near the actor Dick Powell (the subject of one of her scrapbooks at home) and watch him "indifferently."[4] Alternately, she savored the frisson of the light touch, on her shoulder, of the sleeve of Paul Heinreid as he moved through the crowd—a thrill intensified by the fact that the other "women who work in the Canteen literally drool when he goes by."[5] Heinreid, she wrote, was "our new Gable now that Clark is in the Army Air Corp."[6]

She had even been kissed, on Hollywood Boulevard, by a perfect stranger, an army air cadet from Akron, Ohio, with whom she had danced earlier in the evening and who later followed her down the street.[7] They began to talk and walk together, and she found herself ignoring her bus stop at Sunset and Vine to wander with him up to Hollywood Boulevard, where they kissed. Hand in hand, she walked with the attractive man she would later describe as a "boy with all that it takes," turning south on La Brea (missing the last bus home). They kissed again on Sunset, then hitchhiked to Beverly (another *event*—holding hands with a strange man in another stranger's car). On noticing that her mother had abandoned her weekly sentinel at the bus stop, and had returned home without her daughter, she realized that her parents must be worried. It was time to part. But not without a final kiss. In that evening's diary entry, she wrote that watching him "vanish into the crowd" was like being in a "typical film romance."[8]

But that was last week—and tonight had yielded its own unprecedented diary-worthy event. It was her first experience of being swept into the wake of a genuine "jitterbug," not just someone who wanted to dance to swing but a particular kind of person. He didn't just *do* the jitterbug. He *was* a jitterbug. This use of the word actually precedes the name of the dance and, in the 1930s, referred only to the most fanatical participants. Lockwood's use of it, and her surprise, is a reminder that even in the 1940s to call someone a "jitterbug" could confer an "outsider" identity from some perspectives. The dance and the dancer were still exotic for some observers (and not only those over thirty), even at this time in which, as many jazz and swing scholars would later argue, jitterbug and swing had been "whitened" and "mainstreamed" as national popular culture. She didn't recognize her partner as a "jitterbug" until they hit the floor.

> He was a tallish slender conservative looking sailor and very nice—I was completely overwhelmed when we started dancing. I was thrown from one end of the canteen to the other and bounced to the roof. I did the shag—Lindy Hop—New Yorker—collegiate—the hurricane—boogy woogy [sic]—suzy Q—trucking—soft shoe and I guess dive bombing!!! But recovering from the shock I did have to laugh as I could just imagine how it must have looked—They *had* to clear the floor all around us— either that or get kicked to death—irregardless [sic] of this unrehearsed production, I had some real fun.[9]

Reflecting on the event, she imagined herself a comic spectacle—an object "danced" by a "conservative looking" sailor whose exuberant jitterbug identity took her—and everyone else—by surprise. She described being stared at by a gaping, star-studded crowd that receded to the sides of the room in self-protection. Nonetheless, she also seized her diary as an opportunity to "right/write" herself, inscribing her new jitterbugging body as flying beyond an old equilibrium and into an exciting and unpredictable present. The world was at war. Still, she spun her tale of lost control into one of utter exhilaration—"I had some real fun"—as part of the process of becoming an independent young woman, free from the more restrictive codes of her parents' generation and a modern national subject who danced "as never before."[10]

Break-away: Footsteps in the Archive

I never met Jane Lockwood, never sat on her couch or talked to her on the phone. Like Dorothy Guinn, she is a person whose voice is a figment of my aural imagination, unconsciously summoned as I read her written words. Her diary is housed at the Margaret Herrick Library at the Academy of Motion Picture Arts and Sciences. As in my encounter with Guinn's USO-YWCA reports, I feel pulled and turned in this encounter in ways that affect how I understand other repertoires and archives. Jane Lockwood maneuvers a subjective twist to my reading of the hostess perspective lampooned by the Andrews Sisters in the movie *Hollywood Canteen* (1944).

The scene begins when Patty Andrews, the ham of the sister trio, drops into a chair after being yanked around the room by a "five-and-a-half-ton Marine." She rubs her feet, pantomiming pain in a comical way. Flanked by her relatively "square" harmonizing siblings, she mugs, clowns, and belts out what begins as a parody of the blues: "I'm Getting CORNS FOR MY COUNTRY at the Hollywood Canteen / The hardest working Junior Hostess you've ever seen."[11] Throughout the number, Patty limps and grimaces, grins and winks, teasing the contradictions of sacrifice and pleasure, corns and glamour, war and fun. The number ends with a good-humored invitation to an endless procession of soldiers, sailors, and Marines to "look us up at the Hollywood Canteen." The "patriotic jitterbug" cheerfully gives up her arches just as she endures gas rationing and dimouts.

Lockwood's diary indicates that she, too, understands her object function—she knows she is to there to attract and comfort soldiers, to follow their leads and perform the surrogate sweetheart. Nonetheless, she also writes her out-of-control jitterbug experience as an acquisition (through dance and writing) of a new and exciting embodied self. While Andrews's patriotic performance is enhanced by the clumsiness of her dance partner, Lockwood's jitterbug story integrates patriotic service with her own off-kilter experience of adventure and pleasure. From her I learn a buoyant double move that I will recognize later in many interviews—an opening for hostesses to dance as subjects

FIG 4.1: Maxine, Laverne, and Patty Andrews (left to right) and Dane Clark, scene still from the number "[I'm Getting] Corns for My Country," in the film *Hollywood Canteen* (1944). WCFTR-39726. WISCONSIN CENTER FOR FILM AND THEATER RESEARCH.

and objects of freedom. Andrews hams it up, sore but steady "patriotic jitterbug" who is "Getting Corns for [Her] Country." Lockwood writes with humor and exaggeration (she is "bounced to the roof") but ends on a different note: "I danced as I have never danced before."

Archives are peaceful places—until they shake us up. My realignment in the Lockwood Collection is a textbook example of Diana Taylor's theory of the relationship between the "archive" of "supposedly enduring materials" and the "ephemeral repertoire of embodied practice/knowledge."[12] In reading Lockwood's diaries, I didn't pretend to share her experience or knowledge, but neither did I encounter her words as "data," "background," or "context." Facing the page yields a different kind of transmission from face-to-face interaction. Nonetheless, this encounter exceeded strict divisions of past/present, stasis/fluidity, text/performance, and mind/body. The formality of the reading room, the rules, the guard, the monumental mood generated by the history and architecture and presidential-like portraits of actors, directors, and producers lining the walls of the Academy of Motion Picture Arts and Sciences—nothing about this experiential sobriety prevented my dance with Lockwood from turning me in new directions.

I spun out from my afternoon with Lockwood's diary to find myself repositioned in ways that demanded new interpretive moves. I tried to pull away from thinking as a spectator of the couple, and drop, more viscerally, into a point of view I imagine would be experienced from the perpetually moving and thinking body of a hostess, facing a steady stream of strangers. Her charge was to make them feel at home, and they were from many places. In facing all the men of the nation and allied nations, rather than the special individual man of normative domestic union (or other absent men whose safety weighed heavily—a brother, her father perhaps, coworkers, and friends), she not only served her country but danced an altered subjective path that synchronized sanctioned behavior with disorderly conduct. I thought of her body, pulled suddenly off balance, absorbing the cheers of the crowd, glimpsing the blur of spectators' faces upside down as she flies through the air, and I thought of her later that night, reorienting her alignment by telling the story in her diary.

Subjectivity on a shifting landscape is rendered sensible, even triumphant, through the pairing of dance and diary. Archived—but fresh—Lockwood's interpretation of her body in kinetic relation to that of a fast-paced and differently moving other moves *me*, as I write on the dance floor of national memory. I cannot know how she would react to my interpretation. I only know what she wrote at the time (at least the parts that live in the archive). I know that someone found them worthy of deposit in this prestigious vault, where researchers could be swept up, disoriented, and reoriented by them.

I open this section with Lockwood's diary because it was one of the places where I began to think differently about the bundle of national nostalgia that I call the "ideal soldier-hostess dyad" as the raced and gendered symbol of the nation at war. What does it mean when the ideal "girl next door" dances in Hollywood? Though not all volunteers were women (or young) and not all military guests were men, this chapter and chapters 5 and 6 explore the gender arrangement of young civilian women as "junior hostesses" and young military men as "our boys" in order to scratch at the surface of that ideological pairing. What is this dance and why does it endure? Any dyad makes a shaky symbol for democracy—really—offering but two roles, as complementary halves of a national whole. What kind of social equality is represented by dividing people in half or reducing communities to pairs? And what about the people who, for whatever reason, don't pair off? A democratic logic that only recognizes the "halves" in a panorama of "halves" and "halve-nots" is not only a bad pun but the complementary social partner of a democracy predicated on those who "fit into" rather than "make up" its design.

If, as Danielle Goldman argues, improvised dance involves "giving shape to oneself by deciding how to move in relation to an unsteady landscape," then when is a couple's dance a "practice of freedom"?[13] No set of moves or dance floor policies can guarantee that participants will all experience or define "freedom" in the same way; nor can they promise that one participant's "practice of freedom," won't obstruct another's. In order to explore the democratic potential of the swing-dancing soldier-hostess couple, I must first part the dyad and try to listen to how participants "navigated shifting constraints" when narrating their bodies digging for a foothold on that smooth iconic surface.[14] I attune myself to observing differences and adjustments. At the point of connection, the dyad is not a unit to observe but my body hitched to another, lighter or heavier, taller or shorter, lax or taut, local or transient, always with its own embodied knowledge, which is never limited to dance. "One does not check one's 'everyday body' at the door," Goldman reminds her readers, and "artistic choices are never separate" from social worlds.[15] On the floor move bodies tutored in high school hallways and football stadiums, city streets, farms and factories, across many different configurations and effects of racial restriction, on subways and movie sets, and, more recently for those in the "soldier" side of the dyad, in basic training, on troop trains, and, as the war years unfold, in combat.

What did it feel like, from many sides, to join with many different bodies in dance in a famous Hollywood club that was also patriotic? And what did former Canteen-goers feel later when remembering themselves in proximity to the larger-than-life images of movie stars paired one-to-one with anonymous soldiers? Again, Lockwood helps me to imagine one embodied perspective of the hostess side of the Hollywood dyad. Dancing among the stars dominates her weekly accounts and shapes her partners' perceptions of her (and of their own experience). In this club, a hostess's ability to represent, to her dance partner, a domestic postwar future worth defending is inextricable from the value-added possibility that she just might be not only a surrogate sweetheart but a real starlet, someone whose face he may recognize and (most important) whose proximity to him will mean something to family and friends. Lockwood is not a starlet, but as a Hollywood Canteen hostess she is happy to be mistaken for one, and she even signs autographs. Her willingness to do so increases her effectiveness as a "patriotic jitterbug,"

FIG 4.2: What does the dyad feel like from its many sides? Actress-hostess Faye McKenzie jitterbugging with military guest; unknown aerial hostess and soldier to the left; and onlookers. BY PERMISSION, BRUCE TORRENCE, HOLLYWOODPHOTOGRAPHS.COM.

just as the photographs of movie stars dancing with ordinary soldiers form a lasting symbol of the friendly nation.

The image of the swing-dancing man in uniform and the glamorous screen actress, nearly always represented as same-race, opposite-sex, young, and white, is rooted in, while trumping, the typical heterosexual welding of the (masculine) battle front and the (feminine) home front that typified canteen dancing outside of Hollywood. The superdemocratic power of the Hollywood Canteen is this extraordinary pairing: the inaccessible Hollywood creature offered by the grateful nation to a lowly private (not to officers). Most hostesses were not so famous as Rita Hayworth, Hedy Lamarr, or Bette Davis. But in this one-of-a-kind place, any hostess could bring him closer to the stars. Perhaps this reorientation as a national subject worthy of dancing with the stars helped him to "right" himself; to access a new kind of self-recognition in the disorientation of going to war.

The star-struck GI in the arms of a movie star: Marlene Dietrich, Barbara Stanwyck, Claudette Colbert—these dazzling images filled magazines, newspapers, and newsreels of the day. You can still find these images on e-Bay, in vintage magazines and faded glossy photographs, and they are reproduced in

FIG 4.3: Publicity photo, actress Linda Darnell in a star-struck soldier-starlet dyad. BY PERMISSION, BRUCE TORRENCE, HOLLYWOODPHOTOGRAPHS.COM.

new and out-of-print books and documentaries about the U.S. World War II home front. Lockwood's diary helps me to cut in on this appealing surface without losing sight of its power. Her account of dancing from disorientation (being danced/"thrown"/"bounced") to reorientation (having "real fun"), from loss of control to new perspective, suggests an analytic possibility for decoupling the soldier-hostess dyad to see what it's made of. I also want to get at that other possibility: a multisided phenomenology of the soldier-hostess jitterbugging couple as consisting of distinct orientations in interrelated motion on a vibrating floor, the full weight of two bodies linked at the touch of two hands, leaning back or crouching forward, moving to the blast of a nearby big band, operating in gravity, velocity, crowd space, and time. Lockwood helps me to imagine one side of the seesaw without conflating it with that of the unknown other side, and without losing the ballast of the other body.

How did the jitterbug-sailor understand the dance from his side of the dyad? Where did he acquire the embodied knowledge that led Lockwood to classify him as a "jitterbug"? Did he classify himself that way? Did he classify Lockwood as a "starlet"? Did he stargaze from her arms (while gearing up the courage to cut in on Linda Darnell)? Did he think her a jitterbug novice (as she classifies herself) or did he perceive her as practiced enough to safely navigate the series of moves—including aerial steps—that she claims to have never experienced? Did he care? What adjustments did he make from what he learned from the touch of her hand, the frame or floppiness of her dancing body, her laughter and flush, or whatever sociality preceded and accompanied the dance? Did he imagine their turn on the dance floor as creating a spectacle, and if so, for whom was he performing? What did he feel when the crowd backed away and watched him jitterbug in uniform with a Hollywood hostess—how did this performance sync up with his sense of himself at a moment of uncertainty, when his directions were in the hands of the navy, not for a known period of time but "for the duration"? Where had he been? Did he know where he was going next?

I presume that he, like Lockwood, was white, since a dance across race would surely have counted among the significant details in the diary. It doesn't seem to occur to Lockwood to mention the race of the sailor or any other of her dance partners at the Hollywood Canteen. (She does, on the other hand, often record her admiration of the "colored" entertainers at the Hollywood Canteen, including the comedian Ben Carter, whom she finds "very clever," and the pianist Hazel Scott, whom she calls a "sepia genius").[16] However, she only identifies the sailor who takes her on this memorable turn on the dance floor as a "jitterbug," and an unexpected one at that. Nonetheless, race underwrites her telling of the story.

When Lockwood inscribes herself dancing from "overwhelmed" object to the modern gendered national subject who claims her own experience, she attributes the shift not to just any of the dance styles practiced at the Hollywood Canteen but to the jitterbug. Her body flies on the field of swing—a complex of dance, style, and music that had originated in African American culture and that by the 1940s, by some accounts, became reimagined in the mainstream as simply "American." The history of American popular culture teems with mainstream (positive and negative) presumptions about what happens to white bodies when exposed to black music. Race is a disavowed component of the patriotic jitterbug, a power-evasive mode of "dancing black" that feels far removed from minstrelsy in its insistence on the national-universal rather than the race-specific.[17] Jitterbug is the national dance that erases black history and histories of racism in favor of a democratic dance of the color-blind leading (and following) the color-blind.

Without explicit reference to race, Lockwood writes her encounter with the jitterbug—the dancer and dance—as embodied difference, an experience that remakes their bodies as free, new, and literally spectacular. I wouldn't expect her to agree with my suggestion that histories of race, racism, and Crow Jim primitivism had anything to do with the power of that experience.[18] However, her listing of her newly experienced moves—*Lindy Hop, boogie-woogie, trucking, soft-shoe*—indexes a history of black dance, as well as a history of white dancers' embrace of what might be called cross-race dance of same-race bodies. Certainly, in the diary the power is the newness of dancing with a "jitterbug." She has not only tried new steps but joined with a body different from her own (and those of previous partners), and there is something about that embodied difference that triggers disorientation followed by reorientation, a swing from object to subject in her narrated memory of the experience.

Jitterbug bodies meant many things to many people in the 1940s. Frank MacDonald observes that public musical concerns and celebrations were attached not to lyrics but to perceived effects of the musical sound on bodies and society. Such debates continued to rage throughout the war, even as swing became national and patriotic.[19] Were jive-talking, jitterbugging hepcats dangerous to the body politic or were they consumers of mainstream, commercial mass culture? Advertisements for *Where Are Your Children?*— "The FIRST Drama of Juvenile Delinquency to reach the Screen!"—depicted individual young white women in various compromised situations: guzzling alcohol, gazing intensely into a man's eyes, pulling the hair of another woman, dangling a cigarette from a lip, and flying through the air, flipped by a fun-loving jitterbug.[20] Elizabeth Escobedo writes that for young Mexican American women, jitterbugging in dance halls was one of the activities that could be taken as an "identifying characteristic" of "pachuca," a category that meant subcultural identity to some and fashion to others but was criminalized in the juvenile courts and demonized in the mainstream press and therefore worrisome for Mexican American families.[21] However, jitterbugging with soldiers in a USO or USO-like canteen, where "good girls" danced with "our boys" within systems of chaperones and rules against meeting outside the club, could sometimes flip these judgments.[22]

Though the mainstream press continued to call swingsters "hep," for many 1940s hepcats, jitterbug dancing had become too mainstreamed to be able to perform transformative identity-work on bodies of any race. For some, jitter-bug dancing was whitened; for others, it was still black, whether that meant it was still rooted in and practiced within African American cultural spaces or was used as a screen for projecting fantasies of blackness as sexy, wild, and unrestrained. For some, jitterbug dancing was the cultural domain of Mexican American youth culture in Los Angeles, performed with its own specific cultural-generational spin as Pachuco Hop by teenagers claiming modern identities different from those of their parents and that of the dominant culture that racialized and criminalized young people of Mexican descent[23] For others, it was the comical antics of white movie teens like Donald O'Conner and Peggy Ryan.

During the week of the Hollywood Canteen opening, the white liberal columnist Ted Le Berthon was chastised at a private Hollywood party when he urged fellow guests to put down their cocktails and join him in swing dances such as "'The New Yorker,' 'The Balboa,'" and "'The Shag'" to the Count Basie records he had been asked to bring. The white woman who hosted the party lambasted him for introducing a "kind of dancing" she associated with "Negroes and high school children."[24] Jitterbug dancing was popular throughout Los Angeles, in the clubs that admitted black customers and in those that did not. Jitterbug contests were held in night spots across the expanse of the racially demarked social geography, including both the predominantly white Hollywood Canteen and the predominantly black Eastside USO.[25] Jitterbugging was popular—the dance of the day—but for some practitioners and spectators it carried associations of racialized difference, unrestrained youth, and lawlessness. An extreme example was the language in newspapers about the unsolved murder of the Hollywood Canteen hostess Georgette Bauerdorf. Though she was violently strangled in her apartment, the story was reported as a lurid cautionary tale of an "oil heiress" who had danced repeatedly with a GI jitterbug" on the evening of her murder.[26] In all kinds of ways the dance, while mainstream and patriotic, retained the allure of popular primitivism—an exciting or threatening touch of the "wild" that helped young white dancers define new generational identities through kinesthetic rupture, as their parents' generation had done with the Charleston.[27]

I referred earlier to two battles over race in the spring and summer of 1943: the so-called Zoot Suit Riots and the less publicized skirmishes over mixed dancing at the Hollywood Canteen. The Zoot Suit Riots made national headlines in a wider variety of media: these riots were sensationalized in Hearst newspapers as criminal activity of racial minorities and were protested in the African American, Latino, and Popular Front press as racial violence perpetuated by white sailors and tolerated by the police. The Hollywood Canteen dance floor battles also made national news in the black press, Popular Front press, and *DownBeat* but disappeared from the mainstream press.

Neither battle appears in Lockwood's diary. She never mentions the Canteen chaos of January 1943 when the African American junior hostess "Miss Tommie Lee, pretty little Pasadena movie player and socialite, was in such demand that white solders cut in on each other" to dance with her.[28] The story that appeared in the black press (and not the white press) reported that the white woman on duty "became upset at what she saw as a breach of social propriety" for "colored and white to be dancing together," and telephoned the Canteen president, Bette Davis. In a move black newspapers hailed as "one more blow" against "color prejudice," Davis replied, "let them dance if they want to."[29] And Lockwood's diary indicates no awareness of other dance floor debates covered by the black press, as well as the music magazine *Down-Beat*, in April and May 1943. The black press and *DownBeat* praised Davis, as well as the club's vice president, John Garfield, and the segregated locals of the musicians union in Los Angeles for threatening to pull their support if mixed-race dancing was banned.[30] Again, these battles were ignored in the same newspapers that lobbed diatribes of racial panic against nonwhite youth in Los Angeles. Swing historian David Stowe argues that the Hollywood Canteen is possibly the best example of "the scale of swing in wartime Los Angeles and the racial tension surrounding it."[31] Nonetheless, the mainstream press ignored the story, despite other debates about the meaning of the jitterbug and shifting parameters of race and gender.

Lockwood, too, misses this story. Even as she dances week after week, her observations of race train only on the acts, never making their way to dance floor demographics. Perhaps she is one of the many dancers who would later claim to have neither cared about nor noticed the races of soldiers. However, my guess is that questions of mixed dancing escape her diary entries for the same reasons that she probably didn't know that the Canteen volunteer Ben Carter, the "colored film comedian" she admired on January 22, 1944, was refused service at a café within shouting distance of her nearest bus stop.[32]

Bracing Ourselves to Go Inside

As in any account of a visit to a crowded dance floor, the foray into the many sides of the soldier-hostess dyad that I am about to present to you is shaped by embodied perspectives of partial remembrances and brief encounters. Admittedly, as author-host, I am setting up an artificial mood of spontaneity out of material I have worked long and hard to wrestle into place before readers encounter it. I do so as a reminder to myself and to readers that this chapter and chapters 5 and 6, people-packed as they are, accommodate merely fleeting impressions of some of the small number of people with whom I danced, in interviews or in archives. Behind these dancers are many others whose stories would have added additional twists. Over two million guests were entertained in this club by three hundred volunteers per week. I interviewed sixty people. We will encounter a British airman who learned to jitterbug from the actress and singer Lena Horne, a black Marine who was not allowed to dance, and a white hostess scolded by other white hostesses for dancing across race. We'll encounter a white sailor too shy to dance, a black chorus dancer recruited from the Eastside, a white soldier who was a professional dancer, and a white radio actress injured in a spin-gone-wrong.

Before we push our way into this crowd, a quick time-space orientation is in order. At no time, in visiting people in their homes, over the telephone, in letters, or via the internet, could I be considered a person in the present talking to people in the past. This illusion asserts itself on the page, but I must push against it and insist on that present moment shared in dances with the living (most of whom have since died). Unlike Lockwood, this group could (and often did) push back. I asked people to share embodied knowledge of their much younger bodies interacting with other young bodies in another time and place—an impossible task. Interviewees asked me why I was interested. Many were acutely aware of the national nostalgia attached to their generation, and shared a variety of opinions about it. They talked to me knowing I was writing a book about a place they had been, a place that was frequently represented in World War II memory.

When narrators told me about their dance floor memories, they also danced with a lingering shadow of the iconic jitterbugging couple as a symbol of the nation. As in a cartoon, the shadows cast by the figures sometimes move in sync and sometimes strike out in contrasting directions. I found myself picking up patterns from narrators who talked to me. The moving in and out of sync with a particular look and feel of the ubiquitous soldier-hostess dyad that circulates in national memory through reenactments, nostalgia, and World War II documentaries is something I'm sure that I "lifted" from my partners. Narrators often told stories in which the crowd backed away, and they and their partner became the main attraction. From time to time I, too, clear the page of other dancers so as to shine a spotlight on a telling performance that affirmed the Canteen's exceptional achievement, exposed its pitfalls, and/or redefined the terms of its dance floor democracy.

We could travel through this crowded dance floor in any number of ways and see and miss different things. But here is the plan. First we will enter the space, exploring different perspectives from either side of various soldier-hostess dyads, noting moments when embodied difference (often raced) is attributed to the democratic success of the dance. For the remainder of chapter 4, we will pair off with a sequence of narrators whose "break-aways" offer several perspectives, while dancing close enough to the frame to mirror the official story. In chapter 5, we will assume more compromised positions vis-à-vis the soldier-hostess dyad that challenge (in whole or in part) the official claims of dance floor democracy at the Hollywood Canteen. Finally, in chapter 6, we will reincorporate the notion of "torque," so as to highlight stories about dancing difference *differently* that seem to not only affirm or critique the official dance floor story but turn it in ways that, from the perspectives of those who tell the story, make it more inclusive, more responsive, and therefore, more democratic.

Parting the Dyad

In order to imagine our own bodies moving toward, into, and through this club, we must first classify ourselves as civilian volunteers or military guests. This determines which entrance will frame our first impressions of the interior, our paths through the room, and our roles in the dance. In the previous chapters, we explored other embodied differences that shape our travels to the club—indeed, race, gender, ethnicity, nationality, class, and sexuality continue to shape our travels inside, as do signs of rank, fame, the information encoded in stripes and medals, and the presence or absence of visible injury. I'll guide us into the room (drawing on authorial privilege to use both doors), but I warn you, it is packed in there. Some of the people we will encounter may seem familiar—you met them in earlier chapters—but there is no time for new introductions. Just smile and keep moving.

As junior hostesses, we file through the back door on Cole with other civilian volunteers. Like Jane Lockwood, we may come from home, a short or lengthy bus trip away. Mary Lou Ramirez arrives with a friend after a long trek by bus and street car west and north from near East Sixth Street and Downy Road. Some living in the heart of Hollywood are close enough to walk. Caren Marsh travels the short distance from her apartment near "Mom" Lehr's similarly named Hollywood Guild and Canteen (which provided dormitories for soldiers). Some drive and many are driven by family members, friends, coworkers, or spouses. Jean Lewin rides with her live-in future husband, Bernie Gordon; Jeni LeGon delivers her carload of chorus dancers up from Central Avenue; Marion Krow drives herself after work in her pride and joy, a 1941 Studebaker. Pearl Gelfand carpools down through the Cahuenga Pass after a full workday at Universal Studios. Martha Goldman lives nearby but usually attends in the company of fellow cel painters and inkers from the Cartoonist

Guild. Claire Lomas shows up on nights when her husband has worked the day shift at the shipyards and can watch the children.[33]

We arrive from movie sets, typing pools, drafting tables, and assembly lines, readying ourselves to mingle with draftees and enlisted military personnel who have been waiting in long lines out in front of the building. Some of our crowd consists of stars and starlets representing the studios that issued our contracts, or as "independent" starlet-hopefuls (a larger number), but most of us who work in the industry hold other nonacting positions, such as secretaries or workers in the feminized sectors of animation. We are chorus dancers, defense workers, and wives of men whose companies and/or unions have pledged to supply volunteers. We arrive at the back door, ready to dance with men who came to see someone else.

As rank-and-file military guests, we travel different routes and enter a different door. But first we must find our way to Hollywood from ships docked in San Pedro, Long Beach, or San Diego, and the training camps and bases scattered throughout the region's deserts, mountains, ports, and valleys, or from Union Station if we came by train. Some are sent here to await deployment to the Pacific. Others have traveled to spend a furlough in Los Angeles—it is home, or a place that will interest people back home. It is a place we or one of our new friends have wanted to see, or maybe we may even aspire to work in the industry. We hope it will take our minds off the unknown future. Those on leave without friends or family in the area have a heck of a time finding lodging, though if we are men in uniform, we have priority over other travelers, in hotels (if we can afford them), YMCAs, and rooms in private homes. Women in uniform find fewer options, but some YWCA lodging has been cleared, and there are dormitories if we know where to look. Additional challenges block us if we are nonwhite, though hospitality awaits if we find the right part of town (or its citizens find us).

We save time if we already have our bearings in Los Angeles. Some, like Tommy Farrell and B. J. Hansen, are locals who know the area well; Mel Bryant has lived here a short time before, trying to get a foot in the door of the movies. However, even locals navigate differentiated social geographies that bring different worlds into reach for different bodies. Much has changed since we left, and our pathways are altered when we are in uniform. Most of us, however, are not familiar with the territory—we visit a place we "know" but have only seen in the movies. We travel in large groups, with a friend or two from our unit, or else, like Johnny Grant, we purposefully lose our army buddies so as to savor our discovery of Hollywood on our own. Some travel hundreds, even thousands, of miles to spend a precious liberty before shipping out. Like Eric Marsh, we are delivered by helpful strangers who pick us

FIG 4.4: Military guests lining up to enter the Hollywood Canteen. BY PERMISSION, BRUCE TORRENCE, HOLLYWOODPHOTOGRAPHS.COM.

up and think this is the best place to deposit us. Entire cohorts are likewise dropped at the door, arriving in bus- and carloads, transported by the military or by civilian volunteers.

Once in the neighborhood, we wade among throngs of other soldiers, sailors, and Marines along the stretch of Cahuenga described by a *Los Angeles Times* reporter as "Hollywood Coney Island." Inching toward the Hollywood Canteen and the nearby Hollywood USO, we encounter other soldier attractions: a penny arcade, novelty shops, photo studios, and peep shows. Even if we are not so lucky as to dance with Rita Hayworth inside the Canteen, we may purchase photographs of ourselves basking in the presence of her wax replica, maybe even copping a feel. However, the reporter observes, we are less inclined to spend our money on peep shows than to plunk our pennies into games that allow us to "shoot shadows of enemy planes out of the sky or that test [our] skill in flying miniature mechanical planes or for baseballs to peg at Hard-Head Sam, the dodging darky."[34] This collapse of Axis planes and the "dodging darky" as targets for U.S. soldiers (and the implied admiration of "our boys" who would rather lob missiles at this conflation of enemies abroad and "darkies" at home than "peep" at naked women), underscores the violent contradictions of race and space inside and outside the supposedly integrated Canteen, as well as the presumed whiteness of war heroes and the racialization of enemies. Encountered by groups of soldiers from segregated troops seeking a memorable experience in Hollywood, "Hard-Head Sam" is only one clue among many that differential treatment of soldiers across race was inescapable for soldiers of color and invisible to most white soldiers—a point reinforced when black soldiers were turned away at nearby nightclubs and eateries and Latino and Asian American soldiers found unpredictable and limited acceptance.

Guided, perhaps, by passersby, we at last make our way to the end of the line that stretches along the wooden fence in front of the Canteen's main entrance and down the street. Because our troops and duties are racially segregated, our social groups at liberty tend to extend the stark division of the Jim Crow armed forces into the exceedingly more confusing and unpredictable social geography of race in Los Angeles. In this line, we wait, moving forward one large group at a time.

Volunteers, too, travel different social space; we live in different parts of town, segregated by housing restrictions that not only separate bodies but differentiate consciousness of racial restrictions. Even the routes that made us Canteen volunteers to begin with are differentiated in these ways, because of employment disparities in the motion picture industry. Hostesses represent all the studios and all of the guilds and unions that include female members. The Screen Actors Guild is well represented by hostesses,[35] as is the American Guild of Variety Artists, the Screen Office Employees Guild, the Cartoonists Guild, and the two segregated locals of the AFM. Aside from the black AFM Local 767, these unions are white-dominated if not exclusively white in the 1940s. While black women worked as actresses, dancers, extras, and musicians, they (and other nonwhite women) were not generally (at least knowingly) hired for other studio work, including clerical.

For black hostesses, the ideological, local, and professional parameters of performing the "girl-from-home" in this part of town are especially complex. Black hostesses include actors, dancers, and musicians; wives of actors, dancers, and musicians; defense workers and Eastside clubwomen. The *California Eagle* reported that the "Race hostesses" are not only a "boon for the colored servicemen" but "in true democratic style, their presence brightens the atmosphere for soldier boys of all races."[36] If we are black hostesses, our victory dance is double, as we embrace black soldiers who might otherwise be left at the sidelines, while entertaining all soldiers of all races. We diversify visions of democracy in Hollywood for the black and Popular Front press

FIG 4.5: Because troops were segregated, military personnel often arrived in race-divided groupings. BY PERMISSION, BRUCE TORRENCE, HOLLYWOODPHOTOGRAPHS.COM.

FIG 4.6: Volunteers at the Cole Street entrance to the Hollywood Canteen. BY PERMISSION, BRUCE TORRENCE, HOLLYWOODPHOTOGRAPHS.COM.

FIG 4.7: While Duke Ellington and Kay Kyser sign autographs on the bandstand, black soldiers and hostesses pose with busboy-actor Jack LaRue. On the far right is Florence Cadrez, Hollywood Canteen board member in charge of black hostesses and secretary of American Federation of Musicians Local 767. BY PERMISSION, BRUCE TORRENCE, HOLLYWOODPHOTOGRAPHS.COM.

but slip from view in most other renditions. We are "being included" in order to "include" black soldiers in an institution already imagined by non-black volunteers and guests as "inclusive," and our inclusion is celebrated and monitored by black Angelenos for whom Hollywood is an important battlefront.[37] We socialize under the watchful eyes of Florence Cadrez, who, the *Eagle* columnist Harry Levette writes, "guards over" us "as carefully as a hen over her chickens."[38] Cadrez protects us. However, she also protects the Race by policing our behavior. The *Eagle* assures its readers that Cadrez "refuse[s] the services" of "the type" of girl who "wishe[s] only an opportunity to flirt" with soldiers.[39]

Between Cadrez and the black hostesses are eight black hostess captains (covering different nights), drawn from Eastside professional women and clubwomen. Some, such as violinist Victoria Rice and Billye Muse (whose husband is Clarence Muse), understand the professional and social stakes of this Hollywood entrance. The *Eagle* praises the captains for their "faithful performance of duty, even when personally inconvenienced."[40] What are the inconvenient fidelities faced by "Race hostesses" who "practice freedom" while navigating the stag line at this purportedly integrated Westside dance floor? How does one perform combined roles of patriotic jitterbug, respectable race woman, and modern young woman claiming subjectivity and agency? What additional concerns face black hostesses who work in the movies (or who wish to)?

What was it like for Mexican American women to navigate this space, occupying what Escobedo describes as a "kind of 'racially-in-between' social position" in wartime Los Angeles.[41] Less spatially restricted than black women, they, too, moved in bodies often read in ideologically loaded racialized ways. Depending on dress, hairstyle, skin color, dance moves, and current events—their bodies might remind police, soldiers, and others of the "pachucas" in the news.[42] If we are Mexican American women, our bodies may trigger associations with sex and violence, as the purported prizes in race wars between white sailors and Mexican American men on the streets of Los Angeles. Our bodies are often posed as the alibis and provocations of the Zoot Suit Riots of the spring of 1943 in which racially divided men battle over who may look at us, date us, desire us, and decide if we are "easy" or "respectable." These anxieties about our fraternization with white servicemen are fueled not only by presumptions of disrespectful intentions but also by fears that "honorable" ones might develop, as Escobedo has pointed out.[43] Because of the classification of Mexican people as Caucasian in California antimiscegenation laws, anxieties about the possibility that this dance could lead to marriage are shared across the mainstream white population, as well as Mexican families and young Mexican American men.[44] Mexican American women move through wartime Los Angeles with greater freedom than Mexican American civilian men.[45] Several of Escobedo's interviewees remembered moving freely to and through Hollywood nightspots, as did Mary Lou Ramirez (later Ochoa), who tells me she never encountered any problems on her Sunday afternoons at the Hollywood Canteen.[46] "It was mostly Anglos," she recalls. Not many Latinos. "But sometimes you can't tell one from the other, so who knows?"[47] Ochoa's comment reminds me of the role of visibility in the social geography of race in Los Angeles, in which skin color and dress differentiated Latina/o navigations of the city.

As our place in the military line nears the building's entrance, we catch a glimpse of the (white) military police and Shore Patrol officers stationed inside. A civilian volunteer stands at the door, perhaps Disney cartoonist Tom Hayward, who clicks us in and stops those behind us from entering. The club has reached capacity. "We could only let in five hundred," he tells me in

2001. "After they came out, then we'd let in five hundred more. Some of these kids would hitchhike up from San Diego—if they'd get there after eleven, they'd miss going into the Canteen."[48] Once inside, some will unknowingly dance with Tom's wife, Louise, who volunteered from 8 p.m. until midnight every Saturday night. Reflecting animation industry demographics, Tom and Louise are white.[49] Louise painted cels for Walter Lance but was seen by the soldiers as a starlet. She tells a story about a soldier who asked for her autograph. "I'm not anyone," she told him, but he didn't give up. "So I signed an autograph for him, and then the guys stood in line and I was signing autographs on one side of the room and Bette Davis on the other." She laughs at this story. It's a good one, right up there with another one about being thrown about the room by a jitterbug—a story nearly identical to Lockwood's (both recurring narratives among former hostesses).[50]

As military guests wait for their hour inside, volunteers around back stand in shorter lines for longer shifts of two and a half hours (and some work both for a total of five). From hostess perspectives, the room is always packed with soldiers, week after week, throughout the war; our bodies increasingly habituated in routines of dance floor democracy. From soldier perspectives, this is a singular event or a handful of visits at most. We must wisely spend this time. Some stick to the sidelines and watch: the show, the dancing couples, the volunteers—or present a challenge for a hostess on wallflower duty who tries to help us "open up." Some clamor for autographs. And some of us will dance. As we do, other fellow U.S. servicemen and Allies continue to wait for our exit. Only after the muffled show they are missing is over and the tables are cleared will they get their chance to stargaze, sightsee, get an autograph, dance, or just look. "A newcomer's impression is apt to be kaleidoscopic," reported the *New York Times Magazine*, listing tables, chairs, a dance floor that looks large enough but isn't; a stage, a snack bar running the length of the room, and predominant, naturally, a hundred junior hostesses whose smiles of welcome belie their backstage theme song, "I lost my feet at the Hollywood Canteen."[51]

If we are soldiers, we are not to imagine how many soldiers our partners entertain week after week but are encouraged to perceive hostess time as leisure, not labor. If we are hostesses, we know that it is unpatriotic for the pleasure to be ours—duty calls us to the selfless production of soldier-pleasure. We are directed to genuinely love the "boys"—but not for private gain. Smiling through the dance and then comparing our "corns" after the "boys" depart is the acceptable avenue for us to be recognized (and to recognize ourselves) for our patriotic sacrifices. But it is possible to do this, and experience other things, too.

One more swoop to the back entrance: we enter the building as volunteers. We show our IDs, greet coworkers, gear up for another after-work evening of chatting, sandwich-making, cleaning up, and dancing under the wagon-wheel chandeliers. But that doesn't mean we don't also stargaze surreptitiously, making sure that we see and are seen by the right people, especially important if we rank among the industry's underemployed. Once inside, we splinter into work groups. Senior hostesses prepare snacks, wash dishes, and watch for trouble. Some junior hostesses, including Jane Lockwood, later graduate to senior hostess. When junior hostess Martha Goldman (later Sigall) married, she transferred to the kitchen, where proximity to dishwasher–movie goddess Marlene Dietrich made up for the lower percentage of stars.[52] Busboys clean up the debris, and the talented ones take turns removing their aprons to sing, dance, recite, or tell jokes on the stage. Musicians and bands perform on a volunteer basis. People deliver and prepare donated food. As junior hostesses, we try to act like we are not working. We chat, listen, and sit with "the boys." And when they want to dance, we follow their leads (helping them if they don't know how). "It was just a maze of going from one partner to another," said Nancy Marlow. "They would break in. You didn't stay with one soldier, sailor or Marine for very long before he'd be tapped."[53] Soldiers look at us, wondering if we are somebody. We beam back, as though they are the most important person in the room. But most of us look over each other's shoulders for famous faces.

Although blatant stargazing was profoundly unpatriotic when enacted by volunteers (whose gazes should dote on GI guests), staring at the actors of the silver screen was encouraged for soldiers. This was the democratic theme of the Hollywood Canteen—stars treating the soldiers as stars while availing themselves of the expected stargaze of soldiers, thus bestowing a privileged subject position to thousands of beholders in uniform. Though white female movie stars dominate the most widely circulating publicity photos, images of black female stars—Lena Horne and Dorothy Dandridge—also found their way into magazines and newspapers (usually ones targeting black readers). Looking at women across race, like dancing across race, held dangers for nonwhite men—another complication of the construction of democratic GI experience at the Hollywood Canteen. Black men had been and would continue to be lynched for less. Military guests were encouraged to stare and to measure national love by the fame of those who looked back, chatted, or danced. The yardstick for democracy, in this economy of celebrity largess, was the same star system that sold tickets at the box office and privileged white male heterosexual viewers.

Actress Marsha Hunt, on contract with MGM throughout the war, volunteered as a hostess captain, responsible for rustling up and supervising twenty hostesses every Saturday night. With six-day shooting weeks and

Sunday the only day off, she recalled, Saturday night could be a challenge when it came to providing hostesses soldiers would recognize from the movies. Sometimes she would be the only "well-known face" and would spend the evening signing "about 1,000 autographs an hour." What she remembered about the soldiers was that they would rush in and look around to see a famous face so they could write home and say "Guess who I saw," or even better yet, "Guess who I danced with?" For these displaced military workers, movie star sightings exceeded ordinary tourist value; they provided "vocabulary," a "way to find common ground." Though she had made over thirty movies by 1942, Hunt said that it was not until volunteering at the Hollywood Canteen that she realized "the astonishing reach of the movies."[54] Jean Forman was a dancer at the Florentine Gardens who volunteered as a hostess at the Hollywood Canteen. She remembered that despite the popularity of the jitterbug, the soldiers enjoyed dancing to dreamier, more romantic tempos because they "wanted to hug and love those stars to lovely slow music."[55] For B. J. Hansen, recalling his viewpoint as a white seventeen-year-old navy enlistee, the hostesses were "very good-looking, really cool girls" with "probably a couple of starlets" among them. "I just liked the glamour of it," he said. "It was always very crowded. And the guys there were a lot more mature, they were coming back from overseas. And so I just kind of stood in a corner. With my eyes wide open."[56]

To say "I danced with Betty Grable," produced connections to family, friends, and strangers. To say "I danced with a middle-aged married woman who types for someone who has something to do with the movies" didn't create the same sense of belonging. However, unless she stated otherwise, it was always possible that she *could* be in the movies, or the mother of someone who was. The Hollywood Canteen hostess was not only a proxy for the girl back home, but a touchstone to the stars and starlets and famous name bands that could connect the soldier with the people back home and transform him, momentarily, from combatant into tourist, expendable stranger to beloved member of a special community. In this way, the starlet-hostess could powerfully represent, without being representative of, the girl back home. She epitomizes—because she isn't—a girl back home. The probability of starlets was enough to lift this dyad beyond its ranks: American exceptionalism at its finest.

Facing Our Partners: Set 1

Now that we are inside the building, we begin to pair off. Our first foray onto the dance floor sets us face-to-face with a soldier, three starlets, and a stand-in. All five are white, and each dances closely with the official story.

Nonetheless, each is different and in different ways tacks between nostalgic sing-along and the dissonance that marks subjective experience. I listen for critical moves and subtle shifts as narrators "write/right" themselves in Canteen stories. We begin this more or less "official" dance, appropriately enough, with the longtime honorary mayor of Hollywood, Johnny Grant.

Break-away: Johnny Grant

The Army Air Corps sergeant who intentionally "lost" his troops on his first night in Los Angeles and became "smitten," not with a particular partner but with the Canteen itself, is nearly eighty-one in 2004, when Tami Albin and I pay him a visit. I had the good fortune of being assisted by Tami, a spectacular librarian at University of Kansas, and an outstanding oral historian, who joined me on some of my research trips and helped me a great deal in tracking down former Canteen-goers.[57] Many people directed us to Johnny Grant, explaining that he had not only been to the club but was working hard to preserve its memory through mounting exhibits, lobbying to erect a plaque on the site, and connecting its legacy to troop entertainment in the present. Through his secretary, we arranged to visit him at the Hollywood Roosevelt Hotel, a twenty-minute walk from where the Canteen once stood. A friendly man with a walking stick welcomes us to sit in the plush surroundings of an earlier era. He is at home here—literally. He lives in a suite on the fourteenth floor. Our interview takes place in the public lobby, but the recording is punctuated by his periodic yelling at tourist children to "knock it off" so he can concentrate. He acts like he owns the place. But when he narrates his first trip to Los Angeles and tells how he hitchhiked to the Hollywood Canteen "every night" for "all three nights" he was in town, he sounds more like the young army disk jockey from North Carolina than the man who has a star outside on the Walk of Fame.[58]

After that first visit, Grant was sent back East, where he hosted the soldier radio show *Strictly GI*. However, even on the other coast, war bond rallies meant proximity to Hollywood stars, and the love affair continued. When the army sent him west a second time, he knew more "Hollywood people." Again, he attended the Canteen all three nights he was in town. He doesn't talk about dancing. He talks about the cooperation he saw among the stars who pitched in for the war effort and how it inspired him to settle in Los Angeles after the war. His narrative leads us out of the 1940s, along a continuous line in which the deejay shuttles between the military and motion picture industries. In the 1950s, he hosted a popular radio show, *Hollywood Live*, on which he chatted to people from the grounds of Universal Studios and at the same time began to organize and travel in USO shows. Between 1950 and our interview in 2004, he visited military troops overseas on fifty-eight different tours. "I think I made the last one," he says, referring to his trip to Afghanistan in 2003. "Steps are getting a little too high. Those little holes to get into the tanks are getting smaller and I'm getting wider."

Grant's relationship to the Canteen past resembles nostalgia, but he uses it repeatedly to emphasize his work in the present, which he seems to think is coming to an end. His narrative weaves together perspectives of the twenty-year-old sergeant who fell in love with the Hollywood Canteen and the eighty-one-year-old honorary mayor who has carried on what he has seen as its vitality. I ask about the plaque that I heard he was planning for the Canteen site. This he confirms, but he is more animated when telling of his work on the recent expansion of the Bob Hope USO at LAX, where the snack bar where volunteers will feed soldiers will be called "The Hollywood Canteen."[59]

While some narrators speak of the difficulty of remembering so far back as the Hollywood Canteen, Grant appears unconcerned by what he doesn't remember. Was it integrated? He doesn't recall. Were military women there? He has no idea. But he thinks he knows someone who can help me. "They did a lot of things over there that Nancy can tell you about." He gives us the number of a starlet in the San Fernando Valley.

Dancing with the Starlets

All junior hostesses must have been aware that they were representing the nation, but this performance was especially concretized for the young actresses, singers, dancers, and models who worked in star-spangled productions. Chorus lines in matching sparkly red-white-and-blue costumes that revealed lots of leg celebrated the "American Girl." Others, more somberly, in simpler dress, gazed at the horizon, chin lifted à la Miss Liberty, as did teenaged Nancy Marlow, the Los Angeles Junior Chamber of Commerce's "I Am an American Girl" of 1941.[60]

Marlow's reign as the "typical American girl" brought tremendous publicity. She appeared in the *Los Angeles Times*, standing on a pillar and steadying a pole that held a flag taller than herself.[61] She appeared on a program with actor Leo Carrillo at the Biltmore Hotel,[62] sang patriotic songs with the City Council,[63] and welcomed newly naturalized citizens to national belonging in a ceremony that included free airplane rides over Los Angeles, "to get a new view of this country."[64]

But Johnny Grant has his own name for the "I Am an American Girl" when he recommends that I talk to her. He calls her "the Canteen Girl."

FIG 4.8: Nancy Marlow (fourth from left). COURTESY NANCY MARLOW.

Break-away: Nancy Marlow

Nancy Marlow lives in Studio City when we visit her on March 27, 2004, but she also once lived at the Hollywood Roosevelt Hotel. She welcomes us into a room next to the kitchen and shares photos of herself as the "I Am an American Girl." Soon after excelling in this patriotic role, she tells us, she stuffed a bathing suit into her purse and sneaked from the hotel down to Vine Street to answer a "Chorus Girls Wanted" call. The show was Ken Murray's *Blackouts of 1942*, which would be followed by the *Blackouts of 1943, 1944*, and so on to become one of the longest running variety shows in Hollywood history. After the initial excitement at being cast (because she "matched" another girl on the short side with large breasts), she realized she had to tell her mother she had become a chorus girl at the El Capitan Theatre. Her mother "accepted it" but walked her "back and forth to the theatre" for the run of the show.[65]

From there, she landed a contract at RKO. When the studio issued a call for volunteers to dance with the soldiers, "My hand shot up right away!" She tells us she started going regularly, sometimes "twice a week. I had more fun than the soldiers, because I was allowed to flirt, and dance: two things that I love doing—*to this day*." Her Canteen memories are vivid, full of laughter and sensory details, beginning with spaghetti dinners with her parents at Casa D'Amore, after which they all walked down Cahuenga and around the corner to the volunteer entrance. There she joined other Canteen workers waiting to show their IDs and sign in. Her parents, in the meantime, would "get lost until they figured it was time to pick me up. And, in I go, to heaven."

At intervals throughout the evening, announcements would blare through the loudspeaker: "Tonight we have the RKO Starlets!" She laughs at the memory of the soldiers cheering the starlets. "They were so adorable, and so wonderful, and loving," and "so excited to be in Hollywood. You'd think I was Bette Davis, you know, who was there a lot, by the way. But, they didn't care, you know? To them, I was a star." Among the highlights of her three years of Thursday nights at the Canteen is winning the jitterbug contest with Artie Steiner, a soldier cast member in Irving Berlin's musical *This Is the Army*.

Dancing with the Starlets (An Aside)

A word is in order concerning the term "starlet," which I originally mistook as a dated diminutive for any beautiful, young actress. When I asked self-described former starlets to define this word, however, I was told that what was important about being a starlet was not only youth and beauty but a basic studio contract. A young, beautiful actress on contract was a starlet if her name did not go above the title (otherwise she'd be a star). "What do you call a man with a studio contract whose name is not above the title?" I asked. This turned out to be a dumb question. "You call him an actor," quipped Jean Foreman.[66] Starlets were being groomed as stars, but few would be promoted. Even so, "starlet" carried cachet not accorded to male actors of similar rank. Some interviewees who were considered "starlets" in the past did not use the term, preferring to call themselves "actresses" or "contract players." I was fascinated, however, by how many actresses in their seventies and eighties referred to themselves as former "starlets." Some sustained glamorous self-presentations. (I can still envision Helene Bank in full makeup and silk dressing gown, graciously ushering us out of the elevator and into her penthouse for an interview over an extravagant brunch.) Others, like Marlow, in slacks, entertaining us in a room next to her kitchen, presented a more "casual attractive" image. All conveyed awareness that as starlets their value as Canteen workers was not only their ability to perform the "girl next door," but their special status as "girls in movies."

Unlike Johnny Grant, Nancy Marlow needs no prompting to think about diversity. The 1940s democratic dance floor in her memory in 2003 is resolutely multicultural. "The place would be just shoulder to shoulder with soldiers and sailors of *every* nationality in the world. And in those days, of course, um, to dance with a black"—she corrects herself—"an *African American*—was rather daring, you know? Or, an Oriental or whatever, you know? Because, what was it—the Forties! It never bothered me at all, if, if they danced well then, they could have been pink, or orange, or whatever. So, I was liberated long before anybody else, because I danced with whoever asked me—and they did!" When I ask if she remembers specific instances of dancing with black soldiers, she replies, "Of course. And they were really the best dancers, too." However, she also says she doesn't remember the races of her dance partners because "it wasn't important to me."

"It wasn't an issue?" I ask.

"No . . . I never heard anyone talk about it or say 'Oh, dear, you've danced with a black guy!' or anything like that. And it didn't occur to me. They were our servicemen." As with many other white hostesses who recalled dancing across race, mixed dancing stands out in her memory as both memorable and unmemorable (because it didn't matter). She remembers not noticing race and values the memory of not noticing as a good thing—a sign of democracy. She remembers dancing with "Chinese servicemen" and "a lot of Hispanics." This is important in her memory. But then again, "It didn't matter to me. I was there to do my part."

When I ask if she remembers black hostesses, she draws a blank. "That's quite a question, because I don't remember seeing a lot of black women, or *any*." She wonders if perhaps this absence of black women from her memory owes to her not "concentrating on anything like that," since race didn't matter to her. Then she wonders where the black hostesses—had they been in the Canteen—could have come from. "I know at RKO at that time . . . there weren't any black starlets."

She suggests that we pay a visit to Margie Stewart, who lives ten minutes away. She steps into the next room and dials a number. I listen to her as she vouches for me. She pauses, and then laughs, and I can hear the muffled buzz of the voice at the other end, also laughing. It seems impossible that sixty years later, the "I Am an American Girl" of 1941 would still be chummy with the War Department's "Army Poster Girl" of 1942–1945. But they were RKO starlets together and neighbors in the Valley for many years. Marlow looks at me and nods, while still on the phone. I stand up and take the receiver. Margie Stewart begins to share some memories of the Canteen. I ask if we could come and record an interview. She gives directions, which I repeat out loud so that they may be heard by Tami, who is not only a great researcher, but a fearless driver of Southern California freeways. I thank Nancy for her time, for the interview, and for making this new connection. In a gracious parting gesture, she slides an eight- by ten-inch glossy out of a folder and

FIG 4.9: Margie Stewart as the army poster girl. BY PERMISSION, JOSH CURTIS COLLECTION.

autographs it for me. I make a mental note to record, as research, the thrill I feel as I accept this personalized glamorous photograph of Nancy Marlow, Hollywood starlet.

Break-away: Margie Stewart

I didn't know we'd be talking with Margie Stewart. However, in a sense, I've already done my homework. I frequently show PowerPoint slides of her in my course on women and World War II. Many groups of students over the year have helped me to analyze the cultural work of the "Army Poster Girl" campaign.

In the posters, "Margie" is shown in many "girl-back-home" activities—knitting, cooking, letter-writing, fishing; in one, she is seated on the arm of a vacated easy chair in front of which wait an empty pair of men's slippers. In another, she is a reluctant Rosie the Riveter, looking lonely instead of spunky (like Rockwell's) as she leaves the world of the home where she belongs, carrying a lunch-box for one. The text on the posters is always in the feminine handwriting of the "girl back home," often presented as one leaf of a multipage letter. There is a double time in the posters—as viewers we read the letter as if we are its recipient in a faraway theatre of war, yet we are also invited to imagine the point of view of the sender back home, daydreaming as she conducts her home front activities. In each of these daily activities, the look in her eyes is one of sadness, longing, searing incompleteness. Her existence depends on the viewer. "Please get there . . . and back!" In class, my students and I talk about the possible effects of these posters on their target audience of homesick GIs, on the construction of ideal American womanhood, and on postwar domesticity; we never speculate about the person whose image was used to do this work.

It doesn't take long to recognize Margie Stewart as the woman in the posters. Like the soldiers, I feel as though I already know her, at least her warm, expressive eyes. But in 2004, her face conveys no trace of worry. Her Indiana accent and colloquialisms survive Los Angeles to evoke another place—a small town in the Midwest (only with streets lined with palm trees and year-round summer). She greets us as though we are old friends, offers us iced tea. We follow her around a corner and through a gallery-like room lined with framed photographs of people we know as stars and she knows as friends, alongside many photographs of herself as a starlet and model. We set up in a cool room, out of the sun; but with a pool in view. She begins sharing her memories, speaking easily about the Hollywood Canteen as though it is a very fresh memory.

"I was under contract at RKO Studios and every Thursday was our night at the Hollywood Canteen." She apologizes for repeating anything Nancy might have already told us. I assure her that is okay, we want to hear her memories. She dispenses the general information—"We danced with the soldiers and drank coffee with them"—and then announces that she has a story: "My birthday was the same as Spike Jones, December 14, so they had a great big cake. I was having dinner with Randolph Scott, and all of a sudden I said, 'We're supposed to be at the Hollywood Canteen!' And so he drove me over right away, and we cut the cake together. And it was a wonderful experience. Almost everyone had the same experience."[67]

It strikes me as telling that a dinner with a handsome actor and producer, interrupted in order to rush to a public double birthday celebration with an equally famous eccentric bandleader could be thought of as a typical experience—but I suppose in her circle of RKO stars and starlets, there are many such stories. Later, I find a photograph of Stewart cutting the cake with Spike Jones in an issue of *Overture*, the union magazine of the AFM, Local 47. "RKO's lovely new starlet" is how she is described, and the article goes on to report that she, Jones, and another "Spike," J. K. "Spike" Wallace, head of

Local 47, all assisted the City Slickers in performing their popular rendition of "Der Fuehrer's Face," a wartime novelty hit.[68] "There wasn't too much to say about it," concludes Stewart, "except when you went, you spent the evening dancing and visiting with the GIS. . . . What would you like to know?"

I want to know what it meant to the soldiers to dance with the young woman who looked out at them from the posters with those worried eyes. Did they recognize her?

"No," she replies, "that was before." The posters were already circulating—they had been made in 1942—but they targeted the soldiers stationed abroad. It was too early in the military tours of those she met at the Canteen to have seen them. Some of the soldiers she met in hospitals, and certainly those she entertained on the European Theater of Operations (ETO) during her two-and-a-half-month tour in 1945, recognized her. But those she encountered as an RKO junior hostess at the Hollywood Canteen "hadn't seen a lot of action" yet.

Like Marlow, Stewart's stint as an RKO starlet followed on the heels of other self-conscious public performances of ideal American womanhood. After completing one year of college, she set off with a friend for Chicago, where she posed for print ads as the ideal consumer for Kroger Coffee, Maytag washing machines, and others. One of the photographers, a retired major, "went to the government and said that instead of having men pointing 'We Need You,' and so forth, why don't we try having a girl do the posters." Twelve poses later, her image was reproduced on "94 million posters" and displayed "wherever there were American GIS." That was in 1942. The same year, a short film advertisement in which she demonstrated "how to open and close a car door" grabbed the attention of director Alan Dwan.[69] She moved to Los Angeles, signed with RKO, and began playing Girl Guide roles in Fibber McGee and Molly movies. The studio strongly encouraged starlets to volunteer at the Canteen on Thursday nights. "As a matter of fact it was no excuse. If you were in town you went Thursday night." She quickly undoes what might be heard as coercion: "But everyone wanted to anyway."

People have different ways of putting together the past in oral narrative. In our interaction, Stewart's mode strikes a rhythm: quick answer, pause of reflection, then slower elucidation that partially undoes, partially reaffirms the initial response. To "What kind of dancing?" she responds "Jitterbug." The one-word answer seems to open a different window, and she changes it to "Anything that the GIS wanted . . ." She laughs, then stops. "The cute young fellas were all scared, they're going away from home for the first time . . . it took their minds off of what was going to happen later."

"Was that on your mind, too?" I ask.

She replies that it "never left" her mind, that they "may not come back, or come back wounded," which is why she spent so much time "doing hospital shows."

About Canteen rules, she says, a hostess must "watch her language" and act like "a lady at all times." She pauses, then continues. "And if any of *them* got out of line, you were to report them immediately." Her elongated tone on the word, "them" is an unusual hint at GIS as anything but innocent boys. I ask if she knows of any such incidents. She does. A fellow starlet who "had someone who got a little out of hand" reported it. "And they asked him please to leave and said we don't condone that." She adds, "But, all in all, I think everyone behaved very well."

When I ask about racial integration, she answers, "Yes." Pause. "But not to a great degree." She thinks back, as though tuning in a picture of the crowd, and concludes, "I think there was a smattering of the various ethnics."

Stewart's career as a starlet ended three years and twenty films after it began, when General Eisenhower requested the live physical presence of the army poster girl on the ETO, as part of a war bond campaign for the GI magazine *Stars and Stripes*. This gig came with a stipulation: the army poster girl was supposed to represent the "girl back home," not Hollywood. She quit the studio, explaining that "the government does not want me to be followed around by a camera from RKO." She even turned down a contract for after her tour of duty. While the doubling of "girl back home" and "starlet" enhanced the dance floor democracy at the Hollywood Canteen, the same could not be said for the visions of postwar security the War Department hoped to convey through the army poster girl.

On the ETO, Stewart traveled as "Margie," a "girl next door" without a last name, movie deal, or even script; mostly "just talking" to the GIS, thousands at a time. What didn't come up in our interview but I learned later was that while following the requirements of this girl-next-door performance, she broke a cardinal rule when, during the first month of her tour, she met and married an officer. A headline in *Stars and Stripes* announcing her marriage lamented, "Margie It Hurts to Print This."[70] Six years after our interview, I found on her website a letter from "Margie" to the GIS apologizing for being selfish when she married Captain Jerry Johnson. Though the marriage was happy and lasted for nearly fifty-eight years, she assured the dwindling population of elderly veterans who Google their army poster girl that she hadn't intended to let them down.[71] The rules of the soldier-hostess dyad held sway, even to the point of haunting a patriotic jitterbug who married above the ranks of the enlisted men.

Break-away: Dorothy Morris and Caren Marsh-Doll

Caren Marsh-Doll (born Aileen Morris) and Dorothy Morris are sisters who grew up in Hollywood, attended Hollywood High, worked in the movies, and volunteered at the Hollywood Canteen. Caren was a stand-in, actress, and dancer at the time, and Dorothy, three years younger, was on contract at MGM. My introduction to the sisters comes from author and collector Josh Curtis, better known as "That Forties Guy" and author of *Sunkissed: Sunwear in the 1930–1950s*. The sisters live near Palm Springs. Because he lives along the way, Curtis suggests that if Tami and I visit Marsh-Doll and Morris we should stop by for a private tour of his collection. We arrange to take him up on that on our return trip from the desert.

The sisters agree to an interview on the condition that I prepare by reading Marsh-Doll's memoir, *Hollywood's Child: Dancing through Oz*, which covers a lot of Canteen recollections. The book takes its name from another of her memorable experiences—she was Judy Garland's stand-in in the film *Wizard of Oz*. Among the Canteen anecdotes in the book is a doozie about the dampening of her popularity among soldiers who had seen her in the movie *Pickup Girl*, a VD education film in which the lesson is that even someone who looks like a "good girl" might carry sexually transmitted diseases.[72] I look forward to hearing more.

We drive east from Hollywood, on a 115-mile rental car journey that spans the geographical gamut of Southern California. We cruise Sunset Strip, take in a bit of mountain air, inch along in I-10 congestion suspended above downtown and then above El Monte. We continue beyond Riverside (where the black soldiers were stationed who attended the grand opening of the Watts USO). We flow at times, then chug, and finally find ourselves sailing in the eerie silence of acres and acres of white wind turbines, made especially surreal by the snowcapped mountains on the horizon viewed through the rippling visual effects of hot desert air. (On our way back, we will pull off and follow the country roads, believing ourselves lost, until we see a young man in fatigues perched atop a vintage jeep. There is no question that we have found the Forties Guy. He will guide us on a tour of his amazing collection and share his lifelong fascination with the era, its style and material culture, music and dance; his dream is someday to open a museum. Thanks to his curatorial passion, and generosity, many of the photographs in this book are reprinted from his collection.)

When we arrive at Dorothy Morris's home, our first topic of conversation is the man who introduced us, toward whom they express great fondness. "Josh is amazing," says Morris. "He knows more about us than any of us."

FIG 4.10: Dorothy Morris and Caren Marsh-Doll, 1940s. BY PERMISSION, JOSH CURTIS COLLECTION.

FIG 4.11: Dorothy Morris's Hollywood Canteen ID card. BY PERMISSION, JOSH CURTIS COLLECTION.

FIG 4.12: Not all junior hostesses were single while they performed the surrogate sweetheart. Dorothy Morris grooms her husband's navy uniform. BY PERMISSION, JOSH CURTIS COLLECTION.

I tell Caren Marsh-Doll how much I enjoyed her book. Indeed, I will understand when many of her answers to my questions begin with "It's in my book." It truly is. However, different things happen in interviews, just as they do on dance floors. When I have set up the tape recorder on the coffee table, I ask about their memories of the Hollywood Canteen. Their recollections flow in the uncanny turn-taking of siblings who have remained lifelong friends. They know each other's minds.

Like most hostess-interviewees, the sisters begin by telling me how important it was to go and how wonderful the "boys" were. As Morris puts it, "Whenever we were free from work we would absolutely go. Sometimes it was every night for a week," which made up for nights missed after long workdays. If you've been up dancing "since six in the morning," adds Marsh-Doll, "you can't dance at night." But, adds Morris, when she and her group of friends, which included actresses Donna Reed and Alexis Smith, found themselves with any free time at all, they "would never ask, 'What do we do?' or 'Should we go anywhere?' it was just automatic. It was part of your duty. There was a war on, and it was a good way to help the boys."[73]

All of this is familiar. But Morris catches me off guard when she answers my question "What were the soldiers like?"

"Each one was so different." She pauses. "The only thing I do remember, is some of them held you so tight and they were so . . ." her voice expresses a sense of desperation to that tight hold. She searches for the right words, and finally puts it into plain speech. "Part of them was so scared"—one last pause—"and part of them was getting a hard on."

We all laugh. Her sister confirms the latter by adding, "I was going to say, I never had a scared one!"

Another funny line, but, again, not entirely said in jest. They are co-narrating an aspect of Canteen dancing they both remember as part of their war work. Continuing on the theme of GI arousal, Morris adds, "I think that's partly what scared them. The sergeants that were the lookouts were there too, and when they saw something like that happening, they would come and get the guy and tell him, 'Go sit down, cool off.'"

"And say 'Sorry, ma'am,'" recalls Marsh-Doll.

"And say 'I'm sorry, ma'am,'" agrees Morris. "You felt very protected there. I know that I did. That's really all I remember. We just felt like you were helping out a little bit of the way." The sisters then discuss the importance of the jitterbug in promoting distance between bodies—"there's no close contact, you're out and in, out and in, all the time," explains Marsh-Doll. Another problem with the "slower dancing," adds Morris, was that the music "was so romantic—you know, the songs—and it got sad." It was better to "keep them moving . . ." Marsh-Doll chimes in: "to real peppy music."

Though Morris and Marsh-Doll share their Canteen memories with great affection, sensitivity, intelligence, and humor, they describe a socially and ideologically complex "democratic dance," with parameters defined, in part, by tempo, genre, lyrics, and form. In narrating their Canteen hostess memories, they recall moving and thinking as simultaneous—a practice of embodied awareness of constraints, openings, partners, and others. To dance the part of the "junior hostess" is to "give shape" to one's own body, while improvising as the embodiment of a national symbol, or rather, half-of-a-national-symbol, of a serial dyad involving other bodies and desires. The sisters' memories of their moves are inseparable from awareness of contradictory parameters (cheerfully saying "yes," trusting others to say "no," figuring out how to move from moment to moment in the gray areas of this setup). Like many narrators, their co-telling connects memories of serving as "political action figures" (objects moved around by another agent, such as the state) and "political actors," who, like the airborne Jane Lockwood, while hardly autonomous, seize subjectivity while dancing on this "unsteady landscape."[74]

I am struck by Morris's experience of "helping out," a requirement that seems not only to divide people into pairs, and pairs into symbols of the nation, but splits each hostess-body in two: (1) a maternal body that soothes frightened soldiers preparing to be shipped off to combat, and (2) a sweetheart body rewarding particular kinds of soldiers who exercise heterosexual desire and self-control.[75] Publicity photos of Rita Hayworth, in bathing suit and high heels, cutting pie in the kitchen and Linda Darnell, in a loose, billowy white blouse, dispensing a pair of milk bottles to a crowd of grinning sailors exemplify this contradictory framing of traditional femininities. Popular song lyrics about Canteen hostesses do not make it any easier to figure out how to perform the "good girl" of the nation-at-war. Not only does the irrepressible Sophie Tucker sing "The longer you make your kisses, the shorter he'll make the war,"[76] but vocalists in the downright "corny" Sammy Kaye Orchestra sweetly remind junior hostesses that "You Can't Say No to a Soldier" if "he wants to dance."[77]

There are many ironies of this construction of the nation worth dying for as the junior hostess who can't say "no." This is a curious figure, the "good girl" who partners indiscriminately with hundreds of soldiers, sailors, and Marines out of love of nation—constructed in opposition to the "bad girl" as the "camp follower" who weakens the nation by partnering indiscriminately with hundreds of soldiers, sailors, and Marines. In order for a junior hostess to distinguish herself from the dreaded camp followers, someone else must "protect her," as do the military police in Morris and Dahl's narrative. But what if a hostess is not protected? And who decides which hostesses warrant protection from which soldiers? How does race impact the construction of the "good girl" who "can't say no to a soldier"? Winchell argues that "it was within dancing and dating that the unavoidable clash between the USO's need to entertain a democratic army and its preference to recruit a specific type of junior hostess occurred."[78] How did this clash play out on the contingently integrated ground of the Hollywood Canteen? Was "protection" reserved for white women? May a "girl" dance across race and still be "good"? Who protected whom when the soldier-hostess dyad crossed race in various directions?

When I ask Dorothy and Caren about interracial dancing, neither remembers encountering black soldiers or hostesses. They are troubled by this

FIG 4.13: A sailor kisses a hostess and poses for the camera, around 1943. Photograph taken by Gilbert Spreckles. COURTESY OF R. JANIE TILBURY.

gap—they hope it was integrated, but they doubt that it was. Dorothy was on contract at MGM at the time and remembers that "even Lena Horne, who was a big star when I was there, when we would go into makeup, she had her own personal person there. Nobody else was around her. They knew she was talented and a star, but nobody mixed. It was like an unwritten law." On the other hand, she remembers her black friends from grade school and high school and recalls that a black teenage boy was the president of her class at Hollywood High.

Time to Clear the Floor

Divided but entwined, former hostesses who volunteered every week for three years and veterans who entered the club for an hour once or twice talked to me about their encounters in this space. Even those who danced close to the official story charted pathways in and out of the ideal. Like all ideals, this one applies different pressures to different bodies. It resembles some more than others, but even in relation to its closest doubles, the ideal is never the same as the bodies that navigate its parameters.

The ideal of the jitterbugging soldier-starlet dyad not only erases but depends on imbalances normalized in the national woodwork, such as the gender norms that construct the couple as man-lead and woman-follow; male soldier and female civilian; and the patriotic pairing of the soldier-sacrificing-his-life with the volunteer-sacrificing-her-Friday-night. Racial hierarchy is reinforced and up in the air—codified in institutions and habits old and new, and exposed as a site of national embarrassment when democratic contradictions of the segregated melting pot are bared to the world. Among the people dancing these contractions are those for whom racial inequity did not happen at the Hollywood Canteen, those who believe the good fight was not only fought but won, those who do not remember race being a problem.

The first set is ending. For some of us, it is time to exit the Canteen for god-knows-where. For others, it is time to play sweetheart to the next five hundred. There are many more people who wish to dance. And many steps we haven't tried. You might want to soak your feet before stepping into chapter 5.

CHAPTER 5

★ ★ ★

Injured Parties

You can't say no, if he wants to dance
If he's going to fight, he's got a right to romance!
—HARRY WARREN AND MACK GORDON, "YOU CAN'T SAY NO TO A SOLDIER" (1942)

I don't jitterbug and I got hurt, but I do love the Hollywood Canteen.
—FLORIDA EDWARDS, IN "JITTERBUG TRIAL GIRL BEWAILS BEING 'ICKY'"
(APRIL 21, 1944)

It was a different thing, a wonderful thing, to have a place where soldiers
could go. But it wasn't integrated in an equal way.
—MEL BRYANT, INTERVIEW WITH AUTHOR (JULY 25, 2000)

On October 31, 1942, Florida Edwards, professional dancer, actress, and former Miss San Antonio of 1930, struggled in the clutches of a "jive-maddened
Marine."[1] Unlike Jane Lockwood's upbeat account of being "thrown from one
end of the canteen to the other," Edwards testifies about a horrendous experience with lasting ill effects. The dance floor disorientation theme that provides
Lockwood an opportunity to "write/right" herself into new subjectivity turns
nightmarish in Edwards's account of being squeezed so hard she cannot escape and then thrown so hard she cannot recover. As in Lockwood's tale, the
crowd backs up in self-preservation, but this time the hostess-body clobbers
bystanders in the sweep of her helpless break-away. Her dance does not end
in applause but in gasps as she crashes backward tailbone-first against the
bandstand—then silence. Barely aware of the tight circle of onlookers who
have gathered around her body, she awakens to the excruciating pain of a
dislocated coccyx and wrenched vertebrae in her lower back.[2] My thoughts
return to Patty Andrews's wink in the film *Hollywood Canteen* assuring us

that dance floor discomfort is a small sacrifice, comically endured. More serious than "corns for her country," Edwards's spinal injury cannot be soothed away by a footbath, song, or diary. Indeed, its effects extend beyond the war; her physical injuries bear lasting economic impacts, cutting in on her chances for postwar prosperity. She will lose her regular acting role on a weekly radio program—thus wages ($55 per week) and career momentum—and will suffer steep hospital bills, impaired ability to travel to jobs and auditions, and continuing discomfort for the rest of her life.[3]

A versatile performer who grew up in a family of vaudevillians, Edwards was no stranger to the physical demands and economic unpredictability of show business. These had been push factors in her family's migration west during the Depression. In Los Angeles, she, her parents, and her brother, Sam, had found work as freelance talent, mostly in radio. Most successful was Sam, who had hit the voice-over jackpot with the advent of animated features. In that milieu he was a star, knocking it out of the ballpark as the voice of Thumper, the rabbit in the 1942 animated Disney feature *Bambi*. He would eventually do much more—but not until after the war. By the time of the Hollywood Canteen's grand opening, his talent belonged to the navy. With Sam's earning power at Disney reduced to the pittance he earned in Special Services, the loss of Florida's weekly radio role struck a significant blow to the family income. If the accident had happened while dancing on the job, she would have been eligible for workers compensation. As a volunteer, however, her rights as a worker are irrelevant. Nonetheless, her volunteerism was work related.[4] It was at the request of her union that she danced one night a week at the Hollywood Canteen. For no other reason would she have made her healthy body available to the belligerent amateur who forced her to jitterbug, a dance she neither knew nor liked. Her only recourse was to sue the Hollywood Canteen, the very institution that had been erected not only to prove that the Motion Picture Industry was patriotic but to protect union workers in the industry from excessive demands for war-related volunteerism.

When Edwards professed "love" for the Canteen in a 1944 newspaper interview,[5] she likely connected it with social bodies beyond the room: her profession, the unions that struggled to protect even freelancers such as those in her family, and the concerted efforts of industry workers to comfort young men who, like her brother, had been conscripted into service. Nonetheless, the only way to survive the economic, professional, and physical damage was to prove that her female part-time worker's body was worth something to these social bodies and that it had incurred something beyond the usual wear and tear. This is an impossible position in national Canteen memory. The court records of what I am calling state memory, following David Theo

Goldberg, are where we must go to hear Edwards "write/right" herself as a person wronged—a claim that is never abstract or individual under the law.[6] As Sarah Jain writes, "How wounding will count and for whom is a political decision that has everything to do with the meaning of citizenship in a given social and political sphere."[7]

The Flip Side of the Soldier-Hostess Dyad

If "Getting Corns for [Her] Country" was the junior hostess's patriotic duty, what fate was in store for the hostess who sued the Hollywood Canteen for $17,250 for an injury inflicted by a dancing boy in uniform? When Edwards is mentioned in historical accounts, it is as a "sour note" in an otherwise up-beat story.[8] The gravity of her fate evades popular culture references, such as the newspapers and the Andrews Sisters' song and dance. An injury of this magnitude seems impossible in the light of the memories shared in chapter 4 in which even hostesses who "can't say no to a soldier" expressed faith in the military police to monitor the limits of bodily consent.

Nonetheless, the fail-safe network of patriotism, jitterbugging, and chaperoning that is taken for granted as mutually beneficial in national Canteen memory—what we might call, *pace* Adam Smith, the invisible hand-clasp of dance floor democracy—did not protect this junior hostess. As Edwards explained repeatedly to judges, attorneys, and reporters, she firmly told the Marine "no," then yelled "NO," then called for help—only to learn that "no" meant nothing from her side of the soldier-hostess dyad. As described in the judge's decision in the appeal, four years after the injury, the Marine "took a grip on her arm and started to 'throw' her around in 'wild jitterbug antics'" while she screamed for help.[9]

That the Marine's race or color is not mentioned in press coverage or court records suggests that he was (perceived as) white, as was the sailor who jitterbugged with Jane Lockwood. If he had been read as Mexican, Asian, or African American, this certainly would have triggered the ready hysteria about white women's proximities to nonwhite men who had long been treated as criminals and predators in public space, in the press, in the court system, and on the informal and volatile "contact zones" of social dance.[10] If his uniform was that of an Allied nation rather than the United States, this too would factor in debates about the Canteen's responsibility to protect (white) American women.

Somewhere in the Canteen, Jane Lockwood also danced—it was her first night as a junior hostess—but her diary makes no mention of Edwards's jitterbug spectacle. The crash was noticed by several other hostesses, however, who later testified not only about this particular incident but on general effects of the jitterbug. This trial helps us to take seriously the discourses of bodily integrity on a dance floor where some partners are risking their lives for the nation, some people are sacrificing their private time, comfort, and dance preferences, and all are compromising or extending bodily autonomy in connection with others. As an archive of state memory, the case helps us to reconfigure a Greatest Generation whose experiences and interpretations of the lines between sacrifice and recognition, injury and consent were different and unequal in unsurprising ways. In state memory of injured parties (whose injuries follow from inequalities built into the state), a case is heard, a judgment is made. In national memory, injury is smoothed away, a small accidental glitch in the greater service of democratic love. An ideal pair still rises to represent the national body into which all contribute and from which all purportedly will benefit.[11]

In chapter 4, we followed stories that moved in close alignment with the official version, while breaking away from time to time to personal perspectives that connected embodied subjectivity to national memory. Stories that upheld the claims of the superdemocratic dance floor in chapter 4 were not without opposing tensions—in fact, this elasticity between familiar nostalgia and idiosyncratic viewpoints brought narratives to life and animated the telling. Similar tensions pull across the stories of this chapter, but this time the narratives are pitched more forcefully against particular strains of Canteen nostalgia. Most of the stories are not as oppositional as Edwards's, though some are, and none takes place in court. Though Edwards files for compensation for a physical impairment and its economic impacts, I use the debates spurred by the trial to take "injury," more broadly defined, as an effect of the idealized soldier-hostess dyad. Which conscripted sacrificial soldier-bodies are worthy of comfort? Which hostess-bodies are worthy of protection (and from whom)? Whose desires are considered "healthy" and whose "injurious" to the nation? Injured parties, in other words, are not only those who incur an exceptionally unruly spin but those whose bodies are already considered unruly.

Whether telling it to the judge or to an oral historian, a narrator who claims injury on the dance floor of the nation attempts to "write/right" herself or himself against terms of citizenship that fail to recognize violence against his or her person. Courts of law and oral history are different in obvious ways, but both are platforms for public hearings. When interviewees shared testimonies of compromised subjectivity and bodily integrity with me in their Canteen stories, the stakes were different from the medical expenses and lost wages sought by Edwards, but these stories also seemed pitched beyond a two-person encounter. People talk to researchers for many reasons.

As a responsible partner, my practice demands careful listening and, in the case of this book, trying to write so as to remix Canteen memory in a way that does justice to all even when contradictions abound. My ears must be open to dissonant, miss-matched, and ineffable relationships. Like Edwards, interviewees who claimed injury did not relinquish love for the Hollywood Canteen. To love a democratic practice or vision is not the same as loving it "right or wrong." The dance of the citizen-subject of the nation-state is perpetually out of balance, especially so in a time of war.

I confess that no one who danced at the Canteen chose this chapter's title, and some whose stories are told here would not have identified themselves as "injured parties." This classification is mine and is not meant to cancel out the other feelings and stories that accompanied most counter-narratives. These are stories of mixed feelings and intimate relations in the often gray areas of democratic sacrifice, injury, and consent. I take care to note whether pushbacks felt soft or firm and observe negotiations of situations when the line between "yes" and "no" is ambiguously drawn, shifting, and confusing. I allow myself space to share my feelings about stories, while noting when they may have felt otherwise to the teller. Dance is not debate, after all; though its effects are endlessly debated.

Jitterbug on Trial

From October 31, 1942, until April 18, 1944, Edwards waited for her day in court. She was bedridden in her parents' home when her regular role on the radio show was recast. Weeks later, as she began to regain the ability to walk, travel was excruciating. Month after month, her physical pain forced her to miss professional opportunities. Finally—after nearly a year and a half—her negligence suit went to trial.[12]

The *Los Angeles Times* covered the proceedings with funny headlines that ignored the bodily damage: "Jitterbug Trial Girl Bewails Being 'Icky'" and "Jive Experts Disagree on Spin."[13] Literally adding insult to injury, the flippant tone of the news reflected the extent to which the idea of same-race violation of junior hostesses evaded the national imaginary of dance floor democracy. From the first day of the trial, the press narrated the story as though the "jitterbug" itself was on trial—its steps as well as the fanatics it was said to attract. To a certain extent, this "spin" is confirmed in the trial records. The arguments followed the dance—with "jive experts" testifying on both sides. On the first day of the hearings, reported the *Los Angeles Times*, Edwards, a "non-jiving radio artist," explained "rug-cutting" to Superior Court Judge Henry M. Willis: "Jitterbugging is a very peculiar dance. Personally, I don't like it. It reminds me of the jungle antics of natives. There is a basic step, and then there are variations. It's the most ungraceful dance I have ever seen." This opinion was disputed by another Hollywood Canteen hostess, Connie Roberts, who took the stand and testified that "the dance did not have to be 'weird' like some people think."[14] The story was illustrated by a photograph of Roberts demonstrating a graceful recovery from an exhilarating spin.

The Canteen's council questioned Edwards's culpability in what, after all, was a couple dance. Perhaps she wasn't firm enough in declining? "Did you just stand still when you told him you didn't jitterbug?"

Exasperated, Edwards explained, "Well, you don't stand still with a jitterbug. They don't let you." She told her story again.

> He had a firm grip on my wrist and I couldn't get away. I just kept calling for someone to come and get me. I yelled "help" several times, and then I opened my mouth and screamed good and loud. But the floor was jammed with people, and the jitterbugs scream anyway in the excitement of the dance. [15]

The next day's coverage spun the story as a hilarious showdown of "jive experts."[16] At one point in the trial, the case turned on the question of whether or not an "Icky" ("non-jive") "follow" can recover her bearings after being spun out and abandoned by a "Hepcat" "lead." In other words, did it matter that Edwards, a trained dancer, did not know how to do *this* dance? She was, in the slang of the day, a self-admitted "Icky" rather than a "Hepcat." The council for each side produced expert witnesses who were simultaneously "Hepcats" and hostesses. In support of Edwards's complaint, Luise Squire held the position that "once a girl is thrown into a spin, she is in trouble . . . unless her partner catches her to stop the spin." Defense witness Roberts, whose qualifications consisted of having learned how to jitterbug as a Hollywood Canteen hostess, disputed this, arguing that it was impossible to be injured in the dance.[17]

Whether or not it pleased the court, it pleased the *Los Angeles Times* very much when the opposing jive witnesses took their dispute into the hallway, where they argued while swinging each other around the room. When Squire failed to topple Roberts in the corridor, Squire argued that she would have thrown harder if she "had been a jive-maddened marine." In addition, "there wasn't any music so we weren't sent." The judge's unfamiliarity with "jive" usage of words like "sent," translated into copy more suitable for high school skits than courtroom news. "They get sent by the rhythm and go out of this world," explained Squire. The judge declared himself an "icky" and adjourned.[18]

Courtroom visuals of opposing hostesses, under the caption "Canteen Cuties," accompanied the next day's story: a smiling Donna Lee Kelton, who had testified that nobody was "rough," and a pouting Florida Edwards, her large eyes peering over her shoulder into the camera. With her face framed by a large picture hat, she seemed to be caught in a coquettish pinup pose despite her frown.[19] The day after that, the trial coverage was not a courtroom story but an amusing Canteen tumble taken by Connie Roberts five hours after closing arguments. As she was quick to point out to reporters, she was not injured.[20] Again, the focus was on the jitterbug alone—as though injury was otherwise impossible in a center that offered surrogate sweethearts for war-bound young men.

On May 2, 1944, the story made national news when the judge ruled in Edwards's favor, finding that "the dance 'constitutes a real danger for one not skilled in its gyrations.'"[21] The headline in the New York Times drew directly from the language of the ruling: "Court Rules Jitterbug Is All Word Implies, Jitter for 'Nervous' and Bug for 'Crazy.'" Therefore, it was the Canteen's responsibility to protect the uninitiated hostess from this dangerous dance. Edwards was awarded damages to the tune of $8,170, about half of what she had asked—but more than counsel for the Canteen had anticipated. Before the check was cut, however, the Canteen Foundation appealed. It would be another two years before the case would be reviewed by the California Supreme Court. In the meantime, the jitterbug would continue, but volunteers would sign waivers when they registered for duty, exempting the Canteen from damages.[22]

On March 28, 1946, Edwards finally received word that California Superior Court Judge C. J. Gibson had upheld the 1944 ruling. Hostesses were volunteers, but their safety was still the Canteen's responsibility. The original decision relied on city dance hall ordinances and found the defendant "negligent." The appeal had posited that a soldier canteen was not at all like a dance hall. Gibson agreed with his predecessor that lack of admission fees should not exempt the Canteen from extending "ordinary protections." In fact, because the plaintiff had been on the premises at the request of the defendant, "extraordinary care" was owed the hostess to "protect her" from injury.[23] As in the trial, the appellate judge was swayed by testimony that the jitterbug was a dangerous activity. Citing Edwards's trial testimony at length, he noted that the hostess "screamed for help" while her partner danced "in a rough and boisterous manner" and that when the "tempo of the music increased," he "became wild with it" and "threw" Edwards away from him, then

> spun her around and then grabbed her and pulled her back to him at least once before she fell. Another hostess, observing a strange expression on plaintiff's face, attempted to reach plaintiff and her partner to ask him to leave the floor, but before she could do so the accident occurred. From this

testimony the trier of fact could reasonably conclude that those in charge of the dance, in the exercise of due care, should have observed the marine's conduct, realized that it was likely to result in injury, and stopped it.[24]

Two courts ruled that the Canteen failed to protect hostesses from a dancing encounter; and both emphasized a kind of dance over a kind of encounter. Nonetheless, the injury, the debate, and the ruling fall out of national memory, and the patriotic jitterbugging soldier-hostess dyad lives on. Finally, four years after the accident, Edwards cashed a check that compensated her for the initial hospital bill and two months' lost work—but nothing more for a career that never got back on track. Where is her experience in swing culture as war memory? And where is the white Marine whose "conduct" is laundered when the dance style is found guilty? Would a nonwhite hostess have even been deemed worthy of such a hearing? Would a nonwhite dancing Marine have been let off the hook?

As we saw in chapter 3, the Marine Corps dragged its feet longer than any other branch of the service in including black men. (It did not admit black women until 1949.)[25] Just as no black Marine could be present at the opening of the Eastside USO, no black Marine had yet been promoted out of boot camp by the time of Edwards's accident. Roosevelt's executive order for Fair Employment in 1941 called for the admission of black men by January 1, 1942, but the Marine Corps stalled, arguing that there was no suitable (segregated) training camp. Technically, black men were admitted starting May 25, 1942, but their service was postponed until their separate facilities were completed that August. It wasn't until December 1942 that the first group was declared trained and stationed elsewhere.[26] No black Marines sought recreation in Hollywood on that October night in 1942 when Edwards was purportedly dragged against her will into a "primitive" dance that reminded her of "jungle natives." Yet, the injured party, many witnesses, and two judges would persist in ignoring the white Marine who hurt her, and blaming the jitterbug in racist language. The drama repeats a familiar racial script (what Angela Y. Davis called the "myth of the black rapist" in her much-cited article by that title), but just as in D. W. Griffith's *Birth of a Nation*, the scene of the white female victim and black aggressor appears to be cast with all-white actors. On the night of Edwards's injury, black Marines seeking entertainment were restricted to the backs of buses, traveling to and from the well-used segregated USO in the black section of Jacksonville, North Carolina. No bands played in that tiny recreation center, yet soldiers crowded outside, waiting to get in.[27]

What did "jitterbug" mean to the clumsy, "jive-maddened" white Marine whose body falls out of the jitterbug trial story again and again? Did he, like

Florida Edwards, think of the jitterbug as the "jungle antics of natives"? Did he, like Jane Lockwood, think of it as an exhilarating route to a new, modern embodied identity? Was he frightened for his life? Where did he learn this dance? Did he understand the dance and big band swing as license for "wild abandon"? Perhaps he badly needed an embodied discharge from whatever tensions "civilization" was presenting him with at that moment—a furlough from his regulated soldier-body through "primitive" release? Perhaps it was the social construction of race, after all, that constituted the danger of the white-on-white jitterbug practice. If so, it is part of the constellation of ideas about race that led Florida Edwards to fear the dance, Jane Lockwood to discover a new body, and Los Angeles judges, newspaper reporters, and editors to focus on the black dance rather than the white dance partner as the source of injury.

Facing Our Partners: Set 2

Sociologist Black Hawk Hancock has developed an approach that analyzes the Lindy Hop among predominantly white revivalists in the 1990s as an embodied everyday practice of race.[28] Like other scholars of swing dance revival(s), Hancock literally danced with interviewees. I did not. Nonetheless, I too sought interactive connection with interviewees in conversations about dancing memories, and took an embodied approach to analyzing social dance in relation to race, gender, bodies, and nation. The dancers I talked to did not approach the jitterbug as a site of "vintage" authenticity but as a popular dance to which they bore a range of relationships, none of which is identical to the memorialized national version.

Whether narrators identified with, exposed the injuries of, or applied torque to the idealized dyad of national memory, they produced different perspectives from those represented in iconic photographs, reenactments, and monuments. A focus on "injured parties" exposes particular cracks in Seward Johnson's sculptural recreations of the famous photograph of the white sailor and Red Cross nurse who, though not dancing, are frozen in a perpetual anonymous kiss.[29] The symbol looms, but for some narrators the limited edition ideal soldier-hostess dyad is taken to task, not only for omitting but for "unequally dispensing injury."[30]

Narrators described a dance that they may or may not have enjoyed, identified with, or known how to do when they did it at the Canteen. Contradictions of democratic ideals attached to dance floor memories in overt and subtle ways. I listened and asked follow-up questions. We tested each other's responses and moved accordingly. I felt myself pulled into different orientations to swing's national potency, a mercurial lurching and blending of white and black, racelessness and multiculturalism, color-blindness and color-restrictedness; race-, class-, and gender-differentiated notions of bodily comfort and disorientation, safety and injury. If the topics did not come up unsolicited, I made a point to always ask about racial demographics and whether military women danced. These questions sometimes elicited a proud reprise of dance floor democracy and sometimes yielded previously unspoken regrets, justifications, denials, reflections, ennui, amnesia, and claims of injury. I address the question of female soldiers in chapters 7–9. For now, I explore how the meanings of the soldier-hostess dyad could flip on racial contact, and how narrators addressed democratic discrepancies.

Break-away: Mel Bryant

"Are you black or white?" asked Mel Bryant, within the first five minutes of our first telephone conversation about the Hollywood Canteen.[31]

So far, I had been leading. I initiated the call (referred by his sister, trumpet player Clora Bryant, whom I had interviewed for my book on all-woman bands).[32] I introduced myself and told him that his sister had mentioned that he had attended the Hollywood Canteen while on leave from the Marines. He said yes, this was true. I asked him if I could interview him for my book (yes, again). Then, I asked him if the dance floor had been integrated, as reported in the black press, the musicians union magazine, and *DownBeat*.

"Don't you believe it, Sherrie," he replied.

I hadn't believed that a dance floor in Hollywood at that time could have easily been integrated, and I was eager to learn more about how the Hollywood Canteen fell short of its stated goals. I knew that Bryant had been a Los Angeles–based actor for most of his postwar life and that he would have a unique perspective as an African-American military Canteen guest who would have already known the limits of Hollywood within the social geography of Los Angeles. Still feeling we were on the same page, I asked my usual follow-up questions: What happened? What were the rules?

This was where Bryant took the lead.

"Are you black or white?" he asked.

"I'm white," I said.

Somehow, I got the sense that this didn't surprise him. However, my racial identification, once said aloud, became a mutually conscious part of our interaction. Our interview turned in ways different from the ways it would have if I had been able to continue to abstractly sense myself as racially neutral (a white habit, as Sara Ahmed puts it,[33] and a researcher habit, intensified by the telephone). Now, as Bryant gave me an answer, it was in the context of what had become an overtly cross-racial dance.

"For black people, integration isn't just about rules. It's about body language and a look on the face. There doesn't have to be a rope across the room. No one has to say anything for you to know when you are not wanted."[34]

I was not the first white person Bryant had explained this to in his lifetime. Asking me to racially identify had a performative function in our conversation, in that it shifted the concept of racial integration out of the realm of policy or intentions and into the realm of embodied knowledge. My questions about "what happened" and "what were the rules" did not get at his embodied experiences, his memories, or what he had to say about the dance floor at the Hollywood Canteen. Race at this point in the interview had to do with different orientations to the basis of the question—what constitutes an integrated social space? What Bryant had to say about his memories of the dance floor did not fit the framework I was operating in, in which a club was either integrated or segregated, in which we could name what was happening and pin down the governing set of rules.

In asking me to racially identify, Bryant reoriented our conversation so that it had room for his embodied knowledge: a Jim Crow childhood growing up in a small segregated Texas town, a career as an actor spent moving through predominantly white crowds in a racially marked body, basic training with other black recruits under white officers at Montford Point, North Carolina, a furlough spent trying to reconnect with his new hometown and interrupted acting career in Los Angeles, and memories of his long postwar acting career. To white Canteen-goers, the presence of a lone black body moving through an otherwise apparently white crowd could be seen as evidence of integration (interpreted as either a symbol of America or caution of un-Americanism in Hollywood, depending on the viewers' visions of how race difference and democracy were interconnected—both interpretations had currency in World War II). However, from the perspective of the person or persons whose burden it is to integrate the room, this same event could register as evidence of white space, lack of integration.

Bryant explained to me, explicitly as one black person explaining something to one white person, how, from the perspective of a black person, the text of the crowd—the "body language" and "look on the face"—could indicate a segregated space, even if a black Marine was welcomed into the club. For Bryant, the "welcome" did not cancel out but facilitated a kind of segregation that could pass as integrated to most people in a Hollywood night spot. (A white former Canteen-goer whom I did not interview, and who asked to remain anonymous, perceived black soldiers as having "a chip on their shoulder," concluding that if there was a racial barrier at the Hollywood Canteen, it was due to black servicemen's reticence to fully participate.)[35] Though all

FIG 5.1: Actor-Marine Mel Bryant at Montford Point. COURTESY CLORA BRYANT.

enlisted and drafted servicemen were "welcomed," according to Bryant, he recounted a particular operation of the Hollywood welcome on his body in what Ahmed has called the "hospitality" model of diversity. "To be welcomed is to be positioned as the one who is not at home," she writes. To not feel "at home" is to be an ungrateful guest who offends the host.[36]

"The Hollywood Canteen is something to be remembered, and something to be regretted," said Bryant. "It was a different thing, a wonderful thing to have a place where soldiers could go, but it wasn't integrated in an equal way."[37]

When I emerged from this first of two telephone interviews with Bryant, I was turning in a new direction. Instead of standing beside him, facing an imperfectly integrated Canteen, I had turned to face him, listening from my body across the telephone lines to his telling of his embodied experience. Considering his dance floor perspective helped me to factor in body language and looks on faces into the social geography of memory at the Hollywood Canteen as a together-but-unequal democratic space—an acutely accurate portrait of U.S. notions of integration as "democracy," written in Bryant's telling of his Canteen memories. One might think that a meaningful discussion of the transmission of body language and looks on the face would lose something in the form of a phone interview. However, the voice-concentrated medium of the telephone is hardly disembodied. It brings bodies up close in a different way.

The next time we spoke—once again, over the phone—Bryant told me he had been thinking a lot about the war years.[38] He wished he had written a book and was glad, he said, to be telling some of his story on the tape that I promised I would send to him. He then told stories that situated his Hollywood Canteen memories within a longer trajectory organized around his life as an actor and singer. We heard part of this interview in chapter 1—the detailed description of leaving his small, segregated Texas hometown and heading off to Hollywood in 1942. It was with a sense of awe and destiny that he conveyed the story of his discovery by Black Hollywood while working at one of the famous cafeterias owned by Clifford Clinton, an antivice politician, antihunger activist, and entrepreneur. He worked at a South Broadway location that featured waterfalls, an organist, and singing waiters. Bryant was not a singing waiter. He was a busboy. However, one night, he sang anyway.[39] There weren't many people in the upstairs section on the night in question. He was cleaning the vacated tables when he recognized a song that the organist was playing and started to sing along while he worked. All of a sudden, the organist stopped. "I looked over and he was beckoning me to come over there to the organ." The organist invited him to sing. "He started at the beginning. I knew the whole song. People came out from under the balcony. They were applauding, and saying 'More!' I was scared to death because I had never sung in front of that many people before, especially in a strange place."[40]

Bryant insisted that he did not know that two of the most successful black actors in the motion picture industry, Ben Carter and Mantan Moreland, were in the audience. Moreland, a comedian, was one of the most frequently cast black actors in Hollywood (famous for popping his eyes and fearing ghosts). Carter was currently playing the unprecedented (for Hollywood) role of a black war hero (a mess attendant who mans a machine gun in a tight moment, like Dorie Miller at Pearl Harbor) in *Crash Dive* (1943).[41] In addition to his struggle for dignified roles, Carter's own heroism among black actors included his role as a talent agent. It was in the latter role that he invited Bryant to go with him to MGM the following day. There, as they walked down the main company street, Carter stopped to introduce Bryant as a talented young man with great promise. "Can he read?" a man asked. Bryant laughed as he told this part. "I was thinking, 'What does this idiot mean? I just got out of school. Of course I can *read*.' But he meant a script." Bryant went into the man's office, read the lines, and was told on the spot, "Well, son, you've got this part. This is going to be your part. We're going to do a picture with you."[42]

Bryant had landed the title role of *Shoe Shine Boy* (1944), a short patriotic feature about a young man trying to earn $2.00 so he can buy a trumpet in a pawnshop. In the film, a white man helps Bryant's character to obtain the horn, thinking he is going to get rich off of the black man's talent, but the musician turns out to be a patriot who wants the instrument so he can play it in the army. The plot somewhat mirrors Bryant's own career. Under pressure to make racially inclusive war films, MGM could have used him again. "They were mad at me," he recalled, "because I signed up and went in the Marine Corps after I finished the picture."[43] In the sixteen months between Bryant's arrival in Los Angeles (July 1942) and his departure for Montford Point (November 1943), he had starred in an MGM film (earning close to $2,000, he recalled, a large amount in the 1940s) and had moved out of "skid row," as he called it, and into Ben Carter's mansion in the Adams Heights neighborhood, also called Sugar Hill. "Nat Cole lived on the corner. Hattie McDaniel lived right on the next corner. Noble Sissle lived across the street. Juan Tizol lived on Hobart Boulevard, right behind Ben. Ethel Waters lived right behind Ben on Hobart. Louise Beavers lived on Hobart Boulevard."[44] He lived among the elite movers and shakers at the center of Black Hollywood and in the home of the man who, according to the *Chicago Defender*, was "responsible for casting of more Negroes in featured and bit parts than any other Hollywood agency."[45]

In April 1944, just a few days before Florida Edwards's case went to court, the *Baltimore Afro-American* announced that "MGM's *Shoe Shine Boy* [was] now shining in the Marines."[46] When the film was shown in his camp, Bryant said, it put him "in good with the officers," who were white.[47] He became a vocalist with the Montford Point orchestra and the drum major for its band and spent the war doing soldier shows under the direction of composer Bobby Troupe.

Bryant's stories of Montford Point, like his stories of Hollywood, tell of navigating a course paved in paradox, swinging between maddening polarities of possibility and restriction. He weaves in and out of Montford Point and the Hollywood Canteen as he tells me about that time—and indeed there are more intersections than one might imagine. A movie star acquaintance from Hollywood—Tyrone Power—was also serving as a Marine in North

Carolina. One day, Power took Bryant to see the swimming pool at nearby Cherry Point, where the white Marines were based. This is a story of his friendship with a big star—but it is also a story of segregated and unequal conditions. Montford Point also had a pool. However, only white officers could use it.

> We're all going to go overseas to die for our country and we don't have [the right to use the] pool on our base? This is Montford Point, an all-black base. Just white officers on the base—*they* can use the pool and we can't. Do you think that's fair?[48]

This story concludes with Bryant's prohibited dip in the pool and subsequent reprimand. The proximity and restrictions from swimming pools and movie stars at Montford Point mirror his stories of Hollywood, where he was successful and well liked but perpetually out-of-bounds, as his Canteen experiences illuminate. When he returned to Los Angeles on his leave, he enjoyed the hospitality of movie stars and the agent who had discovered him, Ben Carter. Wearing his Marine uniform, he boarded the Red Car up to Hollywood, hoping to renew prewar professional contacts. Of course this entailed visits to the Hollywood Canteen. His voice is slow and low when recounting his approach.

> The Canteen was a very strange place. You know, you'd go up to the front door, like usually you'd go with two or three other buddies in the service. And they would sit you down on one side of the building, and the whites on the other side of the building. And the first time they did that, I was wondering what was going on. Are they leading us to slaughter? I thought they were going to drop us off in a pit or something. We couldn't dance with any of the stars.[49]

Slaughter. Pit. Word choices, rather than the even keel of his measured speech, convey the anger and hurt he ascribed to the experience of unequal togetherness.

I asked if there were black hostesses on the nights he was there, to which he replied, "No, no. Oh, no."

"So you're describing a *kind* of segregation?" I asked, still on a mission, it seems, to classify the place as inclusive or exclusive.

"That's what it was," said Bryant. Again he advised me to take stories about integration in Hollywood with a grain of salt.

> I've heard some of those tales about how we were welcome anywhere. The Ambassador Hotel is there in Hollywood. I went to see Lena Horne there. The man took me and sat me right in the kitchen almost. I couldn't see

Lena for the kitchen door . . . It's almost embarrassing to tell you some of those things that happened in those days, how people treated you because of the color of your skin, without getting to know you, or knowing anything about you.[50]

I returned to the question of rules and policy, only this time I was more careful to work it as one dimension of the unpredictable, improvised volunteer setting of unequal togetherness he had described in our first conversation. Did rules factor into the body language, facial expressions, and being led to a far corner of the room?

"There had to be a rule, Sherrie, for it to be that blatant. It was so obvious that we were separate. Like later on they said, 'Separate but equal,' but we weren't equal." He was, of course, paraphrasing the now historic *Brown v. Board of Education* decision (1954) of the U.S. Supreme Court that overturned legalized segregation in the United States, a reminder that legal precedent would not incorporate this logic until a decade after his Canteen visits and military service.

"If it was really equal, it wouldn't need to be separate," I echoed.

"No," said Bryant, "We'd be all together.

As we wrapped up our conversation, Bryant talked about the movies and television shows he did later on, his relentless efforts to integrate professional and public spaces in Las Vegas and Hollywood throughout his career, and the lingering exclusions. Painful among his postwar examples was his story of being denied entry when he tried to go see his former Marine captain, Bobby Troupe, perform at a nightclub.

Just before we hung up, I pulled us once more toward the Hollywood Canteen. I asked if he remembered any black volunteers at the club, celebrities, perhaps. Or was it only white people entertaining the soldiers?

Mel paused for a minute. "I remember Louise Beavers said she was going out one night, but I don't know if they let her in or not." He chuckled. "I'm sure they must have. Surely they wouldn't turn her out. Because she had just done that picture, *Imitation of Life* with Claudette Colbert, where she played the black lady that made a fortune for the white woman." He laughed. "Yeah, I'm sure they let *her* in!"[51]

There was the rhetorical mode again—a critical, not literal, spin—that extended Bryant's analysis of "together" but "not equal" as the basis of inclusion of the Hollywood Canteen, the neighborhood of Hollywood, and the Hollywood motion picture industry. His punch line implies that black people were allowed in these together-but-not equal spaces only within the same social relations as depicted in the movies—never equals, always at the service of white people. His participation in the uncomfortable tangle of a soldier-actor relegated by race to the far corners of the room excludes him even while including him in a space that was advertised at the time, and celebrated for decades afterward, as the apex of progressive movie star–soldier hospitality. His presence may have supplied evidence for some dancers that the Canteen was simply and easily integrated. However, Bryant, throughout our interview, pushed back at this interpretation, exposing the injuries incurred in the democratic dance of the color-blind leading the color-blind.

As with all accounts, Bryant's story should not be taken as representative of all members of a social group. Indeed, African-American servicemen did not all experience, remember, and narrate the Canteen in the same ways. In a 1996 interview, navy messman William Henry described his visit to the Hollywood Canteen as a highlight of his return from the Pacific. Three buses came to his base in San Diego and delivered him and his fellow troops to the door. "Bette Davis, Tallulah Bankhead, and their whole gang was down there all—all the old chicks—movie stars [of that time] . . . just for us . . . Dorothy Lamour, Hedy Lamarr, and all of them—we danced with them over there! They didn't segregate us. They rolled out the red carpet."[52] Likewise, in September 1944, a society columnist for the *Cleveland Call and Post* reported that the Hollywood Canteen had proven it was "all it's cracked up to be" for black Marines stationed at Camp Pendleton, in Ocean Park, California.[53]

In addition, though black hostesses are absent from many accounts, including Bryant's, and Avanelle Harris spoke of not being welcome at the Hollywood Canteen (chapter 3), some African American women did serve as hostesses and recounted a range of experiences (we will hear from Jeni LeGon in chapter 6). Black celebrities, including Lena Horne and Dorothy Dandridge, appear as Hollywood Canteen hostesses in memoirs and histories of black Hollywood, as well as black newspapers, and the local papers also list less famous black women.[54] Perspectives resembling Bryant's are absent from black newspaper stories about the Hollywood Canteen, which invariably narrate the club as a site of progress, hope, and inclusion for black soldiers—either as a club with "No Jim Crow" or as a place where battles were not only fought but won. The presence of black soldiers dancing with anyone they wanted and of the plenitude of black hostesses and the fact that some big stars advocated mixed-race dancing told stories of double victory. A story like Mel Bryant's did not.

However, in his telling, the duplicity of the Hollywood Canteen—wonderful and inclusive on the one hand, hierarchical and exclusive on the other—also deserves remembrance. To tell a story in which his subjectivity can be recognized, he must narrate the failure of the democratic dance floor. And to narrate its failure, he must establish its democratic intent. "Bette Davis tried, but the powers that be won out." He narrates his Canteen inclusion as a barely open door—like that of the MGM commissary, the lounge in the Ambassador Hotel, casting calls in the motion picture industry, and even interviews with Hollywood historians, such as myself. These barely open doors, in his stories, must be used again and again, under uncomfortable and sometimes humiliating circumstances, if they are ever to provide equal entry. His narrative techniques, like his analysis, are developed over time, through embodied experience, knowledge, and practice. To perform, in our interview, the stickiness of this door seemed a way for him to refuse the position of political action figure (serving others by supplying evidence of integration) and to claim injury as a political actor (making room for his embodied knowledge). His stories of together-but-not-equal integration at the Hollywood Canteen deal with the right to enter (unlike most Hollywood nightclubs), spatial restrictions (being led to one area with other black servicemen), prohibition from dancing with the stars (who are white women), and feeling a chill that he knows is only legible to other people with embodied knowledge of daily racism. Even the construction of stargazing as proof of democracy is injurious when the stars on display are white women and the beholder is a black man in a white part of town.

Bryant's stories link his Canteen stories with other Hollywood memories, an endless reel of exclusions, insults, and slights that were endured in plain sight of others but easily escaped the notice of most of the white people in the room. Like Florida Edwards, he "writes/rights" himself as a person wronged in a place he wants to love.

Break-away: Tommy Farrell

A convivial white eighty-two-year-old man is talking and laughing as he swings open the door to his sunny cottage. Tommy Farrell wears a pink Oxford shirt with a maroon ascot, and his hair is brilliant white and styled. His look and delivery carry an aura of Hollywood glamour. When he visited the Canteen he was a soldier. However, before, during, and after his military service, he was also an actor, dancer, and comedian. He is the son of a famous actress of stage and screen, Glenda Farrell, best remembered as the gum-smacking, wisecracking gun moll in the movies she made in the 1930s while Tommy and his fellow troops were growing up.

Tommy Farrell does not tell his stories as claims of injury, but he does open the floor to a wider range of white soldier bodies than the "jitterbugs" encountered by Jane Lockwood and Florida Edwards. Like Sam Edwards and Mel Bryant, he spent his soldiering days in Special Services, with the plan to work in Hollywood (the industry) after the war. However, unlike Bryant, Tommy Farrell's talented body is white, and unlike both, he enters as the son of a star who lights the way (and will always outshine him). Like Florida Edwards, he is a hoofer who is protective of his body in this democratic playground where skill doesn't matter. However, because he is a soldier, not a hostess, he can say "no" when it doesn't feel right. Contrasting Bryant's experience of unequal togetherness, Farrell tells of doors opening that exceed those available to ordinary white soldiers. He tells stories of Hollywood exceptionalism, but he also tells of the Canteen's importance for other GIs who were not Hollywood insiders.

> It was the only *good* place in the country where the boys could go but the officers couldn't. *They* could go anywhere. The GIs didn't have money to go anywhere. They paid us off in playing cards. It didn't last very long, but it was a great place.[55]

Farrell ushers Tami and me to our seats in the living room. Tami operates the recording equipment, but she also doubles the audience and he plays to us both. He sits facing us. We are in guest position, enjoying his personal gallery, neat rows and columns of framed professional photographs that document a long career in vaudeville, theatre, and motion pictures. On more narrow walls, near, doorways, four- by five-inch framed snapshots line areas above and below light switches. He is up again, guiding the tour. He points out his various dance and comedy partners; his movie roles, mostly in westerns, in which he was always cast as "the young deputy or the girl's brother"; and memorabilia of his World War II days acting in Moss Hart's soldier show, *Winged Victory*. While shooting the film version, the GI cast spent the summer of 1944 at Gardner Field, in Taft, near Bakersfield. While there, he made many trips to Hollywood, but not the usual spots. "Hoofers didn't go ballroom dancing—that was for peasants." He frequented the professional dance hangouts, the "Rainbow Studio on Highland" and "Perry's on Vine," where the studios waived their usual fee of $3 per hour for the GIs. However, he did visit the Hollywood Canteen.

"Canteen stories!" he announces. He tells us he was afraid he wouldn't have anything—"But the memory worked!" He has ten minutes of material, which he delivers with great physicality and showmanship, cheerfully repeating parts he can tell we have missed, and acting out scenes and characters from his chair. His stories are little gems—expertly told—always ending with a funny or poignant point of emphasis.

"It was fun for me, because I always knew somebody—friends of my mother's. The first time I went to the Canteen, Barbara Stanwyck was there. She had a big bunch of people around her, all the GIs and sailors and so forth. I worked my way through the crowd. When I got close, she said, 'Tommy!' " His body now gets into the act—he is doing an over-the-top Stanwyck—arms outstretched—takes a beat—then pantomimes an onlooker turning to stare in puzzlement at the random GI who inspires such passion from this famous movie star. "And I loved it!" Back to Stanwyck's deep diva voice: " 'Dance with me!' So we danced." Similar scenes unfolded every visit. Another time, it was Jayne Wyman. On another night Joan Blondell intercepted him: " 'What are you doing here?' I said, 'Same as everyone else.' She says, 'Let's dance.' " He again mimes the double take of an onlooker. "Everyone is staring, going, 'Who is he?' " He pauses, then delivers his punch line: "They're still doing that!" This is a joke, playing on his unique position as Hollywood insider who is recognized by the stars but not the public. He laughs and we join him.

I ask him what the dancing was like at the Hollywood Canteen.

He replies that it was too crowded for serious dancers. "I hope I'm still dancing with the same person!" he joked, mimicking a soldier bobbing in the crowd, helplessly squished among too many dancers to know what's going on.

When I ask about the dance skills of soldiers at the Hollywood Canteen, he explains that "every fifth or sixth number would be slow so the boys could do the GI Shuffle." This is a joke—a term for holding a hostess close without knowing how to dance. Nonetheless, when my follow-up question betrays my assumption that many soldiers wouldn't have known how to *jitterbug*, he corrects me. "Oh yes they did! Oh, boy, did they *ever*! The army, navy, Marines, Air Force, the Coast Guard, every branch of the service." When the fast swing tempos hit—he claps his hands—"they'd all be up."

"How did they learn?" I ask.

"They'd learn from watching," replies Farrell, "and from each other. Some of them couldn't dance a step. A couple nights out, and they were dancers."

I ask if they did aerial steps—flipping partners in the air à la Jane Lockwood and Florida Edwards. "There was no room!" he exclaims. "If you lifted a girl off the floor you'd kill eight people!" Another joke with a grain of truth.

When I ask if black soldiers danced, he says yes, but that they "usually didn't" dance with white women. He recalls that "there were always black ladies to dance with." He reflects on the question, and adds, "It was a terrible time." He then jumps to the 1950s, to tell of racism he witnessed against fellow entertainers. In one story, he and his partner open for Dorothy Dandridge in Las Vegas, where he learns that "she couldn't go into the casino, or the bar."

Most painful, she wasn't even allowed to attend the "closing night party they had in the main room." As the headliner, it was her name that drew in the revenue. Her race still meant that her body was valued less than the pair of dancing and joking white men in the opening act.

Though Farrell doesn't identify himself as a person wronged (quite the opposite, in fact), he does describe the Hollywood Canteen—and the entertainment industry at large—as a place where things could go wrong.

Differently Dancing Bodies

Farrell's Hollywood Canteen dance floor narrative, unlike most scholarship on social dance, makes room for beginners who "learn from watching," who sometimes make poor choices (like aerial steps when space didn't permit). On reflection, he narrates racially differentiated parameters of who could dance with whom. As a professional hoofer, he highlights additional concerns about entrusting his body to a democratic dance floor where practical experience of dancing with others doesn't matter.

Dance encounters are shaped by combinations of embodied knowledges, which is not to say that embodied knowledge is always (or only) shaped by embodied knowledge *of the dance*. Whether we are talking about the steps of the jitterbug or the navigation of inherited myths and professional constraints, there is a difference between embodied knowledge and self-conscious attempts to get one's body to do something new that has not yet been incorporated but learned and approximated from watching others. People learned their moves by looking across the room, remembering what felt good before, trying to replicate what they saw in the movies, and improvising on whatever cultural associations they had picked up about the practice. Any or all of these orientations might occur simultaneously within couples and/or nearby in various combinations as bodies entered into brief contracts on a crowded dance floor. Even if both bodies bore embodied jitterbug knowledge, there was no telling how these will correspond; regional differences in where the pulse is felt could be enough to stultify a pair of dancers, even if each has achieved optimum torque in the past.

The soldiers, sailors, and Marines were disoriented at the baseline—their private lives had been interrupted. Removed from family, friends, jobs, school, as well as from familiar social geographies of race, and undergoing the reorientation of physical and mental military discipline, their bodies and identities underwent regimes of realignment that affected who they were and who they would become. Some were experienced and some were inexperienced in socializing with people of other races and classes, and some were experienced and some were inexperienced social dancers.

FIG 5.2: Optimum torque is not guaranteed. BY PERMISSION, BRUCE TORRENCE, HOLLYWOODPHOTOGRAPHS.COM.

Some jitterbugged for the first time at the Hollywood Canteen. As they tested their moves with dancing strangers, their bodies interpreted the felt sensation and perceived expectations of swing music and the pounding feet and whipping in and out of nearby bodies. Also shaping their emotional, sensate, and intellectual selves-on-leave was the cumulative embodied knowledge picked up from navigating many social geographies of race, in hometowns, military bases, and the confusing landscape of Los Angeles.

Toes are stepped on, hostesses are flung, and couples collide with other couples. Sometimes when a dyad loses its internal grip, someone is embarrassed, or even hurt. At other times, falling down is an occasion for hilarity (as when John Wayne and Adele Mara topple backward in opposite directions in *The Fighting Seabees* [1944]). Even under less dramatic circumstances, we may safely presume that little, if any, of this group activity is experienced, understood, remembered, or described later in identical ways from its many sides. "We danced with the soldiers and they were charming and they were nice and I was happy to help them," said white actress Helene (Angus) Bank, who danced at the Canteen three nights a week with friends from Los Angeles High. She laughed when I asked if the soldiers were good dancers. "Some were. They could throw you around!"[56]

"Most of the soldiers were great at swing," recalled Claire (Lomas) Rosen, a white hostess who loved to jitterbug. She also noted that many were "shy and troubled" and "not all of them got on the floor."[57] Rosen did not work in the motion picture industry but was recruited when the call went out for volunteers at the shipyard where her husband worked. She made sandwiches from the plentiful but unpredictable food donations, but what she really wanted to do was dance. She started ballroom dancing at the age of twelve and continued to cut a rug as often as possible in her eighties—mostly on cruise ships. Dancing at the Canteen, however, had its problems. Like several other former hostesses, she mentioned that soldiers got "fresh" with hostesses. However, the bigger problem that she highlighted in our interview—and that others did not tend to bring up—were the fights among soldiers, which she remembered were either "over a hostess, or somebody made a remark. If it was a black guy, you know, if he got too close to a couple dancing, they'd cuss, and that would start a fight." I asked her who started the fights. "It all depends," she answered. The white soldier might start it if he thought a black soldier was getting "too close" to a white soldier dancing with a white hostess, or the black soldier might start the fight after the white soldier made a "a cuss remark."

When I asked about black hostesses, Rosen remembered none on the nights she was there. "They may have come at another time." She did "remember a few Mexican women." Rosen said that she danced with soldiers of "different races," adding, as did many white hostesses, that race did not matter to her. "Race has never been a problem with me all my whole life. I think just because you have a different color, that doesn't make you a bad person." However, she also recalled Canteen space as a place where race mattered to many others, where proximity of black soldiers to white women and white dancing couples caused white soldiers to fight and "cross words" of white soldiers toward black soldiers—hate speech—caused black soldiers to fight. Hollywood memoirs and histories describe fights as rare and easily quelled by the band playing "The Star-Spangled Banner."[58] However, in Rosen's memory they were constant: "every time I was there, there was always a problem."

Democratic dancing for a hostess meant following, as the phantom girl-from-home would, making the man feel good, even if he is stepping on toes. She might be a good or a bad dancer; she might identify as a "jitterbug," she might have never jitterbugged before, she might enjoy jitterbug amid a broad range of popular dance repertoire, with expectations varying according to age.

Dancing with the (Surrogate) Starlets

Many movie magazines conveyed funny stories about actresses who said they didn't jitterbug but then changed their minds out of patriotic loyalty to the young men. These stories are of sacrifice but not regret.[59] No actress I interviewed narrated anything resembling Edwards's attempt to get out of a dance. However, several former hostesses who were not in the industry or worked off-screen shared strategies for avoiding the dyad.

Former RKO secretary Marjorie Lewin said no: "I said, 'I'm not getting a broken arm here!' You had to be an Amazon or double-jointed to survive *that*. I said, 'That's not for me.' And so I took the coatroom."[60] Screen reader Aniela "Niel" McAuliffe danced, but only when duty called. "Let me preface it, above everything else: It is not part of my nature to like dancing."[61] She danced at the Canteen because she "did whatever was asked of me." McAuliffe managed to avoid the jitterbug but shuddered at the memory of other hostesses being swung "half parallel with the floor," even though there wasn't enough space for such activity.

Ninety-six-year-old Pearl Gelfand burst into peals of laughter when she described herself as a thirty-five-year-old Universal Studios secretary who was called away from the snack counter to dance with the soldiers "when they didn't have enough young stars."[62] When I asked if she enjoyed dancing, she qualified her answer: "Well, I enjoyed serving the young men. Yes, I loved to dance. But after a day at the studio . . ." Again, the thought makes her laugh. "I didn't know if I was dance material!" When I asked if she jitterbugged at the Hollywood Canteen, she stared at me. Her jaw dropped. She did a classic double take. "Oh no, no!" Seeing that I am serious cracked her up even more. "It isn't that I didn't want to," she explained. "I don't think I would have been very good at it!"

I might never have imagined the preponderance of nonstarlet industry hostesses if I hadn't visited the Motion Picture Home. This unique retirement home is one of the projects of the Motion Picture Relief Fund, founded by film industry workers in 1921, to organize care for longtime union members when they could no longer work. Among those who launched this program were Charlie Chaplin, Mary Pickford, Douglas Fairbanks, and D. W. Griffith. Under the direction of actor and director Jean Hersholt, the Motion Picture Country House and Hospital opened on September 27, 1942, the week before the grand opening of the Hollywood Canteen.[63] The timing of my research catches this confluence full circle, as some of those who had volunteered at the Canteen in their younger days were living out their last days in the Home.

The fabulous landscaping (old Hollywood–style, with topiary animals) and friendly, informative guide (director of affairs Elisa Foster) contribute to a first impression that we are embarking on a tour of the "Retirement Home of the Stars." However, as with the labor history of the motion picture industry, in which it wasn't only or even primarily the Screen Actors Guild that broke down the stronghold of Los Angeles as the "Citadel of the Open Shop," it isn't only actors and actresses who reside here but secretaries, painters, carpenters—anyone who belonged to any one of the movie guilds or unions for twenty years is eligible. I meet five former Canteen-goers at the Home on May 25, 2003; the majority of them were nonactress hostesses.

Break-away: Aniela "Niel" McAuliffe

A flushed and talkative white woman in her eighties sits straight up in bed and asks me what my motivation is for "doing a Canteen story" and whether I understand anything about "this unique industry."[64] She lectures Foster on the importance of properly telling the industry's story "to the world so we don't lose our preeminence." On a recent hospital stay, she was "appalled at what television is like." She looks directly into my eyes, leans forward, and stage-whispers, "Your book could make a difference."

I ask her if she has memories to share about the Hollywood Canteen.

She counters, "If you are going to write about the Hollywood Canteen, you are going to have to write about the workers in our industry." We are a visiting party of three: me, Foster, and Tami (behind the video camera), but McAuliffe's speeches are pitched for a larger audience. "Bette Davis was just an actress in SAG [Screen Actors Guild] who used her voice and power" to get it "going." The studios provided the raw material. "But"—she raises her eyebrows—it was "the union workers" who "put it together.' "

My memory of this interview foregrounds a formidable woman in pink pajamas interrupting her stories from time to time to criticize our failure to dress properly and bring calling cards. She lectures me on how to do research, Foster on contacting donors, and Tami on how to lose weight. It wasn't until I transcribed the interview that I grew sympathetic to the relationship between her frustration with her declining memory and her impulses to instruct her younger visitors on professional conduct. Criticizing us seemed to have a remarkable effect on her ability to regain her footing, and back she would go to stories that mattered to her about the Canteen. Listening to the interview later helped me to understand that the intellectual capacities that failed to retrieve details in 2003 had been her trusty weapons in the many "good wars" she fought during her career: her proud participation in the motion picture industry labor movement, her struggle to rise professionally in a gender-segregated sector of that industry, and her later battles as a researcher at war with industry-wide ageism. Sadly, I had not yet put this together during our in-person interaction.

"I'm a strong union person," she tells me, again and again. However, she is miffed when I ask her which one. I am too stupid to write a book. She returns to the point, which is not "which" union but the importance of the labor movement in the motion picture industry, including the Hollywood Canteen. Because of battles fought by union members for their fellow workers, she is able to reside in this cottage now that she is too old to work.

She tells her memories of moving to Los Angeles during the war and supporting her mother by writing synopses of novels for the studios—she was a screen reader, or "what is today called a story analyst," she explains. I ask if she was in the Screen Readers Guild. She is exasperated with me. "Honey, you've got to earn your way into a union." She explains how difficult it was to survive freelance as an independent, and tells how she was helped out by a clerk at Pickwick Books on Hollywood Boulevard, who let her "go in there and pick up a book, take it home, and return it without any damage to it." During the night, she would peruse and summarize the novel at "twenty-five bucks a reading." She developed an interest in the industry and learned of the preparations for the Canteen. "I don't know if it was at the Actors Lab or some other organization. I've forgotten. I mean, it was sixty years ago, kid. I joined up and I was one of the first ten girls."

Like many other volunteers and guests, injury was never far from her mind while at the Canteen. She entertained soldiers while her own brother was missing in action and she was unable to find out the fates of relatives in France and Austria. Some details resemble more nostalgic renderings: she lovingly describes the building, the music, the entertainment. Then she raises her voice and announces: "I want a plug for our unions, our union members." She tells the story of the refurbishing of the old barn: her version does not star Bette Davis and John Garfield by candlelight—instead she foregrounds union workers donating their labor to transform a dilapidated dump into a glamorous nightspot. She promises to send me a comprehensive organizational chart and then becomes angry when she can't remember where she put it. Foster indicates that it is time to move on. We thank her and prepare to leave. Her parting instruction rings in my ears: "You can't do it without charts!"

Break-away: Marion (Krow) Saphro

Nonactress industry hostesses may have been mistaken for starlets on the dance floor, but those I spoke with made sure I understood the other kinds of work that went into making movies. Secretaries described their work as glamorous and exciting, often telling about the "pictures" they worked on and famous people they knew. Unlike starlets and other on-screen workers, who tended to emphasize their affiliations with particular studios (contract players found job security, at least for a few years), the offscreen workers tended to emphasize union membership. Secretaries in the motion picture industry at this time had bargaining rights through the Screen Office Employees Guild. This was unusual not only among clerical workers throughout the open shop city of Los Angeles but across this labor sector nationwide.[65]

Marion (Krow) Saphro was a secretary who worked for producer William Dieterle, "who made *The Devil and Daniel Webster*," "Valentine Davies, who wrote the original story of *Miracle on 34th Street*," and others.[66] As we sit with her in her cottage at the Home, she expounds on the difference made by the Screen Office Employees Guild. "I started out working for fifteen dollars a week, and as soon as the union came in, I was making forty dollars a week. Boy!" She adds, "As long as I had to work for a living, working in the industry was the best thing that ever happened to me."

During the war, she lived with her mother three miles to the south of the Canteen, on Fairfax and Wilshire. She would have been about thirty-one, she estimates, when she danced every week at the Hollywood Canteen.

> The reason I did was I had two brothers in the service and I was being very patriotic. That was the best I could do. And that's all I did, really. There weren't any particular anecdotes that I can remember. I danced with black soldiers, white soldiers, whoever was there.

Perhaps it is my "Uh-huh," uttered at that very moment, or perhaps this is where her telling performance has taken her before. Either way, the topic of dancing across race seems to bring the scene closer to mind, and she finds that she does, indeed, have a "particular anecdote" to relate. It isn't about dancing with black soldiers so much as about a subsequent "altercation" with other white women volunteers.

"A couple of the gals—none of whom I knew, really—said, 'Why are you dancing with *them*?' . . . And I said, 'Why? Because they're in the service and they're here and they don't rub off, you know?'"

I ask if it was unusual in those days to dance with someone of another race.

"I suppose," she replied, "But I've always felt that way. I wasn't being—what is the word I want? When you get old, the words don't come when you want them—I wasn't trying to *demean* anybody. I didn't think I was doing him a favor."

About the white hostesses who pulled her aside and tried to discourage her from dancing with black soldiers, she explains, "if they didn't want to, that was their problem and if they had those kinds of feelings, then I felt sorry for them."

When I ask about black hostesses at the Canteen, she grows silent. Finally, she replies that it is "a very sad commentary" that she cannot remember any. About the white hostesses, she concludes, "The only altercation I had with them was when I danced with a black man." She remembers that it "bothered" her but that she tried not to "let it take over." She figured that the other volunteers "were just people who were there to dance, as I was. If that's the way they felt, fine. I can't change the world."

Her Canteen work lasted until her marriage in late 1943. "And that took care of that because my husband had come home from the war and he had been wounded. So I had to take care of him, so that was more important than the Canteen at that time."

In this chapter, we have heard Canteen stories from a variety of perspectives that admit evidence of injury, or its potential, in different ways. We have heard from a hostess injured on the dance floor by a white Marine and looked on as a black dance is blamed for the problem and the problem is swept under the rug. We have heard from a black Marine who is not allowed to dance and a white soldier-dancer who sees the Canteen as too crowded and full of novices to be a place he would go to dance with strangers. We have heard from white hostesses who figure out how to get out of dancing, a white hostess scolded by other white hostesses for dancing with a black man, and people who build into their dance floor stories the collateral damage of war. Taken together, this selection of differing accounts of who can't say no and who can't say yes powerfully unsettles the ideal of the Hollywood soldier-hostess interaction as an innocent and natural unfolding of "dance floor democracy." Nonetheless, all contribute collisions, commotion, and disconnections that produce a more inclusive vision than the official version.

Break-away: Margaret Halsey, Stage Door Canteen, New York

During the same period when white hostesses tried to discourage Marion Krow (Saphro) from dancing across race, another white woman in her early thirties was training hostesses in interracial comportment at the Stage Door Canteen in New York.

In chapter 1, I addressed the differences of the social/spatial geographies of race in Los Angeles and New York. Surely these cities' differences shaped experiences, perceptions, and memories of integrated dancing at the two clubs and different strategies of hostess training, chaperonage, and policing. We will quickly break-away here to peruse Halsey's memo to white junior hostesses of the Stage Door Canteen in New York, the "super-democratic" club on which the Hollywood Canteen was patterned. It is possible that some guests and visitors of the Hollywood Canteen also read this memo, which was published in the left-leaning news magazine PM and then reprinted in *Negro Digest* in October 1943—though the readership of white nonleftists would have been negligible. My interviews with former Hollywood Canteen-goers turned up no mention of the memo or of Halsey's later books about race relations at the Stage Door Canteen. Nor did former volunteers recall any particular training for hostesses about race on the dance floor.

Halsey had limited prior experience of socializing across race, prior to the crash course of her Stage Door Canteen work, and she drew on this personal fact to understand her trainees' ignorance and create effective teaching moments. She found that sometimes an unflinchingly direct address to white hostesses was necessary to optimize the chances of democracy on the dance floor. Though most of the hostess meetings she facilitated were integrated, in the spring of 1943 she called a special meeting of white hostesses.[67] Her pre-meeting memo opened with the preamble to the Declaration of Independence: "We hold these truths to be self-evident: That all men are created equal."[68] She reminded her volunteers that they had agreed to socialize with men of the many different races and ethnicities of soldiers passing through New York. She then talked frankly about the challenges this goal presented to white hostesses and offered some preliminary food for thought for their upcoming meeting, a step-by-step lesson of the kind that would later be called "unlearning racism."

To those hostesses who struggled with deep prejudices that intensified on the dance floor, she wrote, "You can't be blamed for having that prejudice in the first place. It was taught to you when you were too young and help-less to be critical." She then spun the privilege of junior hostess work as an opportunity to develop critical faculties and techniques and to employ these as a point of national pride. She also confronted rumors that integration was a Communist plot. "The Reds and long-haired radicals only want to tear [the Constitution] down. The people who deny Negroes democratic equality ac-tually are tearing it down." She debunked the scientific basis of race. Then she ripped into what Angela Davis would later call "the myth of the black rapist." It wasn't the question of equality that evoked prejudice in most white host-esses, she argued, it was the "unconscious," "arrogant," and institutionalized fear that "no male Negro can so much as glance at you without wanting to get you with child"—and this, Halsey argued, was a myth. The "truth" about this fear was "economic and historical" and could be "summed up in two extremely unromantic little words: Cheap labor."

The white hostess played a role in upholding or undermining white supremacy, she argued, depending on whether she turned away from the black soldier as "sub-human," or toward him as a social equal. By refusing to dance with a black soldier, the white hostess did not protect her virtue, nor did she prevent racial violence. Instead, she made "it possible for employers all over the county to get Negroes to work for them for less money than those employers would have to pay you."[69] Unlike Marion (Krow) Saphro, Halsey believed that convincing other white women to dance across race *could* change the world.

Halsey then parted the social construction of the white hostess/black soldier dyad to try to help white hostesses imagine the dance from the point of view of a black soldier. If racial progress seemed evident now, it was largely due to the fact that black soldiers and defense workers were needed in the war effort. There was no reason to believe that full equality would be conceded by the system that had been built on and continued to benefit from racial hierarchy. Likewise, a black soldier had "no reason to believe that he won't be snubbed by one of the girls on our shift or openly insulted by a Southern [white] soldier" who believed he was "superior" and was historically conditioned to uncritically believe that he must guard "the honor" of white women, and put down "Negro revolt."[70]

Her later books about her experiences at the Stage Door Canteen (*Some of My Best Friends Are Soldiers, a Kind of Novel*, 1944, and *Color Blind: A White Woman Looks at the Negro*, 1946) expanded on her own politicization about race as a white woman who had encountered no "Negroes" except as subservient laborers until she supervised junior hostesses at the Stage Door Canteen. The first book fictionalized and the second set into memoir the practical steps she and her hostesses developed collectively over time to back up the ideological claims of equality. Despite the title of her memoir, *Color Blind*, her topic is the hard work it took to aspire to interracial dancing in a country where interracial democracy had yet to be achieved:

> at this point in the history of these United States, you could not just invite Negro servicemen into your canteen and call it a day. If the no-discrimination policy had behind it the highest ideals of American thought and feeling, it had in front of it a veritable miasma of legends, myths, fairy tales and sweeping but inaccurate generalities.

This hard work against the weight of history included such practical measures as training white hostesses on graceful responses to the "problem of 'rescuing,'" when white soldiers would "cut in immediately" when a "Negro serviceman asked a white girl to dance." The white hostess was to gently explain that "we made no differentiation in our treatment of servicemen and that 'rescues' were unnecessary." She could then suggest that the white soldier was welcome to "cut back in a few minutes."[71] It also included separating myths from emotions and acknowledging the work it takes to change personal feelings produced by histories of power. Techniques included focusing on black soldiers' feelings instead of one's own (and understanding that these were also complex, differentiated, and conditioned by history), getting to know the black hostesses better, and making an effort to converse with black soldiers who seemed the "most intelligent, responsible, and mature." These activities could not only democratize the dance floor but help one unlearn the undemocratic myths one had inherited as a white American woman.

The social geography of the Stage Door Canteen was no less complex than the Hollywood Canteen (even the explicitly integrationist busboy Carl Van Vechten held different views from Halsey, writing to his friend Langston Hughes that racial tensions dissipated when black soldiers overcame their insecurities).[72] However, the New York example does raise the question of the effects of the social geography and the spatial expanse of Los Angeles on hostess training with regard to race. We have seen that the Inglewood USO arranged special training on interracial hospitality for white hostesses (including members of the American Daughters of the Confederacy). However, Hollywood was reputed to be more liberal and progressive than places like Inglewood.

If Hollywood hostess training included debunking of racial myths, it wasn't detected by me or the at least equally interested FBI. We know that black hostess captains supervised black hostesses, and white hostess captains supervised white hostesses. We know that Cadrez not only organized black hostesses but served as one of two African Americans on the Canteen board, and was secretary for the black local of the musicians union, which, along with the white local, threatened to boycott if a ban was placed on integrated dancing. It is possible that Halsey's memo may have been distributed and discussed, given the battles over integrated dancing at the Hollywood Canteen, and coalitions among black volunteers and board members and white Hollywood liberals and leftists, including Canteen executive secretary, Jean Lewin.

However, even without knowing the travels of Halsey's memo, we can point to other known differences between Broadway and Hollywood that affected dance floor demographics on the West Coast, and that made their way into on-screen movie canteens. One is the movie industry's tighter rein on off-the-clock photo opportunities of its talent. Movies created intensive up-close familiarity with its stars, and the industry protected its investments by controlling how that intimate knowledge was constructed and perceived. A well-placed spread featuring a female movie star dancing with a same-race GI was good for the box office; interracial dancing could lower the value of those bodies for producers, agents, and investors. This most assuredly affected interracial dance floor encounters and decisions. The same pressures that hindered a screen hostess's freedom to say "no," made it risky for her to say "yes" to a soldier of another race if photographers were in the room. Certainly actual hostesses found multiple ways to navigate the constraints—but the ideal had both national and professional effects.

The idealized soldier-hostess dyad that constructed a wartime vision of postwar prosperity comes with a bundle of built-in social inequalities. In producing the apparently white couple as color-free, colorblind, and democratic, the specificities of bodies disappear, while upholding "together but unequal" mobility, consent, and bodily integrity. The dance is white *and* multicultural, integrated *and* segregated, mandatory *and* off-limits, freely chosen *and* tightly policed. Hostesses must be protected in order to construct them as good girls; and they must be white to be considered capable of social injury. The myth of "good" white womanhood relies on their "protection" from "black men." People of color are "good girls" and "good boys" when, like the black soldiers in the section remembered by Bryant, they "stay in their place." White hostesses who dance across race threaten to devalue the idealized "good girl" of the soldier-hostess dyad. White soldiers must desire women, but their behavior toward them swivels depending on race and class constructions of valuable white virgins to marry and racially and classed others to grope. For these very reasons, racialized communities were often especially protective of respectability and safety of young women-of-color, especially in areas and situations governed by what Sara Ahmed calls, "white space." Ahmed is not referring to places only inhabited by white people, but places where people of color are either invisible (because they don't disrupt the "comfort" of white space) or hypervisible because they stand out. "The moments when the body appears 'out of place' are moments of political and personal trouble."[73] In Claire Rosen's memory, black soldiers stand out for white soldiers when they move "too close."[74] In Mel Bryant's memory, black soldiers stand out when he walks in the room.[75]

The color line on the "integrated dance floor" in segregated Hollywood proved especially potent, from many directions, in producing a patriotic jitterbug couple in national memory. This is a slippery line, one that disappears and reappears, a color line that sometimes *must* be crossed in order for the dance floor to represent democracy (in *DownBeat*, the black press, and the

Popular Front press of the day and autobiographies of Lena Horne, Bette Davis, and other movie stars); and, at the same time, a color line that *must not* be crossed (the possibility of such a thing is absent from the *Los Angeles Times*, publicity shots in movie magazines, and newsreel footage, for example). Because the music most remembered is swing, and the dance most often evoked is jitterbug, the disappearing/reappearing color line is about not only the interaction of bodies with bodies but the slippery associations of swing culture as its mercurial yet deeply embodied meanings worked on bodies of dancers and chaperones.

Stories that explicitly turned on the possibility (or not) of dancing across the color line were sometimes told as evidence of dance floor democracy, sometimes as "sad commentary" and outright critique. And sometimes they provided narrative occasions for torqueing back.

CHAPTER 6

★ ★ ★

Torquing Back

Torque: "Turning force." The magnitude of torque determines the rate
of change of rotational momentum.
—KENNETH LAWS AND ARLENE SUGANO, *PHYSICS AND THE ART OF DANCE* (2002)

Each accented phrasing or accelerating torque or momentary stillness is
an instance of thought.
—SUSAN LEIGH FOSTER, "TAKEN BY SURPRISE" (2003)

Depending on which way bodies turn, different worlds might even come
into view.
—SARA AHMED, *QUEER PHENOMENOLOGY* (2006)

I am grateful to whatever cyber-routings of metadata led Ian Walters to my
website, where he discovered our shared research interests.[1] He found it while
searching for a photograph of Lena Horne at the Hollywood Canteen to send
to his Uncle Eric for his ninety-first birthday. Eric Marsh was a white British
pilot in the Royal Air Force (RAF) when he attended the Hollywood Canteen
in January 1943 and received a jitterbug lesson from Lena Horne. Walters's
web surfing led him to my posted call for interviewees at the same time he
located the perfect photograph of the glamorous star (on the stage) at the
Hollywood club.

   He contacted me by email to see if I was still seeking stories. If so, an
interview might be arranged. Eric, as Walters explained, "ran a pub in England for many years and the storytelling goes with the territory."[2] I'd love to
interview Uncle Eric, I replied. Because Eric's hearing and eyesight were failing him, Walters advised that such a meeting would probably need to be via
the ancient method of cassette tape exchange through the mail, which was

his uncle's preferred mode of correspondence, but that I could initiate it with a letter, followed by an attempt to connect by telephone. When I made the call, I had difficulty making myself intelligible to the friendly-sounding man on the other end of the line, but he assured me he knew who was calling and why, and shouted his transatlantic promise to send me a cassette tape with his Canteen memories. Less than two weeks later, I found, in my mailbox, a package from Hertfordshire, the first of a remarkable series of tapes from Eric Marsh.

> Hello, Sherrie. It's Wednesday morning, right? I thought I'd better start getting something on tape for you as promised on the phone. I don't know quite whether or not this is going to come out.[3]

The moment the cassette began to play, I could tell that Walters had been right about his uncle's gift for vividly relaying his oral accounts of the past. He provided the tactile details that made me feel as if I was there. From time to time, at a particularly exciting moment, Marsh would interrupt himself to stop and start the tape recorder to make sure he had pressed the buttons correctly. There was always something about the story that kept me tuned, even heightened the narrative tension, as I waited to see if he would find his way back to audibility. At ninety-one, technologically unsure (referring to his tape recorder as a "camcorder"), nearly blind, and hearing impaired, Marsh came and went, sometimes explaining that he was renarrating a long section he had accidentally not recorded the first time around. Nonetheless, he managed to produce a riveting twenty-five minutes of Hollywood Canteen memories for a complete stranger.

This was only the first of a long series of tapes in our exchange. I dug out my old cassette recorder and spoke into it, thanking him for the previous tape and asking additional questions. Marsh recorded his answers and asked me some questions. And so it continued. I loved each tape but could tell that making them was an arduous task, so in each tape I made I tried to give him an "out," so he could gracefully not respond. The tapes kept coming until his nephew convinced him that he had helped me immensely and it was okay to stop. On the tapes, he spoke to me as one speaks to a friend; he laughed, he wept; a couple of times he asked me to try to find information about people he had met in 1943. Like many narrators, he blended his Canteen memories with commentary on wars in the present—twice alluding to his concerns about meetings between Tony Blair and President Bush then currently in the news and speaking about the boys who were "dying needlessly" in the Middle East. Then he'd return to his memories of his dancing body in his blue RAF uniform at the Hollywood Canteen, "where they couldn't do enough for the boys." His stories sprung the tensions of affirmation and critique: the Canteen was heaven, and war is hell; it was a different time, and the world is still at war. Keeping these pulls in play throughout, his tape-recorded performances spun alternate visions of swing culture as war memory at the Hollywood Canteen.

As already shown, when narrators told personal Canteen stories they did so in interaction with an official memory of the Hollywood Canteen. Some closely matched the footsteps of the soldier-hostess dyad, dancing in ways we might easily recognize when we see the jitterbugging pair in movies, museums, and memorials. Others pushed against the nostalgia in explicit critique, exposing the contradictions of a democracy defined as a couple dance, where some people can't say no and some can't say yes; where some people are beloved, others invisible. As "telling performances," oral narratives are more than the ordering of words revealed by a transcript: they are tactical embodied entanglements with storytelling physics. Most narrators danced a combination of moves, though the stories highlighted in chapters 4 and 5 struck a more or less "linear acceleration" in relation to Canteen nostalgia—either flowing with or pushing against. In this chapter, I turn the spotlight on storytelling feats that seemed to approximate the "rotational acceleration" of swing dance torque.

When I think of torque as a move within narrative performance, I am not just referring to instances in which people talk about achieving an exhilarating level of turning power with a partner (although many narratives about torque in the past also seem to me to apply torque in the telling). For me, torqueing back happens when people narrate dancing memories in such a way that they channel the expectations connected to the typical telling of democratic dancing and then lean at a bit of different angle, bend the knees a little more, shift the play of pattern and surprise, and apply just the right amount of turning power, timed and weighted for optimum release. These are the moments when throwing one's body into the Canteen story produces something else—not the usual story, not a counternarrative, but a different kind of dance floor democracy.

For this final set, we face, in sequence, two narrators who, at least in my dance with them, seem to neither wholly confirm or critique the dominant narrative but draw power from its nostalgic juice while tilting with and against its gravitational pull to produce a version of the dance floor that is *more* democratic, from each speaker's point of view. My purpose in this division of story lines is not to crown the dancers of chapter 6 as winners of the jitterbug narrative contest but to populate the dance floor not only with different stories and experiences but also different moves and strategies, which gather around the social geography of memory that makes up my archive. Stories that attempt and sometimes achieve torque swing beside those that bask in warm identification with visions of ideally matched misty-eyed soldiers and adoring hostesses, as well as with visions that cast such scenes as sites of not being heard and not being seen, of fights, sleights, injuries, and exclusions. Keep the commotion alive—the comfort and pain, affirmation and interruption—as we step onto the dance floor with Eric Marsh and Jeni LeGon.

Break-away: Eric Marsh

Eric Marsh's route to the dance floor at the Hollywood Canteen began in England when he was "called up for service in 1940." After spending his first two years in the RAF as a flight mechanic, he "remustered to the pilots' course" which took him far away to Bowden, Alberta, Canada, about sixty miles from Calgary. After his training, he spent a four-week leave in Los Angeles and then went home to England to see his wife and five-year-old daughter. He was then "posted out to the Middle East, and then the Far East," where he "finished up on B24s in Burma, just off Imphal, off the Indian border." He did not get home again until "Christmas, 1945." By the time he returned, his daughter was eight years old. He hadn't seen her for three of her formative years but still considered himself one of the "lucky ones"—he survived the war.

Marsh completed his flight training in the snow-covered Canadian prairie at the tail end of 1942. He recalled that there was so much snow that flight training at Bowden included skiing instructions and pilots were fitted for skis in case of emergencies. When his training ended in January 1943, he was awarded a twenty-eight-day leave. "And my chum and I said, well let's go down to Hollywood. And somebody said, 'Well, you'll never get there in the time.'" It was fifteen hundred miles from Calgary to Hollywood.

Nevertheless, the two RAF pilots talked to some American GIs who were stationed in Calgary who told them, "Come to the air base, and when there's a kite going south, we'll put you on it." They went to the air base and soon found themselves "hopping from plane to plane" across North America. When they reached Los Angeles, they hitchhiked by car, telling the drivers that they were Hollywood bound. Their final ride thought it best to drop them off at the Hollywood Canteen. On the tape, Marsh told of entering the building and immediately finding everyone "most effusive. They couldn't do enough for us. The first thing, they wanted to give us a cup of tea, and a bun, or whatever you like to call it. And I think the person who served us that particular day was Rita Hayworth."

The two British airmen knew no one in Los Angeles, but they did have a contact from a family in Calgary with whom Marsh had played cards on

FIG 6.1: Eric Marsh, British Royal Air Force, poses with his plane, 1942. COURTESY ERIC MARSH.

the weekends. The woman who may have been Rita Hayworth dialed the number for him, and the friend of his new friends in Calgary turned out to be a cameraman at RKO. This man whom they had never met not only picked them up at the Canteen but offered them hospitality for their entire stay, including the loan of his car during the day while he was at the studio. Every day Marsh and his friend went sightseeing, and every day they "called in on the Hollywood Canteen."

"And then we went in one evening," he said, chuckling at the memory, "and that's the evening that I first saw Lena Horne. I was dumbfounded. She was absolutely beautiful, absolutely beautiful. But," he added with gravity, "she was having rather a rough time, in general, [because of] the fact that she was colored. This, of course, to us, meant nothing. But, in America, at the time, as you know—I'm not stating anything that everybody doesn't know—but colored people were classed as second-class people in *those days*. So she was rather a little bit reluctant to come over and talk to us."

During this part of the story, Marsh took his time, admitting that he didn't know how all the pieces came together that led to his dance with Lena Horne. He guessed it had something to do with bandleader Harry James, "that's Betty Grable's husband," he explained, in case I didn't know. Marsh recalled that he and his friend were watching the dancers but were reluctant to try to join in, since they didn't know how to jitterbug and didn't know anyone. He watched as Harry James approached Lena Horne and talked to her.

> And he must have said to her, "Look, these two boys have come from Canada, they're from England, they're on leave, and they'd like to have a dance." So rather reluctantly, I thought—I don't know—she came over and she said, "I understand you'd like to have a dance?"

His friend "didn't dance a step," explained Marsh, but he and his wife were "considered rather good dancers over in England," and he jumped at the chance to dance in Hollywood with Lena Horne. "We got on the floor. Well, I was gone. I was gone, Sherrie. I mean, she was so lovely, you know, and that fact that I was holding her in my arms . . ." He laughed. "Well, the missus had better not see me like this!"

Eric's dance partner noticed right away that he was having some difficulty picking up the jitterbug, that it was new to him.

"What sort of steps do you do over there?" asked Lena Horne.

He acted out his response, as if to her, into the tape: "Our steps are mostly slow. It's the waltz, the slow fox-trot, or the tango, but none of this jiving and jitterbugging."

Horne suggested, "Well, you lead me and let me try yours."

Into the tape recorder Marsh narrated how he took over the lead and gave the instructions as they danced: "Slow, slow, quick-quick, slow, slow, quick-quick, turn, turn . . ."

> Well, of course, being a professional hoofer herself, it was easy. She picked it all up in no time, and in matters of seconds, Lena Horne, and this un-known bloody airman—that's me!—were dancing. And the rest of the gang, everybody, all the GIS, the sailors, and WACS [Women's Army Corps members], the QAS [nurses of the British Army], all the girls, all of them were all standing around in a circle watching Lena and I doing this dance . . . When the dance finished, they all clapped like mad!

Marsh's thrill and disbelief about this moment told fifty-three years after the fact bears striking resemblances to Jane Lockwood's immediately scribbled tale of the crowd backing away and cheering as she danced with the jitterbug-sailor. However, the scene is also different from Jane Lockwood's in many ways—the dancing is negotiated, the lead and follow switch back and forth, the jitterbug is rejected for the slow fox-trot, the dyad crosses boundaries of nation and race, and a very famous movie star is the hostess. Instead of a white hostess careening into a new embodied experience via an African American dance, an African American hostess easily moves across styles to dance the slow fox-trot British-style with an RAF pilot who takes the opportunity of the telling to comment on U.S. racism of World War II. He apologizes when he tells me about the racism he "didn't know then" but now knows that Horne experienced, but I hear that he wants to make sure I know this part of the story, and I hear him reading that history back onto his memories of her reluctance. As in Lockwood's diary, there is something significant about the high point of the crowd backing away, applauding the dancing couple. However, this is not so much a story of loss of control resulting in an exciting new subjectivity as it is a story about finding ways to connect across difference in a time of war. In a humbler sense, this is also what we did in this intergenerational international cassette exchange—reaching across different differences in a different time of war.

As Marsh's daily visits to the Canteen continued, they now included dancing with Lena Horne, and his dance floor democracy was retooled as a two-way exchange: transmitting and receiving equally across difference. The next time Lena made a "beeline" for him, he said to himself, " 'I'm not going to be shy. I'm going to learn this jitterbugging.' So I said to her, I said, 'Let's forget this English dancing.' "

Despite the fact that most interviewees said that the Canteen was so popular that it was emptied of servicemen every hour to admit five hundred more so that all comers could have a visit, in Marsh's memory his jitterbug lesson with Lena Horne lasted "two or three hours," by which time he was good enough for Lena Horne to tell him, "You'll pass muster anywhere. In fact, if you put on our uniform, they'd think you were a GI dancing like that." Being told that he could pass as an American GI was not necessarily a compliment for a British airman, but coming from Lena Horne, Eric took it as such and thanked her.

"And that's how I come to know jitterbugging."

Marsh believed that his dances with Lena Horne brought increased attentions from other stars. "Once people had seen Lena Horne come up to me—which, as I said, which was quite a bit on her part considering the social standing in those days—*everybody* came up. Betty Grable came over. Would I like a dance? *Would I? Crikey!*" With Grable, he did the slow fox-trot and the jitterbug as well.

The next star he recalled approaching him for a dance was Hedy Lamarr, "without a doubt, one of the most beautiful women in the world." He laughed, apparently at the memory of himself dancing with the great beauty. "And so, of course, to dance with her, again, was seventh heaven."

Next was Claudette Colbert. After their dance, she invited him to RKO for a cup of tea in her dressing room, where she gave him a photograph of herself, "which she signed, 'Eric Marsh, Best Wishes, Claudette Colbert.'"

In the meantime, driving their host's car, Marsh and his "chum" saw the sights of Los Angeles—at least the Westside, which was what he remembered. In Hollywood, they saw Grauman's Theatre, where they took photographs of the "film stars' hand prints in the cement." In Beverly Hills, they drove around looking at the homes of the stars. "But our biggest enjoyment was to get back to the Hollywood Canteen."

In Marsh's story, his RAF service inspired instant recognition and hospitality at the Hollywood Canteen. "The minute they saw two blue uniforms—they couldn't do enough. We just cannot forget it. My chum, unfortunately, was killed, so he will have no memories, obviously, because he's not here." His voice grew somber as he told of fate of his friend who made the plane-hopping trip and accompanied him on so many memorable evenings before they both were sent to battle. His friend was killed in Egypt in 1944, the year after their trip.

"Now, I'm just going to test this again, dear. Hang on," he said. "I think everything's all right. I hope so." When he returned to the tape, he added a selection of details, meeting Cab Calloway, seeing zoot suits for the first time, long before they had "caught on" in England. "Everyone was so affable," he said, but his mood again turned serious. He announced that he had one more story to tell about Lena Horne, a painful memory of something that had "endeared her" to him.

"I remember there was a young GI come in, he'd been caught by a Japanese flame-thrower, and he was horribly disfigured, in fact, he virtually had no face at all." I could hear the thickening in his voice. He paused for a moment before continuing. "I'm afraid it's very difficult to talk about this, dear." He took a breath.

> Lena Horne went straight up to him, gave him a hug, and a great big kiss. And you could have heard a pin drop. And then the yells and the clapping that went on afterward, you know. She made that boy's life by doing that simple thing.

Marsh again left spaces between his words: "that . . . simple . . . thing." The pitch of his voice rose, and I could hear that he was beginning to weep.

"So, they are rather remarkable memories." He was quiet for several seconds. "Sorry, I'm getting a little bit choked up." He laughed at himself for crying into a tape recorder. "I shouldn't be, should I? But there you are." He started talking again about the ineffectiveness of wars to end wars, and the "boys dying needlessly" in the present. He stopped himself. "I dare not get into politics, because I'm afraid I would wax very, very lyrical." He laughed, and then remembered he wanted to mention "another very lovely star, Eleanor Powell. What a lovely girl." His voice was still full of emotion as he pulled together his impromptu conclusion to the tape.

> Those sorts of people made life worth living for the boys that were giving their lives. We might as well be honest about this. It made their life. I mean, they went away—probably went back to the front, or where ever they were going to. Back to the jungle, back to the air, and probably wouldn't come back again. But that particular time was their moment.

He apologized for being "morbid," and then signed off as he would a letter: "All the very, very best from Eric Marsh."

In my response tape, I asked him if he remembered, in addition to the reticence he perceived in Horne's first approach, any signs of racial division at the Canteen. In his response, he said that although he could not recall whether black GIs danced, he did remember their presence at the Canteen. He remembered that when Lena Horne kissed the disfigured GI, "it was noticeable that he was white and she was colored." He also remembered that after the initial stunned silence had broken and cheers shook the room, the applause especially emanated from one corner. "The clapping that went on in the black section of the club was fantastic," he told me. By choice or by design—he couldn't say which—black GIs sat grouped together at the far end of the room.[4]

Eric Marsh had come to know about Lena Horne's unequal treatment in Hollywood as a contradiction in U.S. wartime democracy. Dancing with her across this rupture had become an important facet of his dance floor memories of the surreal window of time he spent between his pilot training in Canada and tour of duty in the China-Burma-India theatre of war. With Lena Horne at the Hollywood Canteen, he remembered himself in a cross-national and cross-racial exchange among allies as a dance of equal give and take, equal lead and follow. From his side of our transnational cassette exchange, he communicated his concerns about Bush-Blair war preparation again and again. From my side, I assured him on tape that I shared his concerns about escalating militarism and the tragedy and futility of war. Talking about Lena Horne brought us together.

As a figure in Marsh's narrative, Lena Horne facilitates understanding across differences, a vision of shared and equal transmission of knowledge. Even as I write, I regret that I do not know more about Horne's perspectives beyond the brief mentions she makes of the Canteen in her autobiographies. How, I wonder, did she experience her side of her many dances, songs, and poses that connected her with soldiers, apparently extending the racial possibilities of the dyad? For the black press, Horne's hostess activities at the Hollywood Canteen offer a vision of integration of the democratic dance floor, too. Horne is celebrated in the black newspapers of the day not for the cross-racial connections that characterize Marsh's stories of her but for completing a black soldier-hostess dyad for black soldiers and for her importance as a glamorous black Hollywood film star whose commitments to Double Victory, the African American campaign to link freedom from racism at home and freedom from fascism abroad, include refusing to perform for segregated audiences. In her autobiographies, the Hollywood Canteen appears in a favorable light, always opposed to the segregated USO camp shows. The black press celebrates her dedication to the black troops—refusing to perform on programs that privileged white soldiers (and prisoners of war), financing her own trips to entertain black troops, and embracing the role of the most popular pinup girl for black GIs. I wish I had had the opportunity to talk to her about the extent of integration at the Hollywood Canteen, but she had entered a well-earned retreat from interviews by the time I arrived at this project. Dancing with the writings and interviews where I did find her public statements about the Canteen, I am struck by the extent to which she does not mention spatial segregation at the club, or a shortage of black hostesses, or pressures not to dance across race. The integration at the Canteen appears as an image of what U.S. democracy should look like, as opposed to the stubbornly entrenched segregation of larger, more powerful and pervasive institutions in the United States—even new ones, like the USO camp shows.

A rich and growing body of scholarship on Horne emphasizes the film industry's and the NAACP's treatments of her, which landed her in a contradictory position: breaking down barriers for the race while finding herself increasingly on her own island of Hollywood exceptionalism.[5] Her navigations of the neighborhood, the industry, and the Canteen did not resemble those of white stars in Hollywood. However, they also diverged from those of other black artists in white Hollywood (who were not allowed to be stars). Her unequal treatment swings both ways. The symbolic use of her body as a new model of black womanhood for the screen has been analyzed by many scholars and Horne herself.[6] The gains she made toward lessening her inequality among white actors and actresses landed her in an uneven and confusing landscape that increased her preferential treatment in relation to other African Americans in Los Angeles and in the film industry. Her successes were portrayed by white Hollywood as proof of the absence of racism, and by black Hollywood as evidence of color and phenotype privilege of light skin and European features, tokenism, and the inability of the industry and screen imaginary to find room for multifaceted, talented, and attractive non-white people. I am reminded of my earlier telephone interview with dancer Avanelle Harris, who spent many a film dancing behind Lena Horne and who told me, "Maybe Dorothy [Dandridge] and Lena were there, but it didn't happen for *us* at the Hollywood Canteen."[7]

Horne's dedication to the integrated dance floor at the Hollywood Canteen occurred, and has been written about, as concurrent and in relationship with her public critique of USO camp shows, her insistence on entertainment for African American troops, and her controversial struggle for more dignified representations and roles for black women in the movies. Her refusal to play servants (in the historic negotiation leveraged by Walter White of the NAACP) was controversial among local black actors, dancers, and extras, whose livelihoods depended on such roles. Her groundbreaking residency in Beverly Hills, just down the street from the Bogarts, is dissonant not only in relation to the long commutes of the black women who sometimes worked in Hollywood movies and as Canteen volunteers but also in relation to the black women who literally "lived-in" Hollywood and Beverly Hills as cooks and maids (such as the mother of fellow actor, dancer, and Canteen volunteer Lennie Bluett).

Other black women who danced in the movies, who were popular among black audiences, and who fought civil rights battles alongside (and behind) Lena Horne included actress, dancer, and activist Maggie Hathaway, who was also a golfer (and early leader in the fight to desegregate the sport). In 1962, she founded the Beverly Hills NAACP.[8] After *Cabin in the Sky*, Hathaway not only appeared behind Horne, alongside Avanelle Harris, Doris Ake, Juliet Ball, and other glamorous black actresses but became Horne's regular understudy (and stunt double for her makeup). In 1944, Hathaway participated in the strike of the black female chorus dancers in *Ziegfeld Follies* (1946). Led by another black actress, dancer, and writer, Alice Key, the dancers on strike (a group that included Lena Horne and drew strength from her high-profile presence) demanded that the black women be paid the same as the white women who danced in the film.[9] Hathaway and Key were both listed in Los Angeles black newspapers as hostesses at the Hollywood Canteen, though it does not appear in their own newspaper writing of the period. At the same time that she was an extra and dancer in Hollywood films, a chorine at clubs such as the Cotton Club in Culver City, and a hostess at the Hollywood Canteen, Alice Key wrote a politics and entertainment column for the *Los Angeles Tribune* entitled "Keynotes." In a scathing 1943 indictment of the segregated policies of the USO camp shows and canteens, she wrote, "So, bring it out in the open USO, change your name to Separate Service Organization; or 'straighten up and fly right,' and give us a real United Service Organization!"[10]

Another black Hollywood Canteen hostess, Joan Douglas, made news in the *Chicago Defender* when she ascended the stage and objected to the use of the N-word by "Captain Jack," a radio host on KDCA. " 'Sir,' she asked, looking him squarely in the eye, 'didn't you say just now to the crowd that 'we must speak American, be American, and act American?' " When he upheld that he had, she announced that he had insulted a group of Americans and owed them an apology. He asked her to apologize for him, and she refused. He was the one who should apologize for his actions. He refused. Hollywood Canteen hostess captain Billye Muse (in charge of black hostesses one night a week and the wife of actor Clarence Muse) wrote a letter of complaint to the radio station. Billye Muse's war work not only included recruiting "10–20 hostesses, who are to report to her at the Canteen one night a week"[11] but also backing them up when their experiences and observations of racism met with ambivalence. In addition, she and other black hostess captains were often called on to rustle up black hostesses at a moment's notice to steady the ever-changing demographic "line."

Mary Ford (wife of director John Ford) was in charge of white hostesses. In an interview with her grandson, she told of occasions when she issued requests for additional black hostesses after word reached the Canteen that large numbers of black military men were heading their way. As she put it, whenever the situation threatened to get "out of line," they were soon "put back in line" by actor Clarence Muse ("a little guy from Harlem") and his wife, Billye. For instance, she recalled, "We were notified at the last minute from San Bernardino that there was a regiment of blacks going through to the Far East and they would like [to see] the Hollywood Canteen. So we called the Muses and they hurried that ball up."[12]

Importation of black hostesses for clubs in locations where black people did not—and were not allowed to—live was a common "solution" for some USOs and USO-like canteens that operated in liberal white spaces. Although the black press critiqued Jim Crow canteens that turned black soldiers away, the same newspapers did not critique importation of black hostesses to integrate clubs in white areas. Instead, the readiness of black communities in supplying last-minute hostesses was celebrated as double victory (against racism at home and fascism abroad), not double labor. In a March 1943 story in the *California Eagle*, Florence Cadrez was congratulated for securing "Mates for Sailors" when a Canteen "Officer of the Day" "received a call from Port Hueneme that 90 Negro sailors were arriving at the Hollywood Canteen in two hours. Through the cooperation of Florence Cadrez, Negro hostess and canteen representative of Musicians Local 767, 30 Negro girls were ready and waiting when the sailors arrived."[13] The dependence of the integrated Hollywood Canteen on the lengthy commutes of black women from the Eastside on an on-call basis must be seen from a variety of perspectives. We could see it as disrupting Jim Crow in Hollywood, as upholding same-race couple dancing on a "together but unequal" space, and even as "protecting"/preventing white women from dancing with black men. What differences might the presence of black hostesses have made in Mel Bryant's narrative? Were things not "out of line" enough on the nights he was there for Mary Ford to call in the reserves? Were black hostesses overextended across greater Los Angeles on those evenings, completing the black dyads at Eastside canteens and far-flung caravans to wherever black troops were camped? Or were black hostesses in the room but not in his memory? What differences would black hostess encounters have made in his interpretation of democracy on the dance floor at the Hollywood Canteen? I don't know.

The list of black women summoned from the Eastside to the Hollywood Canteen by Mary Ford, Billye and Clarence Muse, Florence Cadrez, and the people on their phone trees included Jeni LeGon, who recalled bringing her chorus line and dance students to the Canteen two or three times a month between November 1942 and April 1943.

Break-away: Jeni LeGon

Jeni LeGon (born Jennie May Ligon) was a well-established dancer in theaters and movies, chorus line organizer, and dance teacher at the time of her Canteen work. When I interviewed her in 2004 and 2005, she continued to enjoy, in her late eighties, status as a master teacher and celebrity amid the tap revival. She maintained an active schedule, traveling the world, giving workshops, and telling about her long career, which extended from the chorus line of the Count Basie Orchestra in the early thirties to a couple of seasons on black vaudeville with the Whitman Sisters and more jobs that she could actually accept as a team with her foster sister, Willa Mae Lane. In our conversation, she situated her Canteen work within a longer story of her career as a dancer in and out of Hollywood and her eventual relocation to Vancouver in 1969. She told me she knew that things had improved in the United States but that she had found Canada a better place to live. "I've had all sorts of horrible things happen to me because my face is brown and I don't like to talk about it, so

I don't talk about the subject. I'm here in Canada, and I've been treated like a person, and I like it."[14]

Though best known as a "hoofer" who preferred to dance in a white tuxedo rather than a skirt, and who performed the athletic tap styles associated with male dancers such as the Nicholas Brothers, LeGon emphasized variety and range of styles within and beyond tap when she told me of her life in dance. The Whitman Sisters, she said, "had a complete show" that included their own band and a line of "eight dancing girls" who performed tap and soft-shoe but also "some Afro-style dancing. Not like Dunham's things . . . these were just kind of off-the-hand; not really authentic, but interesting . . . The dancing was very varied. We did waltzes, and all that sort of thing. And we had, by that time, too, we had one soloist *en pointe*, a little black girl *en pointe*, yeah, she was very good."[15] The Whitmans were famous for the sister team of Alice and Bert, the latter of whom performed in pants. In Jeni's opinion, Alice was the best of all the dancers. "Oh, she was just an excellent dancer. I mean she did it all. She could do all the ballet-style like Eleanor [Powell]. And then she could hoof."[16]

LeGon arrived in Los Angeles in 1934 at the age of seventeen, when she and Willa Mae were recruited for a job that didn't materialize. The team went their separate ways, and as a solo artist LeGon caught the attention of Earl Dancer, who became her manager. She signed a multiyear contract with MGM. In *Ali Baba Goes to Town* (1937), she descends a stairway in turkey feathers and tap shoes; her role is a figment of Eddie Cantor's character's imagination in a larger dream-amnesia sequence that makes up the bulk of the movie. While Cantor sings "Swing Is Here to Sway" in blackface and an "Arab" costume, and a chorus of African American extras, singers, and dancers—dressed as nonspecific happy "natives" of the white imagination—pretend to play the swing soundtrack on prop "primitive" instruments, LeGon executes eighty-seven seconds of tap artistry, much of it on her toes, leading up to a sequence of toe-stand arabesques. Toe-stands were among the "flash" steps considered the purview of male "hoofers"; indeed LeGon is one of the few African American women solo "hoofers" we can see in the entire history of the movies. Her ballerina gestures feminize the steps without detracting from her tap chops, and in emphasizing the black woman's toe-stand as ballet *pointe*, she challenges dance stereotypes of race and gender at the same time.[17] To the uninitiated, "hoofing" and "hoofer" may not sound like positive descriptions of a tap artists' trade, but indeed "hoofing," now more likely called "rhythm tap," is the cream of the dance and usually reserved for men. Behind her in the "Swing Is Here to Sway" number, another future Canteen volunteer, Lennie Bluett, in loincloth and feather headdresses, "plays" his

FIG 6.2: At least three future Hollywood Canteen volunteers in the number "Swing Is Here to Sway," in *Ali Baba Goes to Town* (MGM, 1937): Eddie Cantor (in turban and blackface), Jeni LeGon (in turkey feathers), and Lennie Bluett (flute-playing chorus member in loincloth). PHOTOFEST.

flute held out in front, adopting the stance of a swing clarinetist: lifting and lowering his instrument, leaning backward, his legs bent at the knees. He towers over the other extras, but it isn't just his height that makes him stand out. He accentuates his sway and two-step background choreography with relaxed hip movements and awareness of the camera. Even in chorus and crowd scenes, he is seldom upstaged. The official star, of course, is Cantor in blackface. However, for those eighty seconds when Jeni LeGon taps on her toes, she steals the show.

In our interview, she stressed variety and professionalism in her career as a dancer and teacher—and the limits of Hollywood for black artists. Her dance sequences were often truncated or cut—a pattern she attributed to the jealousy of powerful white women stars. She landed a role in a London production of *Follow the Sun*, which ran for a year. On her return to Los Angeles, she worked in films as well as in Central Avenue theaters and nightclubs. In 1941, she helped her brother, Alfred Ligon, to purchase books in preparation of opening the first black bookstore in Los Angeles, which stayed in business until 1994.[18] She ran her dance school out of the same building on East Jefferson in the Central Avenue district. She hired dancer Archie Savage and a

Russian ballet teacher from St. Petersburg who "had never worked with black people before." She created shows with her students, and they performed in theaters. "My girl dancers—all sixteen of them were *en pointe.*" She told a story of a program she showcased with her students after the school closed. It included a ballet number as well as a piece honoring Congo Square in New Orleans, set to a poem by Paul Laurence Dunbar. Afterward, a writer from the *Los Angeles Times* told her the show was great—then added, "But I don't think the times are right for black girls *en pointe.*"

In the midst of her varied career—running her dance school, performing with her chorus line, dancing in clubs and theaters and in the movies—she received a call from "someone at the Canteen" who had discovered she had a chorus line of other black women. "They just called me directly and asked me if I could bring the girls down. At first I objected," she explained, since they made it clear that they were calling her because "they needed black girls to dance with the black boys." She replied, " 'Well, I don't like that.' And they said, 'Well, that's the rules,' or something like that." She thought it over and decided to take her dancers up to the club. "I figured, well, the boys were putting their lives on it, so it didn't hurt us to do that, you know. I didn't like it particularly."

And so her Canteen story begins with compromise. She agrees to go, not out of approval of the Canteen as a symbol of democracy but in order to support black soldiers who will be ignored otherwise in a club that white liberals think is integrated. Black hostesses, in her interpretation, were imported to protect white hostesses from black men who were presumed to be predators of white women. LeGon's memory places black hostesses in the same project as the Shore Patrol in protecting whiteness, promoting a particular vision of freedom from which they did not benefit. She recalled that the city had far more welcoming places for black soldiers in the Eastside. "They could come to the black clubs, in the black neighborhood, which was Central Avenue, of course. We had a whole bunch of clubs and they could come there and have a ball if they wanted to, you know. But the Hollywood Canteen was supposed to be top dog . . . so, naturally everybody wanted to go . . . because it was Class A."

> But one night . . . there was one white boy on the floor dancing with different girls and they weren't dancing very well, and I was dancing with one of the black boys, and [the white boy] was watching me and I was watching him because he was such a damn good dancer, you know? So, anyway, what turned out was that he came and asked me to dance with him and I said sure. And we went out and started jittering, and everybody on the floor moved out and let us take the floor and we just had a ball. And he

and I danced all over that bloody room that time. And everybody just stood back and cheered and carried on, and it was really fun. I mean, you know, just the black and white thing and that was the end of it, but this particular night, we showed them it just didn't have to be that way. We were just rhythmically wedded, you know what I mean, we just danced similarly and we were good together. And so that's what it was. He'd throw me out and I'd come back, we'd do the boogie, all that sort of business. It was just a fun thing, and we were having such a good time, he and I, you know, enjoying one another's ability to do the things that we could do together, not having seen one another or known anything about one another before.

LeGon represents herself as a political actor who intervenes in her intended role as a political action figure. She torques back by narrating herself and her dance partner as modeling alternative notions of dance floor democracy, as other national subjects watch and cheer. In saying "yes" to the white soldier, not because she "can't say no" but because she thinks he is a damn good dancer, she is saying "no" to a nation that imagines black male predators and white female prizes. And in narrating this dance as taking place in a segregated environment, she says "no" to Hollywood's claims to color-blindness—as a part of town, an industry, or a dreamscape, inside or outside the Canteen. In addition, in narrating her white male partner as dancing *well*, and their dance together as achieving a more effective *torque* than either of them had been able to achieve with their same-race dance partners, she says "no" to what Jon Michael Spencer calls the "essentialist color-line," the logic that says white men can't dance or swing and black women can't dance *en pointe*.[19] In highlighting this particular dance in relation to less satisfying partnerships leading up to it, her story acknowledges that democratic outcomes were not achieved for and by every Canteen-goer in every pairing but at the same time stakes a compelling claim for its potential. Her hopeful and positive picture of integrated dancing at the Hollywood Canteen is not depicted as representative, guaranteed, or taken for granted. It is achieved in the moment, among thinking dancers cocreating embodied connections through mutual attentiveness to each other's moves. In this "we showed them" story, in which the "we" is herself and a white male partner working well together, and the "them" is the other people at the Hollywood Canteen, LeGon claims agency for black hostesses and mutually attentive dancers of all races as people who figure out how to work well together through dance. Her story of dancing across race at the Hollywood Canteen torques back, which is not to say that it is a counter-narrative. While critical of the official story, her story locates democratic potential in a vision of interracial jitterbugging at the Hollywood Canteen.

The idealized image of the soldier-hostess jitterbugging couple at the Hollywood Canteen was presented as a national icon from the moment the club opened in 1942. It has been rolled out periodically ever since. The first person narrations touched on in this chapter and chapters 4 and 5 have traced the steps that link memories of dancing at the Hollywood Canteen with notion of national unity and likeability, but also have faced the nostalgia from many perspectives and stretched it in many directions. Even stories that caressed the sentiments attached to the nostalgia offered insights into the difference it makes to imagine the dyad from one or another side—to think more like dancers about dance floor democracy.

As I listened to former Canteen-goers navigate the social geographies of memory, narrating in the present their youthful swing dancing bodies moving through patriotically charged space, I heard refrains of the unified feel-good version of World War II, danced in different ways. The variety of flows, and pushes, and turns that materialized when people told stories that danced with and against the footsteps of the idealized jitterbug couple conjured a conception of dance floor democracy with less and more room to move than that of the idealized Canteen. They reveal not only more restrictions but more interpretative space, less predictable outcomes, more critique.

In fact, one could say that in their differences, dissonances, and sporadically achieved *torque*, these stories suggest more democracy than the ideal, if the goal of a democratic dance floor is not just to stage "big shots being friendly to little shots" or promote dyad-democracy in which wholeness is achieved by dividing people in half and matching (some of) them in ideologically appropriate pairs. The variety of perspectives on the Hollywood Canteen pooled in these three chapters suggests a dance floor democracy that is *not* unified but that creates a space where all orientations pull, all touches transmit and receive signals, and all bodies (even injured ones) are weighted into the equation.

However, it wasn't just the military men and civilian women who participated in tracing, touching, and torquing the steps of the soldier-hostess dyad. In the next part, we will explore the perspectives of some (then) young civilian men and military women who narrated their memories of participating in the Hollywood Canteen outside the soldier-hostess dyad.

PART III WOMEN IN UNIFORMS, MEN IN APRONS

★ ★

DANCING OUTSIDE THE SOLDIER-HOSTESS DYAD

CHAPTER 7

The Dyad from Without

A new doorman, quite the dashing figure, drew cold glances from a couple of tables of service men when he tried to be too pleasant. Later a soldier with a group looked at him and said "A 4F." The others were embarrassed, laughed, and tried to shut him up, saying "You mustn't say things like that." "Well, he is," smiled the other. "Well, be more— more tactful or something." they said, still having trouble concealing their mirth. It was a good lesson for me for they didn't take that attitude toward me.
—DONALD VINING, DIARY (DECEMBER 25, 1943)

As required by Marine Corps regulations my friends and I were dressed in our Marine Corps uniforms for our big night on the town. We were full of anticipation as we reached the front door of the Hollywood Canteen. However, the star dust was about to be brushed from our eyes.

The front door to the Hollywood Canteen had a gatekeeper. His appearance made no impression on me, but his words did. He told us we could not come in. He directed us to go around the building to the back. At the back of the building we were allowed to enter the back door and climb the stairs to the balcony. From that vantage point we were permitted to sit quietly and watch the servicemen dancing with young women in beautiful gowns on the main floor.
—MARIE PROULOX, IN LINDA CATES LACY, *WE ARE MARINES!* (2004)

From December 1943 to November 1944, aspiring writer and studio janitor Donald Vining volunteered weekly alongside other hosts and hostesses at the Hollywood Canteen, where he stargazed as he worked.[1] To the music of the big bands, Vining carried a tray laden with dirty dishes back and forth across the room, guiding it around, behind, and above the heads of jitterbugging soldier-hostess dyads. Deftly maneuvering between clusters of tables around the dance floor to the designated areas of the kitchen, he collected abandoned plates, washed dishes as needed, and carted whatever needed to be transported between the kitchen and the snack bar and back.

What he did *not* do on the dance floor of the Hollywood Canteen, however, was dance; nor was he authorized to converse at length with military guests. Neither a soldier nor a hostess, Vining's ticket to dance floor democracy was his volunteerism as a busboy. His war work consisted of cleaning up after young men his own age whose bodies indicated an entirely different category of civic belonging than his own, a difference immediately legible in dress: they wore uniforms, he wore civilian clothes, and over those, an apron. Still, like a dancer, his repertoire required quick crowd assessment, crucial for continuous movement without dropping the endless stacks of trays and dishes and cups in his care. His attention scanned and settled not only on people but on openings between them. He noticed tactile details—the trays, for example, were smaller than those he had carted at the Stage Door Canteen in New York (March–August 1943) before traveling west. They were also *cleaner* because of the portable sandwich cuisine rather than the gobs of "cake icing and watermelon messiness" that gummed up the trays in the other canteen—giving him more time to observe the official entertainment and equally entertaining sociality among movie industry hosts and military guests. While there was less variety in the acts, he noted, there were more stars showing up at the West Coast club, since film actors worked by day and had their nights free.[2]

Draft-aged and apparently able-bodied—capable, in any case, of meeting the requirements of busing tables in a joint that served three thousand military guests a night—Vining was well aware of the resentment his civilian volunteer body might elicit from men in uniform. The sandwiches, music, stars, and dance partners were for them, but it was his privilege—however hard he had to work—to be part of the scene every week for the duration. He could not partner with stars and starlets while they danced and mingled, but his proximity to them was in some ways more intimate, as he worked alongside them while they also bused tables, washed dishes, made sandwiches, and served at the counter. Publicity about celebrity busboys, such as Spencer Tracy and Gig Young, showed them signing autographs as well as busing tables and often carried captions indicating their impending inductions. However, the dance of the noncelebrity, draft-exempt civilian busboy demanded humility as part of his performance of stateside elective KP. As he moved through this space, he watched the behaviors of other young male volunteers for clues to the way to mingle in this crowd without attracting the resentment, envy, and suspicion that followed young civilian men in this time of war.

On Christmas 1943, Vining observed intently as the new doorman stumbled in his role. The gatekeeper was "too pleasant," "dashing," and handsome!—all missteps in a system of civilian male dance floor democracy. Draft-age civilian men attracted suspicion; the possibility that they were "crazy," "lazy," "perverted," "criminal," and "contagious" was etched into public consciousness. Rosie the Riveter gained acceptance as a temporary defense industry worker in the public imaginary. (In fact, some of the young women who danced as hostesses also worked a shift at Lockheed and other defense plants, though many were probably imagined by their dance partners as starlets.) The young woman who volunteered at the Hollywood Canteen in a party dress was a patriot. However, the man out of uniform needed an alibi—he was going overseas next month, he was too young, too old. He might redeem himself by expressing his disappointment about a minor medical discovery—flat feet or an irregular heartbeat—that he was obligated to bitterly resent and perhaps fight to have waived. Expressions of disappointment were de rigueur in this highly gendered civilian-military dance of sacrifice, service, and rationed wartime pleasure. He must keep hidden all hints of uninterrupted career, education, family, sweetheart, or sense of personal safety. Vining watched men in uniform as they watched civilian men, trying to decode what it was that caused one to draw their ire and another to fly under the radar. What were the best options for performing his serving body in this economy of looks that reflected the questions of others? How could he do so without denying his own subjective experience?

After witnessing the group of soldiers as they poked fun at the "dashing doorman," he turned to his diary. That night, he contemplated the ugly event, deciphering the sequence of refracted looking, movement, and space in which the doorman had been marked as an object of derision. He concluded this entry with a lesson that would affect his own repertoire of behavior as a Canteen volunteer: "Too much charm in a man draws suspicion and doesn't become them. I had begun to suspect I'd be wise never to try charm again and now I see that it's the worst thing one can do with other men."[3]

Break-away: Busboy in the Archive

I never interviewed Donald Vining (1917–1998). He passed away just before I began the research for this book. Still, I ran into him repeatedly while searching for dancers at the Hollywood Canteen. My search for interviewees drew friendly tips from fellow web surfers, at least two of whom recommended Vining's published diary excerpts.[4] Intrigued by the perspectives recorded and published in his *Gay Diary* (1979), I found my way to the hundreds of pages of typed single-spaced diary pages he donated to his alma mater, Yale University. I allocated two days for Yale—foolishly thinking that would be sufficient time to tackle the three and a half linear feet of paper, mostly diaries (1928–1929, 1932–1958, 1971–1985). Adjusting to the vast landscape of carts and boxes before me, I narrowed my scope to the war years.

The diaries beckoned again at the Manuscripts and Archives Division of the New York Public Library while I was looking for something else. I gave in to the pull and revisited Vining's accounts of 1944, just in case I had missed something—and wound up spending another day absorbing his day-to-day observations, once again imagining myself moving through Canteen space through Vining's point of view. This time, I noticed different details, people, and events, and I "heard" my guide in new ways: another reminder that although *being* Vining and reading his diaries are not the same thing, and entering an archive and entering a nightclub are different activities for sure, the two do have some things in common. I rushed to make the most of my encounters with Vining's papers during quick out-of-town trips. As at the Canteen, the intimacy of this dance was overseen by chaperones, in this case the vigilant professionals who preserve the life of paper that can so utterly enrich our life in the flesh.

My moves outside the soldier-hostess dyad, in this chapter and in chapters 8 and 9, begin with my archival encounters with Vining, because he opens many perspectives and pathways. Like diarist Jane Lockwood, Vining did not conclude his Canteen night until he reclaimed it through narrative. He chronicled his shifting embodied perspective into observations about the military guests, the stars and starlets glimpsed, or even spoken to, often lingering on fleeting flirtations that may have lasted longer in the writing than the real-time Canteen encounters. However, unlike the female civilian volunteers of his age group, Vining's reports of his navigations through Canteen space chart perspectives connected to, though resolutely outside, the soldier-hostess dyad. His perspectives take in other events and people that did not appear in other sources, including a group that also participated largely outside the soldier-hostess dyad: military women.

In chapter 8, I will dance with the servicewomen I found who had been at the Canteen, most of whom told of not being allowed to dance there. My archive for that chapter is primarily the responses I received from a call for memories that I posted in the online database of the Women in Military Service for America Memorial in Washington, D.C., in the spring of 2001: "Did you ever dance at the Hollywood Canteen?"[5] This posting quickly circulated in military women's listservs, newsletters, and reunions. Letters and emails poured in, often with return address labels and electronic signatures indicating the sender's rank and service branch. Most of these communications were fleeting, just long enough for the transmission of a quick report of exclusion, compromise, or explanation. There was some variation, but a strong patterned emerged in a narrative arc in which *exiting* the Canteen, rather than entering, was the turn that "writes/rights" the subject. Not all women veterans told the same story, but strains of misrecognition and reorientation ran through most.

My dances with civilian male volunteers in chapter 9 take on quite a different array of shapes, narratives, moves, personal contacts, and directions. The networks of communication that exist for the servicewomen do not exist for civilian men who volunteered as busboys at the Canteen. My encounters with civilian men were often facilitated through introductions: someone would hear of my work and tell me of someone who had gone there. Usually, this narrator would turn out to be a civilian woman or military man, but on occasion I would meet a male civilian volunteer. Because of the passage of time, perhaps, or because of the stigmas attached to draft-aged civilian men during World War II, the male volunteers did not usually talk about why they weren't in uniform at that time. For the same reasons, I didn't ask. The two longer "break-aways" in chapter 9 provide busboy observations that settle on different details from Vining's in many ways but that also facilitate alternative views that complicate the dance.

Draft-aged civilian men and military women had much, and little, in common. There is no reason to believe that they identified with one another. Nor is there any reason to presume that either group attended the Hollywood Canteen having any more or less sense of service to others, to the nation, or to the four freedoms—or any less or more desire for fun or release—than civilian women and military men had. Both groups were often the brunt of jokes and the objects of resentment, misrecognition, and invisibility, even as they volunteered their labor and time to support the war effort. Did the presence of actual military women and draft-aged civilian men at the Hollywood Canteen potentially throw off balance the primacy of the soldier-hostess dyad, with its projection of a powerful vision of postwar normalcy (conservative and youthful, multicultural and white, at the same time)? Or did their presence provide useful "others" against which to shore up idealized norms?

The Hollywood Canteen, like most other sites of soldier entertainment, inherited and incorporated flows of gender management that permeated home front public spheres. Feminine respectability and masculine (and emasculated) humility underwrite the rules and experiences and memories concerning military women and civilian men. Military women could be separated from, while helping to forge, the soldier-hostess dyad by being elevated above it. At the same time, their effectiveness as soldiers was often neutralized in popular culture by comic portrayals that constructed military women as immature, goofy, man-crazy girls. In *Here Come the WAVES*, Betty Hutton exclaims to Bing Crosby, "I—*even I*—replaced a man. Johnny, there are fellas out there chasing Zeros around that were taught to fly by me. Me! Susie Screwball!"[6] This ostensibly pro-WAVE speech rationalizes servicewomen's value by minimizing their skills.

Civilian men at the Hollywood Canteen participated in the construction of military masculinity by following gender-differentiated rules for volunteers—while hostesses were supposed to be vivacious and charming, busboys recalled being told to keep their socializing to a minimum. At the same time, on the stage, the self-deprecating humor of comedians such as Bob Hope constructed military masculine ideals by portraying civilian men as cowardly, out of shape, and sissified. Performances such as Danny Kaye's "Melody in 4-F" (often performed at the Canteen) portrayed disciplining of masculinity as a comical regimen that could take pathetic, abject male bodies and build them into war-ready 1-A condition. As servicemen applauded and laughed, their civilian counterparts carried their dirty dishes to the kitchen.

Regardless of their labor, circumstances, intentions, motivations, commitments, and/or desires, women in uniform and men out of uniform often acted as lightning rods for national anxieties about gender stability and national unity. The purpose of a lightning rod is not to harness power but to neutralize trouble. However, perspectives gather from those subject positions, and memories adhere in the thinking bodies that moved in these spaces. People made sense of their experiences by telling embodied stories of Canteen visits from the vantage points of these very different routes outside the soldier-hostess dyad. In pushing them together, I am looking for that trouble.

Dissonance in 4-F

Vining could very well have been in uniform, rather than an apron, had he differently answered a key question in the psychiatric round of his physical exam. "Do you get along with women all right?" His vision exam classified him for noncombat duty, but it was his equivocations to the women question—his stammering and hesitation—that completed the plummet of his 1-A to 4-F, earning him the medical tag "Sui generistic 'H' overt." By the time his file was shipped back to his hometown draft board in Bordentown, Pennsylvania, this tag had been translated into "homosexualism-overt." As a gay man who was already "out" among family and friends, to have this sort of note in his official record had less devastating effects than it did for many others. In his diary, he wrote, "I don't give a hoot for my own part. It's only the effect on Mother, who's really known about town."[7] Nonetheless, as a dedicated pacifist, Vining perceived this sexual alibi for his military absentia as a misdiagnosis. His sexuality was decidedly not the foundation of why he did not want to serve in the armed forces—in fact, in many entries, he rues the ethics he holds that will not allow him to explore the homosocial opportunities of military service. Draft exemption due to sexual orientation was not consistent with his ethical code (and was, of course, problematic in light of the many gay soldiers who did serve, as well as in light of the medical classification of those of all sexual orientations as gay and their suffering as a result of this "outing" at the draft board). Still, even with all of the ethical problems involved, the draft exemption that resulted from what Vining saw as an illogical consequence of being identified as gay was more convenient than the alternatives.

If Vining's sexual orientation had not earned him a 4-F, he was prepared to follow through with a plan that more accurately represented his motives for seeking draft exemption. Vining was a "moral pacifist": not a member of a historic "peace" church (like the Society of Friends or the Mennonites) but an individual whose antiwar stance was a matter of political conviction and conscience. This was something he believed he could prove in court, using pacifist entries from his prewar diaries. Being classified 4-F was only preferable to him on economic grounds. A conscientious objector (CO) camp run by the Quakers might have been able to waive the $35/month room-and-board fee for a pacifist without means (even a nonchurchgoer such as himself), but the loss of his wages would cause hardship for his dependent mother and grandmother. His janitorial job in the Hollywood motion picture industry provided rent for a furnished apartment and left him enough money to send home. As he had previously rationalized in New York while busing tables at the Stage Door Canteen, volunteering at the Hollywood Canteen gave him a way to do something for the men and women in service without supporting militarism itself.

Although national memory preserves the sense that the draft was respected by most Americans during World War II and that COs were reviled, it is worth remembering that pacifism was more tolerated at the onset of World War II than it had been in World War I and that the first peacetime draft in U.S. history (1940) was controversial in its time and barely passed. Cynthia Eller writes that the legal parameters of CO status during World War II expanded beyond membership in historic peace churches, due to anti-war activism and lobbying by those very churches committed to pacifism, to include all those "'who by reasons of religious training and belief' were 'opposed to war in any form' and to allow them to either serve as noncombatants in the army or to be engaged in 'work of national importance under civilian direction.'" The Burke-Wadsworth Bill, passed on September 16, 1940, promised that draftees would not be sent outside the Western Hemisphere, "except in American possessions and territories," and conscripted service would be for no longer than one year. When this was extended to eighteen months in 1941, it only passed in the House by a single vote. Not until the attack on Pearl Harbor was the Selective Service Act amended to permit draftees to be sent anywhere the U.S. military wished to send them and to extend the length of service to "the duration of the war plus 6 months."[8] Despite this increased official tolerance for pacifists, cos during World War II, whether or not they participated in war work and war-related volunteerism, were constructed as, and popularly considered "shirkers, not workers," cowards, possibly queer, and/or "un-American." Politically, the general public perceived them much as they perceived Communists. Nonetheless, these categories were markedly different, especially after June 22, 1941, when the Soviet Union and the United States were joined as allies in the war and American Communists rallied in support of the war effort.

Out gay man, pacifist, "4-F," and would-be "co"—Vining's subject positions combine several unpopular orientations, any one of which would clash with normative ideals of military masculinity (constructed as heterosexual, combat ready, healthy, and 100 percent behind the war effort). Of course, not all draft-exempt men shared any, or all, of Vining's "outsider" positions (and not all drafted and enlisted men were heterosexual or fit all the other categories of normative military masculinity).

In contrast to diarist Jane Lockwood, who narrates the pleasures of being the center of attention when she dances with the exuberant, jitterbugging sailor, the crowd backing away to make space for the spectacle, Vining logs himself as a stealth observer—not one who peers in from the sidelines (as the military women were invited to do) but a witness-participant who catches the sights, the sounds, the heat of kinetic energy from the center of action, while flying under the radar, tray in tow, perpetually in motion, weaving in and around the men in uniform and the Canteen hostesses. Nonetheless, that doesn't mean that he does not find his own ways of recognizing and enjoying the looks of others, even of exchanging admiring glances, or of positioning himself in ways to look at the young men of his generation. In his diary he records his attractions in ways that would have been considered harmless and even patriotic (in a moderate "khaki-wacky" sort of way) when observed in a youthful hostess but would have been seen as threatening to military masculinity, even predatory, if detected in Vining's visible performance. On his first night as a volunteer, December 17, 1943, he writes: "Went over to the canteen about nine and had to stand in line a while to register. As there was a window from which I could observe the floor and as my eye lit on a gorgeous sailor, I didn't mind. I could have just sat and looked at him for at least 48 hours without tiring."[9]

He writes about looking at handsome men and about his sexual aspirations and fantasies, who he'd like to be with; he also records the care he must take in concealing his glances:

> Honestly, I could just settle for looking at some of those fellows. I'd ask no more than just to be able to rest my eyes on them without having to look the other way now and then. I stare anyway, but once in a while I do remember that one is taught not to and look the other way.[10]

Sara Ahmed in her book *Queer Phenomenology* poses the question: What difference does it make to turn one way and not another? For Ahmed, the "queer" in "queer phenomenology" is not rooted in identity and object choice but is about directional orientation within a network of straight lines that run through fields of power such as gender, sexuality, race, politics, and other strong social currents. Vining self-consciously and repeatedly adjusts his alignment as he works. How he turns affects which "worlds come into view" for him, as Ahmed puts it, and these in turn affect who he becomes, how he turns, and so on. In remembering that "one is taught" not to look at other men, Vining feels the pull of what Ahmed calls the "straight line." He also "queers" the "straightening effects" by leaning away, charting a "slant-wise" orientation that helps us not so much to debunk the democratic dance floor as to consider additional dissonance in the ways people moved through it and how it appears from slantwise perspectives.[11]

His diary entries track his day-to-day lessons in Canteen space as he learns how to move within it as a desiring subject with a low profile.

> The kitchen isn't a bad place to work because if there are any celebrities present, they go thru there on their way in and out. But of course one sees no service men, and from my point of view it is therefore not so desirable.[12]

In entry after entry, Vining "writes" himself into the national "we" of the Hollywood Canteen, not exactly by "righting" himself in relation to the Canteen or even by "righting" the Canteen so that the picture includes him. Instead, he writes the shifting landscape from a tilted and partial perspective—again, a dancing narrative that maps the constraints of the club, as well as his moves, from his perspective as a gay man, a "4-F," and a lifelong pacifist. He looks, he stops looking, he stares anyway, he catches himself, he looks away, he writes about it later. He steals his pleasures on the democratic dance floor and again, more freely, in his diary (a writing form in which confessions and secrets are straight lines, after all). He struggles with his conscience about whether his Canteen work is at odds with his pacifism, while performing that service as humble.

Vining records the blockages and pathways against and through which he veers off the line, finding a way through dance floor democracy in much the same way he navigates the crowd without dropping trays of dishes. In feeling the pull of dominant wartime masculinity, while also feeling his unfitting relationship to it, he leans away, recording insights into not only his own difference, but the ill fit of gender norms to much of what he sees. Through observation, overhearing of gossip, and new working friendships he gathers information about masculinity that is actually *useful* to him.

On Sunday, January 23, 1944, a fellow volunteer tells him that actor Alan Ladd, who is on the "short side," wears "lifts and also had to have his ears pulled back with some sort of suction device they fasten on." Vining seems delighted when he concludes, "Thus is a leading man constructed." The same night, the free-flowing gossip of his workmates verifies his hunch that the handsome actor Van Johnson is gay. It is an all-round jackpot night when he makes the happy discovery that Lon Chaney and Broderick Crawford, two actors he perceives as patently unattractive, have beautiful young wives.

> Perhaps it's not beyond hoping that I may someday enjoy possession of handsome fellows who now see me and move on to other pastures. Of course the setup is not quite the same, but still . . . [13]

But what kind of setup is it? On April 20, 1944, he reports, "There were so many handsome and attractive men in today that I was simply surfeited," and wonders if Hollywood exceptionalism is exerting a dulling effect. "Good looks are so common one's senses don't respond as they would to pulchritude where it is in its normal proportion."[14] He describes the soldiers who look at him, those who are handsome, those who are too chatty and awkward, those who stick around, and those who wander away. He struggles, not with his sexuality per se, but with his concerns about his political commitment to pacifism in light of how much he is enjoying entertaining the troops. A queer, male, pacifist, co civilian at a wartime dance for military men and civilian women, Vining nonetheless finds much at the Canteen to suggest visions of a better world.

He writes of his joy at watching two men—one in the uniform of the army and one in the Marines—jitterbugging together:

The spotlight was turned on them and they went to town, whirling around in each other's arms, legs flying every whichway. Somehow it looks perfectly all right for two men to jitterbug together, since it's a very strenuous dance and one that minimizes bodily contact except of the hands. I wish I could jitterbug. It's wonderfully barbaric and exciting, albeit not graceful to watch.[15]

While his pleasure in the soldier-soldier dyad queers the Canteen line in some respects, in perceiving the jitterbug as a "barbaric and exciting" pathway to white gay liberation, he travels the same straight line of whiteness as Lockwood's dance with the jitterbug-sailor. He also struggles with his compromised position as a Canteen worker who is supporting the troops from a pacifist orientation.

He is pulled in another queer pacifist direction when he finds himself bursting with admiration for military women. On April 2, 1944, he writes of an inspiring vision of gender democracy in his observations of a coeducational group of Marines.

It was grand to see men and women marines working together, in one instance, singing together. It made it seem as tho [sic] men and women were really in this war together, something one doesn't ordinarily feel in America, most women taking a back seat. There should be many times the women in service than there are and they should work closely with the men. Many good marriages might result, with couples that knew how to work side by side. [16]

There are many ironies to Vining's idea for what would be good for "men and women in America" amounts to heterosexual companionate marriage among military personnel. However, his diary is full of surprising pulls and turns in his detailed narrations of his thinking body darting in and out of sudden openings and beholding the unexpected. He is drawn to differently gendered bodies in the Hollywood Canteen for what they say about inclusiveness, equality, and power sharing. In this sense, the mixed-sex singing Marines, like the same-sex jitterbugging military men, *did* present a queer image of democracy in that they bend the norm—in this case, by performing sex difference of equal rank.[17]

He objects to what he sees as the overt marginalization of military women. On June 11, 1944, he observes that the isolated room where military women are sent when they enter the Canteen has been improved. A ceremony has even been held to move them from what he describes as their "awful little cubby hole" at the back to their newly opened segregated balcony near the stage.[18] He remains attentive to their plight, and the following month he describes the mezzanine space where military women were waited on by a designated busboy (usually actor Rod Cameron during Vining's Sunday afternoon shifts). On July 30, 1944, he writes, "Rod doesn't much like his job of waiting on the service women, not just because of their adulation, but also because of the running up and down stairs it entails, I gather."[19] On August 20, 1944, Vining, himself was "detailed to wait on the women, and a very attractive lot they were, too," he wrote, "especially the Marines, who seem in general to be the best-looking women in the service. It kept me stepping for awhile and then died down."[20]

What did the dance floor look like from the point of view of a good-looking Marine Corps WR (Women's Reserve) from her perch in the mezzanine? What sense of belonging was conferred when civilian men took turns running upstairs with snacks while she watched dancing couples on the floor? Marie Proulox had the "stardust brushed from her eyes" when she and her friends were refused entry in their WR uniforms.[21] They didn't even make it inside to an isolated observation room. Marie Haynes, a WAVE, remembered that she was gazing down at "servicemen dancing with the movie stars" when "an actor named Rod Cameron" gave her a kiss on the cheek. Her account does not confirm the "adulation" of servicewomen toward Cameron that Vining records. "He was not one of the better known actors," she recalled, but he did "come up in the balcony and mingle amongst us." He gave her his autograph before he went back down the stairs. "We did enjoy listening to the dance music and watching the servicemen and actresses dancing. I don't know why we sat in the balcony and [were] not invited to dance."[22]

In the symbolic economy of the Hollywood Canteen, as with most other sites of civilian entertainment of military personnel, women in uniform and young men out of uniform were not easily incorporated into the national body. In this trio of brief chapters, I dance uncomfortably between these disparate groups. This is an awkward connection, like Rod Cameron running up and down the stairs, "mingling" with excluded Marie Haynes who watches the dancers below. However, most of the dancing in this book is pitched toward awkward pairings, drawing insights from pathways, viewpoints, memories, and narratives that are racially differentiated, and always multidirectional and partial. For the civilian men and military women who navigated this space (or tried to), the opportunities for misrecognition, dissonance, and alternative visions of the democratic dance floor are intensified through their different degrees of alienation from the Canteen setup of the soldier-hostess dyad. Taken together, they stimulate awareness of the shifting possibilities that opened and closed inside the building and outside the idealized couple.

Not invited into the dance but present (running humbly through it in an apron or watching it in uniform from a "respectable" remove), civilian men and military women share chapters 7–9. Other than Vining's admiration for military women, there is no reason to believe that they particularly identified with one another. I pair them not to equate their experiences but because thinking of them together stretches Canteen memory in interesting and useful ways. Their heavily managed participation also shapes World War II nostalgia. To tune in their memories, stories, and interpretations shines light through gaps between the floorboards we might otherwise dance right over.

CHAPTER 8

The View from the Mezzanine

Military men and women regardless of race or creed, wearing the uniform of any one of the United Nations will be admitted to the canteen.
—"HOLLYWOOD WILL HAVE STAGE DOOR CANTEEN FOR BENEFIT OF SOLDIERS,"
NEW YORK AGE (AUGUST 29, 1942)

I just remember feeling like a second class citizen having to stand up there watching others having fun on the dance floor.
—LORRAINE (MITCHELL) BEAR, EMAIL TO AUTHOR (APRIL 4, 2001)

Three weeks before Donald Vining took to heart the ridiculing of the excessively "dashing" doorman and altered his own behavior as a civilian volunteer, Kathryn "Kit" (Ludwig) Welter learned her own lesson in ambiguous civic belonging at the Hollywood Canteen.[1] She remembered the exact date, in fact: December 3, 1943. Like the Marine WR Marie Proulox and her friends, when Ludwig (her name at the time) and a fellow navy woman took their leave in Los Angeles, they donned their uniforms and set off for the famous military recreation spot. Unlike Proulox, however, the two were admitted by the doorman.[2] Still, after navigating the Canteen portals, they were not cleared to dance.

In Welter's letter to me in 2001, she told a story in which she and another WAVE approached a group of friendly looking servicemen, whom she referred to as the "other GIs." At the very moment of pre-dance frisson, this mutual pull was disrupted by a civilian hostess (presumably following Canteen rules), who altered the physics of the moment by telling them that they are "not allowed in the 'dancing, mingling, eating, and fun area.'" Instead of welcoming them into the center of patriotic Hollywood hospitality, the hostess diverted them to a balcony, where they "could sit and watch all the 'dancing, mingling, eating and fun.' Naturally we were very disappointed and mad, as we made a very quick exit. . . . But we did get to glance at Hedy Lamarr and Susan Hayward."[3]

Welter narrates what seems at first an utterly torque-denying pathway of identification—she is suspended between pulls in opposite directions. She is simultaneously beckoned in and guided out; her Canteen-belonging is recognized by the "other GIS" and denied by the civilian hostess. Nonetheless, she ends her story with a critical twist. Offered the alternative of watching others enjoy an experience they had stood in line to embody, these two navy women choose to leave it rather than take it. With feet planted firmly on the moral high ground, Welter and her friends push off from the Hollywood Canteen and back into the streets. Their "quick exit" rejects Canteen parameters that celebrate military men and civilian female dance partners even as it siphons off the women in uniform who are simultaneously soldiers and women who want to dance. The concluding flourish of her "writing/righting" her point of view is to "glance at Hedy Lamarr and Susan Hayward" as they storm out of the club. On the street, they will embark on a new search for welcoming recreation, their identities and itineraries shaken, not shattered—but their expectations revised.

I received Welter's story by email, in answer to my web postings asking for military women's memories of the Hollywood Canteen. Like most of the communications I had with women veterans, her story suggests that at the Hollywood Canteen, military women, like civilian men, were considered "not hostesses" and "not soldiers" and therefore outside the sanction of the soldier-hostess dyad. As a military woman, Welter's rejection from that dyad is both opposite from and similar to that of Vining's. The same qualifications that would have authorized Vining for dancing and visible expression of pleasure—military service and a uniform—render Welter's body unacceptable on the democratic dance floor. As a member of the newly formed women's branch of the navy, she has spent the war years teaching "instrument flight" to pilots in Beeville, Texas—national service, yes, but not traditional. If she had *stayed in her place* (according to rapidly war-converted rules of gender), that place could have easily accommodated mingling, dancing, and having fun with servicemen at a Canteen or the USO. Welter and her navy friend were both from Los Angeles, where the opportunities for civilian women to mingle with servicemen would have been plentiful. As a junior hostess, her service would have included "mingling, dancing, and having fun" (but not eating—the food is for the Boys). Her role as a surrogate "sweetheart" of the nation would have then been considered traditional—and thus more patriotic—than joining the navy. To a military woman, Canteen pleasure and isolation from that pleasure were offered hand in hand. She could accept the view from the mezzanine, or reject it. But there were many ways to dance those steps, and many ways to tell about it later.

(Not) Dancing in a Crooked Room

In her analysis of African American women's claims for civic belonging in a nation that misrecognizes them at every turn, Melissa Harris-Perry uses the example of post–World War II "field dependence studies" in which people were told to "stand up straight" but not told that the room was crooked. Some subjects aligned themselves by righting themselves to the room, unwittingly standing at a tilt in order to sync with the slanted furniture and walls. Others aligned themselves to their gravitation centers, even when this landed them off-kilter in relation to the physical appointments of the room. Harris-Perry draws on options for alignment faced by the human subjects in this experiment with those of black women in the United States, always caught in the conundrum of having to figure out "which way is up."[4] In this analysis, it is the race and gender stereotypes that constitute the "structural constraints" or field within which black women stand up, either at a tilt or in alignment with the crooked room. To line one's self up according to crooked constraints is painful. And to stand in alignment to a gravitational center that isn't recognized by the room, or the community, or the state is painful. Both orientations are that of misrecognition—or social recognition limited to moments when one is off-balance. It is easy to begin to misrecognize oneself and difficult to command more acceptable recognition under such circumstances.

Military women arriving at the Hollywood Canteen, only to be offered the choice of sequestering themselves on a balcony to peer at dancers below or leaving altogether, faced the truncated options of standing in a crooked room. Structural constraints affecting military women's ability to be recognized at the Canteen did not begin at the Canteen but in a set of regulatory gender norms that constructed women who would join the military as nontraditional, sexually loose, or lesbian (not "good girls"). In order to make the idea of military women "stand up" in relation to the state, the architects of the women's branches in World War II worked to construct military women as respectable, chaste, and easily convertible back to domestic ideals after the war. These constraints and options for alignment operate differently across race and class. For black women, the structural constraints affecting military women were especially fraught, since claims to public recognition were compromised by historical constructions of black women as lascivious or asexual, angry or unquestioningly loyal to whites. The battle for black women's acceptance into the armed forces was one of the civil rights campaigns of World War II, with the ground being full citizenship for African American women through respectability, opportunity, and full citizenship for all African Americans. The state's recognition of African American women as "respectable" was a high-stakes imperative, not only for black women but for black people generally. The black press coverage of black military women's activities on leave emphasized respectability, education, and uplift. Discussing how she responded to rampant stereotypes of black military women as prostitutes, former WAC Dovie Roundtree told Janet Simms-Woods in an interview that she had a variety of ready responses, including pointing out that "there were many more white women in the military than there were Black women."[5]

Furloughs of African American military women are frequent topics in the society pages of black Los Angeles newspapers. When nine black WAVES were stationed in San Diego in March 1945, they were treated by the black community and black press as celebrities.[6] Among the Los Angeles area clubs that admitted African American military women was the Negro Extension branch of the Long Beach USO (though a YMCA-USO report noted tensions in "feelings between uniformed girls and civilian hostesses")[7] and the Eastside USO. But I don't know about the Hollywood Canteen.

Among the African American women veterans I contacted, no one remembered going to the Hollywood Canteen, nor did their inquiries through friends, organizations, and newsletters locate anyone who did. Nor did I find evidence in the black press of African American military women visiting the Hollywood Canteen, though stories abounded that reported on black community entertainment in Los Angeles of black WACs from race- and gender-segregated units and, by the end of the war, WAVES. This is not to say that African American military women did not enter, or try to enter, the Hollywood Canteen, but I do want to highlight this absence—the fact that I don't know, that I couldn't find out, and that no one I talked to knew—as a telling limitation of my dances with Canteen-goers. In my dance "outside the dyad" in chapters 7–9, all the civilians are men, and all the military women are white.

Otherwise, my search for military women from World War II was easy and fruitful between 2000 and 2010, thanks to networks of community that had been formed in the 1940s, maintained through reunions, newsletters, holiday cards, and organizations, and strengthened by the internet. These were the networks through which I heard from African American women veterans who attempted to help me to find out if black WACs and WAVES attended the Hollywood Canteen. It is through these same networks that I found Kit (Ludwig) Welter and many other white women veterans who shared their memories of inclusion, partial inclusion, and exclusion.

Military women, whose uniformed female bodies presented a categorical problem to military recreation sites everywhere they appeared, were supposedly welcomed at the Hollywood Canteen. The sign above the door said "Servicemen," but the "servicemen and servicewomen" conjunction appeared in many contemporary and historical references to the Hollywood Canteen visitors. Bette Davis biographer Whitney Stine wrote that when the Canteen closed on November 22, 1945, it had "entertained, with the highest-priced talent of the land, more than 3 million servicemen and servicewomen."[8]

I always made it a point to ask interviewees if they remembered military women on the dance floor. Junior hostess Nancy Marlow couldn't remember seeing women in uniform but offered a possible explanation: "I like boys and so I don't remember seeing them!" She laughed, and then added, "However, if a WAC asked me to dance, I would have danced."[9] Margie Stewart remembered "a sprinkling of military women."[10] "Once I danced with a WAVE," said soldier-actor Tommy Farrell. "Oh, she was a hell of a dancer. We made a hole in the floor there—a lot of people watching!"[11]

However, most of the women veterans with whom I communicated shared memories consisting of limited inclusion or outright exclusion. There were exceptions. Shirley Rothstein, a Navy Hospital Corps veteran, remembered dancing, writing to me, "You bet I did and I have a picture to prove I was there in 1945. I loved to dance and at almost 83 years old, I'm still truckin'!!"[12] Ellie Latham, a WAVE stationed in Port Hueneme, remembered going with navy women friends in 1945 to the Canteen, where she was not only welcomed but brought up to the front to enjoy birthday cake among other service personnel born on that day.[13] Mildred Kosanovich, a veteran of the Marine Corps Women's Reserve (WR), told me that she met many entertainers through her role as general clerk for special services at Camp Pendleton but sometimes hitchhiked with another woman Marine to Los Angeles, where they would stay at low-cost dormitories and sightsee. At the Canteen, she remembered singing a song on an audio letter to her parents and then being asked by many servicemen to repeat the performance on audio letters to theirs.[14]

More numerous were memories of differential treatment. Senior Master Sergeant (Retired) Charlotte D. Mansfield wrote that when she and fellow sergeant Bertha C. Brownback went to the Hollywood Canteen, "We were told service women were not admitted to the canteen. Brownie argued a bit with the doorkeeper—a woman—to no avail and we left."[15] Jean M. Woodcome wrote that she and another WAVE stationed at Port Hueneme were turned away from the front door. However, while standing outside on the corner, they discovered an alternate route.

Ronald Reagan and Jane Wyman walked by—said good morning and then disappeared in the back door of the Canteen. We decided to try that. We asked the doorman to let us in to see the stars, etc. He finally told us to go up some stairs in the back and we had 2 chairs and could look out a cut-out window—no glass. From there we could watch all the dancers and just enjoy the music and all goings-on.[16]

Woodcome attached to her letter the xeroxed picture of the Canteen interior that I had included in my request for information. In pen, she had drawn a circle around a small window high on a side wall. This was by far the most detailed account of the separate quarters for military women that anyone recounted to me.

We enjoyed many Sat. nites & Sunday mornings & afternoons up in that loft. One time I had my picture taken with Spencer Tracy & that was a big thrill. After the war, we were allowed in the front door, but sat in the mezzanine near the front, and some male actors would wait on us (do not remember any famous ones). When I went downstairs and saw pictures on the wall, one of them was of me and Tracy. How I wish I had asked for that as I'm sure it was thrown away when the Canteen closed.

"I loved being backstage in our loft," Woodcome wrote, spinning the "loft" as a special perk, like a box seat. However, I couldn't stop thinking about the WAVE watching from above while her photo with one of Hollywood's biggest names hangs downstairs on the foyer wall—an advertisement for democratic inclusiveness at the Hollywood Canteen.

Betty Sue Wimberly, a WAVES veteran, remembered going "in a back door, up some stairs to a mezzanine, where we looked down on the dance floor and listened to the band."[17] Likewise, Jo Neilan recalled that she was "ushered through a hall up to a dark area and could look down on the dancers through peep holes. I remember seeing Bette Davis and Robert Montgomery. Those were the only stars I remember. We did not question it, I guess, but now I wonder why we were not allowed to join in the crowd and dance with the servicemen."[18] Jean Woodcome wondered if they were not allowed to dance with servicemen because "we would be in competition with the starlets."[19] Indeed, Anne Campbell recalled being informed that the reason she and her fellow WAVES were being ushered "to the mezzanine" in 1942 was that the Canteen had its "own hostesses."[20]

Responses to differential treatment ranged from memories of taking it in stride (not expecting to be included) to memories of feeling disappointed and angry and to critiquing the situation on retrospect. R. Janie Tilbury (formerly Rita Bevins) wrote, "We, as military women during that time, felt that the USOs were mainly for men, and the women welcomed there as hostesses were civilians. Not entirely true, of course, but that was the climate of the times."[21] (She also noted that the "Skipper" at the naval air station in Alameda, where she was stationed in 1943, "almost had a stroke the first time he saw one of the WAVES" walk past his office "in dungarees." From then on, they were instructed to walk "IN BACK" of the building, rather than in front of it, "in case he should be looking out the window!"[22]

Meghan Kate Winchell writes that organizations such as the USO specifically mobilized female volunteers "to perform 'women's work' that did not challenge gender norms."[23] The inclusion of military women, who were stigmatized as defying traditional gender roles, disrupted the dyad that held this dance in place. No matter with whom she danced, a jitterbugging military woman did not appear to forecast gender roles unchanged by war. The "good girl" in a party frock, wearing very little makeup (so as not to be thought a sexually available "patriotute" or "khaki-wacky")[24] was the preferred Canteen conduit for moving men from "citizen to soldier and back to citizen."[25] Even Hollywood Canteen starlets were encouraged to show up with fresh faces. Former busboy Bob Alden remembered marveling at the beauty of Ingrid Bergman, Susan Hayward, and other actresses with very little or no makeup.[26]

The attractive and feminine but sexually unavailable "good girl" was also the preferred "type" of the women's branches of the armed forces. To gain institutional support, these newly formed women's branches had themselves to be seen as uninterested in and incapable of toppling traditional gender roles. This was a tremendous public relations problem that needed to be tackled in order for the women's branches to be created—despite the need for military workers and the precedent of women having already served in the U.S. armed forces in World War I. Leisa D. Meyer's now classic analysis of gender and sexuality and the creation of the WAC describes the problem succinctly: how could the nonoverlapping categories of "women" and "soldier" be combined without "masculinizing" American women or "feminizing" the U.S. armed forces?[27] Because the "female soldier" was seen as a threat if she was seen as permanent, she had to be constructed as temporary and different; replacing a man so he could fight—a Rosie the Riveter in a different uniform. Women defense workers, after all, were only acceptable so far as they were "pitching in" for the war effort and eager to relinquish their jobs. Because military women were seen as a nontraditional woman, automatically arousing suspicions of being loose or lesbian, a figure needed to be constructed of a female patriot who was especially respectable, educated, moral, "good" even to a greater extent than the "good girl" who was the ideal Canteen hostess. Like the draft-aged civilian man, the military woman performed acceptability as a national subject in relation to her apparent sacrifice of pleasure and desire for the duration. If her purpose was to "free a man to fight," as much of the propaganda that justified her existence affirmed, then why should she take *his* sandwich at the snack bar or cut in on *his* last dance with a civilian woman before shipping off? By this logic, her membership in the "we" of the democratic dance floor presented a paradox of a guilty proxy. She wasn't a proper guest. She wasn't a proper host. If including her was the democratic thing to do, then managing that inclusion while protecting the dyad was a gatekeeper's puzzle.

Military women on leave discombobulated the logic of many organizations set up for the purpose of entertaining service personnel. While these women shared some of the same insults incurred by civilian draft-aged men, as the brunt of comedy sketches, cartoons, and jokes, their constant negotiation of the respectability politics that had been deployed to justify their existence presented additional barriers. Military women were more likely to be provided with a quiet space to write letters home than a youth-culture party atmosphere with swing music and dance. In Los Angeles, military women were provided dormitory space at the Figueroa YWCA and the Hollywood Studio Club and were welcome in nightclubs. However, their welcome at the Hollywood Canteen does not appear to have been a given.

Still, the Hollywood Canteen was more welcoming to military women than were many other dance floors for the troops. New York's Stage Door Canteen did not admit servicewomen (or claim to). One year after it opened, however, it began to provide separate Sunday afternoon tea dances for military women, providing some recreation for them while constructing them as far too respectable to want to jitterbug at night.[28] The Women's Committee of the Philadelphia Stage Door Canteen justified their refusal to admit WACs in 1942 by saying that the women's "uniforms would detract from the party atmosphere" (apparently the men's military uniforms did not).[29] Marie Bennett Alsmeyer, who served in the WAVES during World War II, recalled not being allowed into the San Francisco Stage Door Canteen.[30]

> It was Easter weekend, 1944 and my friend Helen and I, both WAVES Pharmacists Mates, 2/c, [Second Class] stationed at Oak Knoll Naval Hospital in Oakland, were anxious to go to San Francisco to hear our small hospital band at the Stage Door Canteen. We walked by the big wooden door twice then mustered up courage to ask the huge Marine sergeant to let us in. He told us in no uncertain terms that it was for SERVICE MEN only. We

finally convinced him that we would not leave and he agreed—but only if we stayed out of sight in the kitchen! We weren't to[o] pleased with what we saw—dozens of beautiful young ladies sitting with OUR boys, eating sandwiches and thick slices of cake. The corpsmen we saw every day at the hospital looked so different in their dress blues out there laughing with young girls in frilly dainty pinks, blues and soft pastel silks. I remember one young airman jumping up to receive his free ticket for a long-distance telephone call "anywhere in America." We stayed until closing time, sitting at a food-laden table in the kitchen. Watching.[31]

Alsmeyer ends her story with patriotic revenge. The temporary insult of watching from the kitchen is resolved when the navy women triumphantly ride back to the base with "our boys."

Watching was the most common dance floor perspective available to most of the military women who shared their memories with me. Watching from afar the added value of celebrity hosts and hostesses at the Hollywood Canteen exacerbated the sting of exclusion for Welter, Haynes, Mansfield, and others. What was special about this Canteen—that the hostess whom an ordinary soldier could chat with and hold in his arms might very well be a movie star—also added to the impact of what was being withheld from those not allowed on the dance floor. This dynamic could also affect servicemen. Race-based exclusion from dancing, though not a universal memory of black soldiers, was Mel Bryant's primary association with the Hollywood Canteen. When Bryant spoke of the Canteen, he emphasized the ways the club's Hollywood exceptionalism highlighted the ways he, as a black man, was considered a second-class citizen in the military, in Los Angeles, and in his chosen profession. When military women are offered "watching" instead of "participating," they are not only invited into a different activity but into a different subject position. For Welter, the experience of being able to "glance at Susan Hayward and Hedy Lamarr" while making a quick and angry exit applies critical torque to Hollywood largess, an ironic comment on the democratic achievement of a "place where Joe Dogface can dance with Hedy Lamarr."[32] A similar scenario is reported by Peter Soderbergh in his book on women Marines where he quotes Inga Fredericksen's account of marching out "en masse" with fellow women Marines after being relegated to the mezzanine. "We all got up together and filed down the stairway, past the servicemen who were still inviting us to dance, past the Bette Davis autograph table and out the door."[33]

Susan Hayward, Hedy Lamarr, and Bette Davis appear in these stories as fleeting, blurry scenery glimpsed by the disappointed and angry military women. Celebrity volunteers excel as signposts of exclusion, for the same reasons they surpass ordinary civilian volunteers as evidence of democracy. They also provide powerful denouements in Canteen narratives in which military women *torque back*. Stung by rejection, Welter, Haynes, and Mansfield march out while a name band plays for dancing military men and civilian women. I imagine them feeling acutely the constrictions of this version of dance floor democracy. I imagine their exit as unnoticed by others. Stories of angry exits trouble the nostalgic predictability of swing culture as war memory by remixing its primary components.

The changed location of the observation area for military women in June 1944 altered the experiences of some. No longer hidden from view but literally elevated above the dance floor, small groups of military women can be seen in some Canteen photographs after this date. However, the improvisatory aspect of a volunteer-run organization, overwhelmed by GI guests admitted five hundred at a time into a crowded club where different people were in charge each night should not be underestimated in historical guesswork as to what actually happened on the ground. Some women veterans who communicated with me remembered being turned away at the door. Others recalled being welcomed into the main room and having a wonderful time. A letter from executive secretary Jean Lewin to members of the board of directors indicates that the Canteen was still debating policies regarding military women's admittance as late as March 5, 1945.[34] I don't expect continuity. Occupying a "new category which proclaimed female soldiers as both sexually respectable and feminine,"[35] military women could scarcely move— let alone jitterbug—without jeopardizing their ability to represent the nation.

Break-away: Lorraine Bear, April 23, 2001

"You've got to be kidding!!!" wrote Lorraine Bear, responding to my post "Did You Dance at the Hollywood Canteen?" in *White Caps*, the newsletter of WAVES National.[36] My queries elicited a variety of spirited answers, but Bear's was unequivocal. She closed her initial email with the droll summation that *other* than her visit to the Hollywood Canteen, her "Navy days in California were enjoyable."[37]

> Servicewomen were not allowed to enter the Hollywood Canteen. I was a Navy Storekeeper (D) second class stationed at Camp Bedilion, Port Hueneme, California from November 1943 until February 1946. Our liberty weekends sometimes took us to Los Angeles or Hollywood. The one time we tried to go to the Hollywood Canteen we were told that only servicemen and civilian women were allowed in. They said we could go up to the second floor to listen to the music and watch the dancing.[38]

I sent her a follow-up, a barrage of questions: What was this second-floor space like, where military women were diverted from the main room? Did the stars go up and visit them at least? Unable to ascertain what a "Storekeeper (D)" was, I asked if she was an officer and if that might have been the reason for her exclusion. I asked who else was in that upstairs room. Was it just military women? Was the mezzanine racially integrated? The WAVES were notoriously slow in accepting African American women. (The first class would not go to boot camp until about a year *after* Bear's attempted visit to the Hollywood Canteen.) Civil rights campaigns fought by the NAACP, the black press, the Alpha Kappa Alpha sorority, and other organizations lobbied for black women's inclusion in the WAVES, but it took two and a half years after it was created (April 1942) for the navy to reluctantly capitulate (October 1944). By that time, Regina Akers argues, "some women who may have been interested earlier in the war might not have been available," and some "might have been reluctant to believe that they would not be victims of the same Jim Crow policy oppressing black sailors."[39] The Marines and the SPARS (the Coast Guard's Women's Reserve, named by the initials of the motto "Semper Paratus Always Ready") never did admit African American women during World War II. However, if African Americans in the segregated WAC had mingled in the upstairs room, the military sex-segregated mezzanine would have been a rare site of racial integration of military women.

She emailed back with as many answers to my questions as she could. First of all, she remembered being led to "small, dark room with 'peek hole' windows." She said it was "was warm and stuffy" and that the windows were so small that "if someone was standing in front" of them, you could not "look down on the dance floor."[40] She did not remember who else was in the room but was certain that she and her friends were not alone, since she remembered the room as being crowded. She presumed these other bodies must have been other military women but remembered nothing about them in particular. She remembered that there were no black WAVES at Port Hueneme and that black men at Hueneme were limited to jobs as cooks and stewards. She did not remember if there were people of other races in the mezzanine.

> I just remember feeling like a second class citizen having to stand up there watching others having fun on the dance floor. No, none of the stars came up to talk to us. We did not stay there long. I, too, remember that the Canteen was touted to be for enlisted personnel only—and that is what we were.[41]

She offered to talk to me more by telephone. When I called her for a phone interview, she situated her Canteen memories in a broader personal history about her military service.

Bear was born and raised in Michigan City, Indiana. As Lorraine Mitchell, she was in her late teens when she went to the movies with a friend and came home with the idea of enlisting in the newly formed WAVES. It wasn't the featured attraction that gave her the idea but a recruiting station outside the theatre. "My dad had been in World War I," she explained. As one of three daughters in a family with no sons, she knew that if any of her family served in this war, it would be in the women's branches. "My friend and I looked at the information. I went home and I said to my dad, 'What would you think if I joined the navy?' And he said, 'I think, it'd be great.'"

The bill creating the naval women's reserve was approved on April 7, 1942, but it would not have been necessary if the Naval Reserve Act of 1916 had not been revised to exclude women in 1925. When the first class of women completed their training in 1942, they were the first WAVES, but they were not the first women to serve in the navy. The earlier navy women were official members of the United States Navy (though they did have to fight to receive benefits). The WAVES, however, were constructed as temporary helpers, not as authentic navy personnel—as the full name emphasizes: Women Accepted for Volunteer Emergency Service.[42]

Like other WAVES, when Bear enlisted, she was first sent to boot camp at Hunter College, after which she was sent to Georgia to train as a storekeeper. She had hoped to be stationed in California and was pleased when "five of us from that graduating class were sent to Port Hueneme. I got what I wanted."[43]

Just south of Oxnard, southwest of Camarillo, and about twelve miles down the Pacific coast from Ventura is Port Hueneme, a natural deepwater seaport, one of the many pieces of property that was taken over by the U.S. military in the Los Angeles during World War II. "It was the largest port of embarkation, actually, on the West Coast at the time. But it was a secret," Bear told me. "It was a big port of embarkation for the Seabees" (vernacular name from CB for Construction Battalion). These were the navy corps who would construct, ship, and load materials for quickly building bases. Port Hueneme was also the site for team training for ACORN (Aviation Construction Ordinance Repair Navy), the teams who would quickly assemble airbases.[44] The work was construction, not combat, but it was extremely hazardous. The men would be stationed at Hueneme for four to six months and then shipped off to build bases. "You get to know some of the fellows." She knew many of those in the three shiploads of men who were "torpedoed and sunk" one day soon after shipping out.

Her job was to disperse money for the payroll department, which meant she counted out the cash for the sailors on payday. They had an option to only take part of their pay and "let the rest ride," but "we still had to have enough

FIG 8.1: WAVES and Seabees at Port Hueneme, 1940s. Snapshot in Lorraine (Mitchell) Bear's scrapbook. COURTESY LORRAINE BEAR.

cash, so that if everybody wanted all of their pay, we'd still have enough money to pay them. She was quartered in Camp Bedillion, where she was one of seventy WAVES and there were seven thousand sailors. She chuckled at this part. "Good odds, right?"

Bear remembered that there were often dances at the base and there was a band. With twenty thousand naval personnel stationed there at any given time, there was also a good schedule of entertainment traveling to the base. She remembered Kay Kyser's band coming out to play. The navy had also taken over the Japanese fishing village at Point Mugu after the Isei and Nisei residents had been interned, and she recalled that she could take the liberty bus up there to go fishing. On weekends, the liberty buses would take passengers to Los Angeles, and although she chose not to return to the Hollywood Canteen, she did go dancing at commercial nightclubs.

"I know that we went to the Palladium, which was a huge dance club. And that was on, I think, Sunset Boulevard, but I am not sure. There were several nightclubs that had entertainment, and we were allowed to go there." She even saw Frank Sinatra sing with Tommy Dorsey's band in Hollywood one night, possibly at the Palladium, she couldn't recall.

We were winding up our conversation. Most of what she told me was how she had come to join the navy and what she remembered of her work and leisure time at Port Hueneme. Before we hung up, I steered her back to the

Hollywood Canteen one last time. I asked her how the people at the Canteen had explained why servicewomen were denied entrance on the dance floor. Did she have a memory of what she *felt* when it happened?

She remembered being disappointed. However, she also remembered that all anyone needed to say was that "it was for service men only. . . . And back then, you know, you accepted that kind of stuff." She laughed. "Nowadays, you'd say 'Hey, that's not right, but back then . . ." She paused. "It was okay."[45]

Okay or not, it shaped her route and the worlds that came into view. I imagine Lorraine Bear, peering down at the dance floor and planning her next move. With a blare of a fifteen- or seventeen-piece big band and several hundred people jitterbugging below, the floorboards must have shaken the walls all the way up to the mezzanine of the old wooden building, emphasizing through vibration the lively physical and emotional connection from which she was excluded. I imagine her storming down the stairs and past the many people who remembered seeing military women at the Canteen and concluded that they were welcome. I wonder if she brushes by busboy Donald Vining, who believes military women are treated shabbily. Maybe she and her friends cross paths with busboy Lennie Bluett before they exit the club and stroll up and around the few Hollywood blocks to the Palladium, where they enter without incident and dance to Tommy Dorsey's band. We met Bluett in chapter 2, where he told of not being allowed into the Palladium to hear Frank Sinatra's debut with Dorsey and boycotting the nightclub ever since for its exclusion of African Americans in the 1940s. We meet up with him again in chapter 9, where he cleans up the mess with other civilian male volunteers at the Hollywood Canteen.

CHAPTER 9

★ ★ ★

Men Serving Men

But can you imagine all those beautiful hostesses and only servicemen are allowed? I know one guy who got dressed up in a uniform so he could get into the Canteen, but they knew he was a fake because the uniform fitted him. [pause] So they threw me out.
—BOB HOPE, RADIO BROADCAST, HOLLYWOOD CANTEEN (OCTOBER 13, 1942)

It was kind of embarrassing, me being seventeen years old. I was glad I had three brothers in the Service and was about to join them.
—DELMAR WATSON

For draft-aged civilian men, including employees of the motion picture industry, appropriate wartime sacrifice frequently included occupying the position as the target of jokes (at best), and, less pleasurable, as the object of shame and suspicion. One had to laugh off the incessant and often self-deprecating banter of male comedians about civilian men as lazy, crazy, and queer, just as military women endured their share of jokes about mannishness, man-craziness, and professional ineptitude. Bob Hope's joke about sneaking into the Canteen ostensibly pokes fun at the military for not being able to provide uniforms that fit (sharing an inside joke with servicemen), but the punch line constructs servicemen as sufficiently masculine to not be troubled by such things while it feminizes and queers civilian men as soft, vain, unconcerned about the war, and taking for granted such comforts such as suits that fit.[1] Working alongside older men (the fathers and grandfathers of the nation) as busboys, cleaning up after the military men and military women, as doormen, as dishwashers, and entertainers, young civilian men improvised a tricky set of moves within narrow limits, as Vining notes in his observation of the too-dashing doorman, which he takes as a lesson for his own self-presentation.

Former child actor Delmar Watson remembered feeling "embarrassed" when he went to the Hollywood Canteen as a seventeen-year-old civilian.[2] He did not volunteer as a busboy but showed up with his brothers Garry and Bobs (the most famous sibling) to make an "appearance." Before the war, the six Watson brothers were known for their sixteen-foot-high human pyramid. By the time of the Canteen appearance, half the pyramid had enlisted, so it was only six feet high. He described feeling "strange" in the Canteen environment. When they walked in, he recalled that his father said, "Listen, you guys, you're here to entertain these guys. If they offer you any food or any drink you don't take any of that. That's for the servicemen." He felt confused about what he was doing at the Canteen at all. "I figured, these guys are not here to see three teenage kids, they want to see some long-legged blonde."

Two months later, he had enlisted in the Coast Guard and was headed to boot camp in Sheepshead Bay, Brooklyn. Even in boot camp, it felt strange to be a Hollywood actor. When asked where he was from, "I'd say 'Los Angeles.'" He never volunteered that he "worked in pictures. I wanted them to know *me*, before they knew some Hollywood jerk." Sooner or later, his fellow servicemen would catch on that they had seen him in roles like Peter the goat boy, Shirley Temple's boyfriend, in *Heidi* (1937), but he was in no hurry for this news to spread. He had worked in 77 movies by the time he was seven years old and over 250 by the time he "retired and went into the Service." After the war, he never went back to making movies. He became a photographer in the Coast Guard. "I'm a realist," he explained. "After you came out of the Service you realized there was a lot more to life than Hollywood."

Only through humble, but perceptible, performances of sacrifice could civilian men, especially young, handsome Hollywood actors, be rendered commendable as patriotic volunteers. John Garfield, for example, could be admired for his well-publicized disappointment at his 4-F classification, for the legitimacy of his exemption (a heart murmur), for his dedication to selling war bonds and entertaining the troops (he was one of the first Hollywood film actors to travel to camps, bases, and battle fronts), and, of course, for using his star power to cofound the Canteen. For some constituencies, he could be admired for fighting for the racial integration of its dance floor.[3] He made public statements expressing agreement with the Screen Actors Guild stance that acting should not be considered an essential occupation and therefore draft-exempt. Garfield fought his 4-F classification, arguing that if he was hardy enough for a rigorous war bond tour, he should be considered well enough to enlist. His brief reclassification to 1-A ended when he suffered a heart attack while working at the Canteen.[4]

Garfield's sacrifices on behalf of fighting men were estimable, in other words, and well publicized. However, for most draft-aged civilian men, negotiating ways to support the war effort on the home front presented problems, especially if they did not take defense jobs but continued in their chosen professions. A particular catch-22 for appropriate volunteerism faced the apparently healthy, young, handsome film actors whose careers not only remained intact throughout the war but were boosted through what has been pejoratively been termed "victory casting." Dozens of young, handsome civilian actors were able to play roles in war films as war heroes as a result of the vacancies left by established male leads who were serving in the armed forces. Often, these lesser-known actors played the ideal soldier, sailor, or Marine onscreen, portraying the glories of the cinema war (including love scenes with beautiful actresses) without danger, horror, sadness, fear, or loss, not to mention the interruption of private life and career. What was the appropriate relationship between civilian draft-aged, draft-exempt men and military men? Was it appropriate for such actors to entertain the troops in army camp shows, for example?

This question was debated in industry meetings and in trade and union magazines. The Educational Committee of the HVC met to discuss the problem of civilian men's appropriate volunteerism on July 21, 1942. How could they support the war effort without upsetting soldiers? Surely it would be worse for them *not* to volunteer their time on behalf of the troops. Rather than enact a decisive policy, the committee ruled that it would be left up to the individual.[5] A 1943 issue of the *Hollywood Reporter* addressed ongoing debates over the problem: Did men sacrificing their private lives in the military wish to be visited/entertained/comforted by their draft-exempt brothers? Or were they insulted by such visits/reminders? The magazine published a message to the "big male stars" from Chief Petty Officer Carroll Sandholdt, who wrote: "while we in the service love the glamour gals, the comedians and the singers, we like to look at favorite leading men too. I always was a sucker for a Garfield picture, and it was a real thrill for me to see him close up." Columnist Frank Pope concluded, "Male stars doubtless were once afraid of the almost inevitable, 'Why ain't you in uniform, bud?' But those days have gone. Every man in the service knows now that when Uncle Sam needs somebody these days, he calls. More than a thousand players now in service prove that."[6]

Reminders of the actors and other film industry workers in the service received a boost at the Hollywood Canteen on October 25, 1943, when a "Hol-

FIG 9.1: Volunteers onstage at the Hollywood Canteen. BY PERMISSION, BRUCE TORRENCE, HOLLYWOODPHOTOGRAPHS.COM.

lywood Hall of Honor" was unveiled there. Volunteers and visitors would see, every time they passed through the lobby, photographs of Hollywood industry men in their authentic (not movie role) uniforms. These included "Captain Clark Gable, Major William Wyler, Lieutenant Commander Robert Taylor, Captain Ronald Reagan, Lieutenant James Stewart, and Chief Petty Officer Victor Mature."[7] While this may have buoyed the respect for men in the industry who were in service, it also highlights the reasons why many others did not feel comfortable showing up. Van Johnson, who was ineligible because of an automobile accident injury, his biographer writes, avoided the Canteen because he thought "the servicemen would resent him."[8] Instead, he visited injured servicemen in hospitals.

Civilian men who volunteered at the Hollywood Canteen may not have referenced these wartime debates in their interviews, but the context of gender sacrifice, resentment, and performances of masculine humility and humiliation are important to bear in mind when considering the dances of civilian men at the Canteen who served, cleaned up, wore aprons, and didn't dance among the stars and men in uniform. Just as the gender constraints were race- differentiated for military women, so were the parameters of civilian men's acceptable performance of gender racially specific.

Break-away: Lennie Bluett, May 29, 2003

African American men, both military and civilian, were no strangers to gender politics of emasculation, being represented as humble or humiliated, and relegation to feminized service work. Black men in the navy, for example, were relegated the kitchens, serving white men in uniform. Picking up the dirty dishes of white servicemen does not disturb gender roles when a black man is the busboy. It is no surprise that Lennie Bluett, a third generation African American Los Angeles resident who spent much of his career and private life battling for civil rights in Hollywood, would situate his Canteen memories in our interview in a longer race-based battle for dignity and opportunity. His Canteen work was memorable but was not narrated as an isolated imposition of rules of gender sacrifice but a longer history of race and gender.

A longtime member of the Screen Actors Guild, Bluett appeared in many of the films that defined the era, including *Gone with the Wind* (one of eleven hundred extras, four hundred of them black, playing the dying and wounded) and *Cabin in the Sky* (where you can see him jitterbugging with Dorothy Dandridge's sister Vivian). He can be seen as the tall flute-playing "native" in the nonspecified "primitive" dream sequence in *Ali Baba Goes to Town* (in which Jeni LeGon wears the turkey feather getup). You can't see him in *There's No Business Like Show Business*, but you hear his voice in the number "Heat Wave," as lip-synched by browned-down white men who replaced the black men hired for the job when it was deemed inappropriate for them to dance with Marilyn Monroe.

A tall man with a warm voice and expansive gestures, Lennie Bluett is already standing in his apartment doorway when we arrive at his building. He welcomes us in, and guides through his open floor plan that feels like a combination piano lounge, living room, and museum of a life lived in the entertainment industry. One wall of his living room is mirrored, and other walls are covered with photographs of family and friends, many familiar faces from film and television. A Barbara Streisand recording plays not-so-softly in the background, and occasionally he pauses between Canteen stories to sing or hum along. He was a volunteer at the Canteen, and over six decades later, at eighty-four, he still spends a good deal of his time volunteering, a connection emphasized by the blue Meals-on-Wheels T-shirt. However, most of the connections he draws between his volunteerism at the Hollywood Canteen and the present of our interview have to do with race—with an emphasis on the battles over space he has fought throughout his life so as to be able to move freely in the company town of his chosen profession. With Bluett, as in my dances with other interviewees, I follow the best I can wherever he goes when answering my questions about the Hollywood Canteen. His stories begin in the Canteen building, but branch out beyond its walls and time periods, as he narrates his body and those of other black people, in the representational, industrial, and civic context of Hollywood, Los Angeles, and the United States.

We share pleasantries about our mutual friend, Clora Bryant, who has arranged for this meeting. Then, settling in for the interview, he leans back in his chair and begins: "I don't have a lot to tell you about the Hollywood Canteen, except a couple of *incidents* you may be interested in." He raises his eyebrows when he says the word "incidents."

"Yes," I encourage him. "Please."

"The first," he continues, "is about this young lady." Like many interviewees, he has assembled a stack of memorabilia to illustrate his story. He reaches for the first item, a faded publicity photograph, a headshot, of a very attractive woman with a pleasant smile. She is familiar to me, but I can't place her. "She was the first black lady to sing with a white orchestra. Her name was June Richmond, a dear friend of mine. She's gone now, has been gone a long time. June was the first black lady to sing with a white band and that was Jimmy Dorsey. Do you remember Jimmy Dorsey . . . or are you too young?"[9]

For some reason, we laugh. I did come along too late to remember the famous big bands of the 1940s the way Lennie Bluett remembers them, but I do *remember* them, in that an image and sound came to mind when I hear the name "Jimmy Dorsey." On the other hand, while I also remembered June Richmond, I had not recognized her picture. Bluett returns to the fact of Richmond's significance several times throughout our interview. He wants me to remember June Richmond the way I "remember" Jimmy Dorsey. And I will. Several times he repeats the statistic of how early she broke the color line by singing with a white band—before Lena Horne sang with Charlie Barnet, before Billie Holiday sang with Artie Shaw.

"Her name was June Richmond," he says once again. "And Dick Haymes, who was a very big singer at that time, who later married Rita Hayworth, was singing on the bill . . ." He tries to remember the band Haymes was singing with, but is unable to come up with it. "Because at eighty-four, your memory goes a bit, you know."

"Dick was singing 'Old Man River,'" he continues. "The initial words to 'Old Man River' were 'N all work on the Mississippi.' Lennie will not speak the word but enunciates the letter "N" in a big booming voice, to get across the point: Haymes *did* sing the word, loud and clear and without apology.

Well, he was rehearsing this. June came out of the wings, because she was to follow him with her songs, and she said, "Hold the phone." She said, "'That word is not permissible here or any place in the world, Mr. Haymes.'" And he was shocked. Because he's a Canadian and he didn't know that word was not a nice word, you know? And he said, "Well, hold the band!" You know. And he said, "What should I say?" And she said, "Well sing what's on the paper." And he said, "I am singing what's on the paper." And that's true. That N-word was on there, it was written like that. But most black singers were doing, "Here we all work on the Mississippi . . ." Or "Darkies all work on the" . . . They were saying Darkies and they were thinking, well, that was better than the N-word, so a lot of people used the word "darkies." So she stopped the show, stopped the rehearsal. And, I think, as I recall, that Haymes did "Darkies all work on the Mississippi while the white folks play." Well, that's one little incident.

This next "incident" that Lennie tells refers directly to the parameters of his own Canteen work. "And, while we were allowed to entertain the troops, and serve them food, and clean up afterward, we were not allowed, we were totally instructed not to dance with the white ladies." In Lennie's memory, it is not only his civilian status as a male volunteer that limited his access to the democratic dance floor, but his race. He remembers not simply being told that civilian busboys must refrain from socializing, but that he is not to dance with "white ladies."

When I ask if black servicemen danced, he states without hesitation that they did. He recalls that they danced with black women, whom, he says, were primarily clubwomen. When I ask what he did as a Canteen volunteer, he replies that he worked as a "server, dancer [on the stage], sweeper, whatever—whatever they needed—or entertained, because I played the piano and sang"—but he did not dance on the famous dance floor.

Lennie was both a busboy and an entertainer at the Canteen, as were many of the civilian male volunteers who were professional actors, dancers, and musicians. While no other former busboys whom I interviewed described being allowed to dance, some civilian men who were entertainers did seem to have danced from time to time. Dean Collins, a white professional swing dancer and dance instructor to the stars, is said to have danced at the Hollywood Canteen as a civilian.[10] Lennie was also a professional dancer who had appeared in films by the time of his volunteer work—and he made a connection between the Canteen and his film career right on the line that was both crossed and maintained in Hollywood when it came to black dancers.

"But we were instructed not to dance." He shakes his head. "And that's so funny because several years after that, I got a call from Twentieth Century-Fox." The director sought black actors to sing with Marilyn Monroe. "They wanted a black feel to the song. We put an *umph* that the white boys didn't do for whatever reason." His laugh is sad and trails off. "But then," he sits forward, "they wanted us to do the dance with her. But in those days, black dancers did not dance with white ladies, including Marilyn Monroe! . . . So when you see the 'Heat Wave' number, I and ten other guys are singing, and . . ." From his chair, Bluett is suddenly performing a pantomime of the voiceless white male dancers who appear onscreen, lip-synching to the black voices and imitating the dance that the black actors had rehearsed.

Lennie's discussion of not being able to dance at the Canteen connects to his larger struggles with marginalization and disembodiment. He is at the Hollywood Canteen, but not allowed to dance. Like black men in the military, he is *right there* but not recognized, his talents underutilized. His narrative maps the Canteen to other Hollywood histories of marginalization—literally—his voice is heard in the number "Heat Wave," but the bodies of darkened lip-synching white dancers are acceptable, while the bodies of the black dancer-singers are rejected. The "Black feel" that is desired for the number cannot accommodate actual black bodies, at least not visible ones.

I mention to Lennie that dance scholar Brenda Dixon Gottschild writes about the phenomenon of dominant U.S. culture wanting black dance but not black bodies. Her elegant phrasing about this cruel irony is actually: "an oppressed people's artistry became the keynote of freedom for a dominant culture that segregated the dancer from the dance, that loved the message but denied and discriminated against the messenger."[11] My rephrasing doesn't do justice to the quotation but gets the gist across, eliciting a nod from Bluett. "Yeah, they want black dance, but not black bodies. I can go along with that. I can *attest* to that."

At this point, Bluett tells the story of black people being denied entry at the opening of the Hollywood Palladium. The stories connected to his Canteen stories span seven decades' worth of narratives about dancing within and against policies and attitudes calling for black bodily removal. Springing from an interview about the Hollywood Canteen, his narratives of movement, action, and perseverance in spite of imposed invisibility constitute significant performances of social torque that apply pressure to a dance floor democracy that simultaneously admitted him and denied him citizenship.

At the end of the interview, Lennie asks if we would like to see some film clips of him dancing. Of course we would. He takes us into the dining room, where he pops in a videotape of the nightclub scene in *Cabin in the Sky*, in which he dances with Vivian Dandridge to the Duke Ellington Orchestra. Just as in his work with Jeni LeGon in *Ali Baba Goes to Town*, you can see Bluett working the fine line, perfecting the art of making himself visible and memorable without stealing the scene from the principles. I don't think it is just because I am in his physical presence that my eye is drawn to his performance within the dancing crowd of underutilized actors and actresses of Black Hollywood. First, he and Vivian Dandridge dance casually on the street outside the club. He appears to be trying to talk her into going inside to dance with him. The featured dancers dance through the door, and then Lennie and Vivian link arms and synchronize a cool side-by-side strut through the door. Ellington's band is playing "Things Ain't What They Used to Be." The crowd leans into the band for the trombone cadenza. Then the Savoy Lindy Hoppers run in from the back to center screen and execute dazzling acrobat steps while the crowd looks on. Suddenly, all of the uncredited dancers, including Lennie, leap into action. Many of the women are dancers who are also working at the Alabam, including Avanelle Harris, and some of them are among the black women who served as junior hostesses at the Hollywood Canteen (Doris Ake, Juliet Ball, Louise Franklin, and Tommie Moore). Lennie winds up behind the crowd in the upper left quadrant of the screen, but he is throwing his hands up in the air as he dances.

I notice Lennie even before he points to the tall young handsome dancer in the famous jitterbug scene in *Cabin in the Sky*. He laughs at his younger self. "That's me in the background, waving my hands—so everybody sees me."[12]

I'm glad I saw Lennie Bluett, in person, and in the movie. I recognize him now in the crowd scenes and dance sequences of movies he was in. I've enjoyed seeing him interviewed by other people on YouTube in recent years. And I'm glad for the ways that my dance with him helps me to conceptualize a multiperspectival, race and gender and military service differentiated dance floor democracy. However, his relative invisibility and the fragile lines of introduction and timing that could have blocked our meeting are also a reminder of those who remain absent to my understanding.

Bob Alden: January 13, 2006

My interview with Bob Alden (born Altman, April 21, 1920) was organized around the fragility of memory—*his* memory, which was letting him down as a result of a stroke he had suffered six months previously. Valerie Yaros, historian at the Screen Actors Guild, had suggested that Bob would be a good person to talk to, if he felt up to it. When I called him to introduce myself, I initially thought he sounded uninterested. I felt sorry to bother him. Then he explained the gravity of his memory problem. He literally didn't know if he would know his name on any given day, let alone be able to help me out with memories of the Hollywood Canteen.

I didn't hold out much hope that he would consent to an interview. Nor was I sure if would be appropriate to interview someone in the condition he said he was in. However, I agreed to his request that I telephone him each morning while I was in Los Angeles. If he had a good day, Tami and I would travel to North Hollywood and we'd give it a try.

When I called him the next morning, he picked up the phone on the first ring and said to come as soon as possible. I jotted down the directions and assured him that if he couldn't remember anything, we would discontinue the interview.

A small, gentle man greeted us at the door of a small cottage in the Valley Village area of North Hollywood. His was one of four detached units in one of the little sets of matching houses that were built all over Los Angeles in the late 1940s. His street, Radford Avenue, had several such clusters of cottages in a row. His unit was small and dimly lit but saved by a window onto the street. He ushered us into his living room. We sat on one side, and he sat across from us in a chair and began to talk before we had the equipment set up. He didn't look well—he moved slowly; in person, you could see him working to remember and speak. The remembering seemed steadier than the speaking, in fact—his speech came out in three or four words and then a pause; then three or four more words, another pause. Nonetheless, he struck me as looking quite a bit younger than eighty-five. He seemed excited to talk. He had been thinking through the night about what he wanted to say and was pleased to have remembered some details and stories about the Canteen, despite his rapidly increasing loss of the ability to name things, to retrieve images and stories and details that had once been at his disposal. His speech was slow, but he was in a hurry to talk.

He began by presenting his Canteen card and the business card from his career as a bit actor. His acting career had been built on his appearance: diminutive and perpetually youthful. If you've ever wondered why there is an uncanny resemblance among messenger boys, newsboys, bellhops, and elevator operators from picture to picture between 1944 and the early 1950s, it is because about seventy-five of them are played by Bob Alden. Though nearly always missing from the credits, Alden (whose business card from those years was designed to make casting directors remember him as "The Little Guy") made a career of fitting the bill for bit parts calling for adult men of small stature, impeccable timing, and a talent for following directions precisely without taking up too much time or space. A good example of Bob in action is the film *Payment on Demand* (1951), in which the plot resolves, and the protagonist couple reunites, only because of a telegram that the unassuming Page Boy, neat in his uniform, delivers to Bette Davis at the eleventh hour. The Page Boy is played, of course, by Bob, thirty years old at the time but not looking a day over eighteen. He described his work:

> She's coming up a gangplank. I'm coming down. I've got to get to the bottom at the same time she does. She's carrying all kinds of packages. I'm carrying a wire on a plate. She gives the packages to her friend. I hand her the wire. And I mean, this, it's something you'd normally do, not thinking anything of it. But you're doing it to the camera. It's a real killer.[13]

Alden had two Canteen cards, one as Bob Alden, the anglicized stage name he took when he became an actor in 1944, and the other issued in 1942 under the name of Bob Altman, which was his family name. His parents were the children of Eastern European Jewish immigrants. He was still going by Bob Altman when he moved to Los Angeles from Cleveland. He admitted in our interview that it may have been in the back of his mind to break into pictures when he moved west, but his immediate motive for moving was that he had been offered a factory job in Los Angeles for $30 per week. In Cleveland, he had done the same job for $16.

He concentrated hard during his interview, berating himself for what he didn't remember, but just as often surprising himself with an unexpected detail: the size of the cups that Coke was served in, at one point, followed by a vivid description of the cooler where they were kept. He remembered his Hollywood Canteen by naming its pieces, as one might draw a room on a blank sheet of paper.

> Outside they had a rope. The servicemen used to crowd in. There'd be too many of them. Fill the building. So they'd open it. And then, outside, they had a Shore Patrolman. Two Shore Patrolmen. [pause]. One was in the navy, and the other was army, I guess, I don't, remember . . .

When he didn't remember something, he quickly moved to the next image, of which he seemed to have an endless supply.

"On the right side of the building there was a big snack bar. It was manned by stars. I remember Sheldon Leonard was one that was very active, Robert Alda . . ." His voice faded while naming actors. He shifted into descriptions of the food.

"They had—the sandwiches were just barely—they were very small. Baloney. I don't remember if there was cheese."

On to beverages: "They served Cokes, milk, coffee. And that was under the jurisdiction of—I mean, it was headed by Chef Milani, I don't know if that's right."

Yes, I assured him. It was Milani, an early celebrity chef of radio and later television. In 1942, Milani's daily radio show, *Dinner for Four, One Dollar No More*, could be heard on KFWB and coast-to-coast on the Blue Network.[14]

"He used to oversee it. The kitchen was run by Marie Hare. Her husband was an old vaudevillian, a star . . . In the back they had a bunch of, um, ladies. One of them was Mary Gray. She was that Irish one, who was everybody's mother in every picture you saw, all the, *Dead-End Kids*, the Irish pictures from New York."

A pause. And then another person or object would join the picture. When in doubt, he returned to the description of the Coke cooler, the counter, the cabinets, which seemed to reorient him—and then described the appointments of the room in another direction. It isn't surprising that these are points of reference in his mental map of the Canteen, considering that his physical orientation was of working the room as a busboy.

> To the left of this Coke display, there was a stage. In the corner of the room, there was a big control room where they did the live shows, and, ordinarily, you know, they had dance records. They had a disc jockey—actually, Jim Hawthorne, who later became quite a local radio deejay, operated that. On that stage, they did all kinds of entertainment for the servicemen. On weekends they had all the big bands. Kay Kyser was very, very much part of it, him, and his College of Musical Knowledge. I mean, it was practically a house band. It was all those big bands and the stars, came in at one time or another to perform. And, of course, the center was a dance floor, there were tables around it. And there's one picture that probably nobody remembers but me. In the men's room, the artists had painted servicemen doing their business at the latrine.

We all laughed. He was right, too. He is the only person who described that particular mural.

Alden continued. "It was a cute touch."

Returning to the touchstone of the Coke cooler, he told a story about Buster Keaton, who used to stand there dispensing drinks on Friday nights. One night Mel Blank was doing a Private Sad Sack routine, Alden recalled, and Keaton started laughing. "Buster was doubled over the pop stand, laughing, tears rolling down his cheeks. I tell ya,' it was the most exciting thing to me. Because whoever saw Buster Keaton *laugh*?"

I asked him what the other busboys did for a living. "They were agents, messengers, and anybody in the industry," he recalled. "There were technicians from the studios. Everybody in the industry was eligible. I mean, there were cameramen . . . there was makeup." It might have been a place where a draft-aged civilian man wore an apron and wasn't supposed to dance, but it was also a place where he wasn't isolated, where he was appreciated, where he was in good company. Alden seemed to have a soft spot for other "little guys," for Buster Keaton and Mel Blank, for instance. Later I learned that part of his inspiration to move to Hollywood had come from an interview he had conducted with Stan Laurel for his college newspaper in Ohio.

When I asked him why he volunteered so many nights a week (at least two, often more), he replied, "I had nothing else to do." Then he changed his answer to, "I loved it." He then posed the question again to himself. "Well, look," he said. "I had a very ramshackle room. I mean, I didn't have a . . ." his voice trailed off. "It wasn't home."

He described the makeshift bachelor apartment he had rented from "a little Scottish woman" and her elderly husband who "wasn't well and used to sleep on the couch." As with the Canteen, he drew the interior slowly, with words, working one detail at a time into a picture of memory. "I mean, my room was a bed. It was a Murphy bed but it wasn't mounted. It just sat there on the floor. The back, you know, leaned down. I had a chair . . . A rustic desk . . . That was it." Most of the time while he volunteered at the Hollywood Canteen, Alden worked as a soda jerk at Thrifty's, where, when he could afford it, he had dinner for 89 cents. After work, his apartment was not a place he "wanted to be around much, except to sleep."

Throughout our interview, we would almost say goodbye, and then he would begin to describe another aspect of the Canteen in detail. During one of the goodbyes, he said, "It's a funny thing, you know. I'm—I'm sitting here now, I'm eighty-five years old, and I'm going downhill, and I'm having physical problems I just started, and I never realized what a wonderful life I had. I never appreciated it, but I had a very, very interesting . . ." His voice trailed off. He picked up again: "a very, very interesting life."

For Alden, remembering his movements through the Canteen seemed to provide a route for claiming significance. He developed his "Little Guy" persona while picking up after the servicemen. The Canteen years were the period in which he launched his film career as a forgettable but frequently working extra. In a profession where unemployment and underemployment were—and continue to be—hazards of the trade and where very few ever play leading roles, Alden made more films than most. "I didn't appreciate the body of work I did. I'm looking it over again. It's wonderful. You probably picked a good time, because I didn't think I'd be able to do much." He died three months later.

A Final Run Up and Down the Mezzanine Stairs

As with the military women, civilian male volunteers navigated the Hollywood Canteen differently from the way military men and civilian women did and in a variety of ways that have been incompletely explored in this chapter. As always, it is important to hold space for other stories, other memories, other civilian men and military women, as well as other civilian women and military men. I exit this section especially haunted by my inability to see black WACs and WAVEs, to know if they were in the mezzanine, and if not, did they try to go and were they allowed in, and if so, what was this rare integrating setting of military women like? I leave part III, not knowing if the reason I didn't find black military women is that they weren't there. (If they weren't, perhaps it was because they anticipated they wouldn't be welcome in Hollywood or at USO-like clubs not operated by the black community? Perhaps their leisure time was protected by black community organizations, by clubwomen, by the YWCA women?) If they were there and were sent to the mezzanine, how might watching the soldier-hostess dyads have felt differently to them, according to race? What difference in reception might they have experienced with gatekeepers, hostesses, and other military women in that small room? I take the time to list these unknowns because not-knowing is also historical.

Historical space also needs to leave room for improvisation. Race and gender management could not have been consistent from night to night, hour to hour, with so many volunteers rotating in and out, and hundreds of new guests showing up several times a night. It was a time and context full of contradictions. All at once, military women were constructed as ultra-respectable and perceived as sexless, hypersexual, or queer. Civilian men were constructed as "either too young or too old," or ultra-humble to the point of blending into the woodwork, and at the same time seen as lazy, crazy, or queer. Racial differentiation of gender constructions and modes of gender management, stakes, and constraints affected where and how military women and civilian men could turn, what torque was possible at the Hollywood Canteen, and where else they might go.

Civilian men who volunteered regularly at the Hollywood Canteen moved in closer proximity to movie stars than most military personnel did. However, they did so while downplaying their own masculinity and pleasure. In doing so, they not only served a soldier-hostess dyad from the outside but performed the outside in a way that helped to produce the "inside," ultimately serving the domestic union of the jitterbugging young men marching off to war and the surrogate sweethearts in party dresses. Along with other forgotten players, military women and civilian men were part of the centrifugal force that pulled together a far simpler constituency as national memory. Excluded from the norm, they nonetheless participated in its construction. Yet they also managed to "right/write" themselves in Canteen space in different ways that contribute to an understanding of its complexity.

Consider the differences among the perspectives of the small number of civilian men encountered in these pages: the gay white pacifist, the embarrassed white teenaged child actor, the African American actor and musician in a longer struggle with Hollywood, and the white "soda jerk" who comes out of the Canteen with a new career as a steadily working small male extra. By imagining the perspectives of invisibilized national subjects—the white woman in uniform who watches from above, the woman of color in uniform whom I did not find (and who may not have been there), the man in the apron who removes the plates and cups without notice (except for the racially differentiated anxiety levels over whether the black busboy will dance on the floor)—perhaps it is possible to cause a little interference in the powerful torque of national identification with the dancing "we."

If military women troubled the construction of American woman even while serving their country and draft-aged civilian men were seen as un-American, what of Canteen-goers with diverse political orientations? The following chapter explores manifestations of political difference on the dance floor, including jitterbugging Marxists—actual and imagined, aggressively remembered and aggressively forgotten—and their state-ordered patrol.

PART IV SWING BETWEEN
THE NATION AND THE STATE

★ ★ ★ ★ ★ ★ ★ ★ ★ ★ ★ ★ ★ ★

CHAPTER 10

(Un)American Patrol

Following the State on the Dance Floor of the Nation

Whether you were Democrat or Republican, war or anti-war, we didn't
have all the crap we got now. They pulled together. . . . Republicans and
Democrats alike. So, it was a more united community in those days.
—JOHNNY GRANT, INTERVIEW WITH AUTHOR (MARCH 23, 2004)

The question of Negro equality is one of the basic planks in the Communist Party's platform. They are constantly raising this question to win
the Negroes over to their influence and if they can maintain the practice
now being put into effect in the HOLLYWOOD CANTEEN, they hope to use
it as an example for other sections to follow.
—FBI SPECIAL AGENT ———, REPORT (APRIL 14, 1943)

Among the bodies of jitterbugging junior hostesses and soldiers, sailors and
Marines, and doormen, senior hostesses, busboys, entertainers, other volunteers, and Shore Patrol and military police officers, circulated at least one undercover agent employed by the Los Angeles Field Office of the FBI.[1] I do not
know the name of the chronicler of Canteen events with whom I attempt to
dance in this chapter. On seventy-eight (out of the eighty-nine) pages of FBI
files on the Hollywood Canteen that were released to me through the Freedom of Information Act, the reporter's name has been replaced by a blank
rectangle and sometimes by a thick black line; sometimes he is called Special
Agent _____. I presume he was a *he*; the pronoun remains even though the
name has been removed. There is a strong likelihood that he was male and
white; no women were employed as special agents at the time, only one black
male agent (not in Los Angeles) was working for the FBI in the entire country,
and very few other people of color were, and then they were only used for
cases in which an agent of a particular ethnicity or race could camouflage

federal infiltration of particular groups.[2] Nonwhite race and ethnicity functioned for FBI assignments similarly to the casting of extras in the movies—as atmosphere, costume, specialty bodies for specialty scenes. It would have made little strategic sense to assign a person of color to Hollywood.

I am less sure whether Special Agent _____ was one person or several, but because all are interchangeable in the files, I, too, shall refer to "him" in the singular. Like diarists Jane Lockwood and Donald Vining, whose dance floor observations open chapters 4 and 7, the G-man on the Canteen-beat unlocks this chapter. Who was he? Possibly he was, among other things, a Canteen volunteer who, like Lockwood and Vining, moved through the crowds with an eye for democracy and then rushed home to write before he could forget. I imagine him moving through Canteen space with special attention to what he could see and the ways he was seen. He needed to see a great deal without calling attention to himself. In this way, like the draft-exempt busboy, his watching must have included reading his reflections in the eyes of others. Prose characteristics that might have provided clues (to his education, his class, and whether he was one person or more) are translated into officious summary; proper names are typed in caps if not marked out. Here is a style sample from the report dated August 12, 1943:

> Source stated that JULES C. STEIN was asked if he knew that CARROLL HOLLISTER, who is practically in control of the Canteen, [blank rectangle spreading across approximately forty-six characters]. Source stated that STEIN replied: "Yes, very definitely."[3]

A child of the Cold War, I can't help but hear the voice of actor Jack Webb as LAPD sergeant Joe Friday on the 1950s television show *Dragnet*: "The story you are about to hear is true. Only the names have been changed to protect the innocent." Like the best secret agent dramas, the files offer private pleasures; I feel the pull to play spy myself. These forty-six redacted characters, for example, while they should frustrate the researcher, present a seductive cryptogram whose solving *feels* like it would be justice. In my notes I have scribbled my guess: "is a member of the Communist Party (44 characters)?" There is, of course, no "solutions" appendix to check my handiwork. I puzzle over each cliff-hanger and take copious notes, but I can never know what is really there. What a tease the FBI turns out to be. All evidence is partial, but this kind flaunts its withholdings.

Nonetheless, I take very seriously my access to what I can see of these files. This access is, after all, one of the civil liberties fought for and won in the 1960s to protect us *from* innocence. It is my right to guess at what records might be held in the concealed hand of the state, to ferret out the file numbers that make it possible to request these records, and then, after a time, either receive or be denied censored access. I have the right to decipher the agent's officially paraphrased words, and I may choose to challenge redactions.[4] The Freedom of Information Act represents a hard-won liberal victory for the free flow of information as a hallmark of democracy, one that I passionately believe in, and protect to the best of my ability.[5] However, like other emblems of American democracy (including integrated dancing at the Hollywood Canteen) this one is not without its contradictions.

If the Freedom of Information Act is a hallmark of democratic government, then why must it be repeatedly insisted upon, fought for and defended by people in unrelenting battle with the state?[6] Nonetheless, to its champions, the Freedom of Information Act of 1966 represents the people's access to the information they need in order to fully participate in democratic society. Only if the people have access to information will their interests "flow" back to their government and shape policy that reflects their will. Among the critics of this premise is Grant H. Kester, who argues that the justifications for the Freedom of Information Act are firmly planted within the limitations of liberalism and are based on the shaky premise that the free flow of "'information,' in whatever form it might take . . . constitutes a progressive movement."[7]

In practice, the Freedom of Information Act is part of a tussle over which government branch gets to decide which information to release and which to withhold, part of a much longer dance, in Kester's words, a "highly ritualized *pas de deux* of accusation and moral censure, solicitation, and coy denial" performed by the "President and Congress over the control of information."[8] It is a dance not so much about *whether* information should flow freely to the people as about which entity is best suited to determine which information, if made freely accessible, will help people and which will harm them. Perpetually in motion, the Freedom of Information Act was amended repeatedly during the time I wrote this book.

In the file I am eventually granted—one of those brown files with the two metal prongs—eleven pages are missing, and much is thickly inked out. Nonetheless, despite these impersonal touches, I can trace some steps, learn some moves, identify some pushes and pulls that help me dance with interviewees, deceased diarists, and other figures encountered through email, telephone, and archival research. I am able to consider the effects of state-ordered surveillance on dancing bodies and the effects of incompletely available classified files, cryptic disguises of agents and willing informants, and thick redactions on what is knowable (and what *feels* knowable) through "freedom of information." Most important, I am able to consider the points of view that were untenable during the period of my interviews, but were considered mainstream at the time of surveillance. Although no one I interviewed claimed a prosegregation point of view, the FBI files recorded a prosegregation mainstream and deemed those who supported *intentional* (as opposed to color-blind) dancing across race as radicals, either Communists or fellow travelers. This is the story I read in the files: the FBI is called to the case when intentional integration is announced, steps up the case when it threatens to become policy, and exits the room when integrated dancing is casually tolerated but not explicitly encouraged, mandated, or protected. The sequence of case files reads as a step-by-step tutorial for the kind of "racial state" project that Goldberg argues seeks "to distribute the means and modes of [racist exclusion] behind a façade of racial dispersal."[9]

As I study these files, I am sometimes seduced into believing that my access to them gives me the veracity behind the veneer; the facts that I need to "speak truth to power" to the national memory of the democratic dance floor. Because of these files, after all, I, too, get to "listen in" on closed meetings of the board of directors about whether or not integrated dancing should be allowed, to watch people take positions that are no longer popular, and to consider a multiplicity of articulations of race, dance, swing culture, and American democracy that were all operating at once. In the heady thrill of these discoveries, I have to remind myself of the democratic dissonance of my access to this evidence: that the violated right to privacy of those under secret government surveillance is imperfectly balanced by my right to look over the shoulder of the government spy. I need to remember my orientation to this "free flow of information," and this means that I must remember, and include in this book, this relationship between my body and that of the undercover agent, as well as those of the people whose words were entered into reports without consent forms, narrated into state memory without their knowledge, and presented as "just the facts." Secret agents, like historians, cannot help but interpret as they document. Their bodies may attempt to evade the documents they produce, but they carry and leave traces. Undercover representatives of the state, however stealth, make a difference in the rooms they enter and to the people they encounter while doing their work—indeed, that difference *is* the work. Performance, says Diana Taylor, belongs "to the strong as well as the weak." Taking my cue from Taylor, who argues that archive and repertoire exist in an interactive relationship, I understand the state-charged body or bodies of Special Agent _____ as contributing to the encounters that later pass as "information" that I request from the state.[10] Surely the presence of Special Agent _____ affected the torque potential of others moving in those spaces and those of us who imagine them later. Dancing with the files allows me to consider the role of the state in shaping what happened at the Hollywood Canteen and how it is remembered.

I use the FBI files as an organizing principle in this chapter because, as with so much state memory, the files re-member much of what has been actively forgotten in national memory. They offer clues about what had to happen in the handclasp between the state and the nation in order for national memory to swing out in such spectacularly different yet compatible ways. In chapter 11 I follow through with this turn, conceptualizing the 1944 movie *Hollywood Canteen* (which continues to circulate) as an example of national memory. By approaching the FBI files and the film as dissimilar, but interlocking, official site visits to Canteen memory, I argue that state and national processes of remembering and forgetting are not the same, and are not opposites (and certainly not a contrast of fact and myth)—but are evidence of a powerful, pervasive dancing dyad that is not easily disentangled. I am interested in the magnetic play between the poles. That two such different versions of the dance floor could be produced by many of the same actors, fighting the same battles, offers a fruitful opportunity to explore this dance of forgetting and remembering. State memory maintains secretly compiled and classified data on racial integration conceived as un-American, then, partially releases its secrets, warts and all (well, not all . . . the people must be protected) in a ritual of freedom of information. National memory actively screens over these troubling connections through narrative diplomacy, generating apparently seamless versions of American freedom, equality, and democracy that work to invite unisonance of national subjects.[11] The files have helped researchers to gain better understanding of the role of the state surveillance in many areas that have been re-narrated in national memory as civil rights romances: the life of Martin Luther King, Jr., for example. I draw from such scholarship.

In addition, I draw from the literary genre in which memoirists who had been tailed by FBI agents interact with files obtained through the Freedom of Information Act. This tradition includes such classics as *Hollywood Red: The Autobiography of Lester Cole*, and more recently *The Gordon File: A Screenwriter Recalls Twenty Years of FBI Surveillance*, by Bernard Gordon, who like Cole, was a blacklisted screenwriter, and union president in the 1940s; Cole of the Screen Writers Guild, and Gordon of the Screen Readers Guild.[12] Both screenwriters belonged to the Communist Party in Hollywood, and both participated in the struggles to maintain an integrated dance floor at the Hollywood Canteen (along with Cole's sister Blanche, and Gordon's future spouse Jean Lewin, both active in the Screen Office Employees Guild). In their memoirs, Cole and Gordon tell stories of their lives in annotated relationship to the files that were kept on their every move. They correct FBI errors: both argue that Hollywood Communists did not *control* the guilds and unions of the motion picture industry (that was "neither a possibility nor . . . goal, Cole writes),[13] nor did they control pre-blacklist movies or plot to overthrow the government. Cole and Gordon also confirm what the FBI got right: both heartily agree that Hollywood Communists cared about and defended racial integration and that the government considered intentional race mixing to be subversive. In the spirit of these memoirs, I offer this chapter about diverse political perspectives at the Hollywood Canteen and the lingering effects of the wartime dance of state memory (by which I do not mean California, but the racially constituted but instrumentally narrated wing of the nation-state, as I have been developing throughout), and national memory as the hegemonic affective production of a "we." In this chapter, I want to drag the state back out onto the dance floor. Did Special Agent _____ consider himself a patriot? Was he, as Gordon wonders of his own personal agent, just another writer like himself, working as a bored screen reader?[14] I don't know. I am dancing with a stranger (a common Canteen experience). My purpose is not to accuse anyone of special treachery; I don't need to uncover his identity to crank up the volume on political dissonance at the Hollywood Canteen. To the same extent as any other narrative of dance floor democracy, *the story you are about to hear is true.* I flip open the files and follow—to the best of my ability.

Dancing with the State, Part 1 (August 4, 1942–March 22, 1943): Causing Surveillance

> UNDEVELOPED LEADS: LOS ANGELES FIELD DIVISION
>
> _____ at LOS ANGELES, will cause some surveillance to be made of the canteen which HOLLISTER proposes to open and a report will be submitted containing the facts relative to the nature of this institution and its attitude toward the armed forces.[15]

In the first report that I am granted, dated August 4, 1942, I learn that Special Agent _____'s task that summer is to investigate a nonexistent canteen for its "nature" and "attitude." If I had access to the reports of June and July 1942, I might know more about what drew the FBI to the earliest stages of this dance. However, I am "protected" by my denied request for those previous documents. Thus, I and readers of this book enter when the door opens for us; a little late to the dance, we nonetheless learn quite a bit about how Special Agent _____ approached his duties. His job description that summer is to gather facts on the "canteen which HOLLISTER proposes to open" and to "cause some surveillance" of a group of people that includes Bette Davis, John

Garfield, and other motion picture industry workers, famous and not, as they plan a soldier recreation center in Hollywood.

Did Special Agent _____ celebrate the night he got his working orders? Surely, this must have been one of the cushier wartime espionage gigs handled by the Los Angeles Field Division. If that was the case, it is unlikely that the Hollywood beat was new to him. From the files I was granted, it appears that the Los Angeles Field Office stumbled on the Hollywood Canteen at the very moment of its inception as an *idea* while tracking the activities of "persons of interest" to the FBI, most particularly HOLLISTER, whose name figures under the report header: "undeveloped lead." Reading further, I learn that the FBI's interest was piqued when an alert, democracy-minded white member of the Teamster's union intercepted a letter that had been sent to the guilds and unions of the motion picture industry. In this letter, the "Committee for Civilian Defense" of Local 47 (the white branch of the AFM) invited other guilds and unions to share in the planning of a servicemen's club in Hollywood patterned after New York's Stage Door Canteen.[16]

What was it about the musicians union letter to the other unions that attracted the FBI? It was no secret that interest was brewing in the guilds and unions of the motion picture industry to organize a Canteen for servicemen, based on the Theatre Wing's Stage Door Canteen in New York. As we already know, when the Hollywood Canteen finally did open in October, it was cheered by even the most middle-of-the-road newspapers and magazines, presented as an inspiring story of patriotism, democratic access to glamour, and selfless entertaining of the troops by some of the most popular and well-known figures in the country. What motivated the FBI to sniff out a noir angle to this story? And what were the *effects* of the FBI *causing surveillance*? What difference did it mean to Canteen operations to have a federal agent lurking on the premises? What difference does it make in our understanding of the democratic dance floor to factor in surveillance—or, in the prescient Foucauldian language of the FBI files—to factor in the disciplining effects of the FBI's charge to "cause some surveillance to be made"? Under the misleading heading "DETAILS," we find a clue among errors from a trusted CNDI (FBI code for "Confidential National Defense Informant).

> CNDI [blank rectangle] called Agent's attention to the fact that Local 399 of the Studio Transportation Drivers Union 319, A.F. of M [*sic*] had received a letter from CARROLL HOLLISTER, Chairman, Sub-Committee for the Canteen, 1521 North Detroit Street, Hollywood, California, with which letter he submitted a tentative program for a "canteen for democracy" which he proposed to organize and set up.[17]

In the "revisiting my files" genre of blacklisted writers, it is customary to poke fun at state bloopers, taking an ironic "high road" in noting that after all, the special agents in the "just the facts" genre are "only human." *We must excuse their little mistakes here and there*—this is the kind of rhetorical move summoned by blacklisted writers such as Lester Cole—"busy as the FBI was with hundreds in Hollywood being watched and monitored, such innocent slips must be forgiven."[18] I take this moment to linger on the small typo or misunderstanding that leads to the mistaken "detail" that identifies the Studio Transportation Drivers as a local branch of the AFM instead of the Teamsters. The AFM and the Teamsters stood at opposite ends of the political spectrum of union involvement at the Hollywood Canteen.

However, of course, this is a cheap shot—scathing in the hands of a writer whose career was ruined or interrupted, who was imprisoned, in the case of Cole—but coy in the hands of a researcher reading these reports in order to analyze swing culture as war memory. The FBI was, of course, very attentive of the political polarity between the Teamsters and more left-leaning guilds and unions, to the point of favoritism toward the former and demonization of the latter. The FBI had already identified many of the motion picture industry guilds and unions, including the AFM, as "Communist," or at least "communist," therefore matching the "blueprint" of "worthy targets" of federal surveillance established by J. Edgar Hoover, first director of what would become the FBI, during the Red Scare of World War I.[19] The Studio Transportation Drivers was the oldest Teamsters local in Hollywood, founded by anti-Communist Ralph Clare, who fought what he believed were Communist elements in his own union and in the other guilds and unions that he believed were becoming Communist controlled (such as the Screen Writers Guild). In 1947, Clare would become the chair of the conservative, anti-Communist Motion Picture Alliance for the Preservation of American Ideals.

So that's one error, a typo, really. The Studio Transportation Drivers was clearly not a subsidiary of the more left-leaning Musicians Union. The FBI knows better and will correct it in future reports. Now for the clue: as I try to follow the ins and outs of codes and procedures of FBI file-speak, I learn that it wasn't simply a concerned citizen who reported this letter to the local (undercover) authorities but "CNDI [blank rectangle]." It appears that the Los Angeles office had a "Confidential National Defense Informant" pipeline to the Hollywood Teamsters. It is likely that Special Agent _____ has a working relationship with this particular informant. I imagine them meeting off-site, to avoid suspicion, and perhaps Special Agent _____ doesn't roam the dance floor at all but picks up the tab at the Thrifty lunch counter, perhaps waited on by Bob Alden. In this business of tracking "persons" and "organizations of interest," one relies on the cooperation of others on the ground and at the top, some of whom have been useful in the past, and this pipeline to the Teamsters is one of them. We know from files on individuals and other organizations in the motion picture industry that many Canteen workers had already been identified as "persons of interest" belonging to "organizations of interest." Carroll Hollister had been followed since at least that previous April.[20] Lester Cole had been followed since 1940.[21] With a little help from loyal friends of the FBI, Special Agent ____ followed people who had been followed before, who had been informed on by people who had previously informed.

Perhaps it was Ralph Clare himself, the ultraconservative founding president of the Studio Transportation Drivers Local 399 (Teamsters), or one of his anti-Communist union brothers who saw something fishy about this call for action and dropped it into the lap of the FBI.[22] In any case, the Los Angeles Field Office forwarded the letter to national FBI headquarters with the promise to "cause some surveillance," and Special Agent ____ was unleashed. The Hollywood Canteen would not open until October 3, 1942—a good two months away. Without even *existing*, the Canteen was already under federal surveillance—and would be until April 26, 1945, when J. Edgar Hoover would become convinced that the Communists had vacated the premises.

Let us examine that suspicious letter, dated July 10, 1942, and signed by the "person of interest," Carroll Hollister, representing an "organization of interest," the AFM. Hollister's political leanings were not difficult to track. His premature antifascism was evident in his early support for the Spanish Civil War, as one of the founders of the Musicians' Committee to Aid Spanish Democracy (through the AFM). He already had his own file, according to the biographer of John Charles Thomas, the famous baritone for whom Hollister worked as an accompanist. As the story goes, Hollister had been followed by the FBI shortly after his move from New York to Los Angeles in April 1942, when a box he had shipped to himself "broke open" to reveal Communist literature. Did the box really break, or was it assisted? The FBI already believed that Hollister had belonged to the Communist Party since the early or mid-1930s.[23] It is no surprise that his arrival in Los Angeles caught the notice of the FBI or that his extracurricular activities were carefully tracked.

The first report from Los Angeles to national headquarters included two attachments: the letter from Hollister to the Studio Transportation Drivers (presumably identical to those sent to other motion picture industry unions), identifying him as chairman of the Sub-committee for the Canteen of the Civilian Defense Committee of Local 47 of the AFM, Los Angeles, and the proposal for the Canteen that Hollister's committee had submitted to the AFM.

Also signed by Hollister, this proposal had been previously delivered as a speech on June 19, 1942, at a full meeting of the Civilian Defense Committee of Local 47 in Hollywood.[24]

Titled "Canteens for Democracy," the speech employs language that would have been as suspicious to the FBI as it was attractive to leftists in June 1942:

> Perhaps not many of the members of our union have heard of the unique "Stage Door Canteen" in New York—a new sort of "people's night club" that has been created by the people of Broadway for the people of the armies, navies and air forces of the United States and the United Nations: a Canteen for freedom and Democracy![25]

Rhetorically, the word "people" is suspect—smacks of populism—appearing as it does three times in the first sentence. A different sort of dancing "we" is conjured by "new sort of 'people's night club'" from the morale-building "we" of the nation reflected in more typical patriotic jitterbug angle. His characterization of World War II as a "people's war for freedom" is another signal that those being called to the dance were a different group from the one "wanted" by Uncle Sam. Also suspect to the FBI would have been the deliberate inclusiveness of the "people" served by the club, as elaborated in the second paragraph: "men of every race and nation fighting against the Axis: no racial distinctions or national prejudices can inject their vicious poison into this democratic club, for there is no 'Jim Crow' here!"[26]

The third paragraph emphasizes the trade union membership in particularly populist terms, calling the "people of Broadway" everyone from the "union artists" who painted the walls to the "union cleaners and rubbish collectors" who kept the club clean and to the union actors and musicians who provided entertainment. The proposal doesn't specify the trades of the "union hostesses" but includes their labor of "friendly conversation" and serving as "dancing-partners" among those who "are there and work without pay, give everything without pay . . . a heartening example of what can be done by trade unions *uniting for Victory!*" The left-leaning Screen Office Employees Guild must have popped into the minds of FBI staff (as it does to mine) as a likely source of union hostesses.

Timing is critical in understanding these associations. Ever since Nazi forces had invaded the Soviet Union the previous summer, phrases such as "uniting for Victory" coming from known leftists would have registered as suspicious to the FBI and other anti-Communists. With this call, the Communist Party rallied U.S. members to support the U.S. entry into the war, after a period of opposition, and to inspire coalitions among Communists and non-Communist left liberals, after a period of distrust. "Uniting for Victory" achieves multiple meanings—conveying not only the unity of Allies against the Axis and the unity of Americans behind U.S. involvement in the war effort but the possibility of reuniting those who had been involved in the former alliances of organizations of the Popular Front that had been shaken by different responses to the Nazi-Soviet Non-Aggression Pact. The period of Canteen surveillance occurs in the "Post-Pact" period of American Communism. The "Pact" refers to the agreement signed by Joseph Stalin and Adolph Hitler in which they promised that their countries would not to go to war against one another. The period of the Pact (1939–1941) divided American Communists from many of the non-Communist leftist and liberal organizations and individuals with whom coalitions had been established during the "Popular Front" period (1935–1939). During the period of the pact, Communists, in support of Russia, took a strong position against the United States entering the war. During this time, the Communist position was to denounce the war effort against Hitler as imperialist. However, after the Nazi invasion of the Soviet Union on June 22, 1941, American Communists immediately shifted their position on the war.[27]

The quick turnabout of the American Communists from denouncing the war to full-out organizing to "win the war" demonstrated the strength of the Party line but also rendered postinvasion positions among liberals and Communists almost indistinguishable. On June 24, 1941, two days after the Nazi invasion of the Soviet Union, a twenty-two-year-old writer, Bernie Gordon, reported to his draft board but was classified as 4-F because of a heart murmur. In his memoirs, he wrote, "While friends of mine were sweating and dying in the fight against fascism, I was left sitting pretty in Hollywood. I felt keenly guilty about this and considered it my duty to do whatever I could to join in the struggle for a better world."[28] This included officially joining the Communist Party, soon after the bombing of Pearl Harbor, and doing whatever he could to support the war effort, which he saw as inextricable from the larger fight for world democracy and therefore deeply interconnected with the fight for the rights of workers, and for racial equality. All of these commitments came together in the battle to maintain an integrated dance floor at the Hollywood Canteen. Physically, the closest he got to the dance floor was driving his future wife, Jean Lewin, to and from the Canteen. However, behind the scenes, Gordon used his union leadership, and his professional and political connections, to fight the good fight, as he understood it, on the democratic dance floor that consisted of politically diverse people in coalition. Trust among the former members of the Popular Front may have been damaged, but alliances were again possible.[29]

Framing the ideal soldier canteen as one "without restriction as to race, class, or creed" and therefore as "a practical demonstration of the very ideals of democracy, freedom, and human brotherhood for which we fight," Hollister sounded an effective call for unity among Hollywood leftists, liberals, some trade unionists (depending on the union), civil rights activists, and/or Communists. His call to dance at a "new sort of 'people's night club'" in support of the "people's war for freedom" was a call for renewal among the Popular Front—and for same reasons was received as a call for surveillance by the FBI.

I picture Special Agent _____, contemplating the case from the dingy one-room apartment that doubles as his office. This image is fiction—neither true nor untrue—a product of the L.A. noir imaginary, as it gathers in my mind, uninvited, but somehow always in the wings. Unlike most of the other people whom I follow in this book, I have no idea where he lived. However, I do know that his job required him to read literature he *might* not want to be seen reading in public, especially if he was to publicly lunch with a known anti-Communist Teamster. It was a matter of routine for a Special Agent on the West Coast to count himself among the small but dedicated readership of the *People's World*.[30] His studies reward him with a lead when he stumbles across a story about the Hollywood Canteen penned by John Gunn, dated August 20, 1942, and finds that Carroll Hollister is quoted.[31] The following week he finds a second Canteen story, also written by Gunn, announcing a benefit for the Canteen to be held on August 29, 1942, at the Four Star Theatre on Wilshire, with a preview of a movie followed by a show at Ciro's restaurant. He relays the list of celebrity hostesses for the event: Betty Grable, Dorothy Lamour, Carol Landis, Kay Francis, Pat Dane, Maria Montez, Jane Wyman, Jinx Faulkenberg, and Janet Blaire. He does not seem to realize that "John Gunn" is the easily decodable pen name of Dalton Trumbo (referencing the author's 1939 antiwar novel *Johnny Got His Gun.*). Trumbo had either just joined or would soon join the Communist Party, but his sympathies with the Party preceded his official membership.[32]

Later on, Special Agent _____ will take notice of Trumbo, when he becomes one of the more suspicious of the Hollywood Canteen board members. However, for now, he is still early in the story. He reports that the Hollywood Canteen opened on October 3, 1942, and that Bette Davis is the president and Carroll Hollister is one of the vice presidents. Overall, this first report is dry, dominated by lists. He lists the guilds and unions involved. He lists other industry-related groups involved in the organizing of the Canteen, including the HVC and the Actors Lab. He records the names of other labor organizations "expected to endorse the Canteen," such as the Trade Union Unity for

Victory Committee. Like me, he is convinced that there must be more to the most publicized origin stories behind the planning and opening of the Canteen.

The origin story traced by Special Agent _____ more closely resembles the versions reported in the black press, some union papers (such as the AFM's *Overture*), and Communist and otherwise leftist papers such as the *Daily Worker* and *People's World* than it does the stories in movie magazines or the *Los Angeles Times*. He locates the "campaign for a canteen" not in the Green Room of Warner Bros., but with a coalition among the segregated Los Angeles locals of the AFM. He identifies the key players from the white Local 47 as including Carroll Hollister and Alex and Sarah Compinsky, and members of the segregated black Local 767, including Florence Cadrez and Baron Morehead. He also notes that this integrated group has the support of J. K. (Spike) Wallace, president of Local 47. Unlike the official story repeated as national memory, and like the black press and Popular Front press, the FBI version by Special Agent _____ reports that it was this initial racially integrated meeting of the segregated musicians that "led to a meeting with Bette Davis, Jules Stein, John Garfield," and others. At the opening of the club, the officers were Bette Davis, president, and several vice presidents, including Carroll Hollister, John Garfield, and J. K. Wallace. Al Ybarra was the treasurer and Jean Lewin was the secretary.

More lists: the Executive Committee included Catherine Baldwin, Billie Burke, Florence C. Cadrez, Lester Cole, Mervyn Le Roy, Mack Millar, George Ramsey, Casey Roberts, William Simon, Doris Stein, Jules Stein, and John TeGroen.

The board of directors—another list (to which I shall return).

A slip on page 4 confirms my suspicions that one informant at the top is Ralph Clare. The name is blanked out to protect "the identity of a confidential source," but the initials of the statement are R.C. Disgruntled about a meeting of the board of directors of the Hollywood Canteen held at the Hollywood Roosevelt Hotel, January 7, 8:30 p.m., R.C. complains that the executive board was not informed of the meeting.

From this meeting, however, additional lists could be compiled for national headquarters. Chairs of the various committees included Doris Stein and Florence Cadrez for the hostess committee (white and black, respectively); Mervyn LeRoy and Harry Crocker for the hosts; Mack Millar would head up the publicity committee. Ann Warner (wife of producer Jack Warner) was in charge of contributions. Producer and agent (and arguably the most powerful person in Hollywood) Jules C. Stein was in charge of business management—and on and on. In charge of entertainment would be Bob Hope (chair). The snack bar committee was headed up by Mrs. John Ford and Billie Burke, the kitchen by Chef Milani.

With the help of his informants, Special Agent _____ follows the money, learning that "the Canteen is supported by donations" and some high rollers were included. R.C.'s report, as quoted by Special Agent _____, states that "$50,000 had been donated by Sol Lesser, producer of the motion picture, *Stage Door Canteen*." Selling places at the "Angel's Table" was another method of raising money. "Celebrities are invited to visit the Canteen and pay $100 per plate and sit at certain tables where they are put on exhibition." More modest fees were collected by "workers who donate their services . . . [and] are required to register and pay $1.00 as a fee." And because "persons of interest" are always relevant, even when they don't show up at the meeting, the report notes that "CARROLL HOLLISTER is now in New York."[33]

If the report of February 4, 1943, was mundane and inconclusive, the lengthy missive of April 14, 1943, picked up the slack. This report, in fact, would earn him the special attention of J. Edgar Hoover himself and promote the case to a higher classification (from "INTERNAL SECURITY-R; CUSTODIAL DETENTION" to "INTERNAL SECURITY-C"). The bulk of the report involved details of a meeting of the board of directors of the Hollywood Canteen on March 22, 1943.

Synopsis of Facts

The matter of white girls dancing with Negro soldiers and Negro girls dancing with white soldiers came up for discussion and disposition. The discussion became quite heated and a motion was made that the officers of the Canteen instruct white and colored girls that they were not to dance with soldiers of different color. The motion brought a storm of protest but was lost by an overwhelming majority. Race riots were predicted.[34]

Though not a member of the board of directors and not present at this discussion, Special Agent _____ collected a detailed report from his well-placed informant, who told him all he needed to know in order to report that the motion for mandating hostesses to say "yes" to dance invitations across race "apparently had been promulgated by the Communist element of the management."[35] The three-page, single-spaced report of the meeting reads like a script—who said what, who got angry, what sides people took—all duly noted and delivered via Special Agent _____ to national headquarters.

The March 22 meeting was chaired by J. K. (SPIKE) WALLACE, from Local 47 of the Musicians Union, and attended by about twenty-five people, "a large percentage of whom were unknown to informant although informant is a member."[36] (Ralph Clare, by the way, was a member of the board of directors.)

Again, the spotlight is on "CARROLL HOLLISTER," who "took the floor and complained about officiousness of the Military Police and Shore Police in questioning soldiers who visited the Canteen, particularly the Negroes." Hollister "defended the practice of mixed dancing—white girls with Negroes and Negro girls with white soldiers—which has been going on for some time in the Canteen. He drew a vivid picture of persecution of minorities under Hitler, particularly of the Jews, and compared it with the persecution of the Negro in America."[37]

These linkages—racism at home with fascism abroad—were commonplace in the national black press; this was the Double Victory campaign, through which many African Americans supported the war effort. However, for the FBI such a linkage, in the black press and elsewhere, flew as anti-Americanism.[38] The remainder of the report reads like a ballot count, naming the names of who supported and who opposed the statement.

The lists of Hollister supporters included any possible associations to Communism. For example, PAUL JAFFEE, who supported Hollister's "impassioned talk," is pegged as "a member of the Executive Board of Laboratory Technicians, Local 683, a Communist-controlled local union of the IATSE."[39]

Those who opposed Hollister's nondiscrimination statement included the powerful agent and head of MCA (Music Corporation of America) Jules Stein (agent of Bette Davis and many of the other biggest stars in the business). Vehemently opposed to mixed dancing was "FLORINE BALES, West Coast Representative of the American Guild of Variety Artists (AGVA)," who "stated that many of the girl members of her union refused to visit the Canteen to entertain because attempts were made to coerce them into dancing with Negroes." Another active Canteen volunteer, popular bandleader KAY KYSER (whose band played every Friday night, free of charge), "stated he was not exactly in favor of mixed dancing but thought it might be ironed out in some manner."[40]

Next, RALPH CLARE (possibly writing about himself if he is the source) proposed a motion to solve this problem by having "officers of the Canteen instruct white and colored girls that they were not to dance with soldiers of different color." The informant notes: "This motion brought a storm of protest."[41]

The first person to object, according to the report, was J. K. WALLACE, who "violently opposed the motion and said that if it were passed he would resign from the Canteen, and that his union, Musicians Local 47, would withdraw as a body."[42]

This outburst convinced Special Agent _____ that the AFM "is completely controlled by the Communist Party." The fact that Clare's anti-mixed-dancing motion loses "by an overwhelming majority" is evidence enough for the informant (possibly Clare himself) that "the Hollywood Canteen is under the control of Communist elements, that it was a Communist inspired project from the beginning."[43]

Break-away: Jitterbugging Marxists

Lee found himself in the bar again. A jive record filled the room with a boogie beat and some of the younger Marxists began jitterbugging. Soon an argument ensued as to the correct manner of executing the steps.
—Chester Himes, *Lonely Crusade* (1947)

As dangerous as the FBI considered the efforts to integrate a dance floor in Hollywood, the commitment of the Communist Party to racial justice was a matter of debate among African Americans in the 1940s, even Communist Party members and those drawn to the Party's earlier activism on behalf of the Scottsboro Boys.[44]

Novelist Chester Himes, who had been very influenced by the Communist Party in his early years in Los Angeles, by the mid-1940s was, cynical about Party overtures to African Americans. His 1947 novel *Lonely Crusade* includes a scathing interracial jitterbug scene of jitterbugging Marxists who care more about the "correct manner of executing the steps" than they do about the dance. White Communist women who dance across race are referred to as "bait" at the end of the Party line—their job is to lure African American men in order to expand the reach of the Party.[45] The protagonist stand-in for Himes in this loosely autobiographical novel, Lee, is warned about Jackie, a white Communist woman, and told to "use a prophylactic," presumably because she had slept with many other "recruits." Lee retorts that he will "use dialectics instead." When he asks Jackie if she is bait, she replies, "We're not interested in recruiting colored people. It causes disunity."[46] Elsewhere, a white union organizer explains to Lee why class trumps race: "We can't have unity and special problems at the same time. They just don't go together."[47]

Himes's skepticism about the Communist Party's wartime antiracist commitments was shared by Loren Miller, the civil rights lawyer famous for trying hundreds of housing covenant cases in Los Angeles. Miller had been very interested in Communism in the 1930s, when the Communist Party had done more for the Scottsboro Case than the NAACP did. In 1934, he wrote an article titled "One Way Out—Communism" for *Opportunity* in which he argued that "Negro nationalism" benefited capitalism because in a Jim Crow society, cultural nationalism could only contribute to creating a separate class of people. Instead, he argued, cross-race, working-class alliances were the only way to change the system.[48] He had traveled to Russia with Langston Hughes and briefly written for the Communist press. He became disillusioned with the Party, however, during the period of the Pact (1939) and the Post-Pact reversal. As Miller told Lawrence de Graaf in his 1967 oral history, during World War II "the Communists had no concern except for victory over the Nazis on the part of the Soviet Union."[49]

Not all African Americans were disenchanted with the Communist Party during the war, however. Charlotta Bass of the California *Eagle* had swung to the left and in August 1943 ran an ad in her paper with a message from Pettis Perry, the African American district chair of the Communist Party (whose office was located at 4414 1/2 South Central Avenue). "Only a few weeks ago we witnessed the scandalous anti-Negro, anti-Mexican riots," wrote Perry. "These were fifth column uprisings against our nation's war effort and against the unity of the United Nations. No amount of evasion, silence or red-baiting on the part of anyone can refute this fact." In support of his case that the Zoot Suit Riots were organized by Nazis and the Klan, Perry asked: How can it be explained that these riots took place on the evening of our invasion of Sicily? How is it to be explained that they developed at the time when Negroes were making their greatest contribution to the war effort?[50]

A regular feature of the *Negro Digest* was the "Round Table," in which well-known figures debated topical issues. Questions were treated from a variety of perspectives and accompanied by a poll. The December 1944 issue of *Negro Digest* selected for its round table and monthly poll the question "Have Communists Quit Fighting for Negro Rights?" Taking a variety of positions on the topic were William L. Patterson, George S. Schuyler, Benjamin A. Davis, Horace R. Cayton Jr., and James W. Ford. Of the readers who responded to the poll, 22 percent were undecided. A slim majority voted no. Those who voted yes tended to feel that Communists had let up on the fight for "Negro rights" either at the moment the U.S. Communist Party supported the war (when Germany attacked Russia in June 1941) by focusing more on the war effort and not critiquing the administration's positions on race equality or in 1944, when the U.S. Communist Party became the Communist Political Association (no longer a political party). Those who voted that Communists had not abandoned civil rights for African Americans cited Communist opposition to Jim Crow in the armed forces and support for the Fair Employment Practice Committee.[51] None mentioned interracial dancing at the Hollywood Canteen to support their position. However, the intraracial debate represented by the poll helps to complicate the political implications of white jitterbugging Marxists dancing across race during World War II and to imagine multiple frames in which this would have incited interest and debate beyond the FBI.

Dancing with the State, Part 2 (May 11, 1943–August 12, 1943): Cataloguing Canteen-Goers

In the spring of 1943, on the eve of nationwide race riots, Special Agent _____ received orders to step up the case. A memo from J. Edgar Hoover, dated May 11, 1943, mandated a game change. Special Agent _____ now found himself working a case of higher priority (INTERNAL SECURITY-C), which entailed compiling a detailed compendium of discreetly gathered information about the "Communist Party affiliations or sympathies" of people involved in the Canteen. He was instructed to conduct "highly discreet" inquiries among "confidential informants and reliable contacts" about the "Subversive and Communist" elements at the Canteen. The memo notes that duplicates of the files on the Hollywood Canteen had been sent by special messenger to the War Department, the Director of Naval Intelligence, and the LAPD. Special Agent _____ had been very successful, it seems, not only at conducting but "causing" surveillance." How satisfying it must have been for him to learn that because of his good work, the Canteen's front doors were guarded by military police and Shore Patrol officers whose superiors had been given a personal heads up by J. Edgar Hoover.[52]

The results of Special Agent _____'s investigations are included in his report to national headquarters dated August 12, 1943. In addition, the lengthy report offers a detailed report from a source who had attended a special meeting of the board of directors that had been held on July 8, 1943, expressly for the purpose of settling "the question of racial discrimination and the propriety of officially endorsing mixed dancing between Negro soldiers and white women hostesses at the Canteen." At present, either this informant or another source notes, "there are colored girls provided for colored servicemen and not long ago a white sailor danced with one of the Negress hostesses."[53]

For the source (possibly Ralph Clare) and for many individuals (according to the report), the connection between Communists and mixed-race dancing was no abstraction—and had been heightened by the race riots that had erupted nationwide that summer: San Diego (June 9), Philadelphia (June 10), Chicago (June 15), Evansville (June 27), Detroit (June 20–21), Harlem (August 1–2)—and of course, the so-called Zoot Suit Riots in Los Angeles, the worst of which raged through June 1943.[54]

What follows is my summary of the play-by-play of that meeting, with its alleged three-hour discussion on mixed-race dancing, as reported to the FBI by Special Agent _____ via his confidential informant. First, the secretary of the Canteen, Jean Lewin, read aloud "two communications, one from the Screen Readers Guild and one from the Screen Office Employees Guild." Both letters "demanded a statement from the Board of Directors of the Canteen of its policy on the question of racial discrimination"; after which "a motion was made by a man who appeared to be a Mexican, name unknown, suggesting that the letters be answered suitably and a copy of the Articles of Incorporation and the By-Laws of the Canteen be enclosed with the answers."[55]

Who was the "Mexican, name unknown," who moves to honor these letters with an official reply? Among the small number of Latinos on the board is Cuban-born Pepe Ruiz, union organizer and business manager of the Screen Cartoonists Guilds, and Raymond Lopez, representing the Makeup Artists. However, the informant identifies both men later in the report (misidentifying the latter board member as "PEDRO LOPEZ, Mexican, occupation unknown"). Whoever he is, the man who makes the motion to settle this question of mixed-race dancing, the fact of his apparent Mexican-ness must have registered as significant to everyone in the room in July 1943, so soon after the Zoot Suit Riots (whom some in the room would have understood as race riots perpetrated by white sailors and others would have attributed to the inherent lawlessness of Mexican and black youth in Los Angeles).[56]

What happened next, according to the report, is that "JULES C. STEIN immediately took the floor and raised objections to the content of the letters," adding that "he was aware that both letters were inspired by those elements within the organizations which these parties represented."[57]

At this point, a Screen Readers Guild representative "jumped to his feet and denied vehemently that there was subversive activity in the Canteen and stated that his organization was free of such activity or that the letter from his organization was so inspired."[58] (Sixty years later, Bernie Gordon will tell me that this could not have been him—it would have "complicated" things for Jean to have him present at such meetings.)

Mr. STEIN apologized in a way for accusing the Screen Readers Guild of being subversive as an organization but reiterated that he knew there were subversive elements in that organization whose motives were other than good for the Canteen and he felt that this constant agitation by these subversive elements would bring on, sooner or later, a serious race riot, in which case the military authorities might be forced to close the Canteen.[59]

As an aside, the informant cannot help but share a chummy exchange between himself and Mary Ford, wife of director John Ford, who "leaned over
and said she wished this 'subversive Communistic stuff' could be kept out of
the Canteen." The source seems rather proud of his quick rejoinder, quoting
himself as saying that the two letters "might just as well have been written
on the stationery of the Communist Party and signed by its Secretary." This
brought a favorable response from Mrs. Ford.[60]

Several pages of notes follow in which the source shares with Special
Agent _____ the discussion pertaining to "whether or not the Board of Di-
rectors should officially endorse mixed dancing." Board members who "took
the floor and spoke in favor of the resolution for mixed dancing" included
"PAUL JAFFEE, CARROLL HOLLISTER, DALTON TRUMBO, HARRY CROCKER,
BARON MOREHEAD, and some others whose names he does not remember."
Those who "took the floor and opposed the motion" included "JULES C. STEIN,
MARY FORD, LINDSAY THOMPSON, MICKEY MORRIS, KAY KYSER, and RALPH
CLARE." [61]

The remainder of the report included detailed discussions of the various
positions expressed by those with strong feelings about the racial makeup of
the dance floor. According to the source, bandleader Kay Kyser, articulated
his opposition to mixed dancing as a labor issue because "if a race riot should
start he and his band of musicians were so situated on the platform that they
could never get out."[62]

Ralph Clare "took the floor and stated he knew that subversive elements
were at work in the Canteen, but their motives were well concealed. He stated
that many of them were known to be subversive and that they were not Nazi
or Fascist, but were of another group equally subversive."

Director Mervyn LeRoy "stated that he would not belong to any organization that practiced racial discrimination."

Jules Stein countered with the statement "that the New York Canteen did
not permit mixed dancing and he could not see why the Hollywood Canteen
could not have the same rule and the same regulations," to which "CARROLL
HOLLISTER then took the floor and contradicted STEIN and said that [mixed-
race dancing] was a common practice" at the State Door Canteen.

Next up, according the informant, was "Baron MOREHEAD, a Negro musician," who reminded the board of the attempt at an earlier meeting "to pass a
motion which would prohibit mixed dancing on the Canteen premises, and
that it was only the action of SPIKE WALLACE, Head of the Musicians Union,
Local #47, in making the threat to take his union out of the Canteen, that
prevented the passage of the motion at the former meeting." Whether or not
such a vote had ever taken place became the topic of debate until enough

people remembered it, at which point an "amendment to the original motion was made" that specified that the letters from the Screen Office Employees Guild and the Screen Writers Guild clarify the Canteen policy on mixed-race dancing, thus:

> It was the policy of the Board of Directors to oppose racial discrimination; that although it (the Board) did not favor mixed dancing, it would be a matter of individual action of those who favored it; that it would not be officially prohibited.[63]

The board exempts itself from racism, while the compromised policy endorses nondiscrimination as a *value* without installing infrastructure to dismantle or oppose existing discrimination. This is a precursor to the now ubiquitous corporate-model "diversity statement," analyzed by Sara Ahmed as "the nonperformativity of antiracism."[64]

Of course, the next challenge was how to "devise a method of procedure for the Canteen that would not be based on racial discrimination but would at the same time tend to protect the Canteen from the possibility of race riots (with race riots presumed, of course, to be caused by racial mixing rather than by segregation and racism). People did what people do at such moments in a meeting: they appointed a committee. The seven-member group charged with this task was a volatile mix of Communists and anti-Communists (both Dalton Trumbo and Ralph Clare were appointed); those who had spoken out firmly for mixed-race dancing (Trumbo, Paul Jaffee, and Baron Morehead) and those resolutely opposed (Clare, along with Jules Stein, Mary Ford, and Kay Kyser). Moorehead was the only person of color. While inclusive of the poles at either end of the political spectrum, the balance tilted toward the anti–mixed dancing position.

With that bit of business out of the way, "a motion was then made and carried that all verbatim statements made in the heat of discussions be stricken from the minutes and that only the results of the meeting be placed on record." However, this democratically executed majority decision was breached, observed the source.

"Secretary JEAN LEWIN appeared to take down every statement made during the discussion on the race question while during the discussion on other matters she was not particularly attentive."[65]

Oral History Break-away 1 (May 21, 2003)

I began this project too late to have the opportunity to meet Jean Lewin, executive secretary of the Hollywood Canteen, who wrote so attentively as board members argued about "the race question," even after the vote

FIG 10.1: Jean Lewin, secretary, the Hollywood Canteen. COURTESY BERNARD GORDON.

carried to strike the discussion from the official record. However, I did meet and interview her widower, blacklisted screenwriter Bernard Gordon, who had been president of the Screen Readers Guild in the 1940s.[66] I had learned from reading his memoir, *Hollywood Exile, or, How I Learned to Love the Blacklist*, that if Bernie Gordon and Special Agent _____ agreed on anything at all, it would be that Jean Lewin was especially attentive to the race question at the Hollywood Canteen. Too invested to simply sit there and jot down what would go in the minutes, she was, as the source suspected and Gordon's memoir corroborates, not only a scribe but a comrade and a fighter in the battle to racially integrate the dance floor. It is in his first book that I encounter the story of Jean traveling to Port Hueneme with Bette Davis to try to get the racist shore patrolman "Mickey" transferred, and about how, when he wasn't removed, Jean organized antiracist volunteers to protect black soldiers, sailors, and marines from Mickey's violent reactions to racial mixing.[67] Upon reading this, I wrote two letters to the author, one in care of his publisher and one in care of the Screen Writers Guild. Gordon replied by email. It turned out that the self-proclaimed "Hollywood exile" was living in Hollywood and willing to tell me what he could about Jean's work at the Canteen.

On the map, the house seemed closer to my hotel than it felt as I hiked uphill from Sunset Boulevard. Bernie Gordon lived on one of those winding, gardened, quiet streets just west of La Cienega that benefits from being both within and above West Hollywood. Wide-leaved, brightly flowering tropical plants, cacti, and pine trees flourished side by side on the street I climbed toward his house. It presented me with a precipitous stairway from the driveway to the front door. I rang the bell, without catching my breath, utterly winded and a little late, yet only having walked about five blocks. A white-haired man answered the door. At his side was his trusty black and white springer spaniel, Rocky II. Gordon offered me a glass of water and guided me to his study in the back of the house.

It always makes me a little nervous to ask people if I can tape-record their interviews. It is even harder when I am aware that the person belongs to a group that has good reason to dislike recording devices. Gordon had a look on his face that was somewhat hard to read—a blend of amusement and outrage, I remember thinking. After pleasantries about the weather and my gratitude for his time, I stammered through my explanation about how recording our conversation would help me to quote him accurately.

He shrugged. "Why not? The FBI already knows everything about me."

I knew Gordon's wry wit from his book, but to experience it in person was something else. He was funny—I laughed—but at the same time I wondered if that was the correct response, aware that he was observing me. Of course, that is always true in the getting-to-know-you dance of the interview, but with Gordon, I accepted at the get-go that I was out of my league in the observation department. Here, after all, was a professional writer—not only that but one who had been spied on and secretly written about by the FBI—and whose career had been interrupted by being written about—and then had his revenge, writing books about being watched and written about. He had just completed his second book, *The Gordon File*, a memoir in which he reprinted and responded to the files the FBI had kept on him personally for twenty-six years.

I set up and tested my equipment. As soon as I hit record, Gordon began to interview me. "How did you get into the Canteen business?" For twenty minutes I talked and he asked follow-up questions. He was especially interested in the FBI files on the Hollywood Canteen that I had obtained, which he had not seen. He asked for copies that he might include in his forthcoming book. I agreed to send to him copies of what had been sent to me and told him how much I appreciated his first book.

"Well," he said with an air of finality. "Now you know what I know."

This was the crossroads; time to either thank him for his time, or try my hand at leading, if only momentarily. I asked him to tell me more about Jean's commitment to racial equality. Where did it come from? And who else, besides Jean, was involved in the battle to integrate the dance floor?

"To begin with," he said, "I have to tell you that we were—my wife and I, and a number of other people—members of the Communist Party back then. And we were the ones that took the position that you had to have it integrated. We wouldn't hold for anything else." He contacted everyone he knew in the trade union movement, "other left-wing people," and asked them "to write letters to the board saying it had to be integrated. I wrote one myself. I was president of the screen readers union at the time."

As Canteen secretary, Jean worked closely with people whose political views on racial mixing and other matters clashed. The board of directors, said Gordon, "consisted of a few people like Bette Davis and Jules Stein," as well as "the business managers of each of the unions," who, he added, "with few exceptions were as reactionary as anybody, especially in relation to the race question."[68]

The producers were uptight about racial mixing, said Gordon, because photographs of their stars and starlets dancing across race could hurt their investments. However, the movie industry was not alone in such institutional concerns. "Remember," he said,

The army was segregated. There was no integration anywhere, except in a few places like the Hollywood Canteen. And the producers all felt that it was very dangerous to have this whole story come out . . . You know, they so much as threatened not to let their stars come and perform at the Canteen if this happened. And so the board had to wrestle with this problem of how to deal with this issue and not lose the cooperation of the studios, which was essential. I was not present. My wife was present. I'd hear the story from her. We weren't married yet, but we were virtually living together. Sinful sex did not start with the sixties. We knew about sex way back then. And, I would hear all the stories of what was going on, and, to some extent I would try to encourage her to fight the battle. She was five feet tall and weighed a hundred pounds and she had a lot of important people to deal with. I was very proud of her because she stuck to her guns and she offended some of those people.[69]

Gordon's pride in Jean and his sense of her as a comrade-in-arms and unconventional person fighting a compromised system expresses another idealized heterosexual dyad present at the Canteen. Although Gordon isn't present inside the Canteen, his tender bundling of his account of her Canteen work, his support of her efforts through the unions, their shared political commitments, and long premarital love affair is a powerful instance of romance and intimacy in the Communist Party, as described in scholarship and memoirs. Writes Daniel Hurewitz,. "Communists of the 1930s and '40s were forging a powerful relationship between their interior lives and political action."[70] In her memoir *The Red and the Blacklist*, Norma Barzman writes:

> It sounds silly and maybe that's why no one mentions it. Hollywood Communist couples had a romantic notion of themselves as the ideal young man and young woman surging forward with the Red flag, the logo of Artkino (Soviet films). Each of those couples saw themselves as a tiny collective that would go out and make the world better. . . . To be together in this enterprise of making the world better brought with it a chest-bursting pride, a heady elation, a belief in the gloriousness of life, which was an integral part of Communist love between a man and a woman. It was so strong and all-pervasive that the ordinary trials of everyday life became small and unimportant.[71]

Bernie and Jean didn't have to jitterbug together at the Hollywood Canteen to perform this powerful democratic romance—in fact, their work together at the center of and behind the scenes of Canteen operations enacts a different vision of democracy from that of the state, or the nation—a vision of a better world. In our interview, Gordon elaborated, "We were fighting for racial equality, we were fighting for trade unions, and other things in this country to make life better." Gordon goes on to tell me about the Communist Party's work on behalf of the Scottsboro Boys.

> That whole business of race relations was a very important one for the Party from the very beginning. That's a very honorable role they played. Here in Los Angeles during the war, there was a great deal of racism against Latinos, the zoot-suiters. And a bunch of them were sent to prison for life on a phony charge, and a friend of mine wrote a pamphlet and exposed the whole thing.

Some Los Angeles Communists worked with farmworkers; some defended criminalized Mexican American youth; some promoted interracial dancing—a tactic of Communist youth since the 1930s. A Communist spin on the "junior hostess" was a popular activity of the American Youth for

Democracy (AYD), whose wartime project, Sweethearts of Servicemen, committed its energies to war work such as writing to keep servicemen "informed about the homefront," serving as hostesses in canteens, including USOs, and visiting hospitals. Explicitly political work included advocating servicemen's right to vote, casting one's own vote for legislation that would assist veterans on their return to civilian life, and learning from and educating GIs on "issues of today," including "doing away with prejudices," as well as having fun.[72] In 1943, the AYD also founded an interracial teenage canteen.[73]

According to the organization's pamphlet, published in 1945, the AYD was "an inter-racial, inter-faith youth organization, dedicated to character building and education in the spirit of democracy and freedom."[74] The Los Angeles chapter of the AYD had one thousand members ranging from ages thirteen to thirty in 1944, according to Los Angeles Daily News columnist Virginia Wright.[75] The Shore Patrol characterized the Los Angeles chapter of the AYD as a menace for its "efforts to propagandize and recruit service men, particularly at U.S.O. centers," and prominently featured the organization in a list of hazards for sailors on leave in a report submitted to the chief of naval personnel: "young feminine members of this newest and most active Communist front organization have been extending invitations to service personnel to attend house gatherings and dances sponsored by AYD."[76] The Shore Patrol report does not mention that members of the AYD also circulated petitions calling for "the establishment of full and equal participation of Negroes in the armed forces of our nation" or that California AYD members collected eight thousand signatures on that nationwide petition, which they hand-delivered to Assistant Secretary of War John J. McClay. Specific suggestions in the petition included several explicitly directed to the secretary of the navy to "Open up all branches of Naval service on a basis of full equality" and "Open up WAVES, SPARS, MARINES" and other women's branches of the armed forces "to Negro women on the basis of full equality."[77]

The report of Special Agent _____ and my conversation with Bernie Gordon are consistent with the Shore Patrol's view that dancing across race was a political commitment of Communists. At one point, Special Agent _____ reports that "it is common knowledge in the Hollywood area that the Canteen has become a meeting place where young Communist girls contact prospects for propaganda purposes and arrange for parties and gatherings on the outside. These girls volunteer to work or entertain at the Canteen for this purpose.[78] Though dancing is not necessarily a prelude to sex, it is important to note the similarity of this obsession with interracial dancing and Communism with LAPD police chief Davis's belief that "one of the primary goals of communist ideology was to encourage sexual liaisons between white women and black men."[79] When I asked Gordon how often mixed-race dancing actually occurred at the Hollywood Canteen, he speculated that it probably didn't occur that often. "It happened and we were happy that it happened. But mostly the blacks stayed together because of the whole attitude that was so prevalent in that time. It was probably very hard for a black man to ask a white girl to dance. Except that we had some Communist young ladies there as hostesses who made a point of breaking the segregation." Gordon could not remember names, but I wonder if Blanche Cole was among them. Blanche followed her brother Lester Cole to Los Angeles in the 1930s, where she joined the Party. In the Depression she could not get the job as a lab technician for which her college degree had prepared her, so she worked instead as a secretary at Columbia Pictures, was active in the Screen Office Employees Guild, and purported to be a member of the Communist Party.[80]

According to Gordon, the battle over the integrated dance floor at the Hollywood Canteen was resolved when "we all put our heads together" and came up with a plan in which "it was not required that any girl, white or black, would dance with any soldier, white or black, that they could turn anybody down" because they "were too tall, too short, too hairy, too hairless, too sweaty, whatever—but not on the basis of race. Another thing that was done was to try to recruit as many black girls as possible to all be there to dance, not just with black soldiers, but with anybody. No discrimination."[81]

How would have Jean Lewin described the policy arrived at by this committee of Communists and anti-Communists, integrationists and segregationists? I don't know. But let's swing back to the meeting of July 8, 1943, where she is spotted taking furious notes on the discussion she is not supposed to write about.

Dancing with the State, Part 2 (Continued, July 8, 1943–August 12, 1943)

The informant cannot see what Jean Lewin writes, but she or he notices that Jean writes most attentively when "the race question" is discussed and that she continues to do so even after the decision is made to strike all but the decision from the record. Lewin continues to write, and so does the source. And so does Special Agent _____. I join this writing group, now four of us, all of us writing about what had been agreed in the meeting to leave out of the record. Who is opposed to mixed dancing, who is for. Who is thought to be a Communist (or fellow traveler) and who is definitely not or whose politics is unknown.

The next ten pages of the report catalogue board members according to this taxonomy in increasingly minute (and increasingly censored) details. In page after page, individual Canteen workers, volunteers, and board members are slotted into one of three classifications in relation to two issues. Each individual is identified as either "for," "against," or "unknown" as to mixed-race dancing and Communism. In no case does a position in one category diverge from a position in another.

Mrs. Mary Ford, for example, with whom the source had previously shared the joke about "communist stationery," is against Communism and against mixed-race dancing. Supporting details include the summary of a story she told about an incident that had disturbed her: one evening "her young daughter was maneuvered into dancing with a Negro soldier, much to her embarrassment and that of her escort, a young white soldier." Mrs. Ford is now hesitant to "let her daughter go to the Canteen."

"DALTON TRUMBO, the writer, and CARROLL HOLLISTER, the radio musician," whom the files presume (correctly, in this case) are members of the Communist Party, are repeatedly pegged not only as "for" mixed-race dancing but as trying to sway "other members of the Board to permit colored soldiers to dance with white hostesses at the Hollywood Canteen." Trumbo is also identified as a writer for MGM and "well-known critic of U.S. government." His book protesting the deportation of Harry Bridges is duly reported.[82]

Canteen president and screen actress Bette Davis, who has supported mixed-race dancing, is reported to be "very sympathetic to Communist activities and should be classified as a fellow traveler."[83]

Spike Wallace, who has already come under suspicion for threatening "to resign from the Board of Directors of the Canteen if the resolution prohibiting mixed dancing passed," is, predictably, catalogued as "fellow traveler."[84]

Most of the section on John Garfield (who was later blacklisted) is redacted. For now, all we are allowed to know (from the realm of knowledge from which Special Agent _____ gathers and reports) is that Florence Cadrez "stated that John Garfield at a previous meeting had strongly favored mixed dancing."[85]

Most of the section on Al Ybarra is blanked out.

Not much remains visible in Jean Lewin's categorization except for the fact that she is secretary of the Canteen and a member of the Screen Office Employees Guild.[86]

Paul Jaffee, already associated with the pro–mixed dancing position, is identified as being affiliated with several leftist organizations: the Laboratory Technicians, Local 683 of IATSE (of which he is recording secretary), the Hollywood Writers Mobilization for Defense, and Labor Unity for Victory. If that isn't damning enough, he has "issued pamphlets protesting the deportation proceedings against Harry Bridges, passed resolutions demanding a second front; passed resolutions on the independence of India; and has urged resolutions on the Negro question."[87]

Florence Cadrez of AFM Local 767 is misidentified as "a member of Musicians Union, Local 47," indicating that she may also have been misidentified by the informant as white. She is correctly identified as one of the original incorporators of the Canteen, a member of its executive board, and among those "in favor of the 'Mixed Dancing Resolution.'" (Later, she will be one of several 767 members who will oppose the merger of the segregated locals. Those who will be for integrating the Los Angeles AFM through the merger of the black union into the white union will be red-baited.)

Lester Cole is listed as a screenwriter who associated with other leftist "writers such as Clifford Odets," but a large chunk of page 12 that seems to be devoted to his pro-Communism/mixed-race dancing politics is obstructed from view.[88]

No political activities are listed for Florine Bale—only that she is a member of the American Guild of Variety Artists and the Hollywood Canteen's board of directors and that she has reliably "protested against mixed dancing at the Canteen and stated that many of the girl members of her union had refused to visit the Canteen to entertain because attempts were made to coerce them into dancing with Negroes."[89]

Also blanked out is much of the section on Jules Stein. What remains we already know: he is a motion picture promoter, against mixed dancing, and reported to have stated that the proposal to allow mixed dancing was "definitely a Communist plot, or Communist plan to stir up trouble in the Canteen." What could be redacted, then, in this heavily inked-out section? I presume that Stein's blank rectangle must include confidential material of another sort than that redacted from the sections on Cole, Trumbo, Lewin, and other suspected Communists. Did Stein also wittingly talk to Special Agent _____? It was at Stein's invitation, according to some sources, that Ralph Clare, a close personal friend of Stein's protégé Lew Wasserman, was invited to serve on the Canteen's board.[90]

Doris Stein, wife of Jules, is listed as "active in the affairs of the Canteen" and catalogued as sharing her husband's positions against Communism and mixed dancing.[91]

Not only Communists and "Communist Sympathizers" are exhaustively named but "Persons known to be Non-Communists and Not Communist Sympathizers." On this different sort of list—a roll call of the innocent—appear those who "have been very active in the motion picture business in Los Angeles, but as far as is known . . . have not taken any stand which would indicate they have participated in Communist activities or have engaged in subversive activities of any kind." Included are Billie Burke, Ann Warner (wife of Jack Warner of Warner Bros.), Bob Hope, and Ralph Clare.[92]

The final list, "Persons named in connection with Canteen whose activities are unknown," includes twenty-three names.[93] We may presume they will be henceforth watched more closely. In fact, many people connected with the Canteen may already presume they are being watched.

The source tells Special Agent _____ that Jules Stein announced *at a board meeting* that "the FBI had somebody" at a previous "Board meeting and that the FBI was definitely interested in Communist activities in the motion picture industry." Further, Stein contributed to the self-surveillance of the board when he delivered the kicker: "that the FBI was getting all the information about the goings-on at the Board meetings on the part of the Communist members."[94]

Despite all of this reportage of surveillance and self-surveillance, pro-Communists and anti-Communists, and the matching positions on dancing across race, most of my interviewees seemed perplexed when I asked what they remembered about the conservative, moderate, liberal, and left political orientations among the members of the motion picture industry who volunteered at the Hollywood Canteen. Nancy Marlow suggested that maybe the college-educated Canteen-goers would have known each other's political views but that this was not something that would have been within her radar. She did, however, detect political differences between *us*, taking this moment in our 2004 interview to tell me, gleefully, "I'm rooting for George Bush, *so there!*"[95] Even actress Marsha Hunt, who was blacklisted in 1947 for her participation in the "Hollywood Fights Back!" campaign against McCarthyism, did not recall political difference at the Canteen. She replied that McCarthyism had not yet occurred and that the "sudden about-face" that the United States would make after the war, when the Soviet Union was suddenly considered an enemy, did not happen until later and that it would have seemed incomprehensible at the time. She said that she did not "hear about Communism or anti-Communism in Hollywood until after the war, when the split was more between reactionaries and liberals than Communists and anti-Communists."[96] Delmar Watson, who had made 250 films by the time he turned eighteen and went into the Coast Guard, said that if I only "got one thing" from my conversation with him, he wanted it to be that the Hollywood Canteen was "the *one time* when Hollywood came together."[97]

And it's true. Much of Hollywood did come together, including groups that traditionally did not agree: unions and producers, Communists and

FIG 10.2: Jean Lewin (front row, third from left); continuing left to right: Bette Davis, Kay Kyser, singing onstage at the Hollywood Canteen. COURTESY BERNARD GORDON.

anti-Communists, leftists, liberals, moderates, conservatives. Stars and extras. The AFM and the Teamsters. Integrationists and segregationists of many stripes (purposeful, casual, activist, or practical). Cooperative or at each other's throats, political adversaries were in the house as people danced, or refused to dance, or were refused dancing across race. Nonetheless, of all the people I talked to, only Bernie Gordon corroborates Special Agent _____'s observation that a vast range of political difference underscores what later emerges as a symbol of political sameness, when the Hollywood Canteen becomes a lens for swing memory as war memory at the Hollywood Canteen.

Break-away: Bernie Gordon (March 28, 2004)

Ten months after my first interview with Bernie Gordon, I once again make the hike from the Ramada West Hollywood to Londonderry Place. This time I leave myself more time to climb. At the top of the hill, Gordon ushers me into his home once again, graciously accepts the bottle of Kansas City barbeque sauce I offer, and suggests that we sit in the garden. Maybe we would see hummingbirds. On the phone, he had indicated that he would like a visit but didn't want to talk about his illness. We sit, wait, but there are no hummingbirds. I find myself wishing I knew him better—maybe I'd know better what to say?—but all I know is our conversations that had begun in his home and continued via email about the Canteen and the Communist Party. So I pick up our conversation from the previous year, but it feels hollow. He complies, but he doesn't light up the way he did before. He supplies information. I write it down.

Suddenly he stops. "What is it you hope to gain from talking to half-dead Commies?" he asks me.[98]

I tell him that I want to understand all of the political viewpoints that brought people to the Hollywood Canteen, so I can better understand the struggles that took place over different definitions of democracy. I want to break open that myth in the national memory that the World War II generation of Americans was simple, patriotic, and united. I want to show that there is much more to learn about how his generation thought about democracy and that I want to make these multiple viewpoints visible again, reactivate the struggle that occurred at the Hollywood Canteen that is now remembered only as an uncomplicated picture of American patriotic wartime unity.

Gordon pauses. "I'll tell you what is right and wrong about that idea," he says, considering his words. "There *was* a struggle. That's true. But it was a struggle of a very small group without power against a very large group with power."

We sit for a long time in silence. I know it wasn't an even playing field. But, then, how do we remember struggles over ideas about democracy that are somehow translated into uncontroversial unity by the time they make it into national memory? How do we think about a dance floor democracy produced by Jean Lewin and Bette Davis and Carroll Hollister and Ralph Clare and Jules Stein and J. Edgar Hoover? Bernie gets up at some point—I think to change the battery in his hearing aid. While he is inside, I see a lovely green hummingbird, but it's gone as quickly as it appeared. When Bernie returns, he looks tired. I thank him for all his help and wish him well.

Bernie Gordon hung in there for three more years. He published *The Gordon File* in 2004 and sent me a signed copy. I wanted to bring him to the University of Kansas to speak about the book, in which he connects the surveillance he experienced in the Cold War and the limits on rights that he saw in the post-9/11 United States. I wanted to introduce him as a member of the Greatest Generation to a midwestern university audience. I pictured his face as he stood behind the podium in the Bob Dole Center for Politics. From there, he would see the World War II exhibit, which includes an actual fragment from of the Twin Towers of the World Trade Center encased in glass, backlit by the Kansas sunlight shining through the biggest stained-glass American flag in the world. I imagined what Bernie might say about this articulation of World War II to 9/11. But synchronicity wasn't with us.

Dancing with the State, Part 3 (October 5, 1943–April 26, 1945)
Leaving the Dance Floor (Safe for Democracy)

Starting in the fall of 1943, the reports of Special Agent _____ began to lose their—shall we say—anti-Communist oomph. The tenor is set in the opening summary of the report of October 5, 1943, when we learn that since July 8, 1943, the only executive board meeting dealt with the topic of "indiscriminate dancing of white and colored people for the alleged purposes of breaking down discrimination along racial lines."[99] In that single meeting, held in early September, the "question of mixed dancing between Negroes and Whites" was revisited, "and it was decided that the rule previously established of leaving this question to the individual for decision would be continued."

The report then summarized what had often been repeated in earlier reports: that "Communists meant to use [the Hollywood Canteen] to bring Negro and White soldiers together and to have the hostesses dance with Negro soldiers, the purpose being to break down discrimination on racial lines." Because this goal proved controversial, "the attempt to force the issue" was "laid aside." The practice of "mixed dancing is being indulged in by individual action," though not to "a great extent." Individual choice, however, did not reflect the goals of subversives. Therefore, "the Communists do not look upon the establishment of the CANTEEN as a great victory. They are not showing the great interest they did formerly."[100]

The next report, dated December 13, 1943, reiterated this shift in priorities:

> The question of mixed dancing of white and colored persons has been tabled for the present. Publicity about canteen [sic] is slackening, and the opportunity for spreading Communist propaganda is not believed to be so successful as had been anticipated. It is reported that Warner Brothers is going to make a picture entitled, "Hollywood Canteen."[101]

In report after report, diminishing interest in the integrated dancing issue was represented not as a triumph of segregation over integration (indeed instances of mixed dancing were noted without the hysteria of earlier reports) but as a triumph of free choice over Communism. Although the "question of mixed dancing by white and colored persons has not come to a final conclusion," wrote Special Agent _____,

> the "personal choice" remedy had been permitted to remain. . . . If whites wish to dance with the colored people, they may do so; and if the colored people wish to dance with the whites, they may do so; but there will be no compulsion or set rule requiring a person of one race to dance with a person of another race.[102]

The absence of "compulsion" to dance across race is connected, in the reports, to "a very noticeable slackening of interest in the project by those who hoped to use it for purposes of spreading propaganda of the Communist variety." Instead, the source noted, "efforts of the Hollywood Communists and fellow travelers have been diverted to a great extent from the canteen" and were "now centering on other front organizations which afford better channels for propaganda activities."[103]

Subsequent reports became increasingly mundane, only occasionally stirring up a hint of Communist plot. Potentially of interest was the flurry of lawsuits between the Screen Actors Guild and Warner Bros. during the making of the feature film *Hollywood Canteen* (1944). At issue were the terms of payment to stars from other studios for cameo roles in the film (Warner Brothers expected patriotically reduced salaries; the Screen Actors Guild fought to protect artists against excessive patriotic volunteerism). This did not provide very interesting fodder, however, since the Communists sided with Warner Bros. instead of the union (because the film promoted the war effort). As the Communists failed to produce un-American activities, Special Agent _____ struggled to unearth interesting copy. I detect ennui in the language of these later reports: "The 'mixed races dancing' controversy has been lying dormant and interest in the Canteen seems to be lagging and the Communists seem to be losing interest."[104]

An occasional blip perks up the pace, but not from expected quarters. It turns out that the most relentless opponent of the "'make your own choice' of dancing partner" was not the subversive Communist element at all. The anti-Communist Mary Ford emerges as the most tenacious person in pushing to keep the "mixed dancing" issue on the table, continuing to insist "that the 'mixed races dancing' question" be revisited, "as she was anxious to get the Negro question settled and desired that this form of dancing be prohibited." Non-Communists had to police their own when Mrs. Ford proved herself so racist that the historically racist and anti-Red LAPD complained about *her*.

> _____ reported that Mrs. FORD has on many occasions reported small incidents to the policeman on duty at the Canteen; that these matters had been discussed with JOHN FORD by the policeman and JOHN FORD had told the policeman that Mrs. FORD was inclined to become agitated and excited about racial matters, especially where Negroes were involved, and Mr. FORD told the officer that he should take Mrs. FORD out of the Canteen if she insisted in making protests which were apparently of little consequence.[105]

The Communist-watch was once again rewarded on February 23, 1944, when "the Hollywood Canteen staged a celebration of the 26th Anniversary of the Red Army of the Soviet Union." The event included a "special Russian show," a "tremendous ovation" for "five Soviet sailors and officers," and a "giant birthday cake inscribed 'greetings to the Red Army on its 26th Anniversary.'" The cake "was presented by BETTE DAVIS, President of the Canteen. Miss DAVIS follows the lead of the Communist elements in Hollywood and is one of their favorite 'fronters.'" Despite the fact that Russia was an ally, Special Agent _____ noted the presence of all things Russian—including the actors and musicians of Russian descent who cheered the Red Army at the Hollywood Canteen, concluding that "this entire program" of "Russian propaganda" was probably the most successful "from the Communist standpoint ever put over by the Canteen."[106]

The trail lights up briefly on August 15, 1944, when three pamphlets produced by "the Workers Library Publishers of New York and having the approval of EARL BROWDER" are found scattered about the Canteen. However, the excitement soon dissipates when the executive board is praised for having become "very sensitive to Communist attempts at propaganda" as a result of "the violent opposition of certain members of the Board to the Communists." Besides, as Special Agent _____ reports, the canteen has not been mentioned in the Communist press for a long time.[107]

The final reports to which I have access continue the recurring theme of Communist exodus. Throughout 1944 and into the spring of 1945, the overall Red-ness of the Canteen seems to be fading, as Special Agent _____ reiterates the message of his source(s): "Communist propaganda and racial equality features of the Canteen have largely disappeared." "The Communists seem to be losing interest in the Canteen because of the fact that as a propaganda instrument it has not been of particular value to them, a member of the Board of Directors" tells Special Agent _____ on February 29, 1944. After a year and a half of state surveillance, it turns out "that servicemen who visit Hollywood and the Canteen are out for a good time and are not interested in propaganda," that they are "hurried through . . . by the hundreds, each group going through spending only from twenty to thirty minutes within the building. This being true, there is little opportunity for contact with them by those Communists who take part in the entertainment or in rendering service to the men."[108]

In the report of May 9, 1944, Ralph Clare says as much himself, quoted by the source. Clare's name—unredacted—casts doubt on my earlier theory that Special Agent _____'s source was Clare. Of course, there must have been many sources. In any case, this one relays Clare's opinion that "the Communists are now losing interest in the Canteen" because "they have learned that the soldiers and sailors come to the Canteen for amusement only; that they are not at all interested in political propaganda.[109]

Special Agent _____ turns his focus to the profits and the reviews of the new feature film *Hollywood Canteen* (1944). Of these, the most controversial is the issue of who will control the estimated $1 million or more that "have come into the possession of the Hollywood Canteen . . . derived principally from the sale of interests in the motion picture entitled 'Hollywood Canteen.'" Without a war to unite them, will Communists, anti-Communists, unions, and producers be able to share the pot? Or (as in U.S. electoral democracy) will a winner take all? Once again, Special Agent _____ generates many pages of divisions of individuals into Communist and non-Communist camps but stops when the board of directors passes "a by-law to continue itself after the war."[110]

The film's reviews are mixed. Special Agent _____ records them all. The *New Yorker* calls it "one of the most majestic bores ever imposed on the American people," an occasion for Hollywood "to pat itself on the back." Walter Winchell finds the "the diversion gamut" of the film to run "from ah to zing." Kate Cameron criticizes "the players in this picture [who] seem constantly awed by their own gracious and hospitable entertainment of the servicemen." From the point of view of the FBI, the movie, for better or worse, was more "starrific" than subversive.[111]

Nor was the actual Canteen sufficiently subversive anymore, it seemed. The current policy, according to the February 1945 report, was that "all races in military uniform may avail themselves of the facilities of the Canteen and be at liberty to choose their own social friends and companions without restraint."[112] A source on the executive board had reported in early January that it had been about a year since any complaints had arisen regarding the issue of racial mixing. So quiet were Communist activities on the dance floor that a source told Special Agent _____ that even "the non-Communist elements" had lost interest, even though the Canteen remained "wholly under Communist domination."[113] The once explosive issue of dancing across race had apparently been settled by a combination of free choice and constant surveillance.

Special Agent _____'s description of the truly American democratic dance floor, as it emerges victorious over the suspiciously un-American democratic dance floor, is both different from and compatible with the compromise described by Bernie Gordon that does not mandate integration or segregation, but that permits hostesses of all races to "turn anybody down for whatever reason . . . But not on the basis of race." And both seem consistent with the version of the Canteen described to me by Mel Bryant: it was a place he and other black men in uniform could *go*, but it was not "integrated in an equal way."[114] In each interpretation, the right of all visitors of all races to enter the room, eat the food, and choose their own companions is balanced by the right of hosts and hostesses of all races to choose *not* to embrace racial equality (as long as they call it something else). Such choice-governed togetherness was admittedly different from Jim Crow, but it was not what Bryant meant by "integration in an equal way," nor was it the Canteen for Democracy that decisively forbade the "vicious poison" of racial discrimination, as envisioned by Carroll Hollister in April 1942. In order for the FBI to be satisfied that racial mixing was compatible with American democracy, all traces of social torque in the direction of intentional racial equality had to be removed. With social interaction restored to the individual realm, "free choice" was safe to roam the democratic dance floor, in a color-blind, "innocent," friendly way. The Hollywood Canteen was now, as far as the state was concerned, an acceptably American activity.

Closing Out the Case

Special Agent _____ stayed on the case until at least April 26, 1945, the date of the last report in the file I have the freedom to consult. In a memo to the Los Angeles Field Division, dated April 19, 1945 (five days after the death of President Roosevelt), J. Edgar Hoover ordered the closure of the investigation of the Hollywood Canteen. He did leave the door ajar, advising that the closed case was "subject to being reopened in the event pertinent information is forthcoming from established sources in the future."[115] It would not be under official surveillance, in other words, although participant-informers would continue to have a pipeline in case they noticed any suspicious activity among their fellow volunteers. Special Agent _____ had successfully "caused surveillance." It could continue without him. Amateur detectives would stay alert to suspicious activities, their eyes trained on instances of intentional interracial dancing, which continued to be seen as Communist inspired.

Surveillance of the democratic dance floor is, of course, consistent with other midcentury FBI preoccupations, in which the Bureau, acting on behalf of the state, equated intentional racial integration with Communism. Angela Davis reminds us that "Martin Luther King, Jr. was repeatedly described by his adversaries as a communist, and not because he was actually a member of the Communist Party, but because the cause of racial equality was assumed to be a communist creation." She urges us to consider this association as a two-way street: "Anti-communism enabled resistance to civil rights in myriad ways and vice versa; racism enabled the spread of anti-communism."[116]

Nonetheless, the civil rights movement is now lovingly recalled as a national romance, proof of triumph of good over evil in the United States, proof that democracy works.[117] Martin Luther King Day is a national holiday—hard won and incessantly controversial in some quarters, it has primarily become a widely accepted occasion for national remembrance and redemption.[118] What this remembrance elides is the relentless surveillance of a citizenry by a state that equated antiracism with Communism and fought them in tandem as un-American activities. When ideas that were once considered radical by the state are mainstreamed as national memory, people stand to lose their histories of democratic dissent and memories of social torque.

This chapter is not a conspiracy theory. It is not an exposé of the way *that crazy racist J. Edgar Hoover wasted taxpayer dollars*. I am not interested in "Othering" Hoover in the name of recuperating an innocent state. In dancing with the state, I learn a variety of moves for remembering and forgetting integrated dancing: as democratic, as Communist; as American and un-American; casual and intentional. The next step in this book is to explore the bonds linking state memory and national memory and explore how their interconnection enabled (and continue to enable) so many (white) people who were (and weren't) there to imagine the swing nation as a color-blind dance floor. We now shift to another point of view: that of film spectators of swing culture in cinematic manifestations that circulate as war memory. As we turn our attentions to the 1944 feature film, *Hollywood Canteen*, we are reunited with a cast that includes many of the same players we have just followed in the files (and excludes others), as they present a very different, yet eerily compatible, production of dance floor democracy.

★ ★ ★

The Making(s) of National Memory

Hollywood Canteen (the Movie)

Now comes the picture, "Hollywood Canteen," to celebrate further the magnificent job accomplished by indefatigable representatives of the public-spirited motion picture industry.
—*HOLLYWOOD REPORTER* (DECEMBER 5, 1944)

According to the producers, every effort will be made to integrate Negroes normally throughout the picture.
—*PITTSBURGH COURIER* (JULY 1, 1944)

For contemporary visitors to the Hollywood Canteen, those of us who enter not from Cahuenga Boulevard as military guests or through the back door as volunteers (or FBI agents) but from armchairs, sofas, or cinema seats, the first glimpse we get of the club is an aerial view of its exterior at dusk. As spectators, we enter Canteen-space through our ability to temporarily cast our identifications at a screen. This screen may be large or small, public or private, beveled or flat; its medium may be a reel of film but probably is video or DVD, Netflix™, or TMC™. Any of these routes directs us toward the rooftop sign on which is written in loopy neon cursive "Hollywood Canteen." From our floating vantage point in the evening sky, we swivel to gaze downward at the main entrance, where soldiers, sailors, and Marines loosely assemble. A Pacific Telephone booth links Hollywood to home, as does the nearby photography stand where military travelers may purchase their own images to send to loved ones. Beyond the Canteen building are a gas station, silhouettes of palm trees at dusk, a hotel. The ambient lights of Hollywood beckon beyond the frame.[1]

We won't see the dance floor until the plot delivers our protagonist inside. His uniform is his ticket. This movie is ours. However, we *do* hear music—as credits roll. First the fanfare, as the Warner Bros. logo pops midscreen, followed by "Jack L. Warner Executive Producer presents . . ." The overture shifts to the sentimental strain we will hear throughout the feature, "Sweet Dreams Sweetheart." Suddenly, strings give way to swing, and the harmonizing voices of the three Andrews Singers sell the theme:

> Manhattan nights can brag of lights
> and Boston has its beans,
> but on the Coast we proudly boast
> 'Bout the Hollywood Canteen . . .

The camera zooms back in to frame the sign, as the western "rope" font lettering is eclipsed by major credits: forty star names dazzle in alphabetical order (forty-six, if you parse the teams and group acts: the Andrews Sisters, the Golden Gate Quartet, Roy Rogers and Trigger). Names of five musical groups fly by: Jimmy Dorsey, Carmen Cavallero, the Golden Gate Quartet (again), Rosario and Antonio, the Sons of the Pioneers—a veritable melting pot of singing cowboys, white swing instrumentalists and singers, an African American men's gospel quartet favored by the Popular Front, and a respectable showing of Latin American musicians and dancers in alignment with FDR's call for movies to demonstrate friendly neighborly relations between the United States and nations south of the border.[2]

Delmer Daves wrote the screenplay. LeRoy Prinz "created and directed" the musical numbers—so many, in fact, that it seems impossible that all the songs and stars on this fast-rolling list will fit in a single film.[3] Production credits follow. Then insignia: the stamp of the International Alliance of Theatrical and Stage Employees (IATSE), the approval rating of the Motion Picture Producers and Distributors of America (MPPDA)—even labor and the producers appear to hold hands.

Break-away: Rule 33

Production on *Hollywood Canteen* began on November 15, 1943, and screeched to a halt on December 22, when the historic battle between producers and unions erupted to stall the shooting, until Warner Bros. and the Screen Actors Guild could agree on the proper line between industry charity and worker exploitation.[4] The actors union had adopted rule 33 just prior to the production of United Artists' *Stage Door Canteen* (1943) to protect actors from being pressured into working for less than their ordinary fees in patriotic benefit films that nonetheless garnered profits for studios.[5] Passed in August 1942, the rule was no secret, but when the Screen Actors Guild attempted to apply it to *Hollywood Canteen* on December 7, 1943, Warners not only dropped the project but sued the union for the costs of production up until the moment of invocation. The guild fought back with a suit of its own. With feet in both camps, the board of directors of the Hollywood Canteen (the club), which was the subject and charity recipient of *Hollywood Canteen* (the film), called a meeting among the disputing parties. The Screen Actors Guild backed off, and Warners promised not to pressure actors. By the time production resumed in May 1944, much of the original talent was no longer available (Joan Leslie, for example, replaced Ann Sheridan as the ideal junior hostess). Sets were reassembled, roles recast, and continuity problems hastily resolved. On New Year's Eve, Warner Bros. released its latest tribute to Hollywood's patriotism, just in time to fit the credit "Copyright 1944."

We Return Our Gaze to the War Musical . . .

The final big names roll to the swell of the romantic lullaby's reprise: "Produced by ALEX GOTTLIEB. Directed by DELMER DAVES."[6] The picture fades to black. The last two notes of the "Sweet Dreams Sweetheart" melody sound, now voiced by Hawaiian guitar instead of violins.

Our viewpoint still originates from the sky, but no longer do we hover over Hollywood at dusk; instead, a tropical island paradise beckons below. Palm trees no longer line the boulevards but rustle their fronds above a white sandy beach.

A disembodied voice cheerfully intones, "This looks like a quiet, peaceful Island in the South Pacific, doesn't it? Well, it is. . . ."—meaningful pause— "since the United States Army took it over!" The tourist fantasy merges with national pride as an American flag is hoisted upward—dutifully tracked by the camera until it waves above the palms, a visual corollary of the earlier pan to the rooftop sign at the Hollywood Canteen.

In a third articulation of signage, war, empire, and home, a soldier in a combat helmet climbs what turns out to be a ramshackle "crossroads-of-the-world" signpost, into which has been nailed a series of rustic destination arrows that point out in all directions. Most are battle destinations: Guadalcanal 850, Tokyo 3252, and so on.

"Is this high enough?" he calls.

"Right up on top!" shouts a voice from below.

He nails the sign "Brooklyn 9982."

Adopting the point of view of the soldier on the pole, we gaze down at two injured soldiers, Corporal "Slim" Green (Robert Hutton) and Sergeant "Brooklyn" Nolan (Dane Clark), as they observe the placement of the new sign.

"Imagine, leaving off Brooklyn, the capital of the world," says the dark-haired one, leaning on his crutches.

"Imagine," echoes his tall, fair-haired friend—though his sense of wonder seems to stem from disbelief that he knows someone from Brooklyn. We never learn where Slim is from, but we discover he awaits a letter (that never arrives) from a "girl in Altoona." Slim *may* hail from Altoona, Pennsylvania, but there are many Altoonas in the United States, literally and figuratively. From a Hollywood perspective, every municipality between New York and Los Angeles is Altoona (except for Chicago, where the Feds chase gangsters). By the same token, whatever positive qualities Slim attributes to the Altoona of his dreams will be matched and improved by Hollywood.

For example, Slim easily replaces his dreams of an actual girl-next-door with visions of actress Joan Leslie, thanks to the film industry, which ships its latest reels to the troops. Soon thereafter, Slim and his favorite movie star will be joined in the flesh at the Hollywood Canteen, when John Garfield and Bette Davis select him from hundreds of thousands of soldiers as most deserving of a dream come true. She even takes him home to meet her parents. Just when the fairy tale seems to be coming to an end, she will see him off at the train. The lesson seems to be that for an ideal GI protagonist, Hollywood is just as nice and pleasant as Middle America, only friendlier, sunnier, and infinitely more faithful. The democratic dance floor includes many nationalities and races. However, Slim will choose Joan, and she will choose him. More than just a movie star, she's a girl-next-door, with a white picket fence and a bounding, lovable family dog. She even shops at the farmer's market.

Slim's friend Brooklyn will likewise find soldier-hostess completion at the Hollywood Canteen. My plot spoiler in the introductory chapter has already given it away that his war injury will be healed on the dance floor thanks to "big shot" Hollywood stars being "friendly to little shots" like him. What I didn't divulge is that Brooklyn also finds his other half, no starlet for him but a not-so-bright script girl (Janis Paige). They seal their attraction not by being singled out for Canteen-sanctioned encounters but by sneaking outside to exercise their "animal instincts." While Slim is coddled by the stars, Brooklyn is humiliated by dashing busboys and sophisticated hostesses. His rewards are of a different grade, but he still wins the affections of a hostess in the B-leagues. His place on the ladder of aspirational belonging is secure. They are not the ideal dyad—that would be Slim and Joan—but they complement it very well; this is the best that a vaguely ethnic (Irish, in this case), East Coast comic sidekick might expect from the genre.

Dancing with National Memory, Part 1: Approaching *Hollywood Canteen* (the Movie)

It is no surprise that *Hollywood Canteen* (the movie) tells a different story about the Canteen from the FBI's. To write a chapter that would ferret out distinctions and expose errors would be a pointless exercise. Instead, we will explore *relationships* between Warner Bros.'s production of an immortal vision of Hollywood's patriotic service and the FBI's surveillance of the visions and practices of the site of that service as a hotbed of un-American activities. Many of the people who worked on this movie were also spied on, consulted, and documented by the FBI. We may *see* more dissent in the files than in the movie, but the making of a film, like the operating of a volunteer-operated wartime canteen, is a complicated process. If the same people appear to move in radically different ways in the film text and in secret reports about board meetings, it isn't because one site is fake and the other real but because these contrasting but interconnected terrains of struggle presented different parameters, pathways, and possibilities for torque.

No movie is made by a monolithic "Hollywood." The final cut—Hollywood branded, War Department and Production Code censored, shaped by tensions among unions, producers, and civil rights advocates—is born of hierarchical and segmented labor, in a profitable and embattled industry, rife with political difference and unparalleled in representational reach. What screens is what survives the constant slew of revisions both small and drastic, often hastily implemented after a memo or meeting. The original treatment, for example, did not open with a sentimental overhead shot of soldiers entering the club, followed by quaint comical dialogue among soldiers recuperating in the jungle. Early versions of the script opened in combat. If those had stuck, we would meet our protagonists in the spray of enemy gunfire and watch them go down (with realism achieved by cutting actual documentary footage of warfare with scenes shot in the studio). We would root for Slim and Brooklyn while medics patched them up and get to know them as they convalesced. Brooklyn would share that his twin brother had already been killed in the war. Slim's close call with amputation would inspire brave comic relief among the pair about the pros and cons of having a right arm. (Brooklyn would quip that lacking one might rescue a guy from marriage.)[7] However, the Office of War Information objected to references to casualties, wounds, and other depressing outcomes. Thus, the approved version skips gunfire altogether and jumps to soldiers watching movies and thinking about women.

Simplistic, but stitched together from different sides representing different interests, this nostalgic text was made by a wildly hierarchical committee, working at different levels in a powerful factory, in a unionized industry in a historically open shop company town, under the watchful eyes of the War Department. *Hollywood Canteen* is "just a movie," but those involved in its making also knew that whatever made it into the frame would impact the official story and lasting memory of Hollywood Canteen (the club) and the wartime service of people in their profession. Film professionals (managers, staff, craftsmen and -women, contract and freelance talent) with clashing ideological perspectives and stakes about how to represent a democratic dance floor were nonetheless joined by the desire to perform well and *work again*, which necessitated creating a successful war musical. This was not a noir occasion for fights, pathos, injuries, or dismantled social norms. It was a celebration of a democratic dance floor, crafted by professionals who disagreed about who should dance with whom but who *knew* how to make a war musical.

To get at the struggles underpinning this film that, from a twenty-first-century perspective, simply couldn't be cornier, I dance with its surface as a national rerun, as well as with the studio archival records of its making, pulling away from time to time to synchronize with the FBI. I trace steps of an intricate dance of national memory (read through this "good war" musical) and the effects of surveillance, classification, and freedom of partial disclosure of state memory (the FBI files). I watch for moments when national and state memories touch; when they blend together, bolt from one another, and blot each other out. And I watch for when they achieve something together that neither could achieve alone.

And some members of the Hollywood Canteen board were aware of FBI surveillance that permeated the club-on-the-ground as well as the film production. Indeed, Special Agent _____ incorporated notes on the making of the film in his reports to the state. The making of the film begins at the tail end of the FBI's conviction that the Canteen's primary purpose is no longer Communist-driven racial mixing. Production spans a shift in FBI methods and interpretations—from the period of intensive surveillance of possible Communists (ammunition for the imminent blacklisting of many), to the "victory" perceived by the FBI when Communists vacate the dance floor. Nonetheless, somehow, all of the contradictions that have been vigorously collected and filed by the FBI disappear with as little trace as possible before the film begins its life as national memory as a harmonious and unified vision.

Even those who weren't aware of the presence of the FBI or of its potential threat to livelihoods of left-of-center and/or integrationist film industry workers were well aware of other constraints in wartime filmmaking. They knew, for example, that any film produced during the war would be previewed by Bureau of Motion Pictures (BMP), the film office of the Office of War Information. This was in addition to, and dissonant with, the continued parameters first set by the Hays Office in 1922 (as self-censorship guidelines for the MPPDA), then tightened in 1934 in response to pressure by the American Legion of Decency (a coalition of religious groups) with the implementation of the Production Code Administration (PCA).[8] Considerations of the promises to the NAACP in the historic summit meetings between Walter White, Wendell Willkie, and seventy leaders of the motion picture industry in 1942 were factored among these new sets of constraints and pathways of possibility. However, unlike the BMP and PCA, the NAACP did not have the power to preview scripts or finished films and require changes prior to release. Having the "pledge" of Jack Warner and other studio heads was not the same as having the power to send a film back to the drawing board, but it did provide a public promise by which to measure outcomes and wield moral authority. At the same time, the BMP was much more closely aligned with the NAACP than with the PCA on representations of race, because the War Department had its own reasons for wanting to downplay the continuing existence of racism in the United States. While the PCA had frowned upon representations of anything approaching equal social relations of white people and people of color, the BMP encouraged inclusion of black soldiers in war films, including black officers from time to time. At the same time the FBI patrolled the Hollywood Canteen (club) for signs of racial mixing as un-American, the War Department, the NAACP, the black press, and industry leftists were temporarily in sync in promoting representations of military racial inclusivity in the movies.[9]

Alongside the many unsurprising differences between the Hollywood Canteen of celluloid longevity and classified state storage, there are points of uncanny resemblance. It isn't always easy to tell the difference between photographs of the actual Hollywood Canteen and photographs of the soundstage and movie-set versions of it. Publicity shots of each site highlight many of the same stars; even when I can detect the difference between the club and the film, I see the same facial expressions, poses, and pairings. While many interviewees were quick to point out the differences between the movie and "what really happened," many also broke away from their stories of Canteen memory to say "I don't remember if that happened at the Canteen, or if it was in the movie."

Dancing in Alternate Universes

In conceptualizing the movie as a production of national memory, I am not suggesting that it is a façade for what was "really" going on. Rather, I conceive national memory here, as I did in chapter 10, as an alternate universe to state memory. The film Canteen and the club Canteen are produced from the same materials, animated by the same sets of different players and stakes. As in the twinned alternate universes of science fiction, what happens in the universe of state memory affects the universe of national memory, and vice versa, while not being the same at all. One isn't a mask for the other as much as it is its eerily similar yet different other side. This is not a simple binary in which complementary opposites join to construct the ideological whole, any more than the dancers on the ground cohered into seamless units. We need to know more about the relationship between state memory and national memory in order to understand swing culture as U.S. war memory.

Whereas chapter 10 examined state memory as practiced through surveillance, partial "free" disclosure, and classified retention, this chapter focuses on the feature film as a player in the production of national memory as a smooth surface that "protects" its citizens from difference while envisioning inclusive democracy. The film, in conjunction with the Office of War Information and other watchdogs and censors, constructs viewers as affective citizen-subjects. The surface of this universe has been professionally scrubbed of evidence of the political antagonisms (tied to racial mixing) that dominated the thick files of the other. I work the film's surface frame by frame and dig between the splices, aided by film industry archives, feeling for commotion in this realm of national swing nostalgia. How do the effects of shifts in migration, race, gender, politics, labor, and war present differently in the club and screen universes, and how do they affect one another? We don't need to dig very deeply to locate rifts in the interests of various unions, the studios, the federal government, the military, black actors and the black press, the Hollywood right and left. The final product, however, must sail without a hitch; all those gaps and junctures that meant so much to the various parties involved in the planning and production—and that tell us so much about war memory today—are translated into continuity problems to be solved so the film can succeed.

Behind-the-scenes research turns up interesting changes from original treatment to shooting script, memos about casting decisions and effects of censorship, problems and solutions; contracts yield home addresses, pay scales, and days worked. My files for this chapter are packed with traces of different people with different stakes, different skills, and different access to power, as they danced as quickly and as profitably as they could, within the parameters of the "war musical." I, too, dance within the parameters of writing about a movie I have difficulty taking seriously. I *break away to back-story* when it tugs at the surface, an ongoing tension. The film, like the club, made the news again and again long before its tangible existence.

Memory in Advance (the Movie)

On September 13, 1943, the *Hollywood Reporter* announced that "Jack L. Warner has completed arrangements for Warner Brothers to produce a story about the Hollywood Canteen"—not a newsreel but a star- and starlet-studded war musical set in the famous club, featuring many of its actor-founders and volunteers. The profits for the film were to be shared among the "Hollywood Canteen, New York Theatre Wing, and affiliated Stage Door Canteens throughout the country." Warners had already released the morale booster/fundraiser *This Is the Army* (1943), which according to the *Hollywood Reporter* was "expected to realize more than $10,000,000 for Army Emergency Relief." Another Warners fundraiser and sure box office success waited in the wings to open that week. Stars who appeared in *Thank Your Lucky Stars* (Warner Bros., released September 25, 1943) had donated their $50,000 paychecks to the Hollywood Canteen. That film, which would eventually earn 1.5 million dollars at the box office, featured many of the same stars and contract players who would appear in *Hollywood Canteen*, including Canteen president Bette Davis (who consented to a comic scene in which she is thrown about the room like a rag doll by a "jitterbug").[10]

The news of *Hollywood Canteen* (the movie) couldn't have surprised anyone in the industry. The United Artists film *Stage Door Canteen*, which premiered earlier that summer (June 24), was, by mid-September, already exceeding box office expectations for United Artists and yielding promised financial donations to the running of both the Stage Door Canteen and Hollywood Canteen. A spokesperson for United Artists would announce that *Stage Door Canteen* had received more "return engagements" than any other United Artists film.[11] The *Hollywood Reporter* stated that profits for *Stage Door Canteen* were 500 percent higher than anticipated.[12]

The announcement that a film would be made about the Hollywood Canteen, spurred on by the success of a film about the Stage Door Canteen, echoes the refrain "If New York can do it, so can Hollywood," which had accompanied the original calls for planning the Hollywood Canteen—except that both film representations of the famous canteens, unlike the planning stages of the clubs on the ground, are Hollywood productions. The first five weeks of the shooting of *Stage Door Canteen* took place not in New York but in "an exact replica" of the New York Stage Door Canteen on a sound stage in Culver City at RKO Pathe Studios. The West Coast bias typical of Hollywood films is legible in each of these Canteen fantasies of opposite coasts. In *Stage Door Canteen*, set in New York, the most wide-eyed and innocent of the three place-name soldiers is "California" (in contrast with the boisterous

"Texas" and the strong silent type represented by "Dakota"). Soon after this canteen film was released, soundstage replicas of the Hollywood Canteen were erected, and into them stepped another sweet and faultless white protagonist, "Slim," a midwesterner this time but readily made to feel at home among Hollywood folks. In contrast, Slim's East Coast place-named buddy, "Brooklyn," provides comic relief with his more awkward fit among Hollywood gods and goddesses who cannot help but make fun of him. Slim elicits misty eyes from the biggest stars. Brooklyn elicits practical jokes, love advice designed to backfire, and laughter held in abeyance in his presence and released behind his back.

Just as many of the people who made Hollywood Canteen (the movie) also volunteered at the Hollywood Canteen (the club), most of the scenes from the earlier Stage Door Canteen (the movie) were populated by Los Angeles–based film industry workers, many of whom volunteered at the West Coast Canteen. The Broadway presence in Stage Door Canteen (the film) was achieved by filming "additional sequences" in New York, featuring Equity stage actors, including Katherine Cornell, Alfred Lunt, Lynn Fontaine, and Helen Hayes, who were active in the running of the Stage Door Canteen (the club). Differences in these lasting representations of the two canteens were scripted, acted, and produced largely from a Hollywood base. Both screenplays, in fact, were authored by the same Californian.

On Location (the Movie)

In the late 1920s, San Francisco–born Delmer Daves abandoned his Stanford law studies to pursue a career in Hollywood. By the time he submitted his first treatment of what would become Hollywood Canteen, he had lived in Los Angeles and worked in the movies for fifteen years, mostly as a writer but also as an actor and aspiring director and producer. The year 1943 was a milestone, marking his directorial debut with Destination Tokyo for Warner Bros., which would debut that December. This film starred some of the same contract stars who would also appear in Hollywood Canteen: the venerable John Garfield and two newcomers, Robert Hutton and Dane Clark, whose careers were boosted by "victory casting," the term for the wartime demand for replacements for already established actors now in the armed forces.

Like many who worked in the industry, Daves did not live in Hollywood. Nor did he live in the San Fernando Valley. He lived in Edendale, located east of Hollywood and north of downtown, once the center of the first West Coast iteration of the film industry in 1908 and in 1943 an artists' community. Daniel Hurwitz describes the group of artists, writers, and film people in Edendale as primarily white but spatially situated in ways more conducive to awareness of communities of color in Los Angeles than many of their counterparts in Hollywood, Beverly Hills, and the San Fernando Valley.[13]

The neighborhood existed in a pocket adjoining Mexican American and mixed neighborhoods in Echo Park, bordered by Temple Street to the south, Riverside Drive to the north, Elysian Park to the west, and Virgil Avenue to the east.[14] Many of Daves's neighbors, including Carey McWilliams, were politically active in cases such as the defense of the young Mexican American people framed in the Sleepy Lagoon murder case of August 1942. Throughout the period of Daves's writing and later production of *Hollywood Canteen*, McWilliams and others organized for the release of the Sleepy Lagoon defendants, incarcerated at San Quentin without due process. I do not know if Daves wrote from home or drafted his scripts in a studio office. Either way, his Edendale orientation, whatever else it meant, involved travels across and between Hollywood, Echo Park, Culver City (United Artists), and Burbank (Warner Bros.).

Just on the other side of Elysian Park lived Twelfth Street/Woodlawn YWCA director Dorothy C. Guinn and her sister Elvira, until early September 1943, when Dorothy accepted another YW leadership post in Pittsburgh.[15] I picture the Guinn sisters attending their farewell receptions and packing up and moving out sometime in between the times when Daves completed the screenplay for *Stage Door Canteen* for United Artists and when he pounded away on his first treatment of the film about the Hollywood Canteen under the working title *One in a Million* (September 14, 1943).[16]

The premise of the film about the Hollywood Canteen was organized around the actual club's eminent celebration of its millionth military guest, which been collecting momentum in preparation and publicity. The project—from conception to treatment to announcement—was timed well to closely correspond to the date on which the millionth guest would most likely walk through the door. It was only two days after the announcement in the trades, and the day after Daves's submission of his first treatment, September 15, 1943, to be exact, when First Sergeant Carl E. W. Bell from Rising Star, Texas, entered the club and found himself escorted to the stage, showered in gifts, and kissed by Lana Turner, Marlene Dietrich, and Deanna Durbin.[17]

Both Canteen films were "war musicals," the "dominant film genre during the Second World War," according to Robert Fyne. By V-J Day, he writes, seventy-five "song-and-dance" films about the war had been released. Of these, a great many focused on famous entertainers singing and dancing for the troops, abroad, and in centers set up for the purpose of soldier recreation.[18] The metaplot for such films is best summed up by the title of the previously mentioned *Thank Your Lucky Stars*, which routes film-viewers' stargazing through the grateful onscreen military audiences watching the actors put on a show. Buoyed by the songs and dances, the soldiers feel loved and return to battle. *Hollywood Canteen* is only one of many that emphasize the heroism of the stars behind the men behind the guns. In such films, the soldier-hostess dyad as symbol-of-the-nation is ever present, fortifying the soldier through the promise of the hostess. A dance, perhaps even a kiss; boys are transformed into men before they march off to war.[19] Movie hostesses hold a key role in this transaction, as stand-ins for a much more powerful and sustaining "sweetheart at home": the motion picture industry. Ideal hostess-soldier dyads seldom jitterbug, but swing music and dance, jitterbug hijinks as novelty numbers, and onscreen performances of popular big bands maintain the democratic atmosphere.

Rumors of Inclusion (the War Musical)

From the moment of rumblings that a film was to be made about the Hollywood Canteen (the club), advance press in African American newspapers reported rumors of inclusion of black actors, musicians, and extras. The *Pittsburgh Courier* captioned a glamorous photograph of handsome Billy Eckstine with the rumor that the "former vocalist with Earl Hines" "may be given a leading role opposite Lena Horne in Warner Brothers' new 'Hollywood Canteen' film."[20] *Chicago Defender* columnist Al Monroe wrote that *Hollywood Canteen* would present Marian Anderson in "her first movie role."[21] Daves's original treatment did, in fact, include concert artist Anderson singing "Ave Maria" and "Lonesome Road" and musician-actor Dooley Wilson performing a duet with Humphrey Bogart. Building on the popularity of *Casablanca* (Warner Bros., 1942), Daves's original plan was to include a scene in his Hollywood Canteen film that opened with an unseen pianist playing "As Time Goes By." The spotlight would reveal a surprise: Bogie himself, not the actor who played "Sam," at the piano. An off-camera singing voice would join in, soon revealed as Wilson. In this treatment, "Bogie smilingly lets the colored man take the spotlight to finish the song." Directions called for "CLOSE SHOTS COLORED SOLDIERS, SAILORS WITH COLORED HOSTESSES," and a script note said: "They are proud of the singer and his popularity with the men, moved by the love song. One colored hostess squeezes the hand of a handsome colored boy. His eyes are moist as he smiles down at her."[22] While not comparable to Eckstine and Horne playing the leads, a representation of cross-racial friendship (however patronizing), and an attractive young black soldier-hostess dyad who are proud in the Canteen would have countered the usual exclusions and stereotypes.

None of these scenes made it to the screen. In the cases of Anderson and Wilson, the omission is due to delays in production due to rule 33. If Eckstine and Horne were ever slated for the leads, I found no trace of it in the scripts or other documentation. For many reasons, casting scoops often prove false in entertainment journalism. The purpose of rumors of inclusion, though, when reported by the black press, was not simply to predict outcomes—but to lobby for studio accountability. Black Hollywood entertainment critics collected and delivered rumors of inclusion to readers who would be affected by the success or failure of new representational possibilities, especially after the seventy producers signed the historic pledge of 1942 presented by Walter White and Wendell Willkie. The relationship between black casting of dignified roles, black audiences' pathways to viewing pleasures, and black people's movements in a world whose imaginary was so intimately entwined with the worlds that played on the screen was never lost on black critics and newspaper readers, but these connections received especial diligence in post-pledge coverage.

As a post-pledge film, *Hollywood Canteen* (the film) was made at a moment when racial inclusion was more on studio radars than had previously been the case. President Walter White of the NAACP beseeched the producers to rise to their historic roles as potential correctors of the race problem. White argued that by "avoiding the perpetuation of the stereotypes" and recognizing the "tremendous eagerness of the Negro soldier to win this war for the preservation of the democratic way of life," the motion picture industry could "raise the morale of the Negroes of this country and throughout the world.[23] Jack Warner was among the Hollywood producers who pledged to improve representations of African Americans in films made at their studios.

Decision-makers at Warners knew that their efforts would later be evaluated by the NAACP and black press according to the standards promised in 1942 and would be ranked among the other films made by other producers who had signed the pledge. The film critics, who had long advocated for an end to stereotypes and increased representations of African Americans in roles that were not only positive but "normal," stepped up to their roles in holding filmmakers accountable to their public promises to the NAACP.[24] Soon after Jack Warner had participated in the historic pledge, Billy Rowe, entertainment critic of the *Pittsburgh Courier*, devoted his column to a history of Warner Bros., with a focus on the studio's unparalleled technical and artistic contributions to the industry. As Leo "K" Kuter had done with his history of Burbank, Rowe spun a picturesque narrative of peaceful westward expansion to the idyllic location of the San Fernando Valley, only with an emphasis on the pioneering achievements of one studio above all others in the motion picture craft. The step-by-step leadership from stunning achievements in silent films to Al Jolson (in blackface) bursting into sound in *The*

Jazz Singer (!) and to films in the present and on the drawing board, Rowe's canon of Warners greatness peaks with an impassioned challenge to the studio to seize the "chance to change a gross evil" by becoming a pioneer in improved representations of African Americans in the movies. With measured praise for the "few cases" in which the studio had "given Negroes a chance to do the unusual" and special notice to the recently released *In This Our Life* (1942), Rowe argued that "the surface has just been touched, and ten percent of the American people are asking Warner Brothers and all those of like profession to give them the same chances and show them up in the same light that has been the lot of ninety percent of them since time immemorial [*sic*]." Referring to the producer brothers' rise from humble beginnings as the sons of Jewish immigrants from Poland to their reigning seats of power in the studio system, Rowe argued that "the Warners could do a great job for a country that has done a great job for them. They could, as they changed the trend of motion pictures in those early days, change the manner in which Negroes are set to the silver screen."[25]

One year after the pledge, black film critics ranked the studios on the extent to which they are met their promises. *Casablanca* (Warner Bros., 1942) had fared well under NAACP and black film reviewer scrutiny because Dooley Wilson not only provided "atmosphere" but played a character whose relationships with white characters were not simply subservient. Nonetheless, by May 7, 1943, the NAACP was demanding the "withdrawal from movie screens of an animated cartoon called 'Coal Black and the Sebben Dwarfs,'" a Merrie Melody production of Leon Schlessinger, distributed by Warner Bros. In this film, "the seven dwarfs represent seven miniature Negro soldiers who are held up for derision by theatre-going audiences." The reporter of a story that ran in multiple black papers, including the *Chicago Defender* and the *Negro Star*, noted the irony in the "American flag [that] floats over the camp in which the soldiers are quartered" as though to confer national sanction to "every established stereotype ever concocted to depict the Negro."[26]

Phil Carter of the *Los Angeles Tribune* acknowledged Warner Bros. for overcoming the "shameful" example of *The Green Pastures* to produce *In This Our Life* (the film in which Hattie McDaniel plays a domestic worker who lives "out," rather than in the home of her employers, and whose aspiring lawyer son, played by Ernest Anderson, is framed by the white racist villain played by Bette Davis). However, Carter, who had been the first African American press agent (for MGM), also found Warner Bros. deserving of his most scathing critique, for *Thank Your Lucky Stars*, the multistar patriotic vehicle that was released at the same time that the filming of *Hollywood Canteen* was announced and included many of the same stars. Carter's sarcasm registered that "the pixies went to work while Jack Warner's head was turned and cast Willie Best as a soldier," acting laconic, and rolling his eyes.[27] Carter's highest marks went to Twentieth Century-Fox for *Crash Dive* (for presenting an African American mess attendant as a war hero, à la Dorie Miller, thus presenting a heroic image of African Americans for the war effort while simultaneously honestly depicting "the Navy's policy of segregation"), *The Ox Bow Incident*, and *Stormy Weather*. He praised *Stormy Weather* for dressing the "dancing girls and boys" in "evening gowns and tails" and wrote that the film "depicted the Negro's ambition for a modern hope and children, respected the chastity of Negro womanhood, and gave major expression to acting talent as shown by Cab Calloway and Florence O'Brien."[28] Alyce Key of the *Los Angeles Tribune* agreed on the distance Warner Bros. would need to go in order to live down *Thank Your Lucky Stars*. Her highest rating went to Columbia for *Sahara* and *None Shall Escape*, in which "a Negro sits in the world court."[29]

Especially of interest were representations of African American soldiers on the screen, in tandem with Double Victory battles against the manifestations of racism in the armed forces: Jim Crow troops, menial labor, the withholding of opportunities for and recognitions of heroism, the grounding of trained Tuskegee pilots, the anchoring of navy men in harbors. As early as February 15, 1941, black film critics reported on relationships between racist conditions facing actual black soldiers, and representations (and lack thereof) of black soldiers in war movies. Harry Levette reported a "very noticeable fact," as far as the black press was concerned, that to date, "except for Monogram's 'Drums of the Desert' that depicted colored soldiers as Senegalese parachutists of British English army, there are to date no films being made that portray the Negro as an important factor in the war."[30]

Inclusion, then, was not just a concern in regard to which stars would be cast but extended to the ways black soldiers and hostesses would be represented on the democratic dance floor. Would black people in the film appear in among the general population of Canteen-goers or just in separate musical numbers that white soldiers and hostesses would watch from the dance floor? If the black soldiers would constitute a visible presence, how would they be represented? Would Willie Best return to the Warners soundstage as a slow-witted GI chased by a predatory marriage-minded shrew, as he did in *Thank Your Lucky Stars*? Or would Warners take a leaf out of the book of United Artists' *Stage Door Canteen*, whose casting of the handsome baritone Caleb Peterson as the humble, decorated war hero had warranted celebration? Would black women be included among the hostesses? If so, would they be represented as mammies and hussies or as attractive, intelligent, young patriots who cared about the welfare of soldiers? All of these questions arose in the post-pledge era of World War II moviemaking, not only for reporters and audiences of multiple publics, or politically divided industry workers and FBI agents, but also for producers hoping to appeal to the increasingly important foreign markets, and keep up with current demands of public relations as well as War Department censors (for whom continuing histories of racism in the United States were a handicap to securing an international reputation as a world champion of freedom, equality, and democracy).

Meanwhile, Back in New Guinea

Slim and Brooklyn—white soldiers in a white unit—continue to wait in their jungle encampment for transport to medical care. We won't know if the film fulfills its rumors of racial inclusion until the two head out to Hollywood for some rest and relaxation. However, first, Hollywood comes to the jungle. A kindly chaplain advises Slim to replace the fickle girl from Altoona with dreams of Joan Leslie, the star of tonight's film. As he watches Leslie flounce around with Jack Carson on an outdoor screen in a tropical storm, Slim is smitten, even when the sound cuts out.

Thankfully, we are spared a scene, recommended by a script doctor, that would have included among the spectators "some jungle natives, in a close-up or two, staring at the screen in bewilderment—the bucks with bones in their noses etc." Such a scene, proposed screenwriter Agnes Christine Johnson, would "make for a swell laugh." She also suggested a shot of "a couple of native girls, stripped to the waist," with a GI "looking at them in disgust and breathing: 'Gosh! What I'd give to see an *American* girl—dressed in white *with frills all over!*"[31] Fortunately, these ideas did not shape the revisions. Instead, Slim learns that all the girls-next-door in all the Altoonas of America can't hold a candle to the Hollywood starlet as a dream of postwar peace and prosperity.

While Hollywood may seem an awful long way from New Guinea, troop movement is easily accomplished in the war musical. We cut away to the hospital ship that carries Slim and Brooklyn to Los Angeles for (off-camera) medical treatment. We meet up with them on their post-op furloughs. Slim's arm is good as new. Brooklyn's crutches have been replaced by a cane. The camera pans across the landmarks, such as the Pantages Theatre and the Equitable Building, to a rousing instrumental version of "Hooray for Hollywood." Street signs shot from the same angle as the earlier "crossroads of the world" post (on which the city name "Brooklyn" was nailed) orient us to the intersections visited by the soldiers: Hollywood and Cahuenga, Western and Wilshire, Coldwater Canyon and Sunset. Soon, however, the idealized white GI and his less intelligent, funny, and likeable ethnic sidekick reach a cultural crossroads at Hollywood and Vine, when Slim wishes to sightsee and Brooklyn prefers to seek out the two things he misses most, beer and women. (The original treatment had him missing "white women," but "white" has been excised.)[32] Slim is content just to watch people "who aren't trying to kill each other"—but he also hopes to see some movie stars, especially his new love, Joan Leslie. The two part ways.

Naturally, the camera follows Corporal "Slim" Green, who wanders the palm-tree-lined streets of Hollywood and Beverly Hills alone. He gazes upon a swimming pool in Beverly Hills. He stands alone at the Hollywood Bowl. He walks into a drugstore, where a wisecracking (but kindly) lunch counter attendant informs him that meeting movie stars is easy for a man in uniform. All he has to do is cross Sunset Boulevard.

Dancing with National Memory, Part 2: Dance Floor Democracy (the Movie)

A wide shot frames the soldier entrance to the Hollywood Canteen across the street. With Slim, we approach the building, joining dozens of soldiers, sailors, and Marines. A side view reveals the long awning, under which flows a stream of enchanted GIs, beckoned by the thumping sound of a swing bass line and happy chatter. Squeezed among other young men, Slim drifts into the cavernous foyer to find himself part of a multicultural, multiracial, multiethnic, and international group. In every crowd scene from here on out, Canteen guests include people who appear to be African American, Latino, Asian American, and white; dressed in the uniforms of the various branches of the U.S. armed forces, as well as those of the various Allied nations (Britain, Australia, Canada, France, China, Russia, etc.). Tall, white, and almost startlingly normative, set off, as he is in this diversely cast throng of extras, Slim cranes his neck to see who is signing autographs. It turns out to be comedian Joe E. Brown, who poignantly refers to each individual soldier as "Son." (It is well known that Brown lost his own son early in the war.)[33] Slim's sweetly disoriented GI-in-Wonderland countenance endears him to all he meets (despite his eerie habit of speaking to people above their foreheads). When he asks Brown if all the big stars really come to the Canteen, his host confirms: "Humphrey Bogart waits on tables, Hedy Lamarr makes sandwiches, and Erroll Flynn sweeps out the place!"

Slim and the other soldiers gawk as Brown, famous for his wide mouth, nibbles a donut in a comical way. However, before Slim can say "Golly," his attention is grabbed by the sonic punch of a nearby big band, kicking off the opening bars of a big band arrangement of "King Porter Stomp," the Jelly Roll Morton piano number that by 1935 had become, via Fletcher Henderson through Benny Goodman, a standard jitterbug number played by all the big bands.[34] His focus shifts toward the rustic wooden entrance to the main room. "Say, isn't that . . . ?"

Brown completes his sentence: "Jimmy Dorsey and his band."

Suddenly, though not abruptly, the film audience is invited to adopt Slim's point of view as its own. If we are disciplined Hollywood motion picture spectators (and odds are that we are, whether viewing in the 1940s or today) we know how to do this without giving it a second thought. Corporal "Slim" Green is our Statue of Liberty, and we are the visitors in his head. It is ten minutes into the film, and we are being treated to our first glance of the democratic dance floor as it has circulated in national memory from December 1944 until the present, indeed for perpetuity. Our first view of the main room is framed by the pine logs of the doorway between the front entry hall and the dance floor. The camera facilitates the quick travel of our gaze to the far end of the room, where Jimmy Dorsey plays the clarinet and conducts at the same time. The stage barely accommodates the eighteen-piece band (nineteen counting its reeds-playing leader). Between us and Dorsey is a line of fans, their backs to us; they have rushed the stage to dig the acoustic power of big band sound up close.

While peering over their shoulders, some of us may even sense from the screen the frisson of immediate sound waves blasting from saxophones near enough to touch. We may even sense, at *our* backs, the swoosh of jitter-bugging soldier-hostess dyads, whose swiveling, whipping, spinning bodies surely shake the barn, sending vibrations up the legs of spectators and musicians. Even nondancing listeners dance more than stand, many nodding in time with the band, some clapping or popping their fingers on alternate beats. The bottom of the frame is dominated by the back of an apparently white hepcat who cocks his head to the right, his shoulders shaking, his entire body bobbing vertically, while he claps his cupped hands on "two and four."

For the film's viewers, the rhythmic excitement of swing culture in motion is approximated by the dynamic jumps in perspective made possible by quick cuts and new camera angles that jog us around the room, usually timed at the beginning of four-bar phrases. The fourth measure ends, and we are suddenly right behind the trombone section. As we peer over the scores on the music stands, we see Dorsey, leading, and beyond him the crowd facing the band, clapping and dancing. If we're quick or are especially looking for people of color, we might see that among the dozen or so jitterbugging couples are at least two couples that appear to be African Americans, as is one of the couples clapping at the foot of the stage. An African American soldier stands among white soldiers and hostesses in the crowd at the right. With the next rhythmically timed cut, we are stationed behind the drummer. Looking over the cymbals, we see another perspective of Dorsey smiling and conducting with economical motions, like wagging his index finger, with his arm casually bent at the elbow. Beyond him, we glimpse another view of the crowd, the murals on the walls. Details fly by. I rewind, replay, and keep my finger on "pause."

All these views lead to a framing of the entire room; a kitty-corner angle shot from the right-hand corner of the opposite wall, aimed toward the left of the stage, and taking in about ten jitterbugging soldier-hostess couples, same-race couples of different races. It is an integrated dance floor where no one appears to dance across race. My research tells me that during the same time Jimmy Dorsey's band is recording and filming this scene, they are playing a six-week engagement down the street at the Hollywood Palladium, where African Americans are not admitted. However, this inconsistency escapes the film. The crowd of soldiers entering the club, gawking at stars, rushing the dance floor, and dancing with hostesses is resolutely multiracial. The hostesses are multiracial in exact proportion to the guests. Same-race couples who appear to be black, white, and Latino dance in close proximity, and no one seems to mind in this happy gathering of military personnel, U.S. and Allies (Canadian, British, Chinese, Free French, Russian, etc.), and civilian volunteers. Everyone dances well in the crowd scenes. Only in the later comedy numbers do they get in each other's way.[35]

Even (white) military women are present, if you look really hard or if you pause the film at select moments. From a large window high above and to the left of the stage, three women dressed in the uniforms of three branches of military service—the WAVE among them most easily identifiable by her white hat—peer down at the saxophones. It is unlikely that a viewer's gaze would even take them in, unless that viewer was predisposed to search for signs of military women and knew where to look.

We cut to a wide view of the audience from the stage, just in time to face the dancers as they pivot to applaud the band. The camera zooms out. A tray surfs the top of the crowd, carried, no doubt, by an agile busboy. For a split second, we may be able to catch another quick glance at the three military women, high above the stage in their special room, rising to give the band a standing ovation. I say "may" because the opportunity does go by awfully quickly. I didn't notice this until I had had rewound and reviewed this scene many, many times. Perhaps actual military women and their loved ones noticed.

Break-away: Making the Dance Floor Look Like Democracy

If the racially integrated dance floor was such a contested space for the people who served the Canteen on the executive board, on the board of directors, and as volunteers, how did these same players come to represent a harmoniously integrated space in the film about the Hollywood Canteen? A partial answer is timing. In fact, the dance floor might have looked different if the shooting had taken place as scheduled. Let's consider the shooting schedules of the earlier *Stage Door Canteen* (in which some people of color speak) and *Hollywood Canteen* (in which only white people speak but extras paired in same-race couples are situated harmoniously on the edges of crowd scenes) alongside the FBI files.

During the first five weeks of shooting of *Stage Door Canteen* (November 30, 1942, and mid-January 1943), the battles over mixed-race dancing at the Hollywood Canteen had not yet exploded in the black, Popular Front, and swing press or the FBI files. The first meeting where the wildly different perspectives on mixed-race dancing would battle it out occurred in March 1943. Hoover would demand detailed reports on Communist/non-Communist (integrationist/segregationist) sympathies in May 1943. By the time *Hollywood Canteen* resumed production in June 5, 1944), FBI interest in the Hollywood Canteen had waned. According to Special Agent _____, the mixed dancing agreement of free choice (free to say yes, free to say no), was last confirmed in September 1943, and the choice to dance across race was rarely practiced. The board had become far more interested in the film's ability to raise funds for the club and preserve its positive image than in fighting over what happened inside it.

What we are left with is a torque-free multicultural dance floor. Nonetheless, the dance floor on the film is vastly more integrated than the images of the Canteen dance floor that appeared in newsreels and movie magazines. No one dances across race; but the dance floor also is not represented as a white one. Nonetheless, whereas the integrated (same-race couples) on the same dance floor may have registered as inclusion, and the extras (if not the stars) are presented in equivalent social positions across race, the arrangement did not go very far to improve conditions of African American actors in a professional sense, since nobody speaks. Ambient equivalence is not the same as social transformation.

If Donald Vining's diary correctly dates the opening of the new servicewomen's balcony to June 11, 1944,[36] Warners acted quickly to move the military women into their new mezzanine on the set immediately after the six-month shooting break. A full-set shot from June 26, 1944 (stage 6), included a painted image of a woman Marine in the window, presumably to plot the presence of military women over the stage for the performance by the Sons of the Pioneers. This scene is one of the places where you can see military women, fleetingly, in and out of long shots. I need to press "pause" on my remote. At any rate, white military women do have a place in this "inclusive" vision. In the balcony configuration to the left of the proscenium, they are serenaded and ignored at the same time. The entertainers never play to them, never acknowledge them. Framed, like pictures, the military women in the movie do not march out in rejection of their exclusion but sit sedately in a space conceived as a place of honor but a place that nonetheless has no room to move, no lines of dialogue, and certainly no room to dance.

The swing has been replaced by an instrumental version of "They're Either Too Young or Too Old," a song popularized by Bette Davis in the recently released Warners "war musical" *Thank Your Lucky Stars*. As the melody of this wistful, comic lament about the shortage of eligible bachelors in civilian life plays in the background, some of the servicemen peer from the foyer for a glimpse of the Canteen's inner sanctum.

Slim asks how much it costs to sit closer. Joe E. Brown tells him that everything is free. "If you see what you want, just reach for it." When Slim is distracted by a beautiful hostess, Brown adds, "That is, *the food.*"

"Yes, sir." Slim blushes. Obedient, well-mannered, and heterosexual, he is the very model of military masculinity.

Brown hails a celebrity escort to show Slim the ropes. Jane Wyman takes him by the arm and begins to lead him into the larger room. Gawking in disbelief, Slim asks if she is "Jane Wyman, the actress," and she replies that she is "Jane Wyman, period."

"My gosh," gasps Slim. "I thought movie actresses made enough not to have to work nights."

His next encounter with the humble and famous comes when Barbara Stanwyck, working behind the counter, hands him a sandwich. Slim confesses that she used to be his favorite until he became crazy about Joan Leslie. Stanwyck works into conversation her awareness that Slim earned a Purple Heart and was wounded in the South Pacific, demonstrating Hollywood's literacy in reading patches, insignia, and medals.

This personal touch leaves Slim speechless.

"Aren't you hungry?" she asks.

"I am, ma'am. But my stomach sort of jumped up into my heart."

In short order, Slim has become a favorite of the stars. The next heart he melts is that of Jack Carson, who now bounds off the stage after a comedic "bad-dancing" routine. Slim chokes when he recognizes Carson as the actor from the movie he saw in the jungle. Carson checks to see if he is okay, and Slim explains that it "kind of gets you" to see someone from the movies up close, especially someone who has "been right up close to Joan Leslie." He invites Carson to join him. The actor agrees, but just for a minute, because "it's against the rules for us busboys to sit down very long."

Slim plies him with questions. He wants to know if Joan Leslie is "really just like the girls back home at heart?" Carson confirms that she is just as nice and single in real life as she is in Slim's dreams.

Like all of the other stars who have been touched by Slim, Carson can't wait to tell Bette Davis, who is signing autographs at the snack bar. Carson describes Slim's love for Leslie as "very funny"—(meaningful pause)—"and beautiful." Jane Wyman calls Slim the "politest guy who ever walked in here," adding that he had told her he would "take on all the Japs in the world for one look at Joan Leslie." This catches Garfield's attention. "That sounds like an easy way to get a one-man army!" The stars make a plan to rush Joan Leslie to the Canteen.

In typical "war musical" fashion, dialogue scenes are interspersed with stage acts. The camera returns to a full proscenium view while the Canteen founders presumably execute a matchmaking scheme off-screen. Onto the stage enter four African American men in shiny faux flight uniforms. One man pulls a bomb on a wagon, one walks beside it, one pushes it, and one rides atop. They gather in front of an onstage airplane and sing about a "ready and steady" troop of flyers ready to "jump at dawn." It's the Golden Gate Quartet. Bill Johnson, who rode in on the bomb, rises to deliver his trademark syncopated spoken words as Orlandus Wilson, Henry Owens, and Clyde Riddick hum in harmony.

> The General had a groovy crew,
> A million lads and I'm telling you,
> There were white men, black men, on the beam.
> A real solid all-American team.

The naming of ethnicities is a typical feature in songs about "all-American" troops, and although black soldiers were not integrated into regular units at the time, the invocation of such a vision was agreeable to the quartet, who previewed the lyrics prior to accepting the engagement. It was certainly preferable to their number in Paramount's *Star Spangled Rhythm* (1942), when they played kitchen workers on the train and sang a lullaby to a well-heeled white couple in the dining car. In their flight uniforms and with a bomb and plane on the set, they strike the opposite end of the representational pendulum. No longer servants to white patrons, they are comrades of soldiers of all ethnicities (and movie people with progressive politics). In this scene—shot while the triumphs of the Tuskegee Airmen are fresh in the minds of (some of) the public—the handsome, dignified singers also signal the readiness of black pilots to fly.

The song was prerecorded on Thursday, August 10, 1944, and then shot on August 11 and 12. On the first day of shooting, eighty-one extras from Central Casting filled the onscreen audience, many of them African Americans.[37] Black hostesses and soldiers beam at the group from around the room.

Can the Extra Speak?

Technically, no. At that point, the extra becomes a bit player. If he or she speaks enough, the bit player becomes an actor. However, for African American film viewers and actors, in Los Angeles and throughout the country, the presence of black extras was a significant stake in representation and labor—and scenes in which black extras held social positions in the crowd equal to those of the white extras constituted progress, when compared to black extras' cinematic history of supplying atmosphere for happy plantations and primitive jungles.

The battle for more dignified representations of nonwhite people and acceptable pathways of identification to a greater diversity of viewers had long been fought by organizations such as the NAACP. These representational battles were inextricable from the civil rights battles in housing and employment. In Los Angeles, the connection was especially concrete for people of color who worked in the industry, who faced discrimination in housing near the studios, exclusion from most studio employment, restricted access to speaking roles, a limited range of types of mostly demeaning roles, few available studio contracts, and discrimination at coffee shops, nightclubs, and restaurants near the studios (and even the commissaries at the companies that employed them).

Novelist Chester Himes critiqued the politics of ambient representation in his unhappy foray into screenwriting in the 1940s. During a meeting about a script for a feature film on George Washington Carver, Himes actually walked out rather than sit in a room as a consenting functionary. "At that time, they had black people out there for décor," he said, about the studios. "They almost always had some black face out there."[38]

In the industry's language of the casting of crowd scenes in films, the behind-the-scenes practice of using black people as "décor" that Himes described was translated into the actual official job description of providing "atmosphere." Atmosphere players, unlike extras, who played "types," were presumed to be unskilled. Different films called for different "atmosphere," just as they called for different sets. Extras hired to infuse the background with a particular ethnic flavor were called "racials." Because "racials" were presumably hired for their "heritage" rather than skills, they were often among the lower paid extras. The pay for extras, according to Lasky, ranged from $5 per day for atmosphere to $15 a day for a "dress extra" (hired for clothing they owned and maintained) and to $20 per day for an extra who performed something dangerous or unpleasant that was classified as a "stunt."[39] The line between atmosphere and stunt could be blurry, and countless "stunts" were performed as "atmosphere" by hungry extras who couldn't afford to risk their places in a labor pool plagued by oversupply. Directors' expectations for "atmosphere players," also called "dog extras," was similar to inanimate materials like sets, locations, props, lighting, and makeup. They were media that directors could use in whatever ways the atmosphere required (except speaking, of course).

And so it is a mixed bag—the fact that black inclusion in *Hollywood Canteen* (the movie) is accomplished by extras and musical specialty acts, however dignified.

When Joan Leslie arrives, radiant in evening dress, she is met by Andrea King, who tells her that Bette is waiting. Bette thanks her for leaving her party and explains:

> Well, you know we don't often show favoritism, but there's a boy out front who was wounded in New Guinea. He was shipped home after two years in the jungle. His doctors gave him an okay to report for his transfer next week so he won't be here long. And all he asks of his leave is a look at you.

"Oh, well, that's easy," beams Leslie. "I'll give him a good look."

John Garfield meets them and announces that he's "fixed everything." He found a hat check in his pocket and gave it to Slim, and now he's going to do a fake drawing, and the winner gets a kiss from Joan Leslie. Bette worries this might be a "bad precedent," and Joan hopes they will "at least be introduced first," but they go along. Joan climbs the stairs to a tiny room and awaits a kiss from a soldier she's never met.

Break-away: " 'Merited Spots' for Colored Soldiers"

The "red check 77" scene is one of the most forgettable in the film but was subject to so many interoffice memos and revisions that it deserves a look. The scene exists to take care of a small piece of business. John Garfield must fool Slim into believing he has won the lottery and the prize is a kiss from Joan Leslie. Garfield ambles by Slim's table and inquires, in a general way, if anyone has "red check number 77." Slim has it, so he wins, to the bafflement of the other soldiers at his table, who didn't receive tickets at all.

Daves's third treatment, dated May 20, 1944, contained the following dialogue between a soldier near where Slim is seated and John Garfield.

SOLDIER: Hi, Johnny! I saw you last in *Italy*!
JOHNNY: What d'ya know! Like it better here?
SOLDIER: Brother, this is Heaven!

The scene gives props to Garfield (and therefore Hollywood) for his recent visit to the Italian front, where he entertained soldiers in the spring of 1944, returning just prior to the return to production. Garfield had been an early traveler to visit the soldiers and had tried repeatedly to have his 4-F replaced by a 1-A so he, too, could fight. Dialogue showing the appreciation of a soldier for Garfield's tour would contribute to his image as a manly patriot as well as civilian volunteer.[40]

On May 25, 1944, producer Alex Gottlieb wrote an interoffice memo to writer-director Daves with a couple of "minor notes."

I think that we owe it to the colored soldiers of our fighting forces to give them a merited spot in the picture, carrying out the same thought that you had in "Stage Door Canteen." I know that colored soldiers fought bravely in Italy in the Cassino campaign, so possibly John Garfield could chat for a moment with a couple of colored soldiers while he is enroute to Slim's table for the business of the #77 red check. I know Garfield is very anxious to do something like this.[41]

The scene in *Stage Door Canteen* to which Gottlieb referred had included an interracial conversation among soldiers in which a black soldier, played by actor Caleb Peterson, modestly accepted a compliment for his Distinguished Service Cross when some less decorated and reverent white soldiers noticed it. At the time of the filming, no Distinguished Service Crosses had yet been awarded to black soldiers. "Although there have been larger screen roles given to Negro actors," wrote a reviewer in the *California Eagle*, "there has never been a finer one written from the standpoint of reflecting credit upon the race." Just two weeks prior to Gottlieb's memo, African American flyers in Italy had made news for heroism that later resulted in four Distinguished Flying Crosses.[42]

Gottlieb's suggestion was met by a minor change in the script. Garfield would now say "Sure—south of Cassino—I remember!" There was no mention, however, in this revision, of the race of the actor who would play the soldier.[43] A week later, a memo from head of the Warners research department Herman Lisseauer to art director Leo Kuter identified a continuity problem with the scene: it is set in September 1943, "whereas the attack on Cassino did not begin until around December 1943."[44] Indeed, while the anticipation, especially in the black press, of the maneuvers leading up to the heroic missions of the nation's first all-Negro Army Air Force Unit, the 99th Fighter Squadron, had been reported as early as September 1943, the Cassino raids were making news just as the Warners memos were flying back and forth.[45] War correspondent Walter White, on leave from the NAACP, witnessed the bombings of Cassino in April 1944.[46] On May 9, 1944, "the 332nd Fighter Group, the first all-Negro group of its kind in the Army Air Forces," attacked more than one hundred fighter planes that were aiming for American bombers. African American flyers were still not permitted to fly bombers, but they were proving their heroism by flying so as protect them.

Lissauer's correction was sent the same day the scene was shot, June 6, 1944. Whether or not it had any effect, what we know is that no "chatting with Negro soldiers" occurs on the way to the red check scene, even though an interior set shot taken that day reveals a nearby table at which four African American extras are seated, two hostesses and two soldiers.[47] Instead the coveted two speaking lines go to dark-haired white actor Kay Dibbs, who may or may not be intended to be read by some audiences as a light-skinned black man. The dialogue is the same, except Garfield responds to the soldier's mention of Italy by saying, "Sure. Just south of Cassino. I remember. Do you like it better here?"

"Brother, this is Heaven," says Dibbs's character.

If the line lingers as a reference to the black soldiers who fought bravely in Italy, its only chance at legibility is with audiences skilled at reading against the grain for that possibility. Mostly it reads as a throwaway line, emphasizing Garfield's tour of the front.

Six days after the shooting of the red check 77 scene, Gottlieb wrote to Martin Jurow, the casting director, inquiring about the availability of Harold Nicholas and Dorothy Dandridge. "LeRoy Prinz would like to use them in connection with Louis Armstrong and the Golden Gate Quartet."[48] Jurow replied that the Nicholas Brothers were getting back together and going with Twentieth Century-Fox, but he would see about borrowing them. He also suggested trying to get Bill Robinson or Bill Bailey.[49]

As in the first round of production, rumors of inclusion flew in the black press as optimistically as in the previous spring. On July 1, 1944, the *Pittsburgh Courier* announced that "Louis Armstrong, his band and the Golden Gate quartet will be among the stellar lights who will be seen in the film. A sizeable number of sepia hostesses will be used in canteen scenes and male actors will find work acting as servicemen."[50]

Armstrong's availability fell through, but on July 27, 1944, the studio was relieved to learn that the Golden Gate Quartet had approved the lyrics to

FIG 11.1: Robert Hutton, John Garfield, and Kay Dibbs, the Hollywood Canteen. The actors are white, but the "red check 77" scene is still ground for discussion about representation of African American soldiers in the film. WCFTR-Negative #617–2. WISCONSIN CENTER FOR FILM AND THEATER RESEARCH.

"The General Jumped at Dawn" and agreed to perform it in the film.[51] On July 28, Gottlieb sent these directions to choreographer LeRoy Prinz: "When we photograph the Golden Gate number, we will have to spot a colored band at one side." That is, (white) studio musicians would provide the music, but sidelining African American musicians would appear to make up the band. "Will you be sure to line up the cleanest-cut, neatest colored musicians possible, with a leader to match?"[52]

Shot two months after the "red check 77" scene, I wonder if the scene presenting the Golden Gate Quartet in simulated flight suits, onstage with a plane and a bomb for props, was meant to compensate for the missed opportunity of the Cassino exchange. Perhaps the proximity of the quartet as flyers, placed sequentially prior to the "Cassino" reference, was meant to add up to a meaningful acknowledgment of "colored soldiers." In any case, the Golden Gate Quartet, at last filmed in a dignified manner, performing a song that could have been heard as "progressive" (though the advances celebrated in the lyrics had not been achieved), fulfilled multiple purposes. The scene would please the War Department, the NAACP, and people sympathetic to the Popular Front. The inclusive and democratic multiethnic platoon was a theme favored by the Office of War Information.[53] The positive representation of black soldiers would fulfill the pledge. The Golden Gate Quartet had two histories with Hollywood. Best known for their film appearances and radio broadcasts, for leftists they were also known for performing politically oriented material and making appearances at places and events of importance to the Popular Front, including their residency at Café Society, their participation in John Hammond's 1938 "Spirituals to Swing" concert, and with Josh White at the seventy-fifth anniversary of the abolition of slavery held at the Library of Congress in 1940.

Whatever the quickly revised dialogue of the "red check 77" scene was meant to achieve, what survives is the handoff of the faux lottery ticket that plucks Slim out of the crowd to collect his privileges. Garfield whisks him away and delivers him to Davis.

"Holy Smoke, You're Mrs. Skeffington, I mean Bette Davis, aren't you? I saw you on the hospital ship even before you were released on the mainland. That's one of the advantages we have over you civilians. We see the newest pictures before you do."

The stars laugh and guide him up the stairs. Opening a door, Garfield announces, "It gives me great pleasure to introduce tonight's kiss giver-outer."

Slim can't believe his eyes. He and Joan Leslie share a dewy moment. And a kiss. She wishes him luck. He says, "Thanks, I'll never forget." He gulps. "I guess I'd better go." The camera catches the emotionally heightened expressions of Davis and Garfield.

The next night, Slim returns with Brooklyn, who had fared poorly with the "dames" on his barhopping adventure. They join the line of soldiers, sailors, and Marines, not all of whom are white, and enter the foyer, this time to the sound of cowboy music. A campfire has been erected on the dance floor. The Sons of the Pioneers are singing about "drifting along like a Tumblin' Tumbleweed." Three barely discernible women in uniform watch from their window above the stage.

"I really go for that cowboy music," says Slim.

"Me, too," Brooklyn replies. "It reminds me of Flatbush."

Suddenly, a horse gallops into the room—it is Roy Rogers and Trigger. Trigger bows and everyone claps. Then the famous horse blows kisses "to the ladies" and everyone laughs. Roy coaxes Trigger to kiss him and then says, "He sure kisses juicy."

This draws peals of laughter form the multicultural crowd.

Now Rogers joins the Sons of the Pioneers in that popular ode to western expansionism "Don't Fence Me In." Then, Roy jumps into the saddle, and

Trigger does a little dance to the music, while the crowd claps. For the big finish, Roy races Trigger back through the soldier's entrance to the building (where he came in). Two MPs and two Shore Patrol officers applaud by cheerfully smacking their nightsticks into their palms.

Brooklyn drifts from movie star to movie star, trying his best pickup lines and failing miserably. Slim is also in a slump. Movie star Irene Manning fawns on him, but only Joan Leslie will do. Suddenly, Patty Andrews sits at their table and rubs her foot. "Owwww! Oh, Irene, do you think dancing will ever come back?" It's a joke—whatever the soldiers are doing hasn't felt like dancing, especially the moves of her latest partner, whom she describes as a "five-and-a-half-ton Marine."

The boisterous Marine returns. "Honey, I'm going to dance your hips right out of their sockets." He jerks her out onto the dance floor, not jitterbugging but jumping up and down while pumping her arms. Most viewers do not know that when this scene was filmed on August 7, 1944, the Hollywood Canteen Corporation had filed its appeal of Florida Edwards's successful suit against the Canteen for injuries inflicted by a raucous Marine. Andrews performs the helpless hostess in the arms of a clumsy Marine as a small price to pay for democracy. She mugs, grins, and bugs her eyes as she belts out the exaggerated blues opening of "I'm Getting Corns for My Country." When Andrews calls out "I'm a patriotic jitterbug" and then mugs at the camera and digs into the lower register to respond "Yeah, yeah, that's what I am," the implicit minstrelsy pops—and then dissipates, one of the film's appearing/disappearing articulations of race and swing. Behind her, an African American soldier and hostess sit at a table, not speaking—dignified, but "extra." After the novelty ode to the junior hostesses, the trio strolls around the room, wistful and earnest—no comedy in this reprise of "Don't Fence Me In." The cowboy genre speaks "America" differently from swing—not a modern multicultural/colorblind/white America but a soothing white overlay of the old pioneer spirit in a time of global war. The Sisters sing it like a lullaby: "Oh give me land lots of land."

Meanwhile, Brooklyn (who earlier betrayed his outsider status to cowboy music by associating it with Flatbush) fares no better in the love department. He finds his way to the kitchen and consults the busboys for tips on heteromasculinity. Unlike the soldiers described by Donald Vining, who regard "dashing" draft-age civilian men as crazy, lazy, or queer, Brooklyn looks up to the actors in aprons as big brothers who know how to attract women. Paul Heinreid and Donald Woods take a break from the suds to listen, amused, to Brooklyn's plight. They cannot help but toy with this east-coaster's desire to flirt above his station. Austrian émigré Heinreid tells him that the problem is that humans have become "civilized" and advises Brooklyn to exercise his "animal instincts." Brooklyn thanks the stars, assuring them that they have his "undying gratuity." But his malapropisms follow him onto the dance floor. Attempting to be suave and purposefully "uncivilized" at the same time, Brooklyn strikes out again and again.

The ideal masculinity of civilian male stars in aprons continues in the next production number, a spectacle of barbershop harmony by the busboy actors, led off by Dennis Morgan and picked up by Joe E. Brown. "Yip" Harburg's special lyrics have Morgan and Brown taking turns with the verses and the busboy chorus piping in at key moments with low-pitched booming support.

> You can always tell a yank
> By the way his glass will clank
> With a guy from Wales
> Or a guy from Minsk
> Or a guy from Kiang—Chow or Pinsk
> You can always tell a yank

It is a song about how well loved the American military is around the world and a portrait of American masculinity as a combination of fighting for the "bill of rights" and the "right to love a girl in tights." It is also another opportunity to represent military members of the Allied nations standing in friendly unity with the Yanks.

Finally, Brooklyn meets his match in the dippy script girl and aspiring actress played by Janis Paige. They step out on to the dance floor, where he makes his move. She turns him down, telling him that she is "all tied up with Humphrey Bogart tomorrow."

Posing above her station, she is no "starlet" but a "little shot" like him, Brooklyn's partner in a comic working-class dyad. It is his "instinctual" hot pursuit of this particular hostess that leads him to forget his injury and his cane in his eagerness to impress her on the dance floor. He has embarrassed himself pretending to speak French with Ida Lupino, but his lack of sophistication will pay off with this cute fellow pretender. Holding her in his arms in a simple fox-trot, he comments, "I like these novelty bands that play music the way it was written."

She agrees, and their connection lasts until he becomes overconfident and makes a fool of himself once again. Joan Crawford takes pity on him and asks him for the last dance of the evening. He is fine until he realizes that his new dance partner is not only a "dead ringer for Joan Crawford" but the real deal. He faints.

Later that evening, in the bunk room of the actual hospitality house run by Anne "Mom" Lehr, the Hollywood Guild Canteen, Slim longs for Joan Leslie, while Brooklyn, in undershirt and dog tag, waxes philosophical on democracy.

"You know, Slim, when we was mildewing in the jungle, I kind of resented these canteens and guys that were lucky enough to be here instead of there. But I don't resent it no more." His speech about the friendliness of the stars as the epitome of democracy inspires him to rise from his bunk. As he sits back down, he has another epiphany.

If he can dance, he can walk! He has fully healed from his war wounds.

The room is full of bunk beds with servicemen trying to sleep, but Brooklyn wakes them all, running down the aisles, even singing "I left my cane at the Hollywood Canteen," a variation of "I Left my Heart at the Stage Door Canteen," a reference to the other movie and other canteen. Teary-eyed, he sits down again and says, "Nothing like a leg of your own to stand on."

On the third night, the two soldiers return to the long line outside the Hollywood Canteen. Inside, the volunteers stand ready to shower the millionth military guest with prizes. Garfield steps up to the microphone and offers to give a "quick rundown" of the Canteen story. In his speech, he credits the idea for the Canteen to the workers in the motion picture industry, who wanted to find a way to say "Welcome to Hollywood and thanks to you guys."

Vignettes of busy people working hard and planning together illustrate Garfield's history. At the mention of volunteers from the unions building, painting, and decorating the club, images of skilled volunteers laboring fill the screen. When he mentions the unions, we see an IATSE meeting with people standing and clapping in agreement. About the hostesses, he explains, "They're not only actresses and secretaries and messengers and script girls, they're grand kids."

As the countdown for the millionth entrant approaches, a sailor picks an inopportune time to be peer-pressured into a blind date with a friend instead of entering the Canteen. A poor choice, it turns out.

Next in line, Slim is the millionth man. Under her breath, Davis accuses Garfield of rigging the contest, but this one is "on the level." Slim's first selection as the ideal soldier was a case of preferential treatment, but this one is random, which somehow confirms the stars' first impressions and justifies their breaking the earlier rules.

Everyone applauds as Slim is kissed by actresses, including Andrea King and Joan Leslie. His gifts include lodging in a luxury hotel, a car to drive for the weekend, and his choice of any actress in town as his date.

He says "Golly." Bette Davis points this out and everyone laughs.[54]

Then he says, "Do you mean I can have a date with Joan Leslie?"

Joan Leslie speaks up. "I'm flattered and honored to be chosen, Slim. I'll try and show you a good time."

"Golly," repeats Slim, and everyone laughs.

Jitterbug Memory?

As in most war musicals, the romantic leads in this movie are not the ones who partake in jitterbugging, except as spectators. On his first night at the Canteen, Slim witnessed some sedate swing dancing when he gazed upon the multicultural dance floor full of same-race couples enjoying the sounds of Jimmy Dorsey. There were no aerial steps, no zoot suits, no lascivious or drunken Marines, no stars, just well-behaved young people enjoying the popular music and dance of the day.

In this later scene, however, when he and Brooklyn take a tour of Warner Bros. studios as part of Slim's reward for being the millionth man, they view a rehearsal of a "modern" ballet fantasy number titled "Jitterbug Ballet," featuring Joan McCracken. In this stylized, dream-like performance, McCracken plays a little girl who tries to interact with soldiers, sailors, and cartoonish portrayals of hipsters wearing zoot suits, or, in the parlance of the day, "zoot-suiters." Everything about the performance is exaggerated—from the set to the facial expressions and to the costumes and the props. McCracken's little girl character goes to a bar and orders a banana split. A zoot-suiter gets the bartender to spike it with a Mickey Finn. We know this is what it is because the can it is in is labeled as such. Now that she is intoxicated, everyone breaks into jitterbug ecstasy. After happily whirling about the set with all the men, McCracken's character is crowned queen of the jitterbug. It is a strange scene that rolls together signs of innocence and drugs, Zoot Suit Riots, criminalization of people of color, white swing royalty, and war, presented as an upbeat montage of modern life.

However, this is Art, and the next scene assures us that traditional family values are alive and well in Hollywood. In a very homey scene, Slim visits Joan Leslie's house (filmed in her actual house), to meet her family (some of them played by her actual family). When Joan's sister, Debbie, says, "I'm Joan's sister, Debbie," she really is Joan's sister, Debbie. Slim meets the approval of Joan's parents when her father notices his Purple Heart. He joins the family for supper. Joan's father says grace,

Meanwhile, in the "B" plot, Brooklyn and his girlfriend make coded plans to meet outside to slip away to smooch beneath the Hollywoodland sign.

They've talked about it and danced about it; now it is time to exercise their "animal instincts."

By Hollywood musical logic, it is time for the Latin acts. Carmen Cavallero and his orchestra play "Voo Doo Moon," a piano feature for Cavallerro and his rhythm section, with the rest of the orchestra jumping in for the "exotic" big finish. Well-known dance act Rosario and Antonio perform a flamenco number on the Canteen tables.

Slim Finds His Voice

On his final trip to the Hollywood Canteen, Slim tells Bette Davis that he wants another chance to address the crowd before he leaves for San Francisco to receive his new orders. He didn't have the right words before but has found his voice. Davis announces that Slim has something to say. Slim faces the crowed and apologizes for only being able to say "Golly" before. Now, he wants to tell his fellow soldiers that although he received special treatment, it was on behalf of them all. "I may be number one million, but I represent everyone who's ever come out here."

His inclusive speech continues in the international, multiethnic listing mode we have already heard throughout the film in songs such as "The General Jumped at Dawn" and "You Can Always Tell a Yank." He announces that he could have been "a Chinese Air Cadet here to learn to fly." He continues, "I might have been one of our good friends from Russia," he adds; "or, one of our own colored boys."

At the mention of "colored boys," the camera cuts to a group of black soldiers and hostesses; one black hostess holds the arm of a black sailor.

"I might have come from the Philippines across the Pacific," he continues, "or from Down Under. Australia, or maybe been a Free Frenchman. I could have been one of the boys in South America, or maybe Mexico."

The camera cuts to a group of Latino soldiers with a Latina hostess.

He lists additional possible countries of origin: he could have escaped from "Norway, or the Netherlands, or Greece, or Poland, or Czeckoslovakia." Each listing is illustrated by a new vignette, showing emotional guests, presumably from those countries, moved by the recognition. "I might have been in a kilt from Scotland, but believe me, you would see my knees shaking right now."

This brings hearty laughter.

And so, Slim explains, it was not as an individual that the stars showered him with gifts. "I was all of you guys rolled into one when they made a short leave in Hollywood a kind of a paradise for me." He praises the hosts for being "as real as they are famous. They wait on us, they wash up dishes. They come up here every night to make us laugh or even choke up a little."

He now speaks in first person plural, assuming his destiny as representative of all. He thanks the stars for "helping us to forget" and assuring them that "after coming to the Canteen, we weren't lonely anymore." He continues. "So, Miss Davis, when I just said 'Golly' last night, I was feeling as grateful as all the boys are, but I just couldn't put it in words. So instead of saying, 'Thanks,' we just say, 'Golly.' I'll never forget."

Davis has joined him on stage. "Thank you, Slim, you've given us something we'll never forget. Wherever you go, our hearts go with you." The crowd responds with a standing ovation. (An "educational" pamphlet released by Warners includes an article explaining how Slim's speech may serve as a "springboard for discussion on Human Relations, on the tensions and conflicts confronting us in the schools today.")[55]

Break-away: Back to the Early Treatments

The gist of Slim's speech is constant from the first treatment to the screen, with significant changes in the details. In the first treatment (September 14, 1943), the line that will become "I might have been one of our good friends from Russia," is "I might have been a Russian, except they're pretty busy lately," followed by "(cheers from crowd)." The inclusion of "One of our own colored boys" is missing from the first treatment; recognition of African American soldiers is only added later on. And one acknowledgment that appears in the earlier treatments is cut later on. When he thanks the stars for helping them to forget "where we've been, or where we're going," the original line had been: "where we've been, or where we're going to end up," with this shooting note: "INTERCUT CLOSE SHOTS OF MEN WITHOUT ARMS . . . ONE WHO HAS LOST AN EYE . . . THE ONES WHO WANT TO FORGET."[56] From paper to film, Russians have been reconfigured from war heroes to good friends, African Americans have been tacked on as allies, and the physical and psychological wounds of war are removed from the picture.

Slim may imagine that he "could have been" Russian, African American, or physically impaired, but it is not, of course, random selection that places him at the center of attention in *Hollywood Canteen* (the movie). Robert Hutton's casting as the "millionth man" is not a bold choice. Even in the film, though his second moment of being singled out of the crowd is random, his first selection as a darling of the stars is a case of preferential treatment. Slim does not know of the ruse behind red check 77. Whiteness often works in this way. He does not have to choose or know about his privilege to benefit from it. Not to know his privilege is precisely the privilege that allows him to imagine his benefits as equally shared among the "we" at the democratic dance floor. It is a "we" to feel very good about.

Dancing with National Memory, Part 3: Exiting the Canteen (the Movie)

Nearly all of the films in this genre reward the special soldier with a special hostess who breaks the rules just for him, by meeting him outside the walls of the Canteen or USO. Resolution requires tension, provided in this film by a sequence of delays and missed connections that obstruct Slim and Joan's goodbye. When she fails to show up at the Canteen, Slim writes her a letter of thanks, sharing that even if her love was not for keeps, she has made him happier than he has ever been before. However, Joan is sincere in her affections—she is only delayed by typical wartime shortages. She has run out of gas! She pushes her car, but the gas station itself is out of gas. Slim heads off to the train station, where military men and civilian women are kissing their goodbyes all around him, including Brooklyn and the script girl. The two buddies board the train.

At the eleventh hour, Joan bursts into the station, having gotten a lift from an army captain. She runs alongside the train and promises to sit with him in the garden swing after the war. Whereas the military police and Shore Patrol officers at the Hollywood Canteen on-the-ground were supposed to discourage such rendezvous, in the universe of the movie it is a helpful MP who lifts the hostess so she may kiss her favorite GI while the train pulls out of the station. The starlet-sweetheart-to the-troops is also a deluxe model of the traditional girl-next-door who loves him for himself.

Conflict Resolution (the Movie)

As the movie nears its big finish, little remains unresolved. The stars have entertained the soldiers, who have in turn thanked the stars. Each soldier protagonist has paired off with the appropriate hostess. Race isn't a problem according to this particular slice of wartime Los Angeles. No one has been rejected from, or hurt on, the dance floor. Civilian actors are patriots and heartthrobs at the same time, retaining their masculinity. Politics are set aside. Anti-Communist Hutton interacts nicely with leftist Garfield and liberal Davis in a film produced by conservative Jack Warner. If a friendly atmosphere is proof of democracy, then the film seems to imply that Warner Bros. should monitor the state and not the other way around. The only problem pending resolution is the world conflict, an issue that exceeds the frame. By this logic, the soldiers must return to combat, fueled by the friendliness of

FIG 11.2: Joan Leslie kisses Robert Hutton on the cheek, the Hollywood Canteen. Note the African American extra (background, left) integrating the frame. WCFTR-Negative #617–14. WISCONSIN CENTER FOR FILM AND THEATER RESEARCH.

the motion picture industry, and fight even harder. With dreams of beautiful Hollywood hostesses dancing in their heads, the soldiers will know more than ever before why they fight, and will do so with valor.

In fact, the original treatment and early scripts envisioned the film's conclusion back where it began, "somewhere in the jungle." Only this time Slim and Brooklyn were to bear no signs of their former injuries. Healthy and strong, they were to crouch in camouflage fatigues, wearing combat helmets, rifles ready. There they were to huddle, fondling their mementos from the Hollywood Canteen. Working-class Brooklyn was to boast to fellow soldiers about the movie stars he dazzled. Idealized soldier-next-door Slim was to savor a private moment with a photograph of beloved girl-next-door movie star Joan Leslie. He was to gazes into her eyes, shining from the eight- by ten-inch glossy she signed for him, "with love." He was to smile when he found red check 77 folded inside the envelope. Fortified by Canteen memories, the two soldiers were to raise their rifles and charge into a rain of bullets. Fade Out.

Hollywood's place in the battle was to be clear to all—not only as a company town full of friendly people but as a defense industry that produced the stars behind the men behind the guns. Hollywood was to be revealed as America's sweetheart, inspiring the troops to fight bravely by screening whatever dreams seemed to make the sacrifices worthwhile, even when actual girls-next-door failed to write and wait.

However, this is not the ending that survives in the film, nor in national memory.

The combat ending was exchanged for the gentler one in which the likeable protagonists do not get pummeled with bullets (reminding audiences of theirs worst fears and losses). As in the early treatments, Brooklyn and Slim still board the troop train that will take them to San Francisco for their next orders. Joan Leslie still races to the station and kisses Slim through the train window. The soldiers still return to battle.

Then, instead of following the soldiers into dangerous territory, the film returns us to the aerial view of the Canteen that accompanied the opening credits. Only this time soldiers, sailors, and Marines are exiting rather than entering the club.

Superimposed over this tableau a close-up of the face of Bette Davis fades in, the size of the screen, à la the title character of the *Wizard of Oz*, only very, very sincere. To all the soldiers, she repeats the lines she told Slim at the end of his speech. After he thanked the stars for helping the soldiers forget, she said—and she now repeats—"You've given us something we'll never forget. Where ever you go, our hearts go with you."

Most viewers, at the time as well as today, will not have danced with the FBI and Warner Bros. Archives, and will not know what else has been forgotten in order for this version of Canteen memory to represent the "something we'll never forget." That Davis and Garfield, and many others, had fought for mixed-race dancing to be allowed at the Canteen; that Davis had toured as part of black USO troop with Hattie McDaniel at the request of the Negro Subcommittee of the HVC; that Garfield had not gotten the scene he was eager to do with a black soldier—these happenings are covered by screen memory, in both the Freudian and Hollywood senses. The memory of Davis and Garfield's preferential treatment of one type of soldier participates in the screen memory that forgets difference and struggle by covering it over with another picture of "what happened" that blocks other possibilities. After viewing this film, one would hardly believe that just months before the film's release Bette Davis had been honored by the NAACP-affiliated Committee for Unity in Motion Pictures as the white actress having done most to harmonize and create goodwill between the races in Hollywood.[57]

The Committee for Unity in Motion Pictures was chaired by Caleb Peterson, the actor who played the soldier with the Distinguished Service Cross in *Stage Door Canteen*. Peterson had traveled with Bette Davis, Lennie Bluett, Lena Horne, and many others on Hattie McDaniel's USO spot show to entertain the Tenth Cavalry. Surely Bette Davis was thinking of more people than Slim Green when she promised that Hollywood would never forget, but the overall impact of the film is one of a monolithic Hollywood patting itself on the back and an idealized soldier held up above all the rest.

This film that flies as a memory of simpler times, innocence, and friendliness as the American democratic spirit of World War II was, in fact, critiqued in its day by many members of what would later be called "the Greatest Generation." A reviewer for the *Daily Mail*, May 19, 1945, found "something slightly ugly in the spectacle of fighting men being encouraged to work up on distant battlefields an emotional frenzy over some pretty actress, returning home, and being kissed out of the depths of her patriotism."[58] Even the "honored guests" depicted in the films rubbed many actual soldiers the wrong way. *Time* printed a letter of outrage from four soldiers who listed "foxhole" as their return address. "It was as though we'd been taken into a millionaire's home, treated like uncouth fools to whom a debt was unfortunately owed, then sent back, dazed by the splendorous kindliness of the mighty, to our six-by-three lives."[59] A Private Joseph Wynn, writing to Jack Warner from "Somewhere in New Guinea," called the film "an insult to the intelligence of every serviceman" and offered the suggestion that when "shooting a picture about men in the service, I think it more advisable getting the viewpoints of a serviceman who's undergone the experiences in accordance to the script."[60]

I wonder if Private Wynn might not have preferred Daves's original treatments in which the film began and ended with its protagonists in mortal danger—a framework that acknowledged the cognizance of soldiers and loved ones? Working with the Warner Bros. Archives, I am struck with how much dissonance is preserved in corporate memory. National reruns of the war musical style repeat the genre's consensus aesthetic while obstructing critical memories of difference, competing interests, and mixed outcomes that are also so much a part of filmmaking, Canteen running, and war memories of multiple publics. This national memory version presents a different behind the scenes drama than that of the state: most of the scrambling about race is aimed at adding diversity to the film rather than criminalizing as un-American the people who advocate for racial mixing. However, the end is eerily similar. The multiracial dance floor still promotes a white ideal dyad that appears to float naturally to the top. The promise of that ideal seals a vision of a postwar normal. The universes are different, but the results intertwined.

Exiting the Canteen (the Book)

In the film, as on the ground, no dance floor, set of steps, or genre of music is a guarantee for democracy. However, dance floor democracy may be a way of thinking about democratic practice as multiperspectival, multidirectional, differentially weighted, and crowded with interconnected bodies-in-motion.

The film *Hollywood Canteen* didn't invent the war musical or star system, but its makers adhered to a model that sought a smooth finish in which every response to emergency appears intentional, coherent, and mutually beneficial. In this way, the war musical approach to swing culture as war memory succeeds by excising any admission of uncertainty, power, difference, and struggle. What if the film had been made along a different aesthetic, one that privileged torque as the democratic potential of swing?

What if our first view of the dance floor had been shot from the point of view of Mel Bryant being led to the sidelines with other black soldiers while Mickey the shore patrolman stared at him and Florida Edwards crashed to the floor in the corner of the screen? What if Jean Lewin saw the look on Mickey's face and whispered to a screenwriter in an apron, who made his way through the crowd to stand guard at the men's room? What if the camera traveled in such a way as to show that we were seeing moments that cannot be seen or known from elsewhere in the room? Here's how it could be: in one panning shot, Marion Krow is pulled aside by fellow hostesses and told she doesn't have to dance with black soldiers; Mary Ford picks up the telephone; Mary Lou Ramirez and her friend dance with white sailors; a shy sailor, B.J. Henson, watches from the sidelines; a fight breaks out near Claire Rosen; and Lennie Bluett greets Lena Horne as he picks up abandoned dishes. Horne takes the stage, and Jane Lockwood flips through the air.

Narrowly framed medium shots could take in radically different views of the same scenes from different perspectives, with just enough clues to let the viewer catch spatial and temporal connections. Here's how it could be. Wide shots take in several different approaches to the jitterbug—all at once. No auditions or rehearsals are held. The dancers improvise unpredictable connections and disconnections, some adjusting for the weight and height and center of gravity of their partners, some moving as if dancing alone. Couplings where dancers achieve flight through communicative achievement of optimum torque appear in the same shot as missed connections, manhandled hostesses, the GI shuffle of the inexperienced, and many soldiers, sailors, and Marines, some of them with visible wounds, watching from the sidelines. Through the foyer, we see three white WAVES attempting to enter the room, and being turned away. At the same time, Jeni Legon arrives with a group of other young, beautiful black women and approaches a group of black military men (but Mel Bryant is already gone). A tight shot takes in a group of handsome sailors from a distance and then drops down suddenly at a forty-five-degree angle to a tray of dirty dishes. The next shot shows Donald Vining as he delivers the dishes to the kitchen, then gazes up at the empty window over the stage, and then turns his head to see Lorraine Bear and her fellow WAVES marching past the autograph table. Bear steals a glance at Rita Hayworth, who is making a phone call for a couple of British airmen.

What if handheld cameras followed the travels of guests and volunteers back to their homes and apartments, YMCA lodgings, bases, crowded furlough quarters, ships, and temporary encampments? The next night, some come back, some don't. We follow some to other night spots, other dance floors configured as democratic, the Fairfax Victory House in the Jewish Community Center, the Twenty-Eighth Street YMCA on Central Avenue (where Avanelle Harris dances with soldiers, Dorothy Guinn makes a speech, and Caleb Peterson holds the first meeting of the Committee for Unity in Motion Pictures), the downtown YMCA (where Mary Lou Ochoa learns Latin dance from a professional dancer who is also in the military), and all around: the American Legion in Beverly Hills, the Prosins' living room in North Hollywood, Ben Carter's mansion in Sugar Hill, the Sayanara Ball at Santa Anita Assembly Center, the USOs in Culver City, Glendale, Boyle Heights, and Long Beach (both buildings, main and Negro extension).

I'm not a filmmaker or screenwriter, and my vocabulary and imagination are stretched in trying to craft an alternate treatment for this movie. I suppose this book is my alternate treatment. This book is my improvisation on swing culture as war memory as a feminist jazz studies scholar who has managed to dance with sixty members of a generation whose moves now affect the way I see and hear the music I study. You may spin out in a different direction. But here is where I lean at the moment of leaving the Canteen behind. Democracy in swing is not in the individual freedom of the break-away. It is not in the in-and-out of the two halves of a whole, or individual and community, or stunning exhibitions of the best of the best. It is in the methodology of the torque, by which bodies of different weights practice their inevitable effects on one another.

Notes

PROLOGUE

1. The epigraphs to this chapter are from "There Is No Color Line at This Coast Canteen," *Chicago Defender*, January 30, 1943, 19; Ahmed, *On Being Included*, 49; the film *Hollywood Canteen* (1944).

2. See, for example, Stowe, *Swing Changes*, 162; Starr, *Embattled Dreams*, 159–182; Bogle, *Bright Boulevards*, 232–234; Tyler, *Harlem to Hollywood*, 144, 151–152.

3. This juxtaposition shows up in many places, but one example was the sequence of photographs and museum cards that I saw in the hallway leading up to the American Sector restaurant in the National World War II Museum, New Orleans, on January 6, 2013.

4. See, for example, Cappelletto, *Memory and World War II*, 9.

5. Maude Cheatham, "Hollywood Canteen Celebrates," *Screenland*, November 1943, n.p., Bette Davis Collection, box 382, scrapbook 45, Howard Gotlieb Archival Research Center, Boston University.

6. Brokaw, *Greatest Generation*, 11.

7. "Hollywood Canteen All-Star Opening," NBC radio broadcast, October 3, 1942, reissued in *The Bette Davis Collection*, CD, Radio Revisited, n.d., available from the website, RadioRevisited.com/index.htm, accessed February 16, 2014.

8. Brooklyn's speech resounds with the "pragmatic tolerance" model that Jane Mummery criticizes in Richard Rorty's formulation of democratic process as an ongoing conversation that "leads to increased understanding and inclusiveness." For Mummery, the flaw is Rorty's failure to define the already included "we" or the eventually included "they." Mummery, "Rethinking the Democratic Project: Rorty, Mouffe, Derrida, and Democracy to Come." *Borderlands* 4, no. 1 (2005), available at www .borderlands.net.au/vo14no1_2005/mummery_rethinking.htm, accessed December 2, 2006. For analysis of continuing prevalence of this model, see Ahmed, *Being Included* (from which the epigraph in this chapter from Ahmed has been taken), 9.

9. Mummery, "Rethinking the Democratic."

10. Schlossberg, *Going Hollywood* (DVD).

11. Monaghan, "'Stompin' at the Savoy,'" 31–85.

12. Clyde Haberman, "A Nation Challenged: An Overview: November 10, 2001; Bush's Exhortation at the U.N., and Firing Up the Hollywood Canteen," *New York Times*, November 11, 2001, 1.

13. Torgovnick, *War Complex*, xi.

14. Emily Rosenberg points out that the "infamy framework" of Roosevelt's famous speech of December 8, 1941, was itself drawn from national memory of "America's most celebrated frontier legends: Custer's Last Stand and the Alamo." Soon after this framework was used to recruit popular support for U.S. entry into World War II, it began a new career as rallying cry in service to the aims of the U.S. military-industrial complex. Rosenberg, *Date Which Will Live*, 12, 28–33.

15. Frascina, "Advertisements for Itself," 75–96.

16. "Airport Information, USO, the Bob Hope Hollywood USO at LAX" available at the website of the Los Angeles World Airports, www.lawa.org/welcome_LAX.aspx ?id=1592, accessed August 12, 2010.

17. Christina Aguilera, "Candyman," Vimeo video, 3:16, posted by Christina Aguilera, February 24, 2011, http://vimeo.com/2034800, accessed February 18, 2014, and "Making of 'Candyman' Music Video," Christina Aguilera, © 2006 RCA Records, A Unit of Sony BMG Music Entertainment," Vimeo video, 21:25, posted by "Mark Roberts Motion Control," September 26, 2012, http://vimeo.com/48948063, accessed February 18, 2014.

18. Bud Forrest Entertainment Inc. website, 2002–2013, "In the Mood: A 1940s Revue," www.inthemoodlive.com, accessed March 3, 2014.

19. McMullen, "Identity for Sale," 130–140. Most Andrews Sisters revival trios are white, though the singer-actor-choreographer Chase Kamata has diversified the shifting personnel of the Victory Belles. National WWII Museum, *The Victory Belles*, CD, n.d., available at the website of the National World War II Museum, http://www .nationalww2museum.org/visit/victory-belles.html, accessed May 1, 2013.

20. "Service before Self," World Trade Center Memorial, Hansen Hall, Robert J. Dole Institute of Politics, University of Kansas, Lawrence.

21. Torgovnick, *War Complex*, 2.

22. Bryant, telephone interview, July 25, 2000.

23. Bear, email to author, April 4, 2001.

24. Torgovnick, *War Complex*, ix. In addition, I share the concern of authors whose work was published in a collection on the marketing of 9/11 at the way the "four plane crashes" and "thousands of lives lost" have been "exploited for profit" politically, militarily, and commercially, and I worry about scholars' complicity in this exploitation, when some of us rushed to make our work relevant by tying it to this single event. Heller, *Selling of 9/11*, 2–5.

25. King, email to author, October 20, 2001.

26. Portelli, *Order Has Been Carried Out*, 15–16.

27. Ibid.

28. King, email to author, October 20, 2001.

29. Watson, interview, November 21, 2004.

INTRODUCTION

1. The epigraphs to this chapter are from Goldman, *I Want to Be Ready*, 5; Davis, *Abolition Democracy*, 20; Foster, "Taken by Surprise," 4.

2. Spada, *More Than a Woman*, 191.

3. Billman, *Betty Grable*, 12.

4. Sturken, *Tangled Memories*, 2–4.

5. Crease, "Divine Frivolity," 209.

6. Foster, *Corporealities*, xiv.

7. Savigliano, "Story of Tango Bodies," 200.

8. Ibid., 199.

9. Ibid.

10. Anderson, *Imagined Communities*, 145.

11. Ibid.

12. Heble, *Wrong Note*, 9.

13. Cappelletto, *Memory and World War II*, 5–8.

14. "Canteen Has Birthday," *Los Angeles Times*, November 1, 1943, A1.

15. *Hollywood Canteen* (Warner Brothers, 1944).

16. *Los Angeles Examiner*, December 20, 1944, sec. 3, 16.

17. "There's No Color Line at This Coast Canteen," *Chicago Defender*, January 30, 1943, 19.

18. John Gunn, "Stage Door Canteen Opens in Hollywood," *Daily Worker*, August 24, 1942, 7.

19. "Eddie Cantor to Play Role of Santa Claus at Canteen," *Los Angeles Times*, December 17, 1942, 16; "Hollywood Will Have Stage Door Canteen for Benefit of Soldiers," *New York Age*, August 29, 1942, 10; Gunn, "Stage Door Canteen Opens."

20. Meyer, *Creating GI Jane*, 5–10.

21. On "war memory," see, for instance, Cappeletto, *Memory and World War II*, 31.

22. Stine, *Mother Goddamn*, 192.

23. Halbwachs, *Collective Memory*, 158–186.

24. Grewal, *Transnational America*, 19.

25. Singh, *Black Is a Country*, 17.

26. Usner, "Dancing in the Past," 87–111.

27. Portelli, *"Death of Luigi Trastulli,"* viii–ix.

28. Whitehead, *Why Jazz*, 10.

29. Dinerstein, *Swinging the Machine*, 258.

30. Erenberg, *Swingin' the Dream*, 52.

31. Spring, "Swing and the Lindy Hop," 191; Stearns and Stearns, *Jazz Dance*, 315–316.

32. Crease, "Divine Frivolity," 209–210.

33. Dinerstein, *Swinging the Machine*, 255.

34. Ibid., 257.

35. For the ethnomusicologist and dancer Christopher Wells, the difference between what looks linear from the outside and what he experiences as a dancer is the "tension and release feel," in which even the slotted send-out associated with West Coast style is hardly linear but is built from the gathering and sending of energy—the send-out may look like two bodies separating along a straight line but is felt as an accelerated circular "whipping out," propelled by the prior gathering of energy; the torque won't work if the velocity is steady. I thank Chris for the personal conversation and demonstration in the hallway at the Society for American Music, Charlotte, North Carolina, April 2012.

36. Laws and Sugano, *Physics*, 70–71.

37. Dinerstein, *Swinging the Machine*, 258–268.

38. Goldman, *I Want to Be Ready*, 1–4.

39. Ibid., 54.

40. Ibid., 22.

41. Foster, "Taken by Surprise," 4.

42. Goldman, *I Want to Be Ready*, 5.

43. Davis, *Abolition Democracy*, 20.

44. Sides, *L.A. City Limits*.

45. Goldberg, *Racial State*, 8.

46. O'Leary, *To Die For*, 3.

47. Melling, "War and Memory," 257.

CHAPTER 1: WRESTLING HOLLYWOOD TO THE MAP

1. The epigraphs to this chapter are from Sides, *L.A. City Limits*, 8; Adela Rogers St. John, "Dear Reader: Hollywood Has Changed!," *Photoplay and Mirror*, March 1943, n.p., clipping, scrapbook 45, box 382, Bette Davis Collection, Howard Gotlieb Archival Research Center, Boston College; Boym, *Future of Nostalgia*, xiii.

2. See, for example, Monaghan, " 'Stompin' at the Savoy," 36–37; Stowe, *Swing Changes*; Townsend, *Pearl Harbor Jazz*; Erenberg, *Swingin' the Dream*.

3. Stowe, *Swing Changes*, 161–162.

4. Fyne, *Hollywood Propaganda*, 124–125.

5. Townsend, *Pearl Harbor Jazz*, 184–187.

6. Spada, *More Than a Woman*, 191.

7. Adela Rogers St. John, "Dear Reader."

8. Oppenheimer, *Passionate Playgoer*, 518.

9. See, for example, Horne, *Class Struggle in Hollywood*.

10. Quoted by Giovacchini, "Hollywood Is a State of Mind," 423.

11. Klein, *History of Forgetting*, 253.

12. Ibid., 249–250.

13. Ibid.

14. Among the many outstanding recent books on Los Angeles history, see Ramírez, *The Woman in the Zoot Suit*, Macias, *Mexican American Mojo*, Kurashige, *Shifting*

Grounds of Race, Hurewitz, *Bohemian Los Angeles*, España-Maram, *Creating Masculinity*, Wild, *Street Meeting*, Parson, *Making a Better World*, Flamming, *Bound for Freedom*, Marcus, *Musical Metropolis*, Deverell, *Whitewashed Adobe*, Sides, *L.A. City Limits*, Starr, *Embattled Dreams*, and Julien, "Sounding the City."

15. "City's White Ways Begin to Fade for Dimout," *Los Angeles Times*, August 18, 1942, A1.

16. Maxine Bartlett, "Dimout Fails to Dim Out Glamour at Gay Preview," *Los Angeles Times*, August 31, 1942, 8.

17. Philip K. Scheuer, "'Talk of the Town' Builds to Stirring Filmic Climax," *Los Angeles Times*, August 31, 1942, 8.

18. Starr, *Embattled Dreams*, 66–67.

19. Eleanor Pitts, "Thousands of Women Active in U.S.O," *Los Angeles Times*, February 10, 1943, B2.

20. Pitts, "Thousands of Women."

21. For an excellent study of USO hostesses, see Winchell, *Good Girls*.

22. Commanding Officer, U.S. Naval Training School, Hampton Institute, Hampton, Virginia, Memo to the Chief of Naval Personnel, "Report on Conference on Negro Naval Personnel, Eleventh Naval District, San Diego, California," March 15, 1944 (pt. 2), Record Group 181, Records of Naval Districts and Shore Establishment, National Archives and Records Administration, Pacific Region, Laguna Niguel.

23. See Julien, *Sounding the City*, 266.

24. Commanding Officer, U.S. Naval Training School, Hampton Institute, Hampton, Virginia, Memo to the Chief of Naval Personnel, "Report on Conference on Negro Naval Personnel, Eleventh Naval District, San Diego, California," March 15, 1944 (pt. 3), 19, Record Group 181, Records of Naval Districts and Shore Establishment, National Archives and Records Administration, Pacific Region, Laguna Niguel.

25. Ruth Frankenberg, *White Women, Race Matters*, 14.

26. "Race Relations—Negro," Armed Services YMCA: USO City Histories (Industrial): Inglewood, Kautz Family YMCA Archives.

27. Ibid.

28. "Thumbnail Survey for USO Directors' Conference, June 18, 1943," Armed Services YMCA: USO City Histories (Industrial): Compton, Kautz Family YMCA Archives.

29. Sides, *L.A. City Limits*, 19.

30. Kurashige, *Shifting Grounds*, 162.

31. "YMCA USO City Histories: Watts," Armed Services YMCA: YMCA USO City Histories: Watts, Kautz Family YMCA Archives.

32. "Nightclubs and Other Venues, Los Angeles," in *The New Grove Dictionary of Jazz*, 2nd ed., ed. Barry Kernfeld, Grove Music Online, Oxford Music Online, http://www.oxfordmusiconline.com, accessed December 30, 2008.

33. Laslett, "Historical Perspectives," 58.

34. Himes, *Lonely Crusade*, 130.

35. "Chester Himes Writes 3 Novels, Wins Award," *Chicago Defender*, October 14, 1944, 16; "Calif. USO Worker Lauds Local Club," *Philadelphia Tribune*, February 24, 1945, 14; Margolies and Fabre, *Several Lives*, 49.

36. Minutes, Meeting of East Anaheim Committee of Management, Long Beach, Calif. Negro Extension, April 20, 1945, Armed Services YMCA: USO City Histories (Industrial): Long Beach (Negro), box 5, Kautz Family YMCA Archives.

37. "Policy Regarding Negro Servicemen at the Municipal Service Men's Club," November 10, 1944, Armed Services YMCA: USO City Histories (Industrial): Long Beach (Negro), box 5, Kautz Family YMCA Archives.

38. Macias, *Mexican American Mojo*, 35–36, 51.

39. "New Beverly-Fairfax Victory House to Open," *Los Angeles Times*, July 11, 1943, A2.

40. "National Jewish Welfare Board Questionnaire on Extent of Participation by Women and Girls in the Direction, Staff, Membership, Program and Activities of Jewish Centers," 1945, National Jewish Welfare Board Army-Navy Division Collection, Center for Jewish History, New York.

41. "Soldiers, Sailors, Marines—Free!" *Los Angeles Times*, March 19, 1943, 17.

42. "Hollywood's U.S.O. Center Opening Attracts Notables," *Los Angeles Times*, February 3, 1942, A12.

43. "Chatter Box," *Los Angeles Times*, March 10, 1942, A5.

44. Roarty, *More Than Entertainment*, 140–192.

45. "USO Officials, Filmland, Army Join Hundreds at USO Clubhouse Opening Sunday," *California Eagle*, July 16, 1942, 1B; "Hollywood Will Have Stage Door Canteen for Benefit of Soldiers," *New York Age*, August 29, 1942, 10.

46. Wilma Cockrell, "Notes A 'Pealin," *Los Angeles Tribune*, July 20, 1942, n.p., clipping, scrapbook 45, box 382, Bette Davis Collection, Howard Gotlieb Archival Research Center.

47. Hopper, "Hedda Hopper's Hollywood," *Los Angeles Times*, August 28, 1942, A11.

48. Halle, *New York and Los Angeles*, 27.

49. Kurashige, *Shifting Grounds*, 45.

50. See Halle et al., "Residential Separation," 150–151.

51. Loren Miller, interviewed by Lawrence de Graaf, April 29, 1967, Center for Oral and Public History, California State University, Fullerton.

52. "Girl Demonstrator Opens Door on Film Contract," *Chicago Daily Tribune*, August 21, 1942, 11.

53. Nancy Marlow, interview, March 27, 2004.

54. Jeni LeGon, telephone interview, November 26, 2004, and oral history, June 27, 2005.

55. Helene (Angus) Bank, interview, January 11, 2006.

56. Virginia McDowall, interview, May 23, 2003.

57. Mary Lou (Ramirez) Ochoa, interview, January 13, 2006.

58. Marjorie Lewin, interview, May 30, 2003.

59. Aniela McAuliffe, interview, May 23, 2003.

60. Gordon, *Gordon File*, 55.

61. Donald Vining, diary entry, November 16, 1943, folder 4, vol. 1, pt. 3, 1942–45, box 7, Diary Digests, Donald Vining Papers, New York Public Library Humanities and Social Sciences Library.

62. Mel Bryant, telephone interview, October 28, 2000.

CHAPTER 2: CRUISING THE CAHUENGA PASS(T)

1. The epigraphs to this chapter are from "K" Kuter, "Works of Art," *Warner Club News*, February 1943, 5, clipping, Bette Davis Collection, scrapbook 45, box 382, Howard Gotlieb Archival Research Center, Boston College; Theresa Nevarez, telephone interview, April 11, 2009.

2. Finler, *Hollywood Story*, 16–17, 256–257, 284–286; Schickle and Perry, *You Must Remember This*, 45–49; Sperling and Millner, with Warner, *Hollywood Be Thy Name*, 139–147.

3. Kevin Starr identifies this genre of Hollywood Canteen narrative in *Embattled Dreams*, 159–182.

4. See, for example, Bette Davis, "Our Hollywood Canteen," *Hollywood Reporter*, November 2, 1943; "Open Letter to the Workers of the Hollywood Canteen," *Variety*, July 13, 1944, 10; and "Hollywood Canteen," *Colliers*, January 2, 1943, n.p., clippings, Bette Davis Collection, scrapbook 45, box 382, Howard Gotlieb Archival Research Center. See also Bette Davis with Herskowitz, *This 'n' That*, 122–124. Among the guilds and unions whose representatives sat on the Hollywood Canteen Corporation and Board of Directors were: Actors Equity, Affiliated Property Craftsmen, American Federation of Musicians (both segregated locals: 47 and 767), American Federation of Radio Artists, American Federation of Amusements and Allied Crafts, American Guild of Musical Artists, American Guild of Variety Artists, Association of Motion Picture Costumers, Building Service Employees Union, Independent Publicists, International Photographers, International Sound Technicians, Lab Technicians, Machinists Cinema Lodge, Makeup Artists, Motion Picture Grips, Motion Picture Hair Stylists Guild, Motion Picutre Illustrators, Motion Picture Set Electricians, Motion Picture Studio Projectionists, Moving Picture Painters and Scenic Artists, Radio Writers Guild, Screen Actors Guild, Screen Cartoonists Guild, Screen Directors Guild, Screen Office Employees Guild, Screen Publicists Guild, Screen Readers Guild, Screen Set Designers Guild, Screen Story Analyists, Services Employees International Union, Society of Motion Picture Art Directors, Society of Motion Picture Film Editors, Society of Motion Picture Interior Decorators, Sound Technicians, Studio Carpenters, Studio Electricians Union, Studio Laborers and Utility Workers, Studio Miscellaneous Employees, and Studio Transportation Drivers. "By-Laws and Articles of Incorporation of the Hollywood Canteen, Inc," August 21, 1942; "Hollywood Canteen, Inc. Board of Directors," September 24, 1945. Personal collection, Bernard Gordon.

5. A typical list-angle: "During the first month of operation the boys in armed forces have neatly packed away some 4,000 loaves of bread, 50,000 half pints of milk, 400 pounds of butter, 1,500 pounds of coffee, 1,000 pounds of cheese in three varities, 2,500 pounds of meat in several varieties, 20,000 oranges, 30,000 gallons of orange juice, 75,000 packs of cigarettes, 1,000,000 pieces of cake, more than 150,000 sandwichese all told, not forgetting to add the pickles, relishes, sandwich spreads and mayonnaise." "There's No Color Line at This Coast Canteen," *Chicago Defender*, January 30, 1943, 19.

6. "Bette Davis Upholds Mixed Couples at Movie Canteen," *Chicago Defender*, January 9, 1943, 1.

7. Kuter, "Works of Art," 5.

8. Barraclough, *Making the San Fernando Valley*, 77.

9. McWilliams, *North from Mexico*, 1949. For an excellent review of McWilliams's work and its impact on Los Angeles studies, see Willard, "Nuestra Los Angles," 807–843 (on "Spanish Fantasy," see 809). An excellent example of ongoing engagement and elaboration of McWilliams's analysis is Deverell, *Whitewashed Adobe*, especially 9–10.

10. Hayden, *Power of Place*, 214.

11. Loewen, *Sundown Towns*, 9.

12. Kuter, "Works of Art," 5.

13. Ibid.

14. Ethington, "Ab Urbis Condita," 190–191.

15. Ross, *Stars and Strikes*, 6.

16. Kuter, "Works of Art," 5.

17. Starr, *California*, 42. For an excellent discussion of the Gabrieleno/Tongva people in Los Angeles in this period, see Ethington, "Ab Urbis Condita," 182–187.

18. Pitt and Pitt, *Los Angeles A to Z*, 70.

19. Gabrieleno/Tongva Tribal Council of San Gabriel, official website, www.tongva.com/, accessed May 15, 2012.

20. Deverell, *Whitewashed Adobe*, 5–10.

21. Pagan, *Murder at the Sleepy Lagoon*, 152.

22. Ibid.

23. Ibid.

24. Escobedo, "Mexican American Home Front," 160–162.

25. Deverell, *Whitewashed Adobe*, 9–26

26. Escobedo, *Coveralls*, 115–120.

27. "Simply put, pachucas and pachucos were Mexican Americans who produced and took part in *pachuismo,* a youth subculture whose most salient identifying feature was a zoot suit during the 1930s, 1940s, and 1950s." Ramírez, *Woman in the Zoot Suit*, xiii, 44–46.

28. Pagan, *Murder at the Sleepy Lagoon*, 160.

29. Kuter, "Works of Art," 5.

30. Ibid.

31. Ibid.

32. Ibid.

33. "Hollywood Canteen Draws Record 'First Night' Crowd," *Los Angeles Daily News*, October 7, 1942, 16.

34. "Film Great Aid Opening of Hollywood Canteen," *Los Angeles Examiner*, October 4, 1942, n.p., clipping, "Hollywood Canteen," box 6, Association of Motion Picture and Television Producers Collection, Margaret Herrick Library, Academy of Motion Picture Arts and Sciences, Los Angeles.

35. Brooks, *Alien Neighbors*, 39, 51–59.

36. "Relocation: Race Track to Metropolis to Ghost Town in Six Months," *Santa Anita Pacemaker*, final iss. (n.d.), 14, Denshō Digital Archive, Seattle.

37. Yoshida, *Reminiscing in Swingtime*, 129–130.

38. Fiset, "Public Health," 565–584.

39. Japanese Americans Relocated during World War II (2005), online database, and 1940 United States Federal Census (2012), online database, both available at the website of Ancestry.com Operations, Provo, Utah, http://home.ancestry.com, accessed March 4, 2014.

40. U.S. World War II Army Enlistment Records, 1938–1946, National Archives and Records Administration, online database (2005), available at the website of Ancestry.com Operations, Provo, Utah, http://home.ancestry.com, accessed March 4, 2014.

41. Torrence, *Hollywood*, 202.

42. Yoshida, *Reminiscing in Swingtime*, 130.

43. Ibid.

44. Ibid., 131

45. Kikuchi and Modell, *Kikuchi Diary*, 81–82.

46. Ibid., 126

47. Yoshida, *Reminiscing in Swingtime*, 163–67.

48. Nagumo, oral history, interviewer unknown.

49. Yoshida, *Reminiscing in Swingtime*, 124.

50. This and subsequent quotes are from Lennie Bluett, interview, May 29, 2003.

51. Jones [Baraka], "Swing," 33–50.

52. This is changing. See Macias, *Mexican American Mojo*.

53. This and subsequent quotes are from Theresa Nevarez, telephone interview, April 11, 2009.

54. On erasures of Mexican Americans from World War II history, see Escobedo, *Coveralls*, 149–154.

55. Smith, *Great Black Way*, 239.

56. Loren Miller, oral history, interviewed by Lawrence de Graaf.

57. "A Film Star Lives Here," *Los Angeles Times*, September 1, 1940, 13; Higham, *Bette*, 188; Sikov, *Dark Victory*, 174–175, 226–228.

58. Edith O. N. S. D. Sawyer, "Visitation Report, Glendale, California," March 10, 1936, YWCA of the USA Records, pt. 3a, Local Association Files, reel 163, Sophia Smith Collection, Smith College, Northampton, Massachusetts.

59. Winnifred Wygal, "Visitation Report," Glendale, California, February 25, 1941, YWCA of the USA Records, pt. 3a, Local Association Files, reel 163, Sophia Smith Collection.

60. Esther Breisemeister, Visitation Report, Glendale YWCA, December 18, 1945, YWCA of the USA Records, pt. 3a, Local Association Files, reel 163, Sophia Smith Collection.

61. Eloise M. Ewing, "Visitation Report, Glendale YWCA," November 10, 1947, YWCA of the USA Records, pt. 3a, Local Association Files, reel 163, Sophia Smith Collection. In 1950, *Chicago Defender* columnist, Tomi Ayers reported on an interesting meeting of Y-Teens in Los Angeles, in which a white teen from Glendale asked African

American Y-women, "what we would do if we lived in a situation such as hers, especially if we didn't particularly like the idea ourselves." Ayers passed the question along to her readers "for general discusson from you. You are perhaps aware of the fact that Glendale is a lily-white suburb which has a more than traditional custom of not selling, renting, or buying from Negroes." Tomi Ayers, "West Coast Roundup," *Chicago Defender*, February 18, 1950, 9.

62. Macias, *Mexican American Mojo*, 35–36.

63. Mary Lou Ochoa, interview, January 13, 2006.

64. Macias, *Mexican American Mojo*, 14.

65. "Bette Davis Upholds Mixed Couples at Movie Canteen," *Chicago Defender*, January 9, 1943, 1.

66. "No Mixed Dancing Curb at Hollywood Canteen," *Chicago Defender*, May 8, 1943, 7.

67. Horne, Arstein, and Moss, *Lena Horne*, 199.

68. Julien, "Sounding the City," 133.

CHAPTER 3: OPERATING FROM THE CURBSTONE

1. The epigraphs to this chapter are from Dorothy C. Guinn, "'Operating from the Curbstone': The Experiences of the U.S.O.-Y.W.C.A. Committee of Negro Women, November 5, 1941–May 15, 1942," 14, YWCA of the USA Records, pt. 3a, Local Association Files, Los Angeles, reel 163, Sophia Smith Collection, Smith College; Mrs. Bert MacDonald, "USO-YWCA Committee Reveals Soldiers' Recreational Needs," *California Eagle*, February 5, 1942, 3A; "Watts USO Hospitality House Has Brilliant Opening," *California Eagle*, February 26, 1942, 7A.

2. Watts, *Hattie McDaniel*, 209–210; Jackson, *Hattie*, 83. Other members included Fayard Nicholas, Mantan Moreland, Ben Carter, Nicodemus Stewart, and Wonderful Smith.

3. Though a member, Bette Davis battled the HVC for special permission to call the stars directly for Hollywood Canteen service instead of obeying the HVC clearinghouse. Davis and Mosley, *Bette Davis*, 114–116.

4. Richardson, *Plays and Pageants*, xlvi, 304–330.

5. "Y.W.C.A. News." *Los Angeles Sentinel*, July 27, 1939, 7.

6. Ruby Berkley Goodwin, "Prejudice Revealed to Hollywood 'V' Groups," *Afro-American*, May 30, 1942, 13.

7. *Follow the Boys.*

8. Dorothy C. Guinn, "Some Learnings from U.S.O.-Y.W.C.A. Experience," Los Angeles, May 15, 1942, YWCA of the USA Records, pt. 3a, Local Association Files, reel 163, Sophia Smith Collection, Smith College.

9. In 1935, for instance, the Hollywood YWCA was accused of promoting Communist sympathies when Langston Hughes gave a talk at a conference at a YWCA leadership meeting at the Asilomar conference grounds, near Pacific Grove, California. Minutes, Public Relations Committee of the Young Women's Christian Association, July 11, 1935, YWCA of the USA Records, pt. 3a, Local Association Files, reel 163, Los

Angeles, Miscellaneous Correspondence and Reports, Sophia Smith Collection, Smith College.

10. "New Y.W. Exec Is Honored," *Chicago Defender*, October 9, 1937, 15.

11. "S.R.A. Executive Loses Job as County Office Abolished," *Los Angeles Sentinel*, February 15, 1940, 1; "Juanita Ellsworth Named to High S.R.A. Post," *Los Angeles Sentinel*, August 17, 1939, 1; "Jurors Refuse Damages for Service Refusal," *Los Angeles Sentinel*, January 18, 1940, 1.

12. "No Jim Crow in Coast Housing Projects," *Chicago Defender*, June 13, 1942, 8.

13. Loren Miller, oral history, interviewed by Lawrence de Graaf; Smith, *Great Black Way*, 235–253.

14. Marguerite K. Sylla, "Study of the Young Women's Christian Associations of Los Angeles, San Pedro, Santa Ana, Long Beach, and Pasadena, and Los Angeles and Its Relation to Cities and Communities in the Surrounding Area, May 28–June 23, 1926," YWCA of the USA Records, pt. 3a, Local Association Files, reel 162, Sophia Smith Collection.

15. "The Young Women's Christian Associations Report of Services to Negroes Submitted to Committee on Services to Negroes," n.d., Armed Services YMCA: YMCA USO Administrative Files, United Service Organizations–related records, box 106, Kautz Family YMCA Archives, Elmer L. Anderson Library, University of Minnesota.

16. Eleanor C. Anderson, "Visit Report, Los Angeles, California, September 16–19, and 24–27, 1942," YWCA of the USA Records, pt. 3a, Local Association Files, reel 163, Sophia Smith Collection.

17. Winnifred Wygal, "Visitation Report, Los Angeles, California, February 24–26, 1941," YWCA of the USA Records, pt. 3a, Local Association Files, reel 163, Sophia Smith Collection.

18. Guinn, " 'Operating from the Curbstone,' " 2–3.

19. Ibid., 6.

20. Ibid., 7–9.

21. Ibid., 2.

22. Ibid.

23. Ibid., 9–10.

24. "Celebrities Attend New USO Opening," *Pittsburgh Courier*, February 28, 1942, 2.

25. "Watts USO Hospitality House Has Brilliant Opening," *California Eagle*, February 26, 1942, 7A.

26. Guinn, " 'Operating from the Curbstone,' " 10.

27. Ibid., 14.

28. "Lily-White Calif. Town Welcomes Crack AA Unit." *Afro-American*, May 30, 1942, 11.

29. "Colonel Views California Scenery," *Chicago Defender*, May 30, 1942, 4.

30. "Goodbye Lieutenant," *Chicago Defender*, May 30, 1942, 8.

31. "76th CA Replaces 369th AA at Burbank," *Afro-American*, June 6, 1942, 21.

32. "White Family Who Played Host to Soldiers, Threatened by Neighbors," *Chicago Defender*, June 27, 1942, 4.

33. Ibid.

34. "L.A., Burbank USO Committees Provide Recreation for Local San Fernando Valley Soldiers," *California Eagle*, June 25, 1942, 2-A.

35. "Hollywood Hostess Defies Neighbors and Fetes Colored Soldiers," *Afro-American*, July 11, 1942, 10.

36. HVC Actors Subcommittee and Advisory Committee Minutes, July 16, 1942, "USO Camp Shows, Inc. (Stage, Radio and Screen) Report of Activities for Sixteen Weeks Ended Oct. 17, 1942," 53. Charles K. Feldman Papers, Louis B. Mayer Library, American Film Institute.

37. HVC Education Subcommittee Minutes, July 21, 1942, "USO Camp Shows, Inc. (Stage, Radio and Screen) Report of Activities for Sixteen Weeks Ended Oct. 17, 1942," 58–59. Charles K. Feldman Papers, Louis B. Mayer Library, American Film Institute.

38. Meeting of the Actors Committees of the Hollywood Victory Committee and Actors Representatives Minutes, July 23, 1942, "USO Camp Shows, Inc. (Stage, Radio and Screen) Report of Activities for Sixteen Weeks Ended Oct. 17, 1942," 61. Charles K. Feldman Papers, Louis B. Mayer Library, American Film Institute.

39. "Bette Davis Entertains," *Afro-American*, September 5, 1942, 10.

40. "Bette Davis Invites Boys to Premiere," *California Eagle*, August 27, 1942, 1.

41. "Bette Davis Stars for Hollywood Canteen Benefit," *Pittsburgh Courier*, September 12, 1942, 24.

42. John Gunn, "Hollywood Canteen Premiere Is the Talk of the Town," *People's World*, September 8, 1942, 5.

43. "Hedda Hopper's Hollywood," *Los Angeles Times*, September 1, 1942, A11.

44. Sidney Skolsky, "Hollywood Is My Beat," *Hollywood Citizen-News*, December 26, 1942, n.p., clipping, scrapbook 45, box 382, Bette Davis Collection, Howard Gotlieb Archival Research Center.

45. "USO Officials, Filmland, Army Join Hundreds at USO Clubhouse Opening Sunday in Paloma Street," *California Eagle*, July 16, 1942, 1B.

46. In August 1942, the Marines who arrived at Montford Point were the first black Marines to serve since the American Revolution. McLaurin, *Marines of Montford Point*, 1.

47. "USO Officials, Filmland, Army Join Hundreds at USO Clubhouse Opening," 1B.

48. Ibid.

49. Lucille Leimert, "Soundings," *Los Angeles Times*, January 6, 1943, A5.

50. Avanelle Harris, telephone conversation, July 25, 2000.

51. Avanelle Harris, "I Tried to Crash the Movies," *Ebony*, August 1946, 5.

52. Avanelle Harris, interview, January 10, 2006.

53. Carroll Hollister, Report delivered to Civilian Defense Committee of Local 47, American Federation of Musicians, Hollywood, June 29, 1942. Included in Report from _____, Los Angeles Field Office, to Director, FBI, August 4, 1942, 6, File 100–13342, Bureau File 100-Hq-259318 ("Hollywood Canteen").

54. Carroll Hollister, "Canteens for Democracy," *Overture*, July 1942, 20–21.

55. Commanding Officer, U.S. Naval Training School, Hampton Institute, Hampton, Virginia, Memo to the Chief of Naval Personnel, "Report on Conference on Negro

Naval Personnel, Eleventh Naval District, San Diego, California," March 15, 1944 (pt. 2), Record Group 181, Records of Naval Districts and Shore Establishment, National Archives and Records Administration, Pacific Region, Laguna Niguel.

56. "L.A., Burbank USO Committees Provide Recreation."

57. Freddie Doyle, "Swingtime," *California Eagle*, July 2, 1942, 2B.

58. McWilliams, *Education of Carey McWilliams*, 99.

59. Pascoe, *What Comes Naturally*, 207–223. For more on relationships between Mexican American women and African American men who met at defense jobs and canteens in Los Angeles during World War II, see Escobedo, *Coveralls to Zoot Suits*, 142–144.

60. Escobedo, "Mexican American Home Front," 164.

61. Pascoe, *What Comes Naturally*, 313.

CHAPTER 4: DYAD DEMOCRACY

1. The epigraphs to this chapter are from Kate Holliday, "Troops Gallop to the Dance: Hollywood 'Victim' Tells of Traipsing," *Oregonian*, December 6, 1942, n.p., clipping, scrapbook 45, box 382, Bette Davis Collection, Howard Gotlieb Archival Research Center, Boston University; Jane Lockwood diary, February 13, 1943, Jane Lockwood Ferrero Estate, Special Collections, Margaret Herrick Library, Academy of Motion Picture Arts and Sciences, Los Angeles—though her surname was Josephs, I refer to her by her professional (and mother's maiden) name, Lockwood.

2. Lockwood diary, February 13, 1943.

3. Lockwood diary, November 21, 1942.

4. Lockwood diary, February 6, 1943.

5. Ibid.

6. Ibid.

7. Ibid.

8. Ibid.

9. Lockwood diary, February 13, 1943.

10. Ibid.

11. The original song written by Leah Worth and Jean Barry hailed the volunteers at New York's Stage Door Canteen but was reworked by Dick Charles for *Hollywood Canteen* (1944).

12. Taylor, *Archive and Repertoire*, 19–21.

13. Goldman, *I Want to Be Ready*, 1–4.

14. Ibid., 5.

15. Ibid., 9.

16. Lockwood diary, May 29, 1943.

17. See, for instance, McMains and Robinson, "Swingin' Out," 87.

18. "Crow Jim" is a term for the kind of racism when white people attribute positive racially determined aptitudes to black people, rather than negative ones. The term calls attention to racist continuity despite swapping denigration for admiration.

19. McDonald, "Hot Jazz," 151–160.

20. *Hollywood Reporter*, November 22, 1943, 12–13.

21. Escobedo, *Coveralls to Zoot Suits*, 25.

22. Ibid., 113–122.

23. Ibid., 108–109.

24. Ted LeBerthon, *Los Angeles Daily News*, October 7, 1942, 23. The following September, he was fired by the *Los Angeles Daily News* for his outspokenness against racism. Julian, *Sounding the City*, 242.

25. T.E.Y., "With the Lamplighter after Dark," *Los Angeles Daily News*, September 28, 1942, 12; Lucille Leimert, "Soundings," *Los Angeles Times*, January 6, 1943, A5.

26. "G.I. Jitterbug Sought in Death of Oil Heiress," *Chicago Tribune*, October 15, 1944; "Miss Bauerdorf, Oil Man's Daughter, Slain by Strangler in Her Hollywood Apartment," *New York Times*, October 14, 1944, 15.

27. Spring, "Swing and the Lindy Hop," 187.

28. "Bette Davis Upholds Mixed Couples at Movie Canteen," *Chicago Defender*, January 9, 1943, 1. I believe that this was possibly actress Tommie Moore, who lived in Pasadena, volunteered at the Hollywood Canteen, and had attended the fundraiser at Ciro's. "Bette Davis Stars for Hollywood Canteen Benefit," *Pittsburgh Courier*, September 12, 1942, 24.

29. "Bette Davis Upholds Mixed Couples at Movie Canteen."

30. "Canteen Heads Have Row over Mixed Dancing: Hot Board Session Fails to Pass Rule Drawing Color Line," *DownBeat*, April 1, 15, 1943, 1, 5; "No Mixed Dancing Curb at Hollywood Canteen," *Chicago Defender*, May 8, 1943, 7; "Race Issue Creates Stormy Controversy at Hollywood Canteen," *New York Age*, May 8, 1943, 10; "No Jim Crow at Calif. Canteen," *Afro-American*, May 8, 1943, 12.

31. Stowe, *Swing Changes*, 161–162.

32. Lockwood diary, January 22, 1942.

33. Mary Lou (Ramirez) Ochoa, interview, January 13, 2006; Caren Marsh-Doll, interview, March 24, 2004; Bernie Gordon, interview, May 21, 2003; Jeni LeGon, oral history, Vancouver, June 27, 2005; Marion (Krow) Saphro, interview, May 23, 2003; Pearl Gelfand, interview, May 23, 2003, and Claire (Lomas) Rosen, telephone interview, June 24, 2010.

34. Art Ryon, "Hollywood 'Coney Island' Draws Soldiers' Pennies," *Los Angeles Times*, January 17, 1944, A1.

35. Extras belonged to the Screen Actors Guild until December 17, 1944, when they voted to leave the union that had marginalized their interests, to join the Screen Players Guild. Lasky, "Off Camera," 151.

36. "Race Hollywood Canteen Hostesses Lauded," *California Eagle*, June 10, 1943, 2B.

37. Ahmed, *On Being Included*, 49.

38. Harry Levette, "Behind the Scenes with Harry," *California Eagle*, April 22, 1943, 2B.

39. Ibid.

40. "Race Hollywood Canteen Hostesses Lauded."

41. Escobedo, *Coveralls to Zoot Suits*, 97.

42. Ibid., 25.

43. Ibid., 22.

44. Ibid.

45. Ibid., 121–122.

46. Ibid., 116–120; Mary Lou (Ramirez) Ochoa, interview.

47. Mary Lou (Ramirez) Ochoa, interview.

48. Tom Hayward, telephone interview, August 24, 2001.

49. For an excellent history of race and labor segmentation in the animation industry, as well as representation of race in animation, see Cohen, *Forbidden Animation*, 50–67.

50. Louise Hayward, telephone interview, August 24, 2001.

51. Frank S. Nugent, "Super-Duper Epic: Hollywood Canteen," *New York Times Magazine*, October 17, 1943, 16.

52. Martha (Goldman) Sigall, telephone interview, June 20, 2006.

53. Nancy Marlow, interview, March 27, 2004.

54. Marsha Hunt, interview, March 27, 2004; account also appears in Hunt, *Way We Wore*, 298–301.

55. Jean (Jeanne) (Foreman) Christ, telephone interview, October 28, 2004.

56. B. J. Hansen, interview, January 11, 2006.

57. Tami Albin is the director of the "Under the Rainbow: GLBTQ People in Kansas" Oral History Project, available at http://kuscholarworks.ku.edu/dspace/handle/1808/5330, accessed March 9, 2014.

58. This and subsequent quotes are from Johnny Grant, interview, March 23, 2004.

59. The expanded Bob Hope USO with its "Hollywood Canteen" snack bar opened later that year. The TV lounge is named for Johnny Grant.

60. "Typical American Girl Chosen for Patriotic Week Events," *Los Angeles Times*, February 10, 1941, A1.

61. "Gettysburg Address Called Exposition of Americanism," *Los Angeles Times*, February 13, 1941, A1.

62. "Typical American Girl"; "Gettysburg Address Called"; "City to Honor Lincoln Today," *Los Angeles Times*, February 12, 1941, A2; and "Tributes Paid Lincoln by City," *Los Angeles Times*, February 13, 1941, A1.

63. "Americanism Holds Stage," *Los Angeles Times*, February 19, 1941, A1.

64. "New Citizens Will Get Free Air Trip," *Los Angeles Times*, February 20, 1941, A2.

65. This and subsequent quotes are from Nancy Marlow, interview, March 27, 2004.

66. Jean (Jeanne) (Foreman) Christ, interview, October 28, 2004.

67. This and subsequent quotes are from Margie Stewart, interview, March 27, 2004.

68. Johnny Whitehead, "At the Hollywood Canteen," *Overture*, February 1943, 14.

69. "Girl Demonstrator Opens Door on Film Contract," *Chicago Daily Tribune*, August 21, 1942, 8, 11.

70. "(She Got Married) Margie It Hurts to Print This," *Stars and Stripes*, July 16, 1945, 8.

71. Margie Stewart, "Letter from Margie," Margie Stewart Website, www.margiestewart.com/Letter_from_Margie.html, accessed July 2, 2010.

72. Marsh-Doll, *Hollywood's Child*, 99–101.

73. This and subsequent quotes are from Caren Marsh-Doll and Dorothy Morris, interview, March 24, 2004.

74. Goldman, *I Want to Be Ready*, 5.

75. Eberwein, "'As a Mother Cuddles a Child,'" 149–166.

76. *Follow the Boys*.

77. "You Can't Say No to a Soldier," Harry Gordon (music), Mack Gordon (lyrics).

78. Winchell, *Good Girls*, 11.

CHAPTER 5: INJURED PARTIES

1. The epigraphs to this chapter are from Harry Gordon (music), Mack Gordon (lyrics), "You Can't Say No to a Soldier" (1942); *Los Angeles Times*, April 21, 1944, 2; Mel Bryant, telephone interview, July 25, 2000.

2. Supreme Court of California, Edwards v. Hollywood Canteen, L. A. No. 19463, 27 Cal. 2d 802; 167 P.2d 729; 1946 Cal. LEXIS 358, n.p., available on database, Lexis Nexis Academic, http://www.lexisnexis.com, accessed February 19, 2014.

3. Beverly Edwards, telephone conversation, December 19, 2005.

4. Beverly A. Edwards and William G. Edwards, "Official Web Biography of Sam Edwards," 2004/2008, available at the website, "'Perfessor' Bill Edwards," www.perfessorbill.com/sam_bio.shtml, accessed February 18, 2014.

5. "Jitterbug Trial Girl Bewails Being 'Icky.'"

6. Goldberg, *The Racial State*, 5–8. I am greatly oversimplifying Goldberg's analysis of "state memory." What is useful to me here is the idea that 1) the modern state is a racial state, and 2) the state tells its own story in abstract, instrumental terms (unlike the affective appeal of national memory). Archives such as court records, FBI files, etc., when read as state memory, provide an interesting counterpoint to an analysis of national memory. Neither is less factual, racial, or contradictory than the other. They operate at different registers, but are entwined.

7. Jain, *Injury*, 58.

8. Mitchell and Torrence, *Hollywood Canteen*, 87–88.

9. Supreme Court of California, Edwards v. Hollywood Canteen, L. A. No. 19463, 27 Cal. 2d 802; 167 P.2d 729; 1946, n.p.

10. See, for example, España-Maram, *Creating Masculinity in Los Angeles's Little Manila*.

11. Goldberg, *The Racial State*, 5–8.

12. Edwards v. Hollywood Canteen, 1946.

13. "Jitterbug Trial Girl;" and "Jive Experts Disagree on Spin in $17,250 Canteen Lawsuit," *Los Angeles Times*, April 20, 1944, A1.

14. "Jitterbugging Described in Canteen Suit Trial," *Los Angeles Times*, April 19, 1944, A1.

15. "Jitterbugging Described in Canteen Suit Trial."

16. "Jive Experts Disagree on Spin."

17. Ibid.

18. Ibid.

19. "Jitterbug Trial Girl."

20. "Jive Expert Witness in Suit against Canteen Takes Spill," *Los Angeles Times*, April 22, 1944, A3.

21. "Court Rules Jitterbug Is All Word Implies, Jitter for 'Nervous,' and Bug for 'Crazy,' " *New York Times*, May 3, 1944, 21.

22. Vining, *Gay Diary 1933–1946*, 343.

23. Supreme Court of California, Edwards v. Hollywood Canteen, L. A. No. 19463, 27 Cal. 2d 802; 167 P.2d 729; 1946.

24. Ibid.

25. Moore, *To Serve My Country*, 3.

26. Even then, many people did not know there was such a thing as a black Marine. Melton Alonza McLaurin relays a story of an African American Marine who was arrested in the Midwest for "impersonating a Marine." McLaurin, *Marines of Montford Point*, 85. See also the website of the Montford Point Marine Association, www .montfordpointmarines.com/index.html, accessed February 18, 2014.

27. Bernard Nalty, *The Right to Fight: African-American Marines in World War II*, History and Museums Division, Headquarters, U.S. Marine Corps, Washington, D.C., 1995, available on the website of the Internet Archive, http://archive.org/details /TheRightToFight, accessed February 20, 2014; McLaurin, *Marines of Montford Point*, 81–82.

28. Hancock, "American Allegory," "Learning How to Make Life Swing," and "Put a Little Color on That."

29. As I wrote, these statues loomed over the San Diego waterfront, and then New York's Times Square.

30. While a very different case from those analyzed by Jain, I draw broadly from her analysis of "American injury culture." Jain, *Injury*, 33–59.

31. Bryant, telephone interview, July 25, 2000.

32. Tucker, *Swing Shift*.

33. Ahmed, *Queer Phenomenology*, 129–130.

34. Bryant, telephone interview, July 25, 2000.

35. Informal telephone conversation with a former Canteen volunteer who wished to remain anonymous, September 6, 2000.

36. Ahmed, *On Inclusion*, 43.

37. Bryant, telephone interview, July 25, 2000.

38. Bryant, telephone interview, October 28, 2000.

39. "Clifton's Cafeterias," 2001, available at the website of Clinton's Restaurants, Inc., www.cliftonscafeteria.com/home.html, accessed May 2, 2010. Clifford Clinton is a fascinating figure in Los Angeles political history. See Hurewitz, *Bohemian Los Angeles*, 122–124.

40. Bryant, telephone interview, October 28, 2000.

41. Carter's character, like Miller, is a mess attendant who mans a machine gun in an emergency, but he does it side by side with Tyrone Power, and with a joke. Power

says, "What are you doing here?" as he takes aim at the Nazis who shoot at his colleagues. "I hate crowds," replies the mess attendant. Both laugh, and then fire on the opposition. *Crash Dive* (1943).

42. Bryant, telephone interview, October 28, 2000.

43. Ibid.

44. Ibid. Sugar Hill was the center of the most famous racially restrictive housing covenant battles in Los Angeles. A *Sentinel* reporter referred to its residents as "veritable guinea pigs" who were testing "the theory of Americanism" that presumed one could live wherever one "chooses." "Says Few Movie Folk Living in 'Sugar Hill' Area," *Los Angeles Sentinel*, January 10, 1946, 9.

45. Ruby Berkley Goodwin, "Ben Carter Free Lancer," *Chicago Defender*, August 2, 1941, 21.

46. "MGM's 'Shoe Shine Boy' Now Shining with Marines," *Baltimore Afro-American*, April 8, 1944, 6.

47. Bryant, telephone interview, October 28, 2000.

48. Ibid.

49. Ibid.

50. Ibid.

51. Ibid.

52. Miller, *Messman Chronicles*, 272–273.

53. Ardelia Bradley, "Social Lights," *Cleveland Call and Post*, September 30, 1944, 7A.

54. See, for example, Bogle, *Bright Boulevards*.

55. This and subsequent quotations from Tommy Farrell are from our interview, May 23, 2003.

56. Helene (Angus) Bank, interview, January 11, 2006.

57. Claire (Lomas) Rosen, telephone interview, June 24, 2010.

58. For instance, see Spada, *More than a Women*, 129, and Davis, *This 'n That*, 128.

59. See, for instance, Edwin Schallert, "While the Films Reel By," *Los Angeles Times*, October 11, 1942, C3.

60. Marjorie Lewin, interview, May 30, 2003.

61. This and subsequent quotations from Aniela McAuliffe are from our interview, May 23, 2003.

62. This and subsequent quotations from Pearl Gelfand are from our interview, May 23, 2003.

63. Motion Picture and Television Fund, "Our History," 2014, available at the website of the Motion Picture and Television Fund, http://www.mptf.com/about, accessed February 20, 2014. Features about the openings of the Motion Picture Country House and Hospital and the Hollywood Canteen ran adjacent to one another in movie magazines. See Elza Schallert, "Hollywood Takes Care of Its Own," *Motion Picture*, January 1943, 24–25, 96–97, which ran adjacent to Myrtle Gebhart, "There's No Caste in the Canteen," *Motion Picture*, January 1943, 28–29, 98–99.

64. McAuliffe, interview, May 23, 2003.

65. On the feminization of clerical work, see Lowe, *Women in the Administrative Revolution*.

66. This and subsequent quotations from Marion (Krow) Saphro are from our interview, May 23, 2003.

67. Halsey, *Color Blind*, 58.

68. Halsey, "Memo to Junior Hostesses," 51.

69. Ibid., 52.

70. Ibid.

71. Halsey, *Color Blind*, 21, 30, 36.

72. See Barnard, *Remember Me to Harlem*, 206–216, especially Carl Van Vechten's letter to Langston Hughes, October 8, 1942, 211–212.

73. Ahmed, *Queer Phenomenology*, 134–136.

74. Claire (Lomas) Rosen, telephone interview.

75. Mel Bryant, Interview, July 25, 2000.

CHAPTER 6: TORQUING BACK

1. The epigraphs in this chapter are from Laws and Sugano, *Physics and the Art of Dance*, 260; Foster, "Taken by Surprise," 6–7; Ahmed, *Queer Phenomenology*, 15.

2. Ian Walters, email to author, February 14, 2006.

3. Eric Marsh, taped correspondence, April 17, 2006.

4. Marsh, taped correspondence, May 16, 2006.

5. See, for example, Williams, " 'Crisis' Cover Girl," and Vogle, "Lena Horne's Impersona."

6. Haskins and Benson, *Lena*; Buckley, *Hornes*; Horne and Schickel, *Lena*; Gavin, *Stormy Weather*; Tyler, *From Harlem to Hollywood*, 129.

7. Avanelle Harris, telephone conversation, July 25, 2000.

8. "Maggie Hathaway—Beverly Hills-Hollywood NAACP Member," *Los Angeles Sentinel*, November 2, 1989, A5.

9. Maggie Hathaway, "Segregation and Integration in Hollywood," *Los Angeles Sentinel*, April 6, 1967, E1.

10. Alyce Key, "Key Notes," *Los Angeles Tribune*, October 25, 1943, 15.

11. "Race Hollywood Canteen Hostesses Lauded," *California Eagle*, June 10, 1943, 2B.

12. Mary Ford, interview with Dan Ford, n.d. Tape 43, "War Years," John Ford Collection, Lilly Library, Indiana University, Bloomington.

13. "Flo Cadrez Gets Mates for Sailors," *California Eagle*, March 17, 1943, 2B.

14. Jeni LeGon, telephone interview, November 26, 2004.

15. Jeni LeGon, interview, June 27, 2005.

16. Frank, *Tap*, 122.

17. Racialized perspectives of who is capable and who is not capable of attaining proper "ballet feet" are still prevalent, often preventing the recognition of black ballet dancers because of the persisting stereotypes about black people's feet as flat and large. Black ballet dancers continue to be plagued by assumptions that they lack the potential arch and point that European dancers are assumed to possess if they are properly trained. Gottschild, *Black Dancing Body*, 108–143.

18. Juana E. Duty, "Age of Aquarian Book Shop," *Los Angeles Times*, March 24, 1982, C3; Seth Mydans, "Riot Leveled a Font of Black Culture," *New York Times*, August 5, 1992, A14; Gary Lee, "L.A. Business People Hold Their Ground—and Their Breath," *Washington Post*, April 15, 1993, A6; Martin Douglas, "Alfred Ligon Is Dead at 96; Owned Renowned Book Store," *New York Times*, August 23, 2002, C11.

19. Spencer, *New Negroes and Their Music*, 21; Gottschild, *Waltzing*, 6–7, 43, 52.

CHAPTER 7: THE DYAD FROM WITHOUT

1. The epigraphs to this chapter are from Donald Vining diary, December 25, 1943, Donald Crossley Vining Papers, Manuscripts and Archives, Sterling Memorial Library, Yale University, New Haven, Connecticut; Marie Proulox, quoted in Lacy, *We Are Marines*, 57.

2. Donald Vining diary, December 19, 1943, Donald Crossley Vining Papers.

3. Donald Vining diary, December 25, 1943, Donald Crossley Vining Papers.

4. Vining, *Gay Diary*.

5. Website of Women in Military Service for America Memorial, www.womensmemorial.org, accessed January 8, 2011.

6. *Here Come the Waves* (1944).

7. Vining, *Gay Diary*, 227.

8. Eller, *Conscientious Objectors*, 26.

9. Donald Vining diary, December 17, 1943, Donald Crossley Vining Papers.

10. Ibid., December 17, 1943.

11. Ahmed, *Queer Phenomenology*, 15–20, 100–107.

12. Donald Vining diary, December 25, 1943, Donald Crossley Vining Papers.

13. Ibid., January 23, 1944.

14. Ibid.

15. Donald Vining diary, February 11, 1944, Diary Digests: folder 4, vol. 1, pt. 3 (1942–45), box 7, Donald Vining Papers, Manuscripts and Archives Division, Stephen A. Schwarzman Building, New York Public Library.

16. Donald Vining diary, April, 2, 1944, Donald Crossley Vining Papers.

17. Same-sex jitterbugging was not necessarily a sign for same-sex attraction in the 1940s—but from a gay or lesbian subject position, such an experience held particular visions of possibility. Tom Canford's fictionalized account of the war experiences of a gay male Coast Guard veteran includes an episode in which John Garfield is persuaded to jitterbug with navy men while the official photographer is preoccupied with starlets. Garfield is presented as doing the boys a favor, but the scenario resonates with gay subjective delight for the protagonist who watches the dance. Canford, *Boy at Sea*, 34–35, 131.

18. Vining, *Gay Diary*, 329.

19. Donald Vining diary, July 30, 1944, Donald Crossley Vining Papers.

20. Ibid., August 20, 1944.

21. Lacy, *We Are Marines!*, 58.

22. Marie C. Haynes, letter to author, September 4, 2001.

CHAPTER 8: THE VIEW FROM THE MEZZANINE

1. The epigraphs in this chapter are from "Hollywood Will Have Stage Door Canteen for Benefit of Soldiers," *New York Age*, August 29, 1942, 10; Lorraine (Mitchell) Bear, email to author, April 4, 2001.
2. This and other quotations are from Kathryn "Kit" (Ludwig) Welter, letter to author, May 29, 2001.
3. Ibid.
4. Harris-Perry, *Sister Citizen*, 28–29.
5. Sims-Wood, " 'We Served America Too,' " 64.
6. Akers, "Doing Their Part," 215.
7. Minutes, Meeting of East Anaheim Committee of Management, Long Beach, Calif. Negro Extension, Armed Services YMCA: USO City Histories (Industrial): Long Beach (Negro), Kautz Family YMCA Archives, Elmer L. Anderson Library, University of Minnesota University Archives, University of Minnesota Library, Minneapolis.
8. Stine, *Mother Goddamn*, 192.
9. Nancy Marlow, interview with author, March 27, 2004.
10. Margie Stewart, interview with author, March 27, 2004.
11. Tommy Farrell, interview with author, May 23, 2003.
12. Shirley Rothstein, letter to author, December 24, 2000.
13. Ellie Latham, letter to author, November 3, 2001.
14. Mildred S. Kosanovich, telephone interview with author, January 21, 2001.
15. Senior Master Sergeant (Retired) Charlotte D. Mansfield, letter to author, October 18, 2000.
16. This and subsequent quotes are from Jean Woodcome, letter to author, November 5, 2001.
17. Betty Sue Wimberly, letter to author, October 18, 2001.
18. Jo Neilan, email to author, April 21, 2001.
19. Woodcome, letter to author.
20. Anne Campbell, email to author, January 26, 2001.
21. R. Janie (Bevins) Tilbury, email to author, June 22, 2000.
22. Tilbury, email to author, June 22, 2000 and June 21, 2000.
23. Winchell, *Good Girls, Good Food, Good Fun*, 1.
24. Hegarty, *Victory Girls, Khaki-Wackies, and Patriotutes*.
25. Winchell, *Good Girls, Good Food, Good Fun*, 1, 5.
26. Bob Alden, interview with author, January 13, 2006.
27. Leisa D. Meyer, *Creating* GI *Jane*, 3.
28. Winchell, *Good Girls, Good Food, Good Fun*, 60–62; Roarty, "More Than Entertainment," 143–192.
29. Lovelace, "Facing Change in Wartime Philadelphia," 160–162; Winchell, *Good Girls, Good Food, Good Fun*, 60–61.
30. Alsmeyer, *Way of the Waves*, 100–101.
31. Alsmeyer, letter to the author, April 27, 2001.

32. "Canteen Has Birthday," *Los Angeles Times*, November 1, 1943, A1.

33. Soderbergh, *Women Marines*, 79–80.

34. Jean Lewin to Maybelle Marr, February 24, 1945, personal collection of Patricia Charles Brown.

35. Meyer, "Creating G.I. Jane," 581.

36. Website of WAVES National, www.womenofthewaves.com/whitecaps/index.htm, accessed February 23, 2014.

37. Lorraine (Mitchell) Bear, email to author, April 4, 2001.

38. Ibid.

39. Akers, "Doing Their Part," 210–211.

40. Lorraine (Mitchell) Bear, email to author, April 11, 2001.

41. Ibid.

42. Akers, "Doing Their Part," 40.

43. Lorraine (Mitchell) Bear, telephone interview, April 23, 2001.

44. Coletta and Bauer, *United States Navy and Marine Corps Bases*, 493–497.

45. Lorraine (Mitchell) Bear, telephone interview, April 23, 2001.

CHAPTER 9: MEN SERVING MEN

1. The chapter's first epigraph is from *Bob Hope Radio Show*, broadcast from Hollywood Canteen, October 13, 1942, included in *This Is Bob on the Air Hope*, CD, Hope Enterprises, 1995.

2. The second epigraph and subsequent quotations are from Delmar Watson, telephone interview, November 21, 2004.

3. Swindell, *Body and Soul*, 177–178.

4. Ibid., 192; McGrath, *John Garfield*, 59–60.

5. HVC Education Committee minutes, July 21, 1942, "USO Camp Shows, Inc. (Stage, Radio and Screen) Report of Activities for Sixteen Weeks Ended Oct. 17, 1942," 58–59. Charles K. Feldman Papers, Louis B. Mayer Library, American Film Institute.

6. Frank Pope, "Tradeviews," *Hollywood Reporter*, December 30, 1943, 1.

7. "Canteen Anniversary Will Honor Industry Service Men," *Hollywood Reporter*, October 25, 1943, 6.

8. Davis, *Van Johnson*, 71.

9. This and subsequent quotations are from Leonard "Lennie" Bluett, interview, May 29, 2003.

10. I am grateful to dancer and dance historian Peter Loggins for sharing information on Dean Collins. Loggins, email to author, September 30, 2009. According to Loggins, Collins was 4-F due to flat feet.

11. Gottschild, *Waltzing in the Dark*, 220.

12. Leonard "Lennie" Bluett, interview, May 29, 2003.

13. This and subsequent quotations are from Bob Alden, interview, January 13, 2006.

14. "Personality of the Week: 'What's Cooking?'" *Doings in Los Angeles*, October 8, 1942, clipping, scrapbook 45, box 382, Bette Davis Collection, Howard Gotlieb Archival Research Center, Boston University.

CHAPTER 10: (UN)AMERICAN PATROL

1. The epigraphs in this chapter are from Johnny Grant, interview, March 23, 2004; Report from _____, Los Angeles Field Office, to Director, FBI, April 14, 1943, 3, File 100–13342, Bureau File 100-Hq-259318 ("Hollywood Canteen").

2. Some women agents were hired prior to Hoover's directorship (1924), but none were agents between 1930 and 1972. Only five special agents prior to 1962 were African American men, hired expressly to infiltrate African American organizations. The only black FBI agent during World War II was John Amos, who was not based in Los Angeles. Newton, FBI Encyclopedia, 36–37, 374.

3. Report from _____, Los Angeles Field Office, to Director, FBI, August 12, 1943, 7, File 100–18780, Bureau File 100-Hq-259318 ("Hollywood Canteen").

4. Many thanks to Nichole T. Rustin, jazz scholar and lawyer, who helped me better understand the Freedom of Information Act.

5. I am indebted to Tami Albin for putting these wheels in motion for me, long before I realized the Hollywood Canteen would have been under FBI surveillance.

6. See, for example, Kester, "Access Denied."

7. Kester, "Access Denied," 213.

8. Ibid., 210.

9. Goldberg, *Racial State*, 5.

10. Taylor, *Archive and the Repertoire*, 21, 22.

11. On the Freedom of Information Act as ritual of denial of the "fundamental contradiction" of liberal state theory, see Moon, "Freedom of Information Act."

12. Cole, *Hollywood Red*; Gordon, *Gordon File*.

13. Cole, *Hollywood Red*, 163.

14. Gordon, *Gordon File*, 69.

15. Report from _____, Los Angeles Field Office, to Director, FBI, August 4, 1942, 6, File 100–13342, Bureau File 100-Hq-259318 ("Hollywood Canteen").

16. Ibid., 6.

17. Ibid., 1.

18. Cole, *Hollywood Red*, 14.

19. Cunningham and Browning, "Emergence of Worthy Targets," 354.

20. Hollister (1901–1983), accompanist to the conservative baritone John Charles Thomas from 1933 to 1945, joined the Communist Party in 1934. On President Roosevelt's death, Hollister gave notice to Thomas, effective May 1, International Workers Day, 1945. Maher, *John Charles Thomas*, 144.

21. Cole, *Hollywood Red*, 176.

22. For more on Clare's anti-Communism, work with the Teamsters Local 399, friendships with Stein and Wasserman, and later activities as chair of the Motion Picture Alliance for the Preservation of American Ideals, see Bruck, *When Hollywood Had a King*, 109–111; also McDougal, *Last Mogul*, 280.

23. Maher, *John Charles Thomas*, 133–134.

24. Report, August 4, 1942, File 100–13342, 2–5.

25. Ibid., 2–3.

26. Ibid., 3.

27. Sbardellati, "Brassbound G-Men," 416.

28. Gordon, *Hollywood Exile*, 4.

29. Sbardellati, "Brassbound G-Men," 416.

30. The *People's World* was "not formally a Party organ," Steve Nelson writes, but functioned as "the Party's voice on the West Coast." Nelson et al., *Steve Nelson*, 257.

31. Report, February 4, 1943, File 100–13342, 1.

32. Navasky, *Naming Names*, 367.

33. Report, February 4, 1943, File 100–13342, 6.

34. Report, April 14, 1943, File 100–13342, 4.

35. Ibid., 1.

36. Ibid., 2.

37. Ibid.

38. See Washburn, *Question of Sedition*.

39. Report, April 14, 1943, File 100–13342, 2.

40. Ibid., 2.

41. Ibid.

42. Ibid.

43. Ibid., 2–3.

44. The epigraph to this section is from Himes, *Lonely Crusade*, 91–92.

45. Ibid., 93, 99, 247.

46. Ibid., 99.

47. Ibid., 141–142.

48. Loren Miller, "One Way Out—Communism," *Opportunity* 12, no. 7 (1934): 214–216.

49. Loren Miller, oral history, interviewed by Lawrence de Graaf, April 29, 1967.

50. Pettis Perry, Communist Party advertisement, *California Eagle*, August 5, 1943, 8B.

51. Lee Wallace, "Poll: 'Have Communists Quit Fighting for Negro Rights?,'" *Negro Digest*, December 1944, 57–70; poll on p. 56.

52. This earlier directive is referenced in a memo from J. Edgar Hoover, Director, FBI, to Assistant Chief of Staff, G2, War Department, Washington DC, May 11, 1943, copy included in Report, February 4, 1943, File 100–13342.

53. Report, August 12, 1943, File 100–18780, 4, 8.

54. McWilliams, *Education of Carey McWilliams*, 112–113.

55. Report, August 12, 1943, File 100–18780, 4.

56. Ibid., 4.

57. Ibid., 5.

58. Ibid.

59. Ibid.

60. Ibid.

61. Ibid.

62. Ibid.

63. Ibid., 6.

64. Ahmed, "Declarations of Whiteness."

65. Report, August 12, 1943, File 100–18780, 7.

66. I am grateful to Garnette Cadogan for helping me to get in touch with Bernie Gordon.

67. Gordon, *Hollywood Exile*, 11–16.

68. Bernard Gordon, interview, May 21, 2003.

69. Ibid.

70. Hurewitz, *Bohemian Los Angeles*, 16.

71. Barzman, *Red and the Blacklist*, 29.

72. "Joe and Jill Delegate Heard," mimeographed pamphlet, n.d., 8, file B5/F11, American Youth for Democracy 1940s, 20th Century Organizations Collection, Southern California Library for Social Science Research, Los Angeles.

73. [1] *Dust Off Your Dreams*, 16–17, file B5/F11, American Youth for Democracy 1940s, 20th Century Organizations Collection, Southern California Library for Social Science Research.

74. Ibid., 2.

75. Virginia Wright, column, *Los Angeles Daily News*, December 1, 1944.

76. Commanding Officer, U.S. Naval Training School, Hampton Institute, Hampton, Virginia, Memo to the Chief of Naval Personnel, "Report on Conference on Negro Naval Personnel, Eleventh Naval District, San Diego, California," March 15, 1944 (pt. 2), 10–11, Record Group 181, Records of Naval Districts and Shore Establishment, National Archives and Records Administration, Pacific Region, Laguna Niguel.

77. "Joe and Jill Delegate," n.d., 5–6.

78. Report, January 9, 1945, 2, File 100–18780.

79. Sides, *L.A. City Limits*, 32.

80. Horne, *Class Struggle in Hollywood*, 89. Another Communist Party member who was active in the founding of the Hollywood Canteen was Helen Slote Levitt, John Garfield's secretary. Levitt, oral history, interviewed by Larry Ceplair, March 8, 1988, transcript, tape 3, side 1, Oral History Collections, UCLA Libraries and Collections, University of California, Los Angeles.

81. Bernard Gordon, interview, May 21, 2003.

82. Report, August 12, 1943, File 100–18780, 10–11.

83. Ibid., 9.

84. Ibid.

85. Ibid., 9, 11–12.

86. Ibid., 10.

87. Ibid., 11.

88. Ibid., 12.

89. Ibid.

90. McDougal, *Last Mogul*, 280; Bruck, *When Hollywood Had a King*, 109–111.

91. Report, August 12, 1943, File 100–18780, 12.

92. Ibid., 15–16.

93. Ibid., 16–17.

94. Ibid., 8.

95. Nancy Marlow, interview, March 27, 2004.

96. Marsha Hunt, interview, March 27, 2004.

97. Delmar Watson, telephone interview, November 21, 2004.

98. Bernard Gordon, conversation, March 28, 2004.

99. Report, October 5, 1943, File 100–18780, 1.

100. Ibid., 2.

101. Report, December 13, 1943, File 100–18780, 1.

102. Ibid., 1.

103. Ibid., 2.

104. Report, March 15, 1944, File 100–18780, 1.

105. Ibid., 4.

106. Ibid., 4, 5.

107. Report, August 30, 1944, File 100–18780, 2.

108. Report, March 15, 1944, File 100–18780, 5.

109. Report, May 9, 1944, 2, File 100–18780.

110. Report, November 14, 1944, File 100–18780, 1, 3.

111. Report, February 22, 1945, File 100–18780, 2–3.

112. Ibid., 1.

113. Report, January 9, 1945, File 100–18780, 1–2.

114. Mel Bryant, telephone interview with author, July 25, 2000.

115. Memo, J. Edgar Hoover, Director, FBI, to SAC (Special Agent in Charge), Los Angeles Field Division, April 19, 1945, included in report, April 2, 1945, File 100–259318.

116. Davis, *Abolition Democracy*, 119.

117. See, for example, Valerie Smith's analysis of the ideological work of ameliorative civil rights movement documentaries, "Meditation on Memory," and Singh, *Black Is a Country*.

118. See the various essays in Romano and Raiford, *Civil Rights Movement*.

CHAPTER 11: THE MAKING(S) OF NATIONAL MEMORY

1. This chapter's first epigraph is from "'Hollywood Canteen' Smash All-Star Entertainment," *Hollywood Reporter*, December 5, 1944, 3.

2. For more on FDR's Good Neighbor Policy on war-related film censorship see Karl F. Cohen, *Forbidden Animation,* 33–34; and Dale Adams, *Saludos Amigos: Hollywood and FDR's Good Neighbor Policy.*

3. "Louis Armstrong Plays in 'Hollywood Canteen,'" *Pittsburgh Courier*, July 1, 1944, 13.

4. "Warners Calls Off 'Canteen' Following SAG Decision," *Hollywood Reporter*, December 23, 1943, 1, 4.

5. Lasky, "Off Camera," 138–139.

6. *Hollywood Canteen.* Warner Bros., 1944.

7. Delmer Daves, "One in a Million," September 14, 1943 (first treatment for *Hollywood Canteen*), United Artists Corp. Records: series 1.2: Warner Brothers Scripts, circa 1928–50, Wisconsin Center for Film and Theater Research, Madison.

8. Cohen, *Forbidden Animation*, 11–19.

9. Koppes and Black, *Hollywood Goes to War*, 61–67, 86.

10. "Davis in WB Pic on Hollywood Canteen," *Hollywood Reporter*, September 13, 1943, 2.

11. "'Canteen' in More Return Dates Than Any U.A. Film," *Greater Amusements*, September 17, 1943, 9.

12. "'Canteen' 500 Pct. over 1st Estimate," *Hollywood Reporter*, September 22, 1943.

13. Hurewitz, *Bohemian Los Angeles*, 79, 161–189.

14. Ibid., 24.

15. "Name New YWCA Branch Head Here," *Los Angeles Tribune*, September 20, 1943, 12.

16. Daves, "One in a Million."

17. "Stars Kiss Canteen Guest 1,000,000," *Los Angeles Times*, September 16, 1943, A1.

18. Fyne, *Hollywood Propaganda*, 124–125.

19. Winchell, *Good Food*, 89.

20. "Ridin' High," *Pittsburgh Courier*, November 13, 1943, 19.

21. Al Monroe, "Swinging the News," *Chicago Defender*, December 18, 1943, 10.

22. Daves, "One in a Million."

23. Harry Levette, "Walter White and Willkie Seek Ban on South-Be-the War Movie Roles," *Kansas City Plaindealer*, July 31, 1942, 2.

24. Levette, "Walter White and Willkie Seek Ban."

25. Billy Rowe, "Rowe Reviews Background of Warner Bros.," *Pittsburgh Courier*, September 26, 1942, 21.

26. "Movie Cartoon Pokes Fun at Negro Soldiers," *Negro Star*, May 7, 1943, 4; "Film Cartoon Funny at Race's Expense," *Chicago Defender*, May 8, 1943, 19.

27. Phil Carter, "Review Hollywood Offerings since White-Willkie Meeting," *Los Angeles Tribune*, November 15, 1943, 18.

28. Ibid.

29. Alyce Key, "Key Notes," *Los Angeles Tribune*, December 27, 1943, 19.

30. Harry Levette, "Influence of War Depicted in New Pics," *New Journal and Guide*, February 15, 1941, 17.

31. Agnes Christine Johnson, "Hollywood Canteen Outline" (1944), United Artists Corporation Records: series 1.2: Warner Brothers Scripts, circa 1928–1950, Wisconsin Center for Film and Theater Research, Madison.

32. Daves, "One in a Million."

33. "Joe Brown's Son Killed," *Los Angeles Times*, October 9, 1942, 1, 7.

34. See Magee, "'King Porter Stomp,'" 22–53. Henderson's famous arrangements include two for his own band (1928 and 1932) and another for Goodman, who recorded it and played it many times, including on the West Coast Palomar debut. The piece had been recorded by Cab Calloway, Chick Webb, Count Basie, Erskine Hawkins, Glenn Miller, Harry James, Bob Crosby, and others (26) by the time Dorsey led his band in Otto Helbig's arrangement in the movie; Stockdale, *Jimmy Dorsey*, 437–440.

35. According to the Daily Production Schedule, this scene was shot on June 17, 1944. Choreographer Freddie Prinz used 202 extras from Central Casting and one stand-in. Daily Production and Progress Reports, Hollywood Canteen special, Box B00194,

Folder 1487, Box 1 of 2, Warner Bros. Archives, School of Cinematic Arts, University of Southern California, Los Angeles.

36. Donald Vining diary, Donald Crossley Vining Papers, Manuscripts and Archives, Sterling Memorial Library, Yale University, New Haven, Connecticut.

37. Daily Production Schedule, Hollywood Canteen, Warner Bros. Archives, School of Cinematic Arts, University of Southern California, Los Angeles.

38. Himes et al., *Conversations with Chester Himes*, 56.

39. Lasky, "Off Camera," 151–161.

40. Swindell, *Body and Soul*, 177–178; 189–191.

41. Alex Gottlieb, Inter-Office Memo to Delmar Daves, May 25, 1944, Hollywood Canteen special, Box B00194, Hollywood Canteen Story File 3 of 4, Folder 2780, Warner Bros. Archives, School of Cinematic Arts, University of Southern California, Los Angeles.

42. "Caleb Peterson Jr. Captures Outstanding Movie Role," *California Eagle*, January 8, 1943, 2B; "Four Win Distinguished Flying Cross in Italy," *Kansas City Plaindealer*, September 15, 1944, 1.

43. [No author shown] (1944), Special Sequences for Hollywood Canteen, United Artists Corporation Records: series 1.2: Warner Brothers Scripts, circa 1928–1950, box 182, folder 11, Wisconsin Center for Film and Theater Research, Madison.

44. Herman Lisseauer, Inter-Office Memo to Leo Kuter, June 6, 1944, Hollywood Canteen special, Box B00194, Hollywood Canteen Research File 1 of 1, Folder 2805, Warner Bros. Archives, School of Cinematic Arts, University of Southern California, Los Angeles.

45. "99th's Commandeer on Secret Mission," *Los Angeles Tribune*, September 20, 1943, 2.

46. Ollie Harrington, "Walter White Sees 99th Bomb Cassino," *Pittsburgh Courier*, April 1, 1944, 1; "Four Win Distinguished Flying Cross."

47. *Hollywood Canteen* photographs, stills, and interiors, Hollywood Canteen special, Box B00194, Folder 3206A, Warner Bros. Archives, School of Cinematic Arts, University of Southern California, Los Angeles.

48. Alex Gottlieb, Inter-Office Memo to Martin Jurow, June 12, 1944, Hollywood Canteen special, Box B00194, File 2 of 4, Folder 1975, Warner Bros. Archives, School of Cinematic Arts, University of Southern California, Los Angeles.

49. Martin Jurow, Inter-Office Memo to Alex Gottlieb, July 3, 1944, Hollywood Canteen special, Box B00194, File 3 of 4, Folder 1975, Warner Bros. Archives, School of Cinematic Arts, University of Southern California, Los Angeles.

50. "Louis Armstrong Plays."

51. Alex Gottlieb, Inter-Office Memo to Leo Forbstein, July 27, 1944, Hollywood Canteen special, Box B00194, File 1 of 4, Folder 1975, Warner Bros. Archives, School of Cinematic Arts, University of Southern California, Los Angeles.

52. Alex Gottlieb, Inter-Office Memo to Leroy Prinz, July 28 1944, Hollywood Canteen special, Box B00194, File 1 of 4, Folder 1975, Warner Bros. Archives, School of Cinematic Arts, University of Southern California, Los Angeles.

53. Koppes and Black, *Hollywood Goes to War*, 65–69.

54. The actual millionth man said, "Gosh, I'm married." "Stars Kiss Canteen Guest." The following year, "man" number 5 million at the nearby Hollywood U.S.O. was a WAC. "Hollywood U.S.O. Monthly Narrative," December 1944, Armed Services YMCA: USO City Histories (Industrial) folder: California, Hollywood, box 28, Kautz Family YMCA Archives, Elmer L. Anderson Library, University of Minnesota, Minneapolis.

55. Berg, "Democracy American Style," 13, Hollywood Canteen special, Box B00194, Hollywood Canteen Publicity Folder, File 683, Warner Bros. Archives, School of Cinematic Arts, University of Southern California, Los Angeles.

56. Delmer Daves, "One in a Million."

57. Leon Hardwick, "Lena Horne Wins Trophy for Best Acting in 1943," *Afro-American*, April 22, 1944, 6.

58. Review in *Daily Mail*, May 19, 1945, page unknown, clipping, Film Reviews, *Hollywood Canteen*, Hollywood Canteen special, Box B00194, Picture File 4 of 4, Folder 1975, Warner Bros. Archives, School of Cinematic Arts, University of Southern California, Los Angeles.

59. Quoted in *News Chronicle*, May 19, 1945, page unknown, clipping, Film Reviews, *Hollywood Canteen*, Hollywood Canteen special, Box B00194, Picture File 4 of 4, Folder 1975, Warner Bros. Archives, School of Cinematic Arts, University of Southern California, Los Angeles.

60. Pvt. Joseph Wynn to Mr. Warner, "Somewhere in New Guinea," January 22, 1945, Hollywood Canteen special, Box B00194, Picture File 4 of 4, Folder 1975, Warner Bros. Archives, School of Cinematic Arts, University of Southern California, Los Angeles.

Bibliography

PRIMARY SOURCES

ARCHIVES AND COLLECTIONS

20th Century Organizations Collection, Southern California Library for Social Science Research, Los Angeles.

American Jewish Historical Society, Center for Jewish History, New York.

Bette Davis Collection, Howard Gotlieb Archival Research Center, Boston University.

Denshō Digital Archive, Japanese American Legacy Project, website at www.densho .org/archive/default.asp, accessed March 3, 2014.

Charles K. Feldman Papers, Louis B. Mayer Library, American Film Institute, Los Angeles.

Walter Gordon Collection, Library Special Collections, University of California, Los Angeles.

Margaret Herrick Library, Special Collections, American Academy of Motion Picture Arts and Sciences, Los Angeles.

Kautz Family YMCA Archives, Elmer L. Anderson Library, University of Minnesota, Minneapolis.

National Jewish Welfare Board Army-Navy Division Records, undated, 1917–1955, 1969, 1974, Center for Jewish History, American Jewish Historical Society, New York.

Records of Naval Districts and Shore Establishment, National Archives and Records Administration, Pacific Region, Laguna Niguel, California.

Donald Crossley Vining Papers, Manuscripts and Archives, Sterling Memorial Library, Yale University, New Haven, Connecticut.

Donald Vining Papers, Manuscripts and Archives Division, Stephen A. Schwarzman Building, New York Public Library.

Warner Bros. Archives, School of Cinematic Arts, University of Southern California, Los Angeles.

Warner Brothers Scripts, c. 1928–1950, United Artists Corporation Collection, Wisconsin Center for Film and Theater Research, Madison.

YWCA of the USA Records, Sophia Smith Collection, Smith College, Northampton, Massachusetts.

NEWSPAPERS AND PERIODICALS

Afro-American
California Eagle
Chicago Daily Tribune
Chicago Defender
Cleveland Call and Post
Daily Variety
Daily Worker
DownBeat
Greater Amusements
Hollywood Reporter
Kansas City Plaindealer
Los Angeles Daily News
Los Angeles Examiner
Los Angeles Sentinel
Los Angeles Times
Los Angeles Tribune
Motion Picture
Negro Digest
Negro Star
New Journal and Guide
News Chronicle
New York Age
New York Times
Overture
Philadelphia Tribune
Pittsburgh Courier
Stars and Stripes
Washington Post

INTERVIEWS AND ORAL HISTORIES

Unless otherwise indicated, interviews and oral histories were conducted by the author.

Alden, Bob. Interview. North Hollywood. January 13, 2006.

Bank, Helene (Angus). Interview. Los Angeles. January 11, 2006.

Bear, Lorraine (Mitchell). Telephone interview. April 23, 2001.

Bluett, Leonard "Lennie." Interview. Los Angeles. May 29, 2003.

Bryant, Mel. Telephone interview. July 25, 2000.

————. Telephone interview. October 28, 2000.

Christ, Jean (Jeanne) (Foreman). Telephone interview. October 28, 2004.

Edwards, Beverly. Telephone conversation. December 19, 2005.

Farrell, Tommy. Interview. Woodland Hills, California. May 23, 2003.

Ford, Mary. Interview with Dan Ford, n.d. Tape 43, "War Years," John Ford Collection, Lilly Library, Indiana University, Bloomington.

Gelfand, Pearl. Interview. Woodland Hills, California. May 23, 2003.

Gordon, Bernard. Conversation. Hollywood. March 28, 2004.

————. Interview. Hollywood. May 21, 2003.

Grant, Johnny. Interview. Hollywood. March 23, 2004.

Hansen, B. J. Interview. Los Angeles. January 11, 2006.

Harris, Avanelle. Telephone conversation. July 25, 2000.

————. Interview. Los Angeles. January 10, 2006.

Hayward, Louise. Telephone interview. August 24, 2001.

Hayward, Tom. Telephone interview. August 24, 2001.

Hunt, Marsha. Interview. Sherman Oaks, California. March 27, 2004.

Kosanovich, Mildred S. Telephone interview. January 21, 2001.

LeGon, Jeni. Oral history. Interviewed by Sherrie Tucker. Vancouver, British Columbia. June 27, 2005. DVD, Coastal Jazz and Blues Society, Vancouver.

————. Telephone interview. November 26, 2004.

Lewin, Marjorie. Interview. Los Angeles. May 30, 2003.

Marlow, Nancy. Interview. Studio City, California. March 27, 2004.

Marsh-Doll, Caren. Interview. Palm Springs, California. March 24, 2004.

McAuliffe, Aniela "Niel." Interview. Woodland Hills, California. May 23, 2003.

McDowall, Virginia. Interview. Woodland Hills, California. May 23, 2003.

Miller, Loren. Oral history. Interviewed by Lawrence de Graaf. March 3 and April 29, 1967. Center for Oral and Public History, California State University, Fullerton.

Morris, Dorothy. Interview. Palm Springs, California. March 24, 2004.

Nagumo, Reiko. Oral history. Interviewer unknown. "Time of Remembrance . . . An Elk Grove Legacy." Elk Grove Unified School District, Elk Grove, California, 2005. Available at the website of the Elk Grove Unified School District, www.egusd.net/tor/flash_video/interviews/r_nagumo/index.html, accessed June 18, 2009.

Nevarez, Theresa. Telephone interview. April 11, 2009.

Ochoa, Mary Lou (Ramirez). Interview. Montebello, California. January 13, 2006.

Rosen, Claire (Lomas). Telephone interview. June 24, 2010.

Saphro, Marion (Krow). Interview. May 23, 2003.

Sigall, Martha (Goldman). Telephone interview. June 20, 2006.

Stewart, Margie. Interview. Studio City, California. March 27, 2004.

Watson, Delmar. Telephone interview. November 21, 2004.

PERSONAL CORRESPONDENCE

Alsmeyer, Marie Bennett. Letter to author. April 27, 2001.

Bear, Lorraine (Mitchell). Email to author. April 4, 2001.

Campbell, Anne. Email to author. January 26, 2001.

Haynes, Marie C. Letter to author. September 4, 2001.

King, Andrea. Email to author. October 20, 2001.

Latham, Ellie. Letter to author. November 3, 2001.

Mansfield, Senior Master Sergeant Charlotte D. Letter to author. October 18, 2000.

Marsh, Eric. Cassette tape correspondence with author. May 16, 2006.

———. Cassette tape correspondence with author. April 17, 2006.

Neilan, Jo. Email to author, April 21, 2001.

Rothstein, Shirley. Letter to author. December 24, 2000.

Tilbury, R. Janie (Bevins). Email to author. June 21, 2000.

———. Email to author. June 22, 2000.

Walters, Ian. Email to author. February 14, 2006.

Welter, Kathryn "Kit" (Ludwig). Letter to author. May 29, 2001.

Wimberly, Betty Sue. Letter to author. October 18, 2001.

Woodcome, Jean. Letter to author. November 5, 2001.

SECONDARY SOURCES

Adams, Dale. "Saludos Amigos: Hollywood and FDR's Good Neighbor Policy," *Quarterly Review of Film and Video* (2007) 24:3, 289–295.

Anderson, Benedict. *Imagined Communities: Reflections on the Origin and Spread of Nationalism.* London: Verso, 1991.

Ahmed, Sara. "Declarations of Whiteness: The Non-performativity of Anti-Racism." *Borderlands* 3, no. 2 (2004). Available at www.borderlandsejournal.adelaide.edu.au /vo13no2_2004/ahmed_declarations.htm, accessed April 2, 2014.

———. *On Being Included: Racism and Diversity in Institutional Life.* Durham, N.C.: Duke University Press, 2012.

———.*Queer Phenomenology: Orientations, Objects, Others.* Durham, N.C.: DukeUniversity Press, 2006.

Akers, Regina. "Doing Their Part: The WAVES in World War II." Ph.D. diss., Howard University, 2000.

Alsmeyer, Marie Bennett. *The Way of the Waves.* Conway, Ark.: HAMBA Books, 1981.

Barraclough, Laura R. *Making the San Fernando Valley: Rural Landscapes, Urban Development, and White Privilege.* Athens: University of Georgia Press, 2011.

Barzman, Norma. *The Red and the Blacklist: Intimate Memoir of a Hollywood Expatriate.* New York: Thunder's Mouth Press, 2003.

Berg, Esther L. "Democracy American Style." In *Movies and Morale: "Hollywood Canteen."* Warner Brothers Pictures, c. 1944.

Bernard, Emily. *Remember Me to Harlem: The Letters of Langston Hughes and Carl Van Vechten, 1925–1964.* New York: Alfred A. Knopf, 2001.

Billman, Larry. *Betty Grable: A Bio-Bibliography.* Westport, Conn.: Greenwood Press, 1993.

Bogle, Donald. *Bright Boulevards, Bold Dreams: The Story of Black Hollywood.* New York: One World Ballantine Books, 2005.

Boym, Svetlana. *The Future of Nostalgia.* New York: Basic Books, 2001.

Brokaw, Tom. *The Greatest Generation*. New York: Random House, 1998.

———. *The Greatest Generation Speaks: Letters and Reflections*. New York: Random House, 1999.

Brooks, Charlotte. *Alien Neighbors, Foreign Friends: Asian Americans, Housing, and the Transformation of Urban California*. Chicago: University of Chicago Press, 2009.

Bruck, Connie. *When Hollywood Had a King: The Reign of Lew Wasserman, Who Leveraged Talent into Power and Influence*. New York: Random House, 2003.

Buckley, Gail Lumet. *The Hornes: An American Family*. New York: Knopf, 1986.

Canford, Tom. *Boy at Sea*. Lincoln, Neb.: iUniverse, 2005.

Cappelletto, Francesca, ed. *Memory and World War II: An Ethnographic Approach*. Oxford.: Berg, 2005.

Cheatham, Maude. "Hollywood Canteen Celebrates." *Screenland* 1943.

Clinton's Restaurants, Inc. "Clifton's Cafeterias." Available at www.cliftonscafeteria.com /home.html, accessed April 2, 2014.

Cohen, Karl F. *Forbidden Animation: Censored Cartoons and Blacklisted Animators in America*. Jefferson, N.C.: McFarland, 1997.

Cole, Lester. *Hollywood Red: The Autobiography of Lester Cole*. Palo Alto, Calif.: Ramparts Press, 1981.

Coletta, Paolo Enrico, and K. Jack Bauer. *United States Navy and Marine Corps Bases, Domestic*. Westport, Conn.: Greenwood Press, 1985.

Crease, Robert P. "Divine Frivolity: Hollywood Representations of the Lindy Hop, 1937–1942." In *Representing Jazz*, edited by Krin Gabbard. Durham, N.C.: Duke University Press, 1995, 207–228.

Cunningham, David, and Barb Browning. "The Emergence of Worthy Targets: Official Frames and Deviance Narratives within the FBI." *Sociological Forum* 19, no. 3 (2004): 347–369.

Daves, Delmer. *Hollywood Canteen*. 1944.

Davis, Angela Y. *Abolition Democracy: Beyond Empire, Prisons, and Torture*. New York: Seven Stories Press, 2005.

Davis, Bette, with Michael Herskowitz. *This 'n That*. New York: Putnam's, 1987.

———, with Roy Mosley. *Bette Davis: An Intimate Memoir*. New York: Donald I. Fine, Inc, 1989.

Davis, Mike. *City of Quartz: Excavating the Future in Los Angeles*. New York: Vintage Books, 1992.

Davis, Ronald L. *Van Johnson: MGM's Golden Boy*. Jackson: University Press of Mississippi, 2001.

Deverell, William Francis. *Whitewashed Adobe: The Rise of Los Angeles and the Remaking of Its Mexican Past*. Berkeley: University of California Press, 2004.

Dinerstein, Joel. *Swinging the Machine: Modernity, Technology, and African American Culture between the World Wars*. Amherst: University of Massachusetts Press, 2003.

Eberwein, Robert. "'As a Mother Cuddles a Child': Sexuality and Masculinity in World War II Combat Films." In *Masculinity: Bodies, Movies, Culture*, edited by Peter Lehman. New York: Routledge, 2001, 149–166.

Edwards, Beverly A., and William G. Edwards. "Official Web Biography of Sam Edwards." Available at the website www.perfessorbill.com/sam_bio.shtml, accessed April 2, 2014.

Eller, Cynthia. *Conscientious Objectors and the Second World War: Moral and Religious Arguments in Support of Pacifism*. New York: Praeger, 1991.

Erenberg, Lewis A. *Swingin' the Dream: Big Band Jazz and the Rebirth of American Culture*. Chicago: University of Chicago Press, 1998.

Escobar, Edward J. *Race, Police, and the Making of a Political Identity: Mexican Americans and the Los Angeles Police Department, 1900–1945*. Berkeley: University of California Press, 1999.

Escobedo, Elizabeth R. *From Coveralls to Zoot Suits: The Lives of Mexican American Women on the World War II Home Front*. Chapel Hill: University of North Carolina Press, 2013.

———. "Mexican American Home Front: The Politics of Gender, Culture, and Community in World War II Los Angeles." Ph.D. diss., University of Washington, 2004.

España-Maram, Linda. *Creating Masculinity in Los Angeles's Little Manila: Working-Class Filipinos and Popular Culture, 1920s–1950s*. New York: Columbia University Press, 2006.

Ethington, Philip J. "Ab Urbis Condita: Regional Regimes since 13,000 Before Present." In *A Companion to Los Angeles*, edited by William Francis Deverell and Greg Hise. Malden, Mass.: Wiley-Blackwell, 2010, 178–215.

Finler, Joel W. *The Hollywood Story*. London: Wallflower Press, 2003.

Fiset, Louis. "Public Health in World War II Assembly Centers for Japanese Americans." *Bulletin of the History of Medicine* 734 (1999): 565–584.

Flamming, Douglas. *Bound for Freedom: Black Los Angeles in Jim Crow America*. Berkeley: University of California Press, 2005.

Foster, Susan Leigh. *Corporealities: Dancing Knowledge, Culture and Power*. London: Routledge, 1996.

———. "Taken by Surprise: Improvisation in Dance and Mind." In *Taken by Surprise: A Dance Improvisation Reader*, edited by Ann Cooper Albright and David Gere. Middletown, Conn.: Wesleyan University Press, 2003, 3–10.

Frank, Rusty E. *Tap! The Greatest Tap Dance Stars and Their Stories*. New York: Morrow, 1990.

Frankenberg, Ruth. *White Women, Race Matters: The Social Construction of Whiteness*. Minneapolis: University of Minnesota Press, 1993.

Frascina, Francis A. "Advertisements for Itself: The *New York Times*, Norman Rockwell, and the New Patriotism." In *The Selling of 9/11: How a National Tragedy Became a Commodity*, edited by Dana A. Heller. New York: Palgrave Macmillan, 2005, 75–96.

Friedrich, Otto. *City of Nets: A Portrait of Hollywood in the 1940's*, New York: Harper and Row, 1986.

Fyne, Robert. *The Hollywood Propaganda of World War II*. Metuchen, N.J.: Scarecrow Press, 1994.

Gavin, James. *Stormy Weather: The Life of Lena Horne*. New York: Atria Books, 2009.

Giovacchini, Saverio. "'Hollywood Is a State of Mind': New York Film Culture and the Lure of Los Angeles from 1930 to the Present." In *New York and Los Angeles: Politics, Society, and Culture: A Comparative View*, edited by David Halle. Chicago: University of Chicago Press, 2003, 423–447.

Goldberg, David Theo. *The Racial State*. Malden, Mass.: Blackwell, 2002.

Goldman, Danielle. *I Want to Be Ready: Improvised Dance as a Practice of Freedom.* Ann Arbor: University of Michigan Press, 2010.

Gordon, Bernard. *The Gordon File: A Screenwriter Recalls Twenty Years of* FBI *Surveillance*. Austin: University of Texas Press, 2004.

———. *Hollywood Exile, or, How I Learned to Love the Blacklist: A Memoir*. Austin: University of Texas Press, 1999.

Gottschild, Brenda Dixon. *The Black Dancing Body: A Geography from Coon to Cool.* New York: Palgrave Macmillan, 2003.

———. *Waltzing in the Dark: African American Vaudeville and Race Politics in the Swing Era*. New York: St. Martin's Press, 2000.

Grewal, Inderpal. *Transnational America: Feminisms, Diasporas, Neoliberalisms.* Durham, N.C.: Duke University Press, 2005.

Halbwachs, Maurice. *The Collective Memory*. New York: Harper and Row, 1980.

Halle, David. "Introduction: The New York and Los Angeles Schools." *New York and Los Angeles: Politics, Society, and Culture: A Comparative View*, edited by David Halle. Chicago: University of Chicago Press, 2003, 1–46.

Halle, David, Robert Gedeon, and Andrew A. Beveridge. "Residential Separation and Segregation, Racial and Latino Identity, and the Racial Composition of Each City." In *New York and Los Angeles: Politics, Society, and Culture: A Comparative View*, edited by David Halle. Chicago: University of Chicago Press, 2003, 150–191.

Halsey, Margaret. *Color Blind: A White Woman Looks at the Negro*. New York: Simon and Schuster, 1946.

———. "Memo to Junior Hostesses." *Negro Digest*, October 1943, 51–53.

———. *Some of My Best Friends Are Soldiers, a Kind of Novel*. New York: Simon and Schuster, 1944.

Hancock, Black Hawk. "American Allegory: Lindy Hop and the Racial Imagination." Ph.D. diss., University of Wisconsin, Madison, 2004.

———. "Learning How to Make Life Swing." *Qualitative Sociology* 30, no. 2 (2007): 113–133.

———. "'Put a Little Color on That!'" *Sociological Perspectives* 51, no. 4 (2008): 783–802.

Harris, Avanelle. "I Tried to Crash the Movies," *Ebony*, August 1946, 5.

Harris-Perry, Melissa V. *Sister Citizen: Shame, Stereotypes, and Black Women in America*. New Haven: Yale University Press, 2011.

Haskins, James, and Kathleen Benson. *Lena: A Personal and Professional Biography of Lena Horne*. New York: Stein and Day, 1984.

Hayden, Dolores. *The Power of Place Urban Landscapes as Public History*. Cambridge, Mass.: MIT Press, 1995.

Heble, Ajay. *Landing on the Wrong Note: Jazz, Dissonance, and Critical Practice*. New York: Routledge, 2000.

Hegarty, Marilyn E. *Victory Girls, Khaki-Wackies, and Patriotutes: The Regulation of Female Sexuality during World War II*. New York: New York University Press, 2008.

Higham, Charles. *Bette: The Life of Bette Davis*. New York: Macmillan, 1981.

Himes, Chester. *Lonely Crusade*. New York: Thunder's Mouth Press, 1986.

Himes, Chester B., Michael Fabre, and Robert E. Skinner. *Conversations with Chester Himes*. Jackson: University Press of Mississippi, 1995.

Horne, Gerald. *Class Struggle in Hollywood, 1930–1950: Moguls, Mobsters, Stars, Reds, and Trade Unionists*. Austin: University of Texas Press, 2001.

Horne, Lena, as told to Helen Arstein and Carlton Moss. *In Person, Lena Horne*. New York: Greenberg, 1950.

Horne, Lena, and Richard Schickel. *Lena*. New York: Limelight Editions, 1986.

Hunt, Marsha. *The Way We Wore: Styles of the 1930s and '40s and Our World since Then*. Fallbrook, Calif.: Fallbrook, 1993.

Hurewitz, Daniel. *Bohemian Los Angeles and the Making of Modern Politics*. Berkeley: University of California Press, 2007.

Jackson, Carlton. *Hattie: The Life of Hattie McDaniel*. Lanham, Md.: Madison Books, 1989.

Jain, Sarah S. Lochlann. *Injury: The Politics of Product Design and Safety Law in the United States*. Princeton: Princeton University Press, 2006.

Jarvis, Christina S. *The Male Body at War: American Masculinity during World War II*. DeKalb: Northern Illinois University Press, 2004.

Jones, LeRoi [Amiri Baraka]. "Swing: From Verb to Noun" (1963). In *The LeRoi Jones/ Amiri Baraka Reader*, edited by William J. Harris. New York: Thunder's Mouth Press, 33–50.

Julien, Kyle. "Sounding the City: Jazz, African American Nightlife, and the Articulation of Race in 1940s Los Angeles." Ph.D. diss., University of California, Irvine, 2000.

Kester, Grant H. "Access Denied: Information Policy and the Limits of Liberalism." In *Ethics, Information and Technology: Readings*, edited by Richard N. Stichler and Robert Hauptman. Jefferson, N.C.: McFarland, 2009, 207–230.

Kikuchi, Charles, and John Modell. *The Kikuchi Diary: Chronicle from an American Concentration Camp: The Tanforan Journals of Charles Kikuchi*. Urbana: University of Illinois Press, 1973.

Klein, Norman M. *The History of Forgetting: Los Angeles and the Erasure of Memory*. London: Verso, 1998.

Koppes, Clayton R., and Gregory D. Black. *Hollywood Goes to War: How Politics, Profits, and Propaganda Shaped World War II Movies*. New York: Collier Macmillan, 1987.

Kurashige, Scott. *The Shifting Grounds of Race: Black and Japanese Americans in the Making of Multiethnic Los Angeles*. Princeton: Princeton University Press, 2008.

Lacy, Linda Cates. *We Are Marines! World War I to the Present*. Swansboro, N.C.: Tar Heel Chapter, NC-1, Women Marines Association, 2004.

Lasky, Marjorie Penn. "Off Camera: A History of the Screen Actors Guild during the Era of the Studio System." Ph.D. diss., University of California, Davis, 1992.

Laslett, John H. M. "Historical Perspectives: Immigration and the Rise of a Distinctive Urban Region, 1900–1970." In *Ethnic Los Angeles*, edited by Roger David Waldinger and Mehdi Bozorgmehr. New York: Russell Sage Foundation, 1996, 39–75.

Laws, Kenneth, and Arleen Sugano. *Physics and the Art of Dance: Understanding Movement*. Oxford: Oxford University Press, 2008.

Loewen, James W. *Sundown Towns: A Hidden Dimension of American Racism*. New York: New Press, 2005.

Lovelace, Maryann. "Facing Change in Wartime Philadelphia: The Story of the Philadelphia USO." *Pennsylvania Magazine of History and Biography* 123 (1999): 143–175.

Lowe, Graham S. *Women in the Administrative Revolution: The Feminization of Clerical Work*. Toronto: University of Toronto Press, 1987.

Macias, Anthony F. *Mexican American Mojo: Popular Music, Dance, and Urban Culture in Los Angeles, 1935–1968*. Durham, N.C.: Duke University Press, 2008.

Magee, Jeffrey. "'King Porter Stomp' and the Jazz Tradition." *Current Musicology* 71–73 (Spring 2001/2002): 22–53.

Maher, Michael J. *John Charles Thomas: Beloved Baritone of American Opera and Popular Music*. Jefferson, N.C.: McFarland, 2006.

Marcus, Kenneth H. *Musical Metropolis: Los Angeles and the Creation of a Music Culture, 1880–1940*. New York: Palgrave Macmillan, 2004.

Margolies, Edward, and Michel Fabre. *The Several Lives of Chester Himes.* Jackson: University Press of Mississippi, 1997.

Marsh-Doll, Caren. *Hollywood's Child: Dancing through Oz, an Autobiography*. Las Vegas, Nevada: Joshua Tree, 2003.

McClung, William A. *Landscapes of Desire: Anglo Mythologies of Los Angeles*. Berkeley: University of California Press, 2000.

McDonald, J. Frederick. "'Hot Jazz': The Jitterbug, and Misunderstanding: The Generation Gap in Swing." In *American Popular Music: Readings from the Popular Press*, vol. 1, *The Nineteenth Century and Tin Pan Alley*, edited by Timothy E. Scheurer. Bowling Green, Ky.: Bowling Green State University Popular Press, 1989, 151–160.

McDougal, Dennis. *The Last Mogul: Lew Wasserman, MCA, and the Hidden History of Hollywood*. New York: Crown, 1998.

McGrath, Patrick J. *John Garfield: The Illustrated Career in Films and on Stage*. Jefferson, N.C.: McFarland, 1993.

McLaurin, Melton Alonza. *The Marines of Montford Point: America's First Black Marines*. Chapel Hill: University of North Carolina Press, 2007.

McMains, Juliet, and Danielle Robinson. "Swingin' Out: Southern California's Lindy Revival." (2000) In *I See America Dancing: Selected Readings, 1685–2000*, edited by Maureen Needham. Urbana: University of Illinois Press, 2002, 84–91.

McWilliams, Carey. *Brothers under the Skin*. Boston: Little, Brown, 1943.

———. *The Education of Carey McWilliams*. New York: Simon and Schuster, 1979.

———. *North from Mexico: The Spanish-Speaking People of the United States*. Philadelphia: Lippincott, 1949.

———. *Prejudice; Japanese-Americans: Symbol of Racial Intolerance*. Boston: Little, Brown, 1944.

Melling, Phil. "War and Memory in the New World Order." In *War and Memory in the Twentieth Century*, edited by Martin Evans and Kenneth Lunn. Oxford: Berg, 1997, 255–267.

Meyer, Leisa D. "Creating GI Jane: The Regulation of Sexuality and Sexual Behavior in the Women's Army Corps during World War II." *Feminist Studies* 18, no. 3 (1992): 581–601.

———. *Creating GI Jane: Sexuality and Power in the Women's Army Corps during World War II*. New York: Columbia University Press, 1996.

———. "One Way Out—Communism." *Opportunity: Journal of Negro Life* 12, no. 7 (1934): 214–216.

Miller, Richard E. *The Messman Chronicles: African Americans in the U.S. Navy, 1932–1943*. Annapolis, Md.: Naval Institute Press, 2004.

Mitchell, Lisa, and Bruce Torrence. *The Hollywood Canteen: Where the Greatest Generation Danced with the Most Beautiful Girls in the World*. Duncan, Ok.: BearManor Media, 2012.

Modell, John. *The Economics and Politics of Racial Accommodation: The Japanese of Los Angeles, 1900–1942*. Urbana: University of Illinois Press, 1977.

Monaghan, Terry. "'Stompin' at the Savoy'—Remembering, Re-enacting and Re-searching the Lindy Hop's Relationship to Harlem's Savoy Ballroom." In *Conference Proceedings: Dancing at the Crossroads: African Diasporic Dances in Britain*, edited by Caroline Muraldo, Mo Dodson, and Terry Monaghan. London: Metropolitan University, 2005, 31–85.

Moon, John. "The Freedom of Information Act: A Fundamental Contradiction." *American University Law Review* 34, no. 1157 (1985), 1157–1189.

Moore, Brenda L. *To Serve My Country, to Serve My Race: The Story of the Only African American WACS Stationed Overseas During World War II*. New York: New York University Press, 1996.

Mummery, Jane. "Rethinking the Democratic Project: Rorty, Mouffe, Derrida, and Democracy to Come." *Borderlands* 4, no. 1 (2005), available at www.borderlands.net .au/vol4no1_2005/mummery_rethinking.htm, accessed December 2, 2006 .

Nalty, Bernard. *The Right to Fight: African-American Marines in World War II*, History and Museums Division, Headquarters, U.S. Marine Corps, Washington, D.C., 1995, available on the website of the Internet Archive, http://archive.org/details/TheRight ToFight, accessed February 20, 2014.

Navasky, Victor S. *Naming Names*. New York: Viking Press, 1980.

Nelson, Steve, James R. Barrett, and Rob Ruck. *Steve Nelson, American Radical*. Pittsburgh: University of Pittsburgh Press, 1981.

Newton, Michael. *The FBI Encyclopedia*. Jefferson, N.C.: McFarland, 2003.

Nichols, Gina. *The Seabees at Port Hueneme*. Charleston, S.C.: Arcadia, 2006.

"Nightclubs and Other Venues, Los Angeles." In *The New Grove Dictionary of Jazz*. 2nd ed. edited by Barry Kernfeld. *Grove Music Online*. *Oxford Music Online*. Oxford University Press. Available on http://www.oxfordmusiconline.com, accessed March 6, 2014.

O'Leary, Cecilia Elizabeth. *To Die For: The Paradox of American Patriotism* (Princeton: Princeton University Press, 1999.

Oppenheimer, George. *The Passionate Playgoer, a Personal Scrapbook.* New York: Viking Press, 1958.

Pagan, Eduardo Obregon. *Murder at the Sleepy Lagoon: Zoot Suits, Race, and Riot in Wartime L.A.* Chapel Hill: University of North Carolina Press, 2003.

Parson, Donald Craig. *Making a Better World: Public Housing, the Red Scare, and the Direction of Modern Los Angeles.* Minneapolis: University of Minnesota Press, 2005.

Pascoe, Peggy. *What Comes Naturally: Miscegenation Law and the Making of Race in America.*Oxford: Oxford University Press, 2009.

Perry, Louis B., and Richard S. Perry. *A History of the Los Angeles Labor Movement, 1911–1941.* Berkeley: University of California Press, 1963.

Pitt, Leonard, and Dale Pitt. *Los Angeles A to Z: An Encyclopedia of the City and County.* Berkeley: University of California Press, 1997.

Portelli, Alessandro. *The Death of Luigi Trastulli and Other Stories: Form and Meaning in Oral History.* Albany: State University of New York Press, 1991.

———. *The Order Has Been Carried Out: History, Memory and Meaning of a Nazi Massacre in Rome.* New York: Palgrave Macmillan, 2003.

Raferty, Judith Rosenberg. *Land of Fair Promise: Politics and Reform in Los Angeles Schools, 1885–1941.* Stanford, Calif.: Stanford University Press, 1992.

Ramírez, Catherine Sue. "Crimes of Fashion: The Pachuca and Chicana Style Politics." *Meridians: Feminism, Race, Transnationalism* 2, no. 2 (2002): 1–35.

———. *The Woman in the Zoot Suit: Gender, Nationalism, and the Cultural Politics of Memory.* Durham, N.C.: Duke University Press, 2009.

Richardson, Willis. *Plays and Pageants from the Life of the Negro.* Jackson: University Press of Mississippi, 1993.

Roarty, Robert C. "More Than Entertainment: The American Theater Wing during World War II." Ph. diss., City University of New York, 2002.

Romano, Renee Christine, and Leigh Raiford. *The Civil Rights Movement in American Memory.* Athens: University of Georgia Press, 2006.

Rosenberg, Emily S. *A Date Which Will Live: Pearl Harbor in American Memory.* Durham, N.C.: Duke University Press, 2003.

Ross, Murray. *Stars and Strikes: The Unionization of Hollywood.* New York: Columbia University Press, 1941.

Sanchez, George J. *Becoming Mexican American: Ethnicity, Culture, and Identity in Chicano Los Angeles, 1900–1945.* New York: Oxford University Press, 1993.

Savigliano, Marta E. "Fragments for a Story of Tango Bodies (on Choreocritics and the Memory of Power)." In *Corporealities: Dancing Knowledge, Culture and Power,* edited by Susan Leigh Foster. London: Routledge, 1996, 199–232.

Sbardellati, John. "Brassbound G-Men and Celluloid Reds: The FBI's Search for Communist Propaganda in Wartime Hollywood." *Film History* 20 (2008): 412–436.

Schickle, Richard, and George Perry. *You Must Remember This: The Warner Bros. Story.* Philadelphia: Running Press, 2008.

Sides, Josh. *L.A. City Limits: African American Los Angeles from the Great Depression to the Present*. Berkeley: University of California Press, 2003.

Sikov, Ed. *Dark Victory: The Life of Bette Davis*. New York: Holt, 2007.

Sims-Wood, Janet Louise. "'We Served America Too!': Personal Recollections of African-Americans in the Women's Army Corps during World War II." Ph.D. diss., Union Institute, 1994.

Singh, Nikhil Pal. *Black Is a Country: Race and the Unfinished Struggle for Democracy*. Cambridge, Mass.: Harvard University Press, 2004.

Sitton, Tom. *Los Angeles Transformed: Fletcher Bowron's Urban Reform Revival, 1938–1953*. Albuquerque: University of New Mexico Press, 2005.

Smith, R. J. *The Great Black Way: L.A. in the 1940s and the Lost African-American Renaissance*. New York: PublicAffairs, 2006.

Smith, Valerie. "Meditation on Memory: Clark Johnson's Boycott." *American Literary History* 17, no. 3 (2005): 530–541.

Soderbergh, Peter A. *Women Marines: The World War II Era*. Westport, Conn.: Praeger, 1992.

Spada, James. *More Than a Woman: An Intimate Biography of Bette Davis*. New York: Bantam Books, 1993.

Spencer, Jon Michael. *The New Negroes and Their Music: The Success of the Harlem Renaissance*. Knoxville: University of Tennessee Press, 1997.

Sperling, Cass Warner, and Cork Millner, with Jack Warner, Jr. *Hollywood Be Thy Name: The Warner Brothers Story*. Rocklin, Calif.: Prima, 1994.

Spring, Howard. "Swing and the Lindy Hop: Dance, Venue, Media, and Tradition." *American Music* 15, no. 2 (1997): 183–207.

Starr, Kevin. *Embattled Dreams: California in War and Peace, 1940–1950*. Oxford: Oxford University Press, 2002.

Stearns, Marshall, and Jean. *Jazz Dance: The Story of American Vernacular Dance*. New York: Schirmer Books, 1979.

Stevens, Tamara. *Swing Dancing*. Santa Barbara: Greenwood, 2011.

Stine, Whitney. *Mother Goddamn: The Story of the Career of Bette Davis*. New York: Hawthorn Books, 1974.

Stockdale, Robert L. *Jimmy Dorsey: A Study in Contrasts*. Lanham, Md.: Scarecrow Press, 1999.

Stowe, David W. *Swing Changes: Big-Band Jazz in New Deal America*. Cambridge, Mass.: Harvard University Press, 1994.

Sturken, Marita. *Tangled Memories: The Vietnam War, the Aids Epidemic, and the Politics of Remembering*. Berkeley: University of California Press, 1997.

Swindell, Larry. *Body and Soul: The Story of John Garfield*. New York: Morrow, 1975.

Taylor, Diana. *The Archive and the Repertoire: Performing Cultural Memory in the Americas*. Durham, N.C.: Duke University Press, 2003.

Torgovnick, Marianna. *The War Complex: World War II in Our Time*. Chicago: University of Chicago Press, 2005.

Torrence, Bruce T. *Hollywood, the First Hundred Years*. Hollywood: Hollywood Chamber of Commerce, 1979.

Townsend, Peter. *Pearl Harbor Jazz: Change in Popular Music in the Early 1940s*. Jackson: University Press of Mississippi, 2007.

Tyler, Bruce M. *From Harlem to Hollywood: The Struggle for Racial and Cultural Democracy 1920–1943*. New York: Garland, 1992.

Usner, Eric. "Dancing in the Past, Living in the Present: Nostalgia and Race in Southern Californian Neo-swing Dance Culture." *Dance Research Journal, Congress on Research in Dance* 33, no. 2 (2001): 87–111.

Vining, Donald. *A Gay Diary 1933–1946*. New York: Pepys Press, 1979.

Vogle, Shane. "Lena Horne's Impersona." In Vogle, *The Scene of Harlem Cabaret: Race, Sexuality, Performance*. Chicago: University of Chicago Press, 2009, 167–193.

Washburn, Patrick Scott. *A Question of Sedition: The Federal Government's Investigation of the Black Press during World War II*. New York: Oxford University Press, 1986.

Watts, Jill. *Hattie McDaniel: Black Ambition, White Hollywood*. New York: HarperCollins, 2005.

Whitehead, Kevin. *Why Jazz? A Concise Guide*. New York: Oxford University Press, 2011.

Widener, Daniel. "Something Else: Creative Community and Black Liberation in Postwar Los Angeles." Ph.D. diss., New York University, 2003.

Wild, Mark. *Street Meeting: Multiethnic Neighborhoods in Early Twentieth-Century Los Angeles*. Berkeley: University of California Press, 2005.

Willard, Michael Nevin. "Nuestra Los Angles." *American Quarterly* 56, no. 3 (September 2004): 807–843.

Williams, Megan E. "The 'Crisis' Cover Girl: Lena Horne, the NAACP, and Representations of African American Femininity, 1941–1945." *American Periodicals* 16, no. 2 (2006): 200–218.

Winchell, Meghan K. *Good Girls, Good Food, Good Fun: The Story of USO Hostesses during World War II*. Chapel Hill: University of North Carolina Press, 2008.

Yoshida, George. *Reminiscing in Swingtime: Japanese Americans in American Popular Muis, 1925–1960*. San Francisco: National Japanese American Historical Society, 1997.

FILMS

Ali Baba Goes to Town. Twentieth Century-Fox, 1937.

Crash Dive. Twentieth Century-Fox, 1943.

Follow the Boys. Universal Pictures, 1944.

Going Hollywood: The War Years. Shanachie Entertainment Corp., 1988. DVD.

Here Come the Waves. Paramount, 1944.

Hollywood Canteen. Warner Bros., 1944.

Shoe Shine Boy. MGM, 1944.

Stage Door Canteen. Warner Bros., 1943.

Thank Your Lucky Stars. Warner Bros., 1943.

This Is the Army. Warner Bros., 1943.

Index

American Federation of Musicians (AFM): in Los Angeles, 41, 250, 255; Committee for Civilian Defense, 100, 249, 251–52; Local 47, 6, 53, 257, 271; Local 767, 123, 191, 271

American Guild of Variety Artists (AGVA), 257

American Legion of Democracy, 287

American Veterans of Foreign Wars, 95

American Women's Volunteer Services (AWVS), 95

American Youth for Democracy (AYD), 267–68

Anderson, Eddie, 77

Anderson, Ernest, 92–93, 294

Anderson, Marian, 292

Andrews, Patty, 107, 109, 110, 146, 309

Andrews Sisters, 109, 110, 148, 282, 309

Andrews Sisters reenactments, xix

Angus, Helene (Bank). See Bank, Helene (Angus)

anti-Communism, 39, 250–52, 254, 263, 269, 272–73, 275–76, 278, 315; and racism, 279

anti-miscegenation laws, 101, 126

archive, 5, 80–81, 202; and "repertoire," 110–11, 246–47

Army, Department of the, 19, 62; enlisted men, 33, 62, 107–8, 121, 130, 133, 138; enlisted men in Los Angeles, 37, 92–93, Japanese American enlisted men, 62; Mexican American enlisted men, 69

Arnold, Edward, 79

Associated Negro Press, 53–54, 90, 92

Bacall, Lauren, 69

Bailey, Bill, 66

Bales, Florine, 257, 271

Ball, Juliet, 189

ballrooms in Los Angeles, 52, 100, 164; Hollywood Palladium, 63–66, 102, 224–25, 233, 299; Palomar, 65–66; Trianon, 37; Zenda, 39, 73

ballrooms in New York: Palladium, 16; Savoy, 28, 67

Bank, Helene (Angus), 46, 133, 167

Barnet, Charlie, 231

Barzman, Norma, 267

Bass, Charlotta, 259

Bauerdorf, Georgette, 117

Bear, Lorraine (Mitchell), xxi, 212, 223–25, 320

Beavers, Louise, 76–77, 79, 159, 161

Bell, Carl E. W., 291

Bergman, Ingrid, 218

Best, Willie, 295

Beverly-Fairfax, 32, 32, 46; Jewish Community Center, 40; Victory House, 34

Beverly Hills, 32, 46, 62, 186, 297; African American residents, 69, 189; Japanese American residents, 62; USO, 34 , 35, 40, 320; whiteness of, 29–30, 76, 291

Bevins, Rita. See Tilbury, R. Janie

Biltmore Hotel, 35, 131

Black dance, 166; and white dancers, 115–16, 154, 233

Black history, 77

Black Hollywood, 49, 66, 69–71, 76–77, 79, 81, 234. See also actors: African American

Black music, 66–67

Black musicals, 99

black press: on African American military women, 215, 222; on black hostesses at the Hollywood Canteen, 191; on black troops stationed in white neighborhoods, 55, 90; on black war heroism, 306; on canteens in black neighborhoods, 88; Double Victory campaign of, 257; on integration at Ciro's benefit, 31; on integration at the Hollywood Canteen, xiv, 6–7, 41, 53–54, 73–74, 118, 177–78; on Jim Crow canteens, 190; on Lena Horne, 188; representations of Los Angeles, in, 43; role in monitoring studio pledge, 287, 292–95, 306; on sundown towns, 72

blacklist, 48, 270, 272, 286; memoirists of, 247–48, 250, 264, 267

blackouts (dimouts), 27, 30–31, 40, 109, 132

Blair, Tony, 180, 187

Blank, Mel, 237–38

Bluett, Leonard "Lennie," 52, 64, 69–71, 92, 95, 189, 192–93, 193, 225, 230–34, 318–19

Bogart, Humphrey, 69, 189, 292, 297, 310

Boyle Heights, 32, 32, 33, 40, 320

break-away, also swing-out, send-out, 11–15, 320, 324n35

Bridges, Harry, 270–71

British Merchant Marine, 46

Brokaw, Tom, xvi, 8

Browder, Earl, 277

Brown v. Board of Education, 161

Brown, Joe E., 297–98, 301, 310

Brownback, Bertha, 216

Bryant, Clora, 155, 231

Bryant, Melvin "Mel," xxi, 48–49, 101, 121, 146, 157, 155–60, 161–64, 177, 191, 220, 278–79, 319–20

Burbank, 32, 51, 52, 91, 93, 291; African American troops in, 89–90; defense plants in, 33, 101; history of, 56, 293; USO, 34, 78, 91, 100–101; whiteness of, 54–55

Bureau of Motion Pictures (BMP), 286–87

Burke, Billie, 255–56

Bush, George W., Jr., xviii, 180, 187

Butler, Loretta, 97

Cabin in the Sky, 99, 189, 230, 233–34, 255, 270–71

Cadrez, Florence, 125, 125, 176–77, 191, 255

Cahuenga Pass, 52, 54–58, 60, 101, 120; battle of, 55–56

California: anti-miscegenation laws, 101, 126; history of, 54–58; racism in, 97; reputation as racially progressive, 87; state dance of, 68; World War II military buildup, 60

California Eagle, 82, 88, 259

Calloway, Cab, 186, 295

Camarillo, 33, 223

Cameron, Rod, 210

Campbell, Anne, 217

Canada, 182, 184, 187, 191, 192, 297

Cantor, Eddie, 93, 192–93, 193

Carson, Jack, 296, 301–2

Carter, Ben, 92, 160; as actor; 158; entertaining the troops, 88, 95; at Hollywood Canteen, 115, 118; as plaintiff in civil rights cases, 71, 102; Sugar Hill home, 76, 78; as talent agent, 49, 159

Carter, Phil, 294–95

cartoonists, 31, 102, 126; cel painters and inkers, 120, 127. *See also* Screen Cartoonists Guild

Cavallero, Carmen, 282, 313

Cayton, Horace R., 259

Central Avenue district, 33, 42, 66, 75, 93, 97, 120; nightspots, 99, 101, 193–94, 259; policing of, by Shore Patrol and LAPD, 35–36, 101; soldier canteens, 37–38; USO, 80, 86–87, 89, 93, 320. *See also* Club Alabam; Eastside

Chaney, Lon, 208

Chavez Ravine, 32, 52, 58

Christ, Jean [Jeanne] (Foreman), 129, 133

Ciro's, 31, 78, 92–93, 254

citizenship, 215, 220

civilian men, draft aged, 210; as brunt of jokes, 199, 203, 212, 219, 226; of color, 230, 232; draft-exemption, 205; entertaining the troops, 228; feelings of embarrassment, 227; feelings of guilt, 253; gender parameters, 204, 208, 211; policing of, 48; public attitudes toward, 201, 206, 226, 239–40; resentment of by servicemen, 200, 229. *See also* Hollywood Canteen, volunteers: civilian men

Clare, Ralph, 250–51, 255, 257–58, 260, 262–63, 271–72, 274, 277–78

Clark, Dane, xvi, 283, 290

Clifton's Cafeteria, 158

Club Alabam, 38, 78, 99, 101, 234; chorus line at, 97, 99; policing of, by Shore Patrol, 101

Coast Guard, xiv, 61, 165, 227, 272, 340n17; band, 32. *See also* SPARS

Colbert, Claudette, 77, 113, 161, 186

Darwell, Jane, 95
Davenport, Harry, 95
Daves, Delmar, 20, 282–83, 290–92, 305, 318
Davis, Angela Y., 1, 174, 279
Davis, Benjamin A., 259
Davis, Bette: autobiographies and biographies, 27, 178, 216; autographs, 64, 127; as champion of integration, 54, 118, 163; as figure in counter-narratives, 170, 220; in film, *Hollywood Canteen*, 284, 302, 308, 312–13, 317; Glendale home, 52, 72; and Hollywood Canteen, 44, 113, 133, 162, 217, 266, 273, 274; and Hollywood Victory Committee, 77, 330n3; *In This Our Life*, 294; request for transfer of Shore Patrol Officer, 264–65; surveillance of, 254, 255, 277; *Thank Your Lucky Stars,* 289, 301; tour with predominantly African American USO "Spot" Show, 77, 92–93, 94, 95, 318; and typical Hollywood Canteen narrative, 41, 53, 61
Davis, Sylvester, 101
de Havilland, Olivia, 107
de Portola, Don Gaspar, 54–58, 60
defense industries: as canteen volunteers, 102, 121, 123; as civilian patriotism, 228; discrimination in, 55; and influx of workers to Los Angeles, 27, 36, 45, 48, 83; integration of, 7, 153; and interracial romance, 101, 333n59; motion picture industry as, 316; plants in San Fernando Valley, 33, 52, 78, 90; workers in, African Americans, 69, 175; workers in, Mexican Americans, 59, 201, 218
Delta Sigma Theta, 82
democracy: access to movie stars as expression of, 221; as complimentary fitting pieces, 181; as conceived in jazz and swing studies, 9–11, 16; as crossings of social divisions, 6–7; and difference, 22, 209; as equal access, 82; as incommensurate with segregation, 80, 252; as largess of the powerful toward the

less powerful, xvi–xvii, 20; as mutually meaningful exchange, 185, 187, 196; perspectives from the dance floor, 3, 15, 18–19; as practice, 85–86; as process that leads to "inclusion," 332n8; racial integration as slippery evidence of, 41, 76, 88, 177–78, 188; as simultaneously multicultural and white, xv; and swing dance, 11–12; as torque, 13–14, 17, 195–96; as undefined core value, 16; world, 253; and writing, xxiv, 4–5. *See also* dance floor democracy; dancing across race; Freedom of Information Act (FOIA); integration
Dietrich, Marlene, 2, 26, 107, 113, 128, 291
Disney Studios, 28, 52, 52
dissonance, 5, 14, 19, 21, 196, 207, 210
Doolittle, General, xix
Dorsey, Jimmy, xvi, 231, 282, 298–99, 312
Dorsey, Tommy, 64, 224–25
Double Victory/Double V campaign, 96, 188, 190, 257, 295; and African American hostesses, 123
Douglas, Joan, 190
DownBeat, 118, 155, 177
downtown Los Angeles, 32, 32–33, 40, 42, 49, 50, 52, 58, 59, 66, 69; Figueroa USO, 34, 39, 73, 86, 219; Pershing Square USO, 35; YMCA and YWCA, 52, 47–48, 320
draft. *See* conscription
Durbin, Deanna, xvi, 291
Dwan, Alan, 137

East Los Angeles, 46–47, 58–59, 68–69, 73
Eastside, 33, 34, 42–43, 46, 52, 76, 78, 87, 91, 101, 119, 194; African American servicewomen in, 95, 215; civil rights attorneys in, 82; clubwomen, 123, 125; Eastside USO, 37–38, 80, 86, 89, 93, 95–97, 99, 102, 117, 153, 191, 215; YMCA, 66; YWCA, 78, 81–82. *See also* Central Avenue district
Ebony, 96–97
Eckstine, Billy, 292
Edendale, 290–91

Edwards, Florida: dislike of jitterbug, 154; *Edwards v. Hollywood Canteen,* 150–53, 309; injury, 146–47; as professional dancer, 163–64

Edwards, Sam, 147, 164

Eisenhower, General, 138

Ellington, Duke, xvi, 61, *125,* 234

Elysian Park, 83, 291

embodiment: embodied knowledge, 13–14, 29, 103, 110–12, 115, 118, 127, 142–43; and memory, xix, 16–17, 18–19; and oral history, 3–5, 119–20, 156–57; and research, 15, 18–19, 246; and writing, xxiv, 1–5

Escobedo, Elizabeth Rachel, 59, 116, 126

Executive Order 8802, 7, 101, 153. *See also* defense industries

Executive Order 9066, 7. *See also* Japanese Americans: internment of

Exposition Park, 87

Farrell, Glenda, 163

Farrell, Tommy, 121, 163–66, 216

Faulkenberg, Jinx, 254

Federal Bureau of Investigations (FBI), xiv, 19–21, 176; Los Angeles Bureau, 243–45, 248–49; and state memory, 246–47, 286; surveillance of Communists, known, suspected, and conceivable, 250–52, 272; surveillance of mixed-race dancing, xiv, 19–20, 176, 254–55, 258, 260–61, 278–79, 287, 300

Ferdinand of Spain, King, 57

Ferrero, Jane. *See* Lockwood, Jane (Josephs, Ferrero)

First National Studio, 51–52

Fleming, Victor, 70–71

Flynn, Erroll, 297

Follow the Boys, 79

Fonda, Henry, 95

Ford, James W., 259

Ford, John, 190, 191, 262

Ford, Mary, 190, 191, 256, 262, 263, 270, 276, 319

Foreman, Jeanne. *See* Christ, Jean (Foreman)

Franklin, Louise, 234

Freedom of Information Act (FOIA), 243–45; contradictions of, 246; as hallmark of democracy, 243–45; post-9/11, xviii; ritual of partial release, 247–48

Gable, Clark, 70–71, 229

Gabrieleno/Tongva people, 57–58

Garfield, John, as champion of integration, xiv, 118, 178, 227, 317; as depicted in typical narrative, 41, 44, 53, 61, 171; fighting his 4F classification, 227–28; in film, *Hollywood Canteen,* 284, 290, 302, 304–6, 311, 315, 317; surveillance of, 248–49, 255, 270

Garland, Judy, 139

Gelfand, Pearl, 120, 169

gender: and African American men, 230; and African American women, 214–15; construction of women's branches of the armed forces, 204, 218; and democracy, 209; good girls/bad girls, 219; intersections of, with race and military status, 234, 239, 288; masculinity, civilian men and, 201, 203–4, 229; and Mexican American men and women, 59; and national subjectivity, 115; norms, 145; norms, and alignment, 207–8; and race, class, and dance, 154–55, 192; and race, constructions of, and African American men, 230; and race and national memory, xv, xix, xxiii; and race and social geography, 120; and race, social memories of, 8, 18; and race and soldier-hostess dyad, 111; and race, and space, 83; servicewomen, 213, 215, 226, 239; wartime changes in, 118; wartime management of, 203, 219; white military masculinity, 203, 206–7. *See also* soldier-hostess dyad

Glendale, 32, 33, 39, 43, 55, 72–73; Japanese American residents, 73; USO, *34;* whiteness of, 72–73; YWCA, 72–73, 329–30n61

Glenn Miller Orchestra: ghost orchestra, xx; reenactments of, xix–xx

Hollywood Canteen (*continued*)
geography of neighborhood, 18, 25, 30, 43–45, 71, 102–3; as founded by guilds and unions, 170–71, 249, 255; history of, 40–41, 61–62; as hub of memory, xxii–xxiv, 3–5, 14–17, 22, 120; jitterbug at, xx, xxiv, 102, 113, 133, 145, 165; memories of exclusion, 96, 199, 210, 212, 215, 217, 221; memories of integration, xix–xxii, 8, 102, 184–85, 266; memories of integration and segregation, 187–88, 194–96; as national memory, xv; official narrative, xvi, 2, 20–21, 26–27, 52; policing of, 126, 143, 148, 243, 257, 264–65, 315, 319; political difference at, 240, 248; press coverage of, 31, 178; relationship with Hollywood Victory Committee (HVC), 77, 330n3; star-gazing at, 128; surveillance of, 245–74, 277–80, 285–86, 288; as symbol of democracy, xvii, 6–7, 100; union-management collaboration, 56–57; as war memory, xviii, 9, 119, 180–81; and World War II homefront nostalgia for, xiii, xix, xx, 9. *See also* Hollywood Canteen, military guests, servicemen; Hollywood Canteen, military guests, servicewomen; Hollywood Canteen, volunteers

Hollywood Canteen, military guests, servicemen, 17, 33, 41, 61, 63, 127; African American, 119, 123, *125*, 155–57, 162; constructed as naïve, xvi, 53; dancing, jitterbug, 108, 163–65; dancing, "GI Shuffle," 129, 165; Marines, memories of dancing with movie stars, 162, 165; memories of integration, 162; memories of segregation, 119, 155, 162; Red Army 277; Royal Air Force, 179–80, 184, 186; remembered as frightened, 142; remembered as shy, 119, 127; as represented in the film, *Hollywood Canteen*, 297, 299, 313, 318. *See also* servicemen

Hollywood Canteen, military guests, servicewomen, xxii, 7–8, 19, 184, 199, 202–4,

209–25, 300; memories of exiting, 220, 221, 225; memories of segregated inclusion, 204, 210, 212, 217, 220; parameters of performance, 203, 214, 239; as represented in the film, *Hollywood Canteen*, 299, 301. *See also* servicewomen

Hollywood Canteen, volunteers, 29, 33, 45, 52–53, 60, 102, 118–23, 124, 127–28, 169, 229; African American, 64, 100–101, 189, 193; celebrity, 6, 21, 220–21; civilian men, 19, 228; conflicts among, regarding racial integration, xiv, 265; doormen, 126, 199; improvisation of, 44, 142, 161, 221, 226, 239; making appearances, 227; members of guilds and unions, xiv; musicians, 257; political differences among, 272; surveillance of, 279; vulnerability of entertainers to over-volunteerism, 40; and worker's compensation, 147; working on canteen-themed movies, including *Hollywood Canteen*, xvi, 20, 44, 290, 300. *See also* Hollywood Canteen, volunteers, busboys; Hollywood Canteen, volunteers, hostesses

Hollywood Canteen, volunteers, busboys, 128, 210, 237; actors, 125, 228; African American, 230, 232–33; and disruption and construction of soldier-hostess dyad, 239–40; draft-aged civilian men, 19, 48, 234–36, 238; occupations of, 237; parameters of performance, 199–206, 226, 232; perceived resentment from servicemen, 229, as represented in movie, *Hollywood Canteen*, 284, 302, 309–10

Hollywood Canteen, volunteers, hostesses, 111, *113*, 120, 255; African American, 92, 95, 96, 100–101, 123, *125*, 125–26, 128, 162, 188–91, 194–96, 234; captains, 92, 95, 125, 128, 176, 190; celebrity, 129, 143, 162, 165, 183–87, 220; Communists, 269; flirting, parameters of, 143, 194–95; injury, 144, 148–54; junior, 194–95; memories of fights, 168; Mexican American, 47, 126; murder of Georgette Bauerdorf, 117;

housing covenants, 33, 36, 303; effects of, on social geography, 38, 40, 42–44, 55, 71–72, 87, 123; and legal cases against, 37, 73, 82, 101–2, 258

Hughes, Langston, 176, 259, 330n9

Hunt, Marsha, 128, 129, 272

Hutton, Betty, 204

Hutton, Robert, xvi, 283, 290, *307*, 314, 315, *316*

I Dood It, 99

immigrants: children of, 66–68, 90; historic intolerance for, in Los Angeles, 42; Mexican, 37, 46

improvisation: of canteen volunteers, 44, 142, 161, 221, 226, 239; and committee work, 78, 86–87; and dance, 11–12, 14, 18, 166, 319; history, 239; and jazz, 11; and memory, 19; and nostalgia, 4; as "practice of freedom," 16, 112; research and writing as, 320

In This Our Life, 72, 92–93, 294

indigenous people: Gabrieleno/Tongva people, 57–58; in Los Angeles, 42, 56; in Spanish Fantasy, 55

Inglewood, 32, 33, 36–37, 43, 72, 176; race in, 36–37, 43, 73; USO, *34*, 36–37, 176

integration: in African American clubs, 38, 41; of Ciro's, 31, 93; Communists' commitments to, 246, 248, 253, 264, 266, 300; Communists' commitments to, limits of, 258; as "Communist plot," 20, 174, 247; defense plants, 101; at the Eastside USO, 37, 89, 99; and embodied knowledge, 153; as "free choice," 269, 275; at Hollywood Canteen, xiv, 6–8, 31, 41, 53–54, 72, 74, 118, 138, 178, 188–89, 194–95, 227, 266, 317; at Hollywood Canteen, memories of, xix–xxii, 8, 102, 184–85, 266; and Hollywood Victory Committee USO "Spot" caravan, 72, 93, 317–18; as "inclusion" of people of color into white space, xv, 126, 156; intentional, 174, 243, 246, 254, 260, 267, 279; as labor, 77, 161, 190–91; liberals and, 176, 194; in Los Angeles, public housing, 82; in Los Angeles, public schools, 43; managed, xv, xxii, xxiv, 19–21, 321n3; multiple definitions of, xv, 16, 20, 191; and national memory, xv, xxii, 7, 9, 20, 103, 123, 245, 247; representations of in war-era movies, 299–300, 302; at the Stage Door Canteen, New York, 100, 174–76; "together but not equal," xxi, 158, 160, 163, 191, 279; at 12th Street/Woodlawn YWCA, 82; two-way, 79; USO clubs, advocacy for, 86, 89–90; at the Watts Hospitality House, 76, 88, 89; of white people into nonwhite social space, 37–38, 41; Young Women's Christian Association (YWCA), 72, 84. See also dancing across race; segregation

Jaffee, Paul, 257, 262

James, Harry, 26, 184

Japanese Americans: and Glendale YWCA, 72–73; internment of, 7, 33, 55, 62; and swing culture, 63–64; at 12st Street YWCA, 82

jazz studies: "democracy" in, xv, 11, 16; historiography, of Los Angeles jazz, 65–66; on white interest in black music, 67; on whitenening and mainstreaming of swing, 108

Jefferson High School, 87

Jewish Americans: and cross-racial sociality, 90; FBI's association of, with Communism, 20; and housing covenants, 40; in motion picture industry, 294; and swing culture, 66, 93

Jewish Community Centers (JCC), 39; in Los Angeles, 40, 86

jitterbug, as a kind of person, 108, 127; fanatic, 151; patriotic, 109–10, 112, 126

jitterbug, dance: aerial steps, 108, *113*, 165; as American, 9–10; as coercion, 146–48; as communicative partnership, 11, 13, 185; and Communists, 240, 258, 260; as dangerous, 152–53; and democracy, xxiv,

Lockwood, Jane (Josephs, Ferrero), xix, *52*, 71, 120, 128; dance, diary-writing, and realignment, 110–12, 184–85, 202, 244; and dance with "a jitterbug," 107–9, 127, 146, 148, 154, 164–65, 206, 209; diaries, absence of mentions of interracial dancing in, 118; perspective of, as swing dancing junior hostess, 114–16, 143

Lomas, Claire. *See* Rosen, Claire (Lomas)

London, Helene. *See* Bank, Helene (Angus)

Long Beach, *32*, 121; USO main club and Negro extension, *34*, 38–39, 215

Lopez, Raymond, 261

Los Angeles, 7, 10, 18; black Los Angeles, 66–67; colonialism, 30, 54, 58, 74–75; in comparison to New York, 40–42; history of, 28–29, 42, 56–58, 60, 66–67; integration, 43, 81–82; neighborhoods, on borders of racially restricted and unrestricted neighborhoods, 36–37, 42–43, 72; neighborhoods, racially restricted, 36, 43, 71–72, 74, 76, 100–101; neighborhoods, racially unrestricted, 36–37, 42–43, 76, 78, 82–83, 88–89, 101; promoted and imagined as white, 30, 56, 69, 74–75, 102; race in, 35–37, 83, 87, 102; race in, as confusing, 37, 83, 87, 102; race in, invisibility of, to most white residents, 43–44, 71–72, 75, 102; racism, 68, 72–73, 101; as represented in movies, 29, 43–44; reputation as racially progressive, 43, 87; segregation, 83–84; Spanish Fantasy narrative, 51, 55–57; spatial expanse of, 31–33, 50, 76, 78; wartime changes in, 48–49, 59, 66, 69, 74, 85. *See also* individual neighborhoods by name

Los Angeles Police Department (LAPD), 35–36, 38, 48, 60–61, 74, 117–18, 126, 260, 268, 276

Ludwig, Kathryn "Kit". *See* Welter, Kathryn "Kit" (Ludwig)

Lunt, Alfred, 290

Lupino, Ida, xvi, 310

MacDonald, Mrs. Bert, 76

Mack, Mae, 38–39

Mansfield, Charlotte D., Senior Master Sergeant (Retired), 216, 220–21

Mansfield, June, 47

Marine Corps: African American enlisted men, 49, 161–62, 337n26; Jim Crow training camp, 96, 159–60; reluctance to admit African American men, 153

Marine Corps Women's Reserves (WR), 199, 209–10, 212, 216, 220; exclusion of African American women, 222. *See also* servicewomen

Marlow, Nancy, 45, 128, *132*, 131–35, 216, 272

Marsh, Eric, 121, *183*, 179–88

Marsh-Doll, Caren (Aileen Morris), 120, *140*, 139–43

Mature, Victor, 229

McAuliffe, Aniela "Niel," 47, 169–71

McClay, John J., 268

McConnell's Restaurant, 71, 118

McDaniel, Hattie, 81, *94–95*, 294; and anti-covenant suit, 102; and Hollywood Victory Committee, 76–79, 91–92; and integrated USO caravan, 72, 93, 317–18; Sugar Hill home, *78*, 159

McDowall, Roddy, 46

McDowall, Virginia, 46

McKenzie, Faye, *12*, *113*

McWilliams, Carey, 29–30, 55–56, 58–60, 101, 291

memory: embodied, xxiii; erasure of, 29–30; "Good War" memory boom, xx; and music, 9; national, x, xiii–xvi, xix–xxi, 3, 4–6, 27–28, 102–3, 149, 153, 240, 298, 317–18, 322n14; oral history and, xxii, 8, 131, 234–35; relationship between personal and national, 14–17, 22, 119–20; relationship between personal and social/community, xxiii, 18–19; relationship between state and national, 20–21, 246–47, 280, 286–88; state, 147–49, 248, 280, 336n6; war, xviii–xx, xxiv, 11, 22

memory studies, xix, 3, 9, 17

Mexican Americans, 7, 30, 67, 75; criminalization of, 58–60, 74, 91; discrimination against, 68–69; in Hollywood, 64–65; housing, 83; in Los Angeles, 33–37, 42, 51; mobility of, 126; provisional integration to white space, 66; racial classifications of, 56, 101; violence against, 55; women, 9, 116–17. *See also* pachucas/pachucos

Mexican Revolution, 69

Mexican War, 58; "Unending," 56, 59

MGM Studios, 28, 46, 49, 70–71, 128–29, 139, 144, 158–59, 163, 192, 270, 294

Milani, Chef, 236–37

military police, 61, 126, 143, 148, 243, 257, 315

Millar, Mack, 255

Miller, Dorie, 158, 295, 337–38n41

Miller, Henry, 47

Miller, J. C. P., 60

Miller, Juanita, 82

Miller, Loren, 72, 82, 102, 258–59

Mitchell, Lorraine. *See* Bear, Lorraine (Mitchell)

Mogambo, 70

Monroe, Marilyn, 230, 233

Montgomery, Robert, 217

Moore, Tommie, 92, 234, 334n28

Morehead, Baron, 225, 262–63

Moreland, Mantan, 49, 88, *95*, 95, 158

Morris, Aileen. *See* Marsh-Doll, Caren

Morris, Dorothy, *140–41*, 139–44

Morris, Mickey, 262

Motion Picture Alliance for the Preservation of American Ideals, 250

Motion Picture Country House and Hospital, 169, 338n63

motion picture industry: labor history, 56–57; migration to San Fernando Valley, 52; migration west, 51; racial disparities in, 46, 70–71, 123, 193, 196–97; racial stereotypes in movies, 78–79, 91, 188–89; rivalry with New York theater business, 41; source of volunteer troop entertainment, 40, 42, 77; under-employment,

128, 147; and World War II, 20–21, 25–26. *See also* motion picture industry guilds and unions

motion picture industry guilds and unions, xiv, 8, 53, 124–25, 147, 170–71, 249, 327n4; race disparities in, 44; relationship with studios, 56–57; surveillance of, 250, 252, 254. *See also* individual guilds and unions by name

Motion Picture Producers Association (MPPA), 56

Motion Picture Producers and Distributors of America (MPPDA), 282, 286–87

movie stars, xiv, 26, 210, 217, 222, 228, 236–37, 239, 257, 266, 273, 276, 282, 287, 289, 290, 297, 299; African American, 31, 37, 188; civilian male stars, 200; as compensation for sacrifice, 186–87; depicted as benevolent, xv–xvi, 6, 27, 30, 53, 74, 284, 311, 314; at Eastside USO, 41, 93; as familiar faces, 129; at Hollywood Canteen, 39, 45–46, 80, 160–61, 178–79, 181–82; at Hollywood USO, 40; in military service, 107, 159–60, 229; as morale boosters, 291–92, 315–17; at other canteens, 34, 44; on USO Shows, 77, 79, 92; on war bond tours, 130, 227; at Watts Hospitality House, 88; whiteness of, 300. *See also* starlets

multiculturalism, xiv, xix, 9–10, 20–21, 83, 102, 103, 133, 154–55, 297, 300, 308; and whiteness, 25, 37, 177, 203, 309, 312

Muse, Billye, 125, 190–91

Muse, Clarence, 81, 88, 92, *95*, 125, 190–91

Muse, Mae, 81

Nagumo, Reiko, 63–64

narrative, xxiii; and community, 5; and nation, 57; and subjectivity, 129–30, 146, 148–49, 202–3, 207–8, 212–13, 220–21

nation: and narration, 57, 247; national identity and belonging, 9–10, 15, 27, 29, 61, 207, 212; as remembering together, 4–5. *See also* memory: national

social geography, xxiii, 2; and embodiment, 83–84; at the Hollywood Canteen, 43, 97, 155, 158, 176; in Los Angeles, 18, 25–26, 30, 35, 36, 58–60, 71–72, 74–75, 91, 117, 123, 126; of memory, 15, 181–182

soldier-hostess dyad, 19, 43–44, 111, 239; African American, 188, 191; alternative visions, 185, 208–9; continued circulation as patriotic symbol, xx, 114, 119, 154; Mexican American, 59; performing from within its halves, 15, 112, 142–43, 196; as represented in war-era films, 26, 284, 292, 298, 310; whiteness of, xix, 318. *See also* soldier-starlet dyad

soldier-starlet dyad, xvii, xx, 26, 61, 111–14, 145, 284

Sons of the Pioneers, 282, 301, 308

Soundies, 26

South Gate, 37

SPARS (Semper Paratus Always Ready): advocacy for inclusion of African American women in, 268; exclusion of African American women, 222

Stafford, Jo, 64

Stage Door Canteen, 26, 256, 282; representations of race in, 295, 300, 305, 318; West Coast bias in, 289–90

Stage Door Canteen (New York), 200, 205; busboys at, 176, 200, 205; as inspiration for Hollywood Canteen, xiv, 40–41, 249; integration at, 100; interracial hostess training, 173–76; separate tea dances for military women, 219. *See also Stage Door Canteen*

Stage Door Canteens: exclusion of military women, 219; San Francisco, 220

Stanwyck, Barbara, 113, 165, 301

"Star-Spangled Banner," 21, 168

Star Spangled Rhythm, 302

starlets, xxiv, 40, 102, 172, 202, 217–18, 289, 296; definition of "starlet," 133; expected to entertain the troops, 45, 136; non-starlets mistaken as, 127, 171, 201; performing "girl-back-home," 129, 135, 138,

315; performing ideal "American girl," 131, 137; possibility of at Hollywood Canteen, 112, 115, 134; starlet-hopefuls, 46, 121, 310; whiteness of, xv, xvii, 26, 54, 134, 266. *See also* soldier-starlet dyad

state: racial, 246, 248. *See also* memory: state

Stein, Doris, 255, 271

Stein, Jules, 244, 255–57, 261–63, 266, 271–72, 274

Steiner, Artie, 133

Stewart, James, 229

Stewart, Margie, 45, *135*, 134–38, 216

Stormy Weather, 99, 295

Studio City, 32, *52*, 90

Studio Transportation Drivers, 249–51

Sugar Hill. *See* West Adams

sundown towns, 33–37; Burbank, 55; Glendale, 72–73

surveillance, 20, 245–73, 274, 277–80, 285, 286, 288; blurry line between research and, 81; effects of, 246, 248. *See also* Federal Bureau of Investigations (FBI)

swing: African American culture, 13, 66, 115; as American, xv, xix, xx, xxiv, 9, 21, 26, 27, 64, 109; as democratic, 14, 16, 25; and Japanese Americans, 62; slippage of race meanings (white, black, pachuco/a, color-blind, multicultural), 10, 102–3, 116–17; "Swing Era" as official narrative, 65; whiteness, 108

swing culture as war memory, xxi–xxiv, 9, 16–17, 20–21, 26–27, 29–30, 102; and national memory, 10, 14, 16, 22, 25, 32, 181

swing culture industry, 25; and race, 28, 64–68; on West Coast, 26–27, 30

swing dance: physics of, 11–13, 324n35; revivals, xvii, 10, 28, 67–68, 154. *See also* jitterbug, dance; Lindy Hop; Pachuco Hop; torque

swing scholarship, 9–10; focus on dance, 11–14, 154; historiography, 5, 65–66; West Coast, 25–26